Mayas in the Marketplace

Walter E. Little

Mayas in the Marketplace

Tourism, Globalization, and Cultural Identity

UNIVERSITY OF TEXAS PRESS AUSTIN

Chapter 7 is a revision of "Home as a Place of Exhibition and Performance: Mayan Household Transformation in Guatemala," which was previously published in *Ethnology* (The University of Pittsburgh) 39 (2): 163–181.

First edition, 2004

∞ The paper used in this book meets the minimum requirements of ANSI/NISO Z39.48-1992 (R1997) (Permanence of Paper).

Little, Walter E., 1963–
  Mayas in the marketplace : tourism, globalization, and cultural identity / Walter E. Little.— 1st ed.
      p.   cm.
Includes bibliographical references and index.
"Chapter 7 is a revision of "Home as a Place of Exhibition and Performance: Mayan Household Transformation in Guatemala," which was previously published in Ethnology (The University of Pittsburgh) 39 (2): 163–181."
ISBN 0-292-70278-7 (alk. paper) — ISBN 0-292-70567-0 (pbk. : alk. paper)
  1. Cakchikel Indians—Commerce.   2. Cakchikel Indians—Economic conditions
3. Cakchikel Indians—Social conditions.   4. Maya business enterprises—Guatemala—Antigua Region.   5. Culture and tourism—Guatemala—Antigua Region.   6. Tourists—Guatemala—Antigua Region—Attitudes.   7. Antigua Region
(Guatemala)—Social conditions.   8. Antigua Region (Guatemala)—Economic
conditions.   I. Ethnology monographs.   II. Title.
F1465.2.C3L57   2004
972.974'00497422—dc22   2003025096

Contents

Figures

Acknowledgments

E thnographies are the result of the collaboration, cooperation, and support of many people and institutions. This one is no exception. Certainly, I am indebted to more people than I probably realize. I offer my apologies in advance to those I overlook; such omissions were not intentional.

Without the permission, interest, camaraderie, friendship, and encouragement of the handicraft vendors upon whom this book is based, my research would not have been possible. Even now, after more than ten years of working and socializing with vendors, I am still amazed by how much of their lives they continue to share with me. We look forward to my annual two- to three-month visits to Guatemala, and as some of them become more successful, we look forward to their visits to the United States. Clearly, our communities are beginning to overlap.

Given the political history of Guatemala, the troubles that handicraft vendors faced and will probably face with the municipality, and the fact that most would prefer not to be named, it is not possible or prudent for me to thank them individually. For these reasons, personal names in this book have been altered. All vendors not only generously contributed to my research, they also made sure that my family and I were safe, entertained, and fed.

Several families in Guatemala deserve special recognition, not necessarily for the help they provided in direct relation to my field research, but for their friendship and how well they took care of me and my family. Their homes were places where I could relax, feel at ease, and develop friendships. Foremost among these is the Simón-Icú family of Comalapa, whose generosity, humor, and goodwill made my daughter announce more than once that she would just live with them. It was with this family that I really learned to speak Kaqchikel. The Tax family in Santa Catarina Palopó and the López Hernández family in San Antonio Aguas Calientes also took me into their homes and befriended, fed, and teased me. The Arreola and Spillari families in Antigua provided me with places to live, but more importantly, they helped me remember that not all Ladinos depreciate Mayas. These families welcomed my Maya friends into their homes and relayed messages to Mayas and to my family when they were not with me in Guatemala.

Had it not been for my participation in Tulane University's Oxlajuj Aj Kaqchikel Maya Language course in Guatemala, I probably never would have done my research on Kaqchikel Maya vendors. At least, I would not have been able to do it the way I did. The founding directors of the course, Judith Maxwell and Robert McKenna Brown, provided a good example of how to work with Mayas and helped me make a number of early contacts. Often just the mention of their good names opened doors for me. All of the Oxlajuj Aj teachers introduced me to Kaqchikel Maya life and language; a few in particular helped me understand my data, entertained me, consoled me when my family was not in Guatemala, looked after me when I was sick, provided me with advice that made living in Guatemala easier, and have never ceased in their efforts to improve my Kaqchikel. These include Waqi' Kej and Ixim Nikte' of Tecpán, B'eleje' Ey of Poaquil, Ix'ey of San Antonio, Ix'ey of Comalapa, Tojil of Santa Catarina, and Waqi' Kawoq of Santa María de Jesús. Both Ix'eys also gave me weaving lessons.

Because Guatemala is a relatively small country, and I conducted research in a city through which most scholars pass, I was able to share ideas and problems with many of them, including Nancie González, Linda Asturias de Barrios, Yoshinobu Ota, Virginia Tilley, Sirvando Hinojosa, David Carey, Jennifer Burrell, Seth Minkoff, Carol Hendrickson, Abigail Adams, Robert Hamrick, Gail Ament, Jim Handy, George Lovell, and David Stoll. Several others in Guatemala helped expand my perspectives on and knowledge of Guatemala, including Vincent Stanzione, Angelica Bauer, Frank Taylor, Frank Mays, Daniel and Carmen Ixayason, Efraín García, Mercedes Apé, Sergio García, Oralia and Everildo Guarán, Iris and Humberto Díaz, Cesar and Emy Xicay, Sarah Matzar, Raxche', Oscar Perén, and María Elena Currichiche.

Over the years, a number of scholars have offered encouragement for this research, listened to my ideas in formation, and provided constructive criticism. At the University of Illinois at Chicago, they include Michael Lieber, Jim Phillips, John Monaghan, Susan Freeman, and Robert Hall. While I was teaching at the University of Oklahoma, weekly lunches with Joe Whitecotton and Stephen Perkins provided stimulating conversation about Mesoamerica. Since graduate school, William W. Wood has been a comrade-in-arms with whom I could hash over theory and method.

Earlier versions of the book were read by Mahir Şaul, Edward Bruner, Alejandro Lugo, and John Watanabe, who also provided guidance as I prepared for fieldwork, did the fieldwork, and wrote up the results. All four of these anthropologists have left their mark on this book through their critical readings of it. I feel fortunate to have had their support over the years.

Many others have read and commented on earlier versions of these chapters, and their comments improved the book. Carol Hendrickson and Robert Kemper critiqued an early version of Chapter 5. Barry Isaac, former editor of *Research in Economic Anthropology,* commented on and made editorial suggestions for Chapter 8. Leonard Plotnicov and anonymous reviewers at *Ethnology* provided editorial and critical commentary for an earlier version of Chapter 7, which is a revision of "Home as a Place of Exhibition and Performance: Mayan Household Transformation in Guatemala," originally published in *Ethnology* (The University of Pittsburgh) 39 (2): 163–181. Rolando Romero critiqued a very early version of Chapter 1.

I had the good fortune of having June Nash, Quetzil Castañeda, and Kay Warren (all originally anonymous reviewers for the University of Texas Press) read the final versions of the manuscript. Their critical readings, tough commentaries, insightful suggestions, and knowledge of the region helped me write a better book.

Generous aid from numerous institutions supported me as I conducted research and wrote this book. This included two U.S. Department of Education Summer FLAS grants in 1994 and 1996, a living stipend from Oxlajuj Aj in the summer of 1995, a Predoctoral Grant from the Wenner-Gren Foundation for Anthropological Research, a Fulbright IIE Grant, and the Bruner Award for Anthropological Excellence. The Center for Regional Investigations of Mesoamerica, SMART, the Archivo General de Centro América, Kaqchikel Cholchi', the Center for the Study of Maya Culture, the Center for Maya Documentation and Investigation, and Saq B'ey provided library and textual resources. While writing the manuscript, I received some support from the anthropology departments of Indiana University Northwest; the University of Oklahoma, Norman; the University of Illinois at Chicago; and DePaul University, Chicago, each of which employed me as a visiting assistant professor. The anthropology department at the University at Albany has supported the final phases of manuscript preparation.

Finally and most importantly, my wife, Wilma Alvarado-Little, and my daughter, Ileana, have given me unwavering support and helped me keep my fieldwork and writing obsessions in perspective. Without them, it is doubtful that I would have endured the trials and tribulations of anthropological fieldwork.

To the memory of Joseph and Manuela Moreno

Mayas in the Marketplace

Introduction: Subjectivity and Fieldwork among Kaqchikel Vendors

Scene I: Ruq'ij Ala', *San Antonio Aguas Calientes, March 1997*

Tomás and Alejandra invited me to celebrate their son's ninth birthday, a gathering attended by numerous members of their family. As is customary, *pepián* (roasted chile and tomato sauce for meat) was served with rice and tortillas. For dessert we ate white cake and drank Coca-Cola. Afterward, the adults discussed family, work, and me while the children played in the courtyard.

We compared the land and rent prices in San Antonio Aguas Calientes and Chicago, as well as other cultural differences between our towns. They were curious to know if the children of Spanish speakers spoke Spanish in Chicago. Was bilingual schooling promoted? Were children embarrassed to speak Spanish? Tomás's mother commented that the public school in San Antonio was giving lessons in Kaqchikel. "It's good that the children are learning it in school, but the lessons aren't very good because the teachers don't speak Kaqchikel."

Her sister laughed, "And you don't know Kaqchikel either. You use a lot of Spanish words when you speak." They all laughed, and someone commented that it is important to know Kaqchikel. In the courtyard the children yelled at each other in Spanish.

"It's really good that you speak our language," Alejandra told me.

"You don't use any Spanish words," commented another relative.

Tomás said to me, "We saw you the other day when we were walking in the Central Plaza in Antigua. You are an *indígena* the same as us."

"Thanks," I answered, "but why?"

Tomás explained, "Because you speak our language well. You like our food. Also, the Ladinos treat you badly."

I replied that I did not understand what he meant.

Alejandra continued, "When we passed through the plaza, we saw that you were with some vendors from Santa Catarina [Palopó]. The Ladinos said foul words to you and spit at you. You are *indígena* like us."

Seizing the moment to talk about identity issues, I asked them what they thought about the debates going on in the newspapers about Maya and Ladino identity. Several of them said that they had seen the editorial columns, but they do not read them anymore. "They only write because they like to talk a lot. We know who we are," one of them commented.

Then someone changed the subject, "In England there is a problem. A lot of cows have been killed because of a bad disease."

"That's true," another said, "because they are mad cows."

We did not return to identity issues.

Scene II: Compañía de Jesús Artisan Marketplace, Antigua Guatemala, May 1997

On my way into the Compañía de Jesús Artisan Marketplace, Delmi waves me over. Her small *típica tienda* (store selling handicraft goods) is on the northeast corner of the marketplace. "Where are you hurrying now?" she asks me in Kaqchikel.

"I have to do an interview inside the marketplace," I answer.

Mayas in the Marketplace

"Wait! It's not good to rush by and not talk to us for a few minutes," she says, motioning me to sit down.

As I squat down to talk, she comments, "You haven't passed by here in many days."

"That's because I moved and then I went to Comalapa," I respond as a group of tourists walks up to her display of textiles, dolls, and key chains.

One asks slowly in Spanish with an American accent, "Where is the post office?"

Delmi tells them and then says in Kaqchikel, "I have to sell maps. If I sell them for Q1 (US$0.17), I would make a lot of money."

We notice that a few elderly women, dressed in threadbare *blusas* (machine-made blouses) and *cortes* (wraparound skirts), have paused and are listening to us converse. One asks Delmi, "Does he know *lengua* [literally "tongue," but used as a synonym for "language"]?"

"No," Delmi answers. "He knows Kaqchikel."

The women look perplexed, and then the oldest one asks me, "Do you know *lengua*?"

"Only a little Kaqchikel," I reply.

"Thanks and praise the Lord that you speak *lengua*." she says, patting me on the shoulder.

Delmi interrupts, "He doesn't speak *lengua*; he speaks Kaqchikel."

"What is Kaqchikel?" the woman asks.

"*Qach'ab'äl* [Our language]," Delmi informs her. "What is your language?"

"*Lengua,*" she replies.

"No. There is no language named *lengua,*" Delmi says. "I speak Kaqchikel because I am from San Antonio Aguas Calientes. Where are you from?"

"Salcaja," she answers.

"Do you speak the same as those from Santa Cruz del Quiché?" Delmi inquires.

"Yes, the same," she answers.

"Then, you speak K'iche'," Delmi tells her.

"I don't know," the woman says. She turns and speaks to the other women with her. When she turns back to Delmi and me, she says, "We speak *lengua*." Then, she asked me, "Do you know a lot [of *lengua*]?"

"A little," I say before Delmi interrupts and says, "He is fluent in Kaqchikel. He is teaching my daughter how to speak it."

The women laugh and one asks (in K'iche') the girl next to Delmi if it's true, but she says in Spanish, "I don't speak Kaqchikel. I only understand a little."

The women laugh and continue in the direction of the Central Plaza.

Tourism, Social Relations, and Identity in Guatemala

Kaqchikel Maya handicraft vendors work and live in places that are situated within a range of local, state, and global political and economic forces. The scenes above illustrate concerns they have about identity, language, and social relations among themselves and with Ladinos and tourists. This book focuses on how Kaqchikel Maya handicraft vendors strategically use different identity constructions for political and economic reasons to help maintain their livelihoods.

In Guatemala, a country that comprises over twenty different ethnolinguistic groups and has a history of discriminatory practices against the Maya and political violence, it is important to understand the types of social relations that exist between different groups of people and then know how the people involved in these relations position themselves socially, politically, and economically vis-à-vis others. In this book, I am less concerned with discussing specific categories of identity, such as ethnic, national, cultural, gender, or class identities, than I am with examining the ways that Mayas, specifically Kaqchikel Mayas, strategically make and use these categories within the contexts of national and international tourism. In other words, instead of pursuing identity categories and identity as an attribute that Mayas have, I treat identity as a process.

Additionally, the two examples of conversations reveal some of the interrelated social and economic issues that have concerned Kaqchikel Mayas since the 1990s, such as crime, language retention, money, tourism, and inequalities (social, political, and economic) between Ladinos[1] and Mayas, among other interests. Tourism is one of the more important institutions around which Kaqchikel and K'iche' Mayas organize their economic lives in Guatemala. *Típica* vendors, those who sell handwoven textiles and handmade crafts, have been a common fixture in Guatemala since at least the 1930s. Although there were significant numbers of them until the early 1980s, when violence against Mayas—a direct result of the conflict between the Guatemalan military and the Guatemalan National Revolutionary Union (Unidad Nacional Revolucionaria Guatemalteca, UNRG)—contributed to a decline in number of tourists, tourism dramatically increased in the postwar 1990s. In turn, the number of vendors selling handicrafts increased for multiple reasons: more tourists (averaging over 500,000 per year since 1990, which represent larger numbers than for any year prior to the violence), resulting in a greater demand for handicrafts; easier within-country travel as the conflict ended; high levels of unemployment and underemployment (46 percent or higher); poor or low wages in the countryside (US$2/day for ten hours' labor); land shortages as a result of population growth in some towns (e.g., San Antonio Aguas Calientes, Santa Catarina Palopó); and low capital investment to enter *típica* sales (a backstrap loom costs around US$1.50, and one need only bring bracelets and some used clothing to get started). Because of changes in politics (the signing of the Peace Accords in 1996 between the government and revolutionaries) and in the infrastructure (building and improving roads has been a priority of recent presidential administrations), Kaqchikel Maya vendors have become commuters. They travel regularly, sometimes daily, between their hometowns and their workplaces in tourism marketplaces.

It is primarily Mayas who create and sell the handicrafts that tourists buy. They also clean rooms and tend gardens in hotels and wash dishes and bus tables in restaurants. The garden produce (tomatoes, peppers, carrots, squash) and commercial crops (maize, beans, broccoli) they grow end up on the tables of hotels, restaurants, and Ladino families that host foreign students studying Spanish. They build the hotels, restaurants, and sites that tourists use. *Típica* vendors, however, have intense connections to tourism because they interact directly with tourists in the marketplace. Other Mayas' relationships to tourism are indirect (in the case of farmers and construction workers) or mediated through their mainly Ladino employers (for hotel and restaurant employees).

How Maya *típica* vendors participate in tourism gives rise to two interrelated problems. First, not only do the interests and practices of foreign tourists affect the ways that Kaqchikel Maya vendors present themselves in the marketplace and in their hometowns, but vendors' participation in these tourism marketplaces has also led to changes in the performance of some gender roles in their households and in how they participate in hometown social and political activities. Furthermore, international tourism contributes to their thoughts about and practice of language and identity among themselves in their hometowns and households.

The second problem relates to how Mayas construct and maintain their identity within a globally oriented tourism market. I argue that one of the more significant components of identity construction for Mayas is their ongoing social relations, but maintaining social relations with others is no simple matter. That Kaqchikel Maya *típica* vendors commute to tourism sites such as Antigua and Panajachel from their hometowns presents both theoretical and methodological problems with regard to how vendors are economically and socially connected to their hometowns and to global markets through international tourism. Hence, the social relations in which they participate span three overlapping social spheres: those with persons from their hometowns; those with other vendors, middlepersons, and craftspersons in the handicraft market; and those with consumers—usually foreign tourists but also Ladinos and occasionally other Mayas.

That international tourists and tourism institutions affect Maya handicraft vendors' lives will be apparent in the coming chapters. However, this is not a study about the impact of international tourism on Mayas. The Mayas described in this book do not have to enter the tourism business. They choose to participate and in the process use various kinds of identity in calculated ways. They work to maintain social relations with residents from their hometowns and other handicraft market participants. These concerns distinguish this study from impact studies outlined by Cristóbal Kay (1989) related to underdevelopment research, and by June Nash (1981) related to world systems analysis. Instead of focusing on the impact of international tourism, this book concentrates on how Maya handicraft vendors participate in this global economy and con-

struct and use dynamic and flexible cultural identities to provide livelihoods for themselves.

There are ethnographic and theoretical gaps related to studies of globalization, international tourism, and locality (or place). Recent anthropological studies of globalism and transnationalism and their relation to
locality, such as Arjun Appadurai's (1996) *Modernity at Large,* Akhil Gupta
and James Ferguson's (1997) *Culture, Power, Place,* and Michael Kearney's
(1996) *Reconceptualizing the Peasantry,* have staked out a theoretical ground
that does not always focus on the day-to-day practices of the people they
discuss. They are mainly concerned with diasporic peoples who maintain
connections with and get news about their compatriots through e-mail,
the Internet, and various forms of mass media. In favorable economic
and political climates, these peoples may return periodically to their homelands and hometowns. Research of this type has focused primarily on
boundary crossing, on how members of dispersed social groups stay in
contact with each other, and on classifying or describing observable features of these peoples' global and transnational interactions.

Instead of working in their hometowns, workers move between their
"hometowns" and places of employment in other cities and even other
countries. With these labor practices, meanings of nation, community,
and identity are changing for those who migrate for work because they
are in regular, intense contact with cultural Others. Increasingly, the subjects of anthropological interest do not fit traditional academic categories, such as primitive and peasant (Kearney 1996). Furthermore, as Nash
(1993b: 20) points out, people from different cultural traditions are linked
through commodities, as when "consuming elite" travelers "search for
identity through consumerism" and form strange alliances with "producing communities" that lead to new forms of handicrafts that are still
perceived as "traditional." Thus, community for Mexican/Zapotec migrant laborers to the United States (Kearney 1996) and for Mesoamerican
producers of handicrafts to tourists (Nash 1993a) is linked in concrete
ways to both local and global economic interests.

According to Appadurai (2000: 1–3), globalization is a "source of
anxiety" for social scientists, activists, and the poor that is reflected in a
"double apartheid." One aspect of this is the separation between aca-

demic debates and "vernacular discourses about the global" that attempt to maintain local and national cultural and economic autonomy. The other aspect of it is that the poor are removed from both "nationalist discourses about globalization" and global discourses "surrounding trade, labor, environment, disease, and warfare." Appadurai (2000: 3) argues that new social organizations, "grassroots globalizations," are emerging that "contest, interrogate, and reverse these developments."

There is nothing unique or profound in this statement. Earlier, Stuart Hall (1997a, 1997b) made a similar observation that people in today's world feel forced to go global but sometimes react by going local— creating new strategies for creating locality and identity. The question should not be Does globalization homogenize or differentiate people and social groups?—a theme also addressed in *Identities on the Move: Transnational Processes in North America and the Caribbean Basin* (Goldín 1999). Instead, globalization studies need to focus on the particular ways that people live in the world, how they work, and how they reproduce their collective identities. Depending on the social, economic, and political contexts and the goals of the persons in question, globalization can be both homogenizing and differentiating. Compared to Appadurai and Hall, Nash and Christine Kovic (1997) offer a concrete ethnographic example using the Zapatista National Liberation Army's uprising to illustrate political resistance to the Mexican government's promotion of global trade and finance. And Marc Edelman (1999) shows how "peasant" can be a political identity and practice for Costa Ricans that also contests globalization. One of the conditions of living and working within the world today is dealing with globalization in specific ways, as the Zapatista revolutionaries in Mexico, the peasants in Costa Rica, and the Maya handicraft vendors in Guatemala are doing.

Rather than map global labor, commodity, and other flows, I describe ethnographically how Kaqchikel Maya vendors who are not displaced from the places where they were born and raised are nonetheless tied to the ways that "global" and "local" converge in the places where they live and work. In thinking about this convergence, I endeavor to fuse Appadurai's theories on the production of locality with John Watanabe's (1990, 1992) theories on Maya practices of community construction to show how Mayas incorporate themselves into the global while continuing to reinscribe significance in the local.

In contrast to most of the research done on globalization and transnationalism, this book looks at the mundane practices of vendors, attending to such things as how they sell to tourists; what foods they eat; how they refer to themselves and others in conversation; and who takes care of children, cooking, and cleaning. In these ordinary practices, one can find evidence of how global processes are part of household organization and local identity concepts. International tourism has contributed a larger palette and more colors from which Maya vendors can construct, maintain, and reflect on their identities as vendors, Mayas, and *indígenas*. I illustrate how these processes are embedded in the daily lives of vendors in their households by paying attention to existential practices.

Furthermore, I have concentrated on the perspectives of people who are the subjects of international tourism and participants in other global processes. This may seem an obvious goal, but with respect to research on tourism, this tends not to be the case. The majority of tourism research is about tourists—their behavior and attitudes—and the sociocultural construction of tourism sites, persons, and objects by outsiders. Castañeda's (1996) research on the tourism/archaeology site Chichén Itzá in Mexico is an important contribution to these issues. A survey of the last five years of the *Annals of Tourism Research* also demonstrates this trend, as do other anthropologically oriented studies, including Pierre van den Berghe's (1994, 1995) research on tourism in Chiapas, James Urry's (1990, 1992) research on touristic gazes, Edward Bruner and Barbara Kirshenblatt-Gimblett's (1994) research on the Maasai, and edited volumes by Marie-Françoise Lanfant, John B. Allcock, and Bruner (1995), *International Tourism: Identity and Change,* and by M. Thea Sinclair (1997a), *Gender, Work, and Tourism.*

Sinclair (1997b) explains that although tourism research has focused on the cultural, economic, status, and power divisions between tourists and persons working in the tourism sector, few studies have focused on the divisions between workers themselves, especially with regard to gender and race. As she notes, the volumes by Vivian Kinnaird and Derek Hall (1994) and Margaret Swain (1995) and miscellaneous articles on sex/prostitution tourism are the exceptions. This research, including the volume edited by Sinclair (1997a), focuses on women's roles, largely positing that women's work is an extension of the domestic sphere and subject to patriarchal relations and traditional cultural gender roles. These studies do not look at the relationships between men and women within tourism, but rather reduce gender to a category pertaining to women only.

Cynthia Cone (1995), Lynn Meisch (1995), and Margaret Swain (1993) offer examples of this gendered research on tourism workers in Mexico, Ecuador, and Panama, but they do not look at the specific ethnographic interactions of female and male tourism workers either. Cone's research compares two different strategies used by Maya women for economic success. Meisch looks at the sexual relations between men from Otavalo and foreign female tourists that is only sanctioned if the tourist conforms to local norms and standards. Swain analyzes the work of Cuna female artisans whose economic success can improve their power within their households, but not in the larger Panamanian society. In contrast to this research, I offer an ethnographic case that illustrates how Maya men and women interact within the tourism industry and how traditional gender roles for men and women are changing in Maya households, contributing to women's economic and political power beyond the realm of the household.

An example of ethnographic research that considers male-female relations within tourism is Nash's (1993c) "Maya Household Production in the World Market: The Potters of Amatenango del Valle, Chiapas, Mexico," which looks at specific ways that global economic forces, of which tourism is one, change local economic and social practices in terms of gender relations and roles. I build on her research by looking at the gender relations of female and male Maya handicraft vendors.

COMMUNITY IN THE GLOBAL CONTEXT

The focus on the existential practices and the opinions of vendors makes it possible to gain insight into the ways that global forces act on them, as well as to demonstrate how localities (places) come to be what they are and how they are used and interpreted. My research fits into an emerging trend in anthropology—represented by works such as Bruner (1999), Nash (1993c), Ortner (1997), and Stoller (1997)—that is trying to bring more detailed ethnographic data into studies of global and transnational processes. This research takes issue with how "community" has been studied anthropologically as a largely self-contained whole, and it calls for a reformation of the concept. As Bruner (1999: 475) remarks of the Batak village where he did research but is equally applicable to other places, it "remains a fixed, bounded locality, but the ways of the outside world now reside within the village and within the minds of the villagers."

Nash (1993c) describes how Maya women's pottery production in Amatenango has become part of a global tourism economy, but women themselves have indirect or limited contact with tourists. The town itself is not a tourism site, though that is changing. Bruner (1999) describes how Balinese villagers participate in tourism by meeting tourists in "touristic borderzones." The borderzone is a performative space, but Balinese persons and tourists do not live in it. Paul Stoller (1997) describes how West African vendors from different ethnic groups migrate to a transnational locality, New York City, and form occupational groups. Kaqchikel vendors, described here, are embedded in global, transnational, as well as Guatemalan national tourism in different ways than the people these ethnographers describe.

Unlike Mayas from Amatenango, the Maya vendors in Guatemala are in direct contact with tourists, tourism guides, and tourism places, such as hotels, restaurants, and sites, that are part of the Ruta Maya tourism system that includes Mexico, Belize, Guatemala, Honduras, and El Salvador. Tourism is concentrated in just a few areas in Guatemala, particularly Antigua, Lake Atitlán, Chichicastenango, and Tikal. The most-traveled tourism routes are located firmly within Kaqchikel Maya regions of Guatemala. If, on average, only 500,000 tourists visit Guatemala in a year, they pass through at least one of these four places. Furthermore, the vendors that received the most attention from tourism organizations and tourists are from two towns, San Antonio Aguas Calientes and Santa Catarina Palopó, that have been fully incorporated into the main tourism routes in Guatemala for seventy or more years. For these Mayas, it is difficult to get out of the touristic borderzone, and people living in these towns have grown up in this performative space. Some have even made their homes and domestic spaces performance areas. Similar to West Africans in New York City, persons from different Maya ethnolinguistic groups come together in the tourism marketplace in Antigua and constitute an occupational group that lives in a transnational space. Unlike the West Africans, however, they are not separated from their hometowns for long periods of time, and their homes are also part of the transnational space.

The ethnographic context in which Kaqchikel Maya vendors are located allowed me to gain insights into how they conceive of, construct, maintain, and use identity. Sol Tax's (1937) theories about Maya identities being situated at the level of the *municipio* (cultural and political community) and how participation in marketplaces heightens awareness of ethnic differences still hold true today in most cases. Mayas continue to use identities that are based on the *municipio,* and marketplaces can still be arenas where these identities are reaffirmed. Mayas today are more conscious of their identities, as well as the political and economic ramifications of using them (see Warren 1998a, 1998b). They use different identities in self-conscious ways that Tax did not explain or anticipate. It is significant to note, however, that community remains as one form of collective identity expression, despite dramatic changes in the economic and political contexts of contemporary Guatemala.

IDENTITY CONSTRUCTION THROUGH SOCIAL RELATIONS

Tax (1941) explains how, historically, Mayas of one town are well aware of other towns' differences and have maintained distinctions among themselves. These distinctions are not preserved by physical isolation, but, according to Tax, by a "system of impersonal relations." Or in Fredrik Barth's (1969: 9) terms, ethnic "boundaries persist despite a flow of personnel across them" and a significant amount of knowledge about others. Although it is not currently fashionable to use Tax's and Barth's theories on identity construction, they are appropriate for positioning some of the theoretical arguments in this book and for framing a theory of identity construction through social relations. The research informing this book draws on Tax's and Barth's theories of how ethnic identity emerges through a dialectic of self-identification and ascription by others, but it moves beyond them to look at how identity concepts in general emerge from the interactions of people within the same group (Kaqchikel vendors and people from their hometowns). The data also show that how identity is used, signified, and negotiated within a group depends on an interplay of factors, including local collective notions of tradition, belonging, work, and beliefs, as they relate to broader national and global contexts.

Tax's and Barth's work on identity construction is not far removed from contemporary and more fashionable discussions of identity as cultural difference that are formulated by Appadurai (1996: 12–16) and cultural theorist Homi Bhabha (1994: 1–2, 162–164). Appadurai's and Bhabha's formulations of cultural difference treat identity as a process. For Appadurai

(1996: 14), this means that identity construction "takes the conscious and imaginative construction and mobilization of differences as its core." For Bhabha (1994: 2), "collective experiences ... are negotiated" within spaces of difference and lead to identities that are more than "the sum of the 'parts' of difference (usually intoned as race/class/gender, etc.)."

Cultural difference is key to understanding Tax's (1937, 1941) descriptions of Guatemalan marketplaces and interethnic relations in the 1930s, as well as the handicraft marketplaces of 1990s Guatemala. Difference becomes manifest through economic and social participation in the marketplace. It is a place where difference is tied to unequal relations of power—economic and political—between social groups. John Comaroff and Jean Comaroff (1992: 52–54) note this about ethnic relations in general where differentiation occurs. Identity relations of social groups today are different than during the period when Tax conducted fieldwork because of the globalization of society, politics, and the economy. This has led to the formation of new ethnicities (Hall 1996a, 1996b), creative uses of cultural identity and difference—in the case of Maya political activists in Guatemala (Warren 1998a)—and the increased internal differentiation of once autonomous sociocultural groups (Kearney 1996; G. Smith 1989). The common thread running through these discussions of identity construction is that it is processual and related to specific power relations rather than lists of traits. For Mayas, identity as a process emerges in part from within "the company of particularly Maya neighbors" (Watanabe 1992: 16). In the contexts of selling in the handicraft marketplace and commuting between the home and the marketplace, Maya vendors especially rely on specific kinds of social relations with particular types of people to maintain, modify, and differentiate their cultural identities.

Few Maya vendors thought about how their economic, social, and political practices were embedded within forms of globalization that structure the marketplaces where they work and communities where they sleep, worship, work, and play. Of greater concern to them was the continuity of social relations that they had with other people and the fostering of new, potentially long-term social relations. Vendors live within different, overlapping fields of social interaction, including family, community, marketplace, and the Guatemalan state. In each of these fields, vendors present themselves to the other people (à la Goffman 1959) and engage them through numerous types of social relations.

Kaqchikel vendors evoked concepts of identity in self-conscious ways, depending on the social context and the social relation in which they were embedded. The multiple identity concepts they used could not simply be explained in terms of boundaries or a dialectic of self-identification and attribution by others (Barth 1969). Certainly, these conditions are important to identity construction, but for vendors involved in numerous social interactive arenas and engaged with different types of social actors, the boundaries are gray because there are so many of them, all overlapping each other. Barth's dialectic is ambiguous, because Kaqchikel Maya vendors, for instance, interact with different categories of people: foreign and national tourists, vendors, middlepersons, police officers, garbage collectors, tax collectors, fellow Mayas from their hometowns, and others. Exactly what is significant and the degree of its significance relates to the time, place, and people involved. Mayas live in a social universe where they are, at the same time, members of families, households, towns, markets, and the Guatemala state. In each of these social contexts, global processes (tourism in the case of these Kaqchikeles) both subjectify and objectify them in observable ways. Identity constructions, hence, are structured around the overlapping constellations of social relations embedded in local, regional, national, and global spaces.

My contribution to identity studies in general, and Maya studies in particular, lies in the recognition that a significant component of Maya identity construction and maintenance is embedded in particular types of social relations. This is quite different from research that has been done on identity concepts within and outside of Maya studies. By referring to social relations, I'm not talking about the ascribed-assumed dichotomy that Tax (1937, 1941) effectively described and Barth (1969) popularized nor identity as cultural difference that was outlined earlier. Other anthropologists have taken up these positions as well as the Weberian-inspired debate over the primordial versus constructed aspects of identity (Fischer 1996a, 1999).

With regard to studying ethnicity or cultural identity, it is too easy to merely look at relations of power and social relations between subordinate (or subaltern or marginalized) groups of people and those who have political, social, and economic control. It is also important to understand local, within-group meanings and uses of identity. As part of their research with Mayas in Guatemala, Hendrickson (1995), Warren (1989, 1992), and Watanabe (1992) have focused on locally conceived and practiced identity. Both Watanabe's and Warren's research also calls attention to the importance of place[2] in the construction of Maya identities.

Their findings are not contradicted here. However, Maya vendors had different relationships with the places they considered home and the other places where they worked and lived. Specifically, I am interested in what happens to Maya identity construction when Mayas spend a substantial amount of time outside their communities and with other groups of people (foreigners, Ladinos, and other Mayas). Although the place called home is the most important locality to vendors, their identities in relation to that place are maintained primarily through ongoing social relations with people from their hometown and regular trips home to participate in highly visible activities. It mattered less that vendors were actually in their towns all the time than that they participated in these ongoing social relations. Similarly, political activists, migratory laborers, and cooperative officials, all of whom work away from their hometowns, also maintain such social relations (Kearney 1996; Nash 2001; G. Smith 1989; Warren 1998a). If an individual did not foster these relations, then vendors and people in the hometown did not recognize that person's claim of community identity. In other words, being Maya is not only about always living in a specific type of locality and doing specific types of Maya practices (Watanabe 1990); it is about interacting socially with others from one's town (for community identity), with others from one's linguistic group (for linguistic identity), and with other Mayas (for Maya and *indígena* identities) on a regular basis.[3] This is not to create the impression that the identities of Mayas are detached from material, historical, and ideological bases. Such conditions would probably create unstable subjectivities, where Mayas would not be sure of who they are. Maya vendors quite clearly know who they are. Simply put, they were not having "identity crises."

IDENTITY USE AS STRATEGY

Maya identities, as will be seen in the coming chapters, are also related to practices of difference, as Tax recognized long ago. Today, however, Mayas are constructing broader collective identities than Tax predicted. This, of course, relates to changes in Guatemalan national politics, mass media, and the global economy. Kay Warren and Jean Jackson (2002b), like Charles Hale (1997), suggest that indigenous activism is tied to identity politics in Latin America. Mayas, like other indigenous peoples throughout the Americas, have organized and spoken about political, economic, and social issues in terms of identity. Indigenous activists and mass media representatives have used each other—indigenous leaders to get their respective causes heard, and the media to sell images of exotic others, much as *National Geographic* has (Hervik 1998; Lutz and Collins 1993). The problem facing Maya political and social activists, as Watanabe (1995: 39) noted early, is that they "need first to persuade other Maya to recognise their lead."

Maya vendors share with Maya activists and other participants in the Maya movement (see Esquit and Gálvez 1997, Fischer and Brown 1996b, and Warren 1998a and 1998b for descriptions of this political movement) the practice of using identity in strategic ways to further their respective causes. Leaders of the Maya movement, such as Cojtí Cuxil (1995, 1997), have emphasized cultural education and specific cultural values (language, dress, cosmology) over economic and material concerns. At the same time, Maya handicraft vendors reject the calculated use of identity for cultural goals, using it instead for economically oriented purposes, though they do draw on some Pan-Mayanist constructions of language, as illustrated in the vignettes opening this introduction. I address the vendors' critique of the Maya movement elsewhere (Little 1998, n.d.; also see Esquit and Gálvez 1997 for an autocritique of the movement), but their main problem with it is that it is not based on the material conditions that are relevant to Maya handicraft vendors or, for that matter, Mayas working in agriculture, factories, or handicraft fabrication.

Maya vendors use identity deliberately in ways that are similar to the indigenous people and workers described in (post)peasant studies such as those by Marc Edelman (1999) for Costa Rica; Michael Kearney (1996) for Oaxaca, Mexico; and Gavin Smith (1989) for Peru, although these anthropologists differ in their views as to what constitutes the "peasant" in contemporary Latin America. Identity is also similarly used in political contexts by Maya activists (Warren 1998a) and other indigenous activists (Warren and Jackson 2002a). Although the link between identity construction and social relations is not part of these authors' discussions, it is not a leap to suggest that social relations play a prominent role in the maintenance and establishment of certain key identity concepts used by the subjects of their books. Costa Rican coffee workers, Mixtec and Zapotec transnational laborers in Mexico, *huasicanchino* laborers in Peru, and Maya handicraft vendors all use identity in intentional ways that are related to the particular conditions in which they maintain their livelihoods. Although cultural perspectives certainly play an important part in how these groups of people use their identities for economic and political gain, they do not use their identities only for narrow cultural goals.

Increasingly, Mayas perform cultural practices before tourists' inquisitive eyes and in anticipation of tourists watching them. In other words, Mayas involved with tourists—and probably others too, especially those involved with the Maya political movement—are self-conscious about their cultural practices and identities. In essence, this means that identity is both a concept held and used by them as well as an explanation of social and political relations.

Shifting Subjectivities of an Anthropologist

Like other anthropologists' field experiences, my fieldwork was shaped by the intersubjective experiences I had with people who live in and visit Guatemala. My first trip to Guatemala was in July 1987. I went as a tourist with mediocre Spanish skills, accompanied by two friends, one of whom is Honduran. She helped us out of trouble by repairing our major linguistic blunders, but on occasion she allowed us to humiliate ourselves with our faux pas. Like other first-time tourists to Guatemala, I was consumed by the institution of tourism but had little direct contact with Mayas. The structures that direct and guide tourists to designated sites are so obvious and so well organized that it is difficult for tourists to have experiences with people and places that are not on the tourism route. Our trip itinerary began with a stop at the Catholic cathedral in Esquipulas, continued with stops in Guatemala City, Antigua, San Antonio Aguas Calientes, Panajachel, Chichicastenango, and ended in Antigua and Guatemala City (Figure 0.1). Despite the population being more than half Maya (according to some estimates, three-fourths or more [Tzian 1994]),[4] we had little contact with Mayas, except in the one place that was *not* promoted for its traditional handicrafts and indigenous population: Antigua.

While in Antigua, I met vendors who helped reshape my personal perspectives about the town as only a Spanish colonial city. From that time forward, it became increasingly Maya for me, as these vendors introduced me to other Maya vendors and middlepersons during subsequent trips as a tourist (December 1987 through January 1988 and December 1988 through February 1989).

My subjectivity shifted dramatically in the summer of 1992 with my first trip as an anthropologist. My small field project was to work as a guide for a tour company in order to learn how U.S. tourists interacted with Mayas and conceived of Guatemala. This project ended in 1994 after another summer of fieldwork in Guatemala, but this time I paid more attention to Mayas' reactions to tourists. The results of this research are described in an essay informed by ethnographic and library research (Little 1995). During the 1992 fieldwork, my subject position was viewed negatively by my Maya friends. They considered my role as guide to be linked to Ladino society. The only exchanges we—the tour group and I—had with Mayas were purely economic.

I worked to undo my subjectivity as a tour guide among my Maya friends and associates in the summer of 1994. This coincided with my beginning Kaqchikel studies and an association with the Oxlajuj Aj Kaqchikel Maya Language and Culture course offered by Tulane University in Guatemala. It also marks the formal start of my research with Kaqchikel Maya *típica* vendors.

Figure 0.1. Major tourism sites and cities in Guatemala. Mayas sell handicrafts at all locations listed. Map by the author.

Mayas in the Marketplace

My association with the Kaqchikel language course produced an ambiguous and controversial subject position in relation to Kaqchikel vendors, especially after my fourth year of participation, when I went from a student and research assistant to one of the course's co-directors. Although my vendor friends congratulated me on getting a position that they considered prestigious and culturally valuable (I was, after all, promoting their language and culture), it caused some problems. For my intensive continuous fieldwork, from June 1996 through August 1998, vendors had my undivided attention, except during the six weeks of the Kaqchikel course. My duties then were so demanding that I could not maintain regular social relations with my vendor friends. They also knew that one of my roles in the course was as employer of Kaqchikel Maya teachers. The first year I assumed co-directorship many vendors pressured me to hire their kin. However, few had the skills or academic credentials to be teachers. Over consecutive summers since 1997, vendors became more aware of my roles in the course and of the necessary qualifications of the teachers.

Despite the sometimes strained relationships with vendors that resulted from my post in the Kaqchikel course, the course introduced me to other Kaqchikel persons, especially those who have chosen academic and political careers. The teachers offered additional perspectives on Kaqchikel life, opened their homes to me when I needed a break from tourists and vendors in Antigua, and taught me about Kaqchikel customs by tolerating and even encouraging my questions. Learning the basics of planting, weaving, church rituals, curing ceremonies, and other customs from the Kaqchikel teachers helped improve my relationships with Kaqchikel vendors and their extended families because they knew that I would behave appropriately and ask questions at appropriate times.

Though my subjectivity has been remade several times over the years, some vendors insisted on acknowledging me in singular ways. For a few, I was never more than a tourist. For most, I was a scholar studying their lives. For many, I was their friend, with a family of my own. My subject position as a father solidified with my daughter's annual (now nine) two-month visits. Her friendships with the children of vendor families helped strengthen my social connections with them, associated me with particular hearth groups,[5] and integrated me into Kaqchikel towns.

Locations of Field Research

George Marcus (1995) describes two different types of ethnographic research that emerged in the mid-1980s. The most common focuses on a single site, a traditional ethnographic approach, where ethnographers are increasingly concerned with the place of these sites within the world system of capitalist political economy. The other type of ethnographic research is "self-consciously embedded in a world system . . . [and] moves out from the single sites and local situations of conventional ethnographic research designs to examine the circulation of cultural meanings, objects, and identities in diffuse time-space" (Marcus 1995: 96). In other words, ethnographic research in this design takes ethnographers to multiple sites.[6]

Not all ethnographic research requires anthropologists to travel. However, in my case, it would have been impossible to learn how Kaqchikel Maya *típica* vendors participated in international tourism and conceived of the collective forms of identity they used and manipulated had I chosen just one fieldsite. Had I been rooted in any one site, I would have missed the important socioeconomic ways that Mayas organize, and are organized by, their families, households, community relations, and marketplaces.

Understanding how identity and labor are practiced in Guatemala necessitates—almost demands—that anthropologists get out of the "little community." This is because not just vendors but also construction workers, schoolteachers, hotel service employees, waiters and waitresses, and other job holders commute between their hometowns and their places of employment. Vendors are part of a commuter culture that emerged in the late 1980s as the war in Guatemala calmed, wages in the countryside continued to decline relative to cost of living, roads and transportation improved, and some job and educational opportunities opened in large cities and tourism sites. Kearney (1996: 122–123) argues that migrants "share structural features with 'commuters' who each day jam expressways, trains, and buses, although such 'migrants' differ from 'commuters' in that they travel farther and stay in their destinations longer."

In Guatemala, vendors do not just "share structural features" with "commuters." They *are* commuters. A big difference between the people that Kearney refers to and the vendors that I worked with is the frequency of travel between their hometowns and jobs. Several have traveled to the United States and Europe, and a small number of vendors,

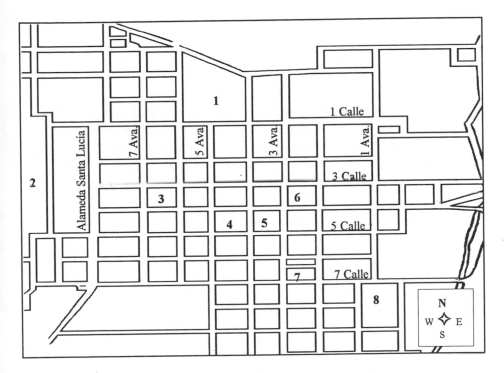

1 - **La Merced Church:** San Antonio Aguas Calientes, San Andrés Itzapa
2 - **Municipal Marketplace:** San Antonio Aguas Calientes, Santa Catarina Barahona, San Juan de Comalapa, Momostenango, Chichicastenango, Totonicapán
3 - **Compañía de Jesús Artisan Marketplace:** San Antonio Aguas Calientes, Santa Catarina Barahona, San Juan de Comalapa, Momostenango, Chichicastenango, Nebaj, Santa Catarina Palopó, Los Encuentros, Sololá, Todos Santos
4 - **Central Plaza:** San Antonio Aguas Calientes, Santa Catarina Barahona, San Andrés Itzapa, Momostenango, Chichicastenango, Santa Catarina Palopó, San Antonio Palopó, Los Encuentros, Sololá
5 - **Cathedral:** San Antonio Aguas Calientes, Santa Catarina Barahona
6 - **La Fuente Saturday Marketplace:** San Antonio Aguas Calientes, Santa Catarina Barahona, Santa María de Jesús, Santo Domingo Xenacoj, San Juan Sacatepéquez, San Pedro Sacatepéquez, Patzún, Chichicastenango, Nahualá, Panajachel, Santa Catarina Palopó, San Antonio Palopó, Todos Santos
7 - **Tanque de la Unión Park:** San Antonio Aguas Calientes, Santa Catarina Barahona, Santa María de Jesús, Santa Catarina Palopó, San Antonio Palopó, Chajul
8 - **San Francisco el Grande Church:** San Antonio Aguas Calientes, Santa Catarina Barahona

Figure 0.2. Primary *típica* vending locations in Antigua, with vendors' principal towns of origin. Map by author.

when business is good, have traveled to, and have business connections in, other countries. This is not commuting, though, and those who have family members living in other countries do not consider their relatives' annual or biannual trips home to be commuting. Commuters, in contrast, maintain regular social and economic connections with at least two localities. They literally have lives in more than one place. This changes how Mayas interact with and live in their hometowns.

My research base and the hub from which I studied Kaqchikel Maya *típica* vendor social relations and identity was Antigua Guatemala. Mayas, mainly from nearby towns, have provided labor and food to the city for nearly five hundred years (Lutz 1994). It has been a popular tourist destination for more than a century and, since the 1940s, one of the places where the wealthy from all over the world come to live and to vacation

Figure 0.3. Major linguistic areas of *típica* vendors in Antigua. Map by author.

Mayas in the Marketplace

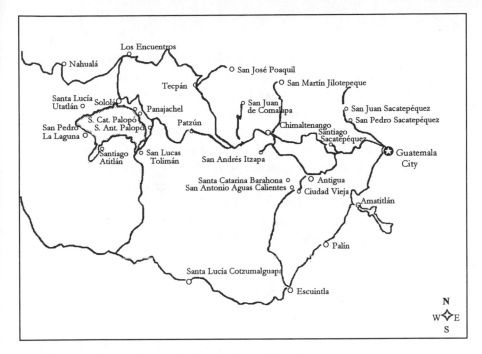

Figure 0.4. Central Guatemalan highlands. Map by author.

and buy homes. It is also a place where tourists, Ladinos, and sometimes even Mayas expect that Mayas should act like "Indians" in order to fit into the touristic scheme of the city. Antigua has become a place for both foreign and national tourists to play and relax but one where Mayas work. The types of jobs they do determine the ways they do or do not demonstrate their Mayanness.

In Antigua I worked mainly with vendors in the Compañía de Jesús Artisan Marketplace and with peddlers. I also regularly visited other vending locations (Figure 0.2). The Kaqchikel, K'iche', and other Maya ethnolinguistic groups who sell *típica* in Antigua are not from Antigua (Figure 0.3). As I became more involved with their lives, it was evident that Antigua, with its many *típica* retail outlets, was an insufficient context for studying vendors' lives and identities. Much of their social, political, and economic lives were still embedded in their hometowns.

My research took me mainly to the Kaqchikel towns of San Antonio Aguas Calientes and Santa Catarina Palopó (Figure 0.4). The advantages of choosing these sites over others were multiple. First, they had been studied previously by other anthropologists. Sheldon Annis (1987) conducted research in San Antonio, and Sol Tax (1946) conducted research in Santa Catarina. These in-depth community studies provided a base from which to measure vendors' interactions with fellow community members. Second, these towns have been connected to international tourism at least since the 1930s. Kaqchikel Mayas who live in these two towns continue to produce souvenirs and handicrafts for tourists. Third, San Antonio and Santa Catarina are relatively well incorporated into the Guatemalan nation-state. Residents of San Antonio have been well connected to Guatemala's administrative and economic centers, and residents of Santa Catarina, until the late 1970s, were dependent on migratory wage labor in the coastal cotton and sugar cane plantations, as well as the surrounding coffee plantations. How they have historically been tied to the Guatemalan nation-state contributes to their interactions with Ladinos and tourists in Antigua.

Methodology

My research methodology took shape because of the intersubjective experiences that I have had with Kaqchikeles over the sixteen years that I have been an anthropologist or tourist in Guatemala. The subject positions that they assigned to me and let me assume allowed me to conduct my research in specific ways. I used common anthropological strategies, but my data collection was also tactical when common fieldwork strategies failed.

This book is primarily based on continuous research from June 1996 through August 1998. Earlier, in the summer of 1992, I studied tourism networks and conducted fieldwork as a guide. In June 1994, I initiated conversations with several vendors in the Compañía de Jesús Artisan Marketplace and other marketplaces in Antigua. I slowly integrated myself into the marketplace, where I could observe the socioeconomic exchanges between vendors and tourists and among vendors themselves. By November 1996, I was well known among the Maya *típica* vendors selling in Antigua, and the Compañía de Jesús Artisan Association (Asociación de Artesanos de la Compañía de Jesús) officially recognized me.

MARKETPLACE AND COMMUNITY

For the period I conducted continuous research, I divided my time between tourism/*típica* marketplaces in Antigua and vendors' hometowns. During the first year, I spent more time in Antigua in the marketplaces.

Mayas in the Marketplace

In the second year, I spent the majority of my time in the hometowns of Kaqchikel vendors.

Even though all vendors spoke Spanish, and many spoke some English (two of the Kaqchikel vendors were fluent enough that they asked me to interview them in English), developing rapport, participating in vendor society, and comprehending their social relations demanded that I converse in Kaqchikel. By June 1996, all my conversations and interviews with Kaqchikel speakers were in Kaqchikel.

During my first artisan association meeting with Compañía de Jesús vendors, they agreed that I had to work for them. My responsibilities included interviewing tourists, assisting with language interpreting (help that most of them did not need), and coordinating a commercial book project by them about their lives. The book project died when vendors argued about how to represent themselves. Most vendors doubted their writing abilities, which contributed to their doubts about what interests tourists. Each month, I reported to them what I learned from conversations with and observations of tourists.

Although I frequently visited San Antonio Aguas Calientes and Santa Catarina Palopó, participating in community functions and learning about the respective people and places, this research should not be construed as a community-based ethnographic study. My main goals were to learn how vendors remained integrated with their hometowns, despite the fact that they spent more time in Antigua, and to observe family life and household activities, paying attention to references to tourism and marketplace.

ANTHROPOLOGICAL STRATEGIES

My research methodology included a number of well-tested anthropological strategies. First, using fieldnotes, audiotape recordings, and videotape recordings, I recorded my observations of the vendors, tourists, and others who entered tourism/*típica* marketplaces throughout Antigua. During the busiest hours of the day, I pretended to be a customer, blending in with the tourists visiting the marketplaces, unless a vendor wanted me to explain something or interpret for her. Castañeda (1996) describes how he was considered a spy by the vendors in Pisté because he was recording his observations of them. In my case, I was a spy too, but vendors employed me to spy on tourists. However, when I talked to tourists, I explained why I was in Guatemala.

Second, I interviewed vendors in all 205 marketplace stalls in the Compañía de Jesús Artisan Marketplace, as well as dozens of street peddlers and vendors in other marketplaces. The interview/survey that I used was based on questions from John Swetnam (1975) and Linda Asturias de Barrios (1994; see Appendix). Although the survey helped me get information about vendors, I used the interview items more as a context for us to talk. Vendors did not just answer the questions, they discussed them with me. If a question in the interview caused vendors to talk about something tangential to my immediate interests, I encouraged them. The interviewing/surveying that I did with them and with tourists was also academic work with which they were familiar. Merely spending the day with them, conversing and observing, seemed too much as if I were goofing off.

Third, I initiated some long, ongoing conversations and was invited to participate in other continuing discussions with several different vendors and their extended families. Most of my data come from these talks. Early in my fieldwork, I overzealously asked a lot of questions. Vendors typically resisted this interrogation, never directly refusing to talk to me, but never answering my questions. The only reason vendors answered my questions in the interview/survey was that they had agreed to it in the association meeting. Several vendors during my early fieldwork said, "*Tawoyob'ej* (Wait), Walter. Stay long enough and you will learn what you want to know." By participating in conversations that were reciprocal and demonstrated a long-term social relation, I was able to learn about the economic and social concerns of vendors, how they used identity concepts in strategic and tactical ways, and how tourism (and other transnational forces) was affecting them.

Fourth, I participated in vendor society as much as they permitted me. The two main social arenas that I was part of were the marketplace and the vendors' hometown. Marketplace participation involved helping them set up and arrange their vending locales in the morning and take down and store their merchandise in the evening, which included carrying *bultos* (large bags/bundles of merchandise) to the warehouses. I learned basic selling techniques and watched vendor stalls when vendors had errands outside of the marketplace. Most of the time my participation was similar to that of other males in the marketplace. I ran errands for female vendors by going to the bank to exchange money, buying food and construction materials in the municipal marketplace, and delivering messages to family members outside of the marketplace. I also helped watch vendors' children.

In vendors' homes, I participated in a number of different ways, performing some "male" and some "female" activities. My objective was to learn as much about Maya life as possible through involvement. I undertook gender-specific tasks related to cooking, in part, because they are of personal interest to me. Vendors were curious about my interests, and fixing meals became a form of cross-cultural comparison for us. I learned how to prepare and cook several dishes served in Maya homes, such as *pepián* (chile and tomato sauce for meat), *ichaj* (greens), *tamales, chuchitos* (a form of tamale), and *pulik* (chicken stew thickened with cornmeal). I learned how to make tortillas. In turn, I taught people how to make pizza, the dish that was most requested. I also took weaving lessons in two towns, San Antonio Aguas Calientes and San Juan de Comalapa. In the former town, I learned some traditional designs, such as the *kumatzin* and *rupam läq,* and finished a small throw cloth. In the latter town, I worked on a traditional *huipil* panel but never completed it. These lessons resulted in my being teased by some, which is explained in Chapter 5. In Santa Catarina Palopó, I learned how to make *pulseras,* commonly known as friendship bracelets. In addition, to these supposedly female activities, I learned and performed several activities associated with men's work, such as preparing the *milpa* (maize field), chopping firewood, or building construction. As one who grew up on a Midwestern farm and roofed during summer breaks in college, these roles were not far from my own background. My log-splitting skills earned me the respect of male Mayas and helped offset their chides about my weaving.

My final strategy was reading the newspapers and discussing the contents with vendors. Initially, I had hoped that such discussions would stimulate their opinions about the Maya movement that received daily attention in the press at that time. They had little to say about this movement. However, since they read newspapers on a regular basis, I learned that there were other topics that interested them, particularly crime and the manner in which the media represented it. They used the information about crime to try to predict how many tourists would visit Guatemala. Newspaper articles also provided neutral conversation topics and information about the United States, about which vendors often questioned me.

Some of my fieldwork was tactical in nature, as I was forced to continually renegotiate my relationships with vendors. This had to do somewhat with the shifting subjectivities that vendors ascribed to me: anthropologist, guide, tourist, Kaqchikel language course co-director, friend, and so on. Depending on what they wanted to get from me, they would ascribe a particular subjectivity to me. I could not begin my day thinking that I was simply an anthropologist.

Typical anthropological practices of making observations, writing them down, and interviewing were disrupted when vendors decided to use me as a translator or culture broker between them and tourists. As Kaqchikel course co-director, they regarded me as a potential employer, tour guide, and, even, tourist. Basically, vendors were interested in reaping some sort of economic benefit from their association with me, either directly by selling merchandise to me or indirectly by using me to convince tourists and Kaqchikel students to buy their merchandise. Because I could not afford (nor did I desire) to purchase items from all vendors with whom I worked, I usually waited until a situation arose in which we could mutually benefit from the exchange.

My relationships with vendors were economic as well as social. Unlike the exchanges between vendors and tourists, which usually ended with the purchase, anthropologists cannot afford to have such limited relationships. With several families, I entered into complicated gift and favor exchanges. This helped me avoid becoming an economic patron to vendors. It also alleviated some of the competition between vendors for my economic resources.

Another related tactic arose when I first began fieldwork, especially from vendors from San Antonio Aguas Calientes and Santa Catarina Barahona. Some had worked with Sheldon Annis (1987) and Robert McKenna Brown (1991, 1998). They knew something about anthropological work and competed to provide services for me, such as shelter, meals, laundry, and transportation. I kindly declined all of these offers. To have hired people to perform these services would have affiliated me with only a few families; the others would have shut me out of their homes and lives.

Instead, I rented a room, then later a small apartment in Antigua, which vendors could visit any time they wanted. At the same time, a couple of my Kaqchikel teachers, one from San Antonio Aguas Calientes and one from Santa Catarina Barahona, invited me to their homes and to various social functions. Our friendships strengthened, and they provided me with guidance on social mores and language. Vendors, however, soon learned that these fellow townspeople were not charging me for food or a place to stay when I visited. Additionally, they learned that these Kaqchikeles and other Kaqchikel teachers would visit me in Antigua. When they realized this, vendors stopped trying to sell me services and instead began competing for me to visit them and started to visit my apartment. In return, I never refused a guest and I tried not to refuse invitations. The end result of this tactic was that I was able to work with a number of vendors and their extended families, even those who were feuding with each other. Although most vendors viewed me as an impartial listener who would not spread rumors or personal information about them, they freely gossiped about each other. Having a place of my own in a neutral location allowed me to reciprocate the hospitality that was extended to me, which also served as a good way to build rapport.

Organization of the Book

Guatemalan society, similar to other complex societies, is composed of different stratified socioeconomic classes, as well as different ethnic and cultural groups. Guatemalans are well aware of these differences. Tourists and anthropologists who are new to the country quickly recognize the overt signs that differentiate these social groups from each other. Many Mayas, especially women, still distinguish themselves from non-Mayas by the type of clothing they wear. With a little effort, a visitor to Guatemala can learn the major social and economic hierarchies that are present. The social categories of people, language, and occupation—for example, Maya, Ladino, Kaqchikel, K'iche', vendor, farmer, factory worker, and others (which sometimes overlap each other)—are meaningful to the members of Guatemalan society and are used strategically by them.

Because of where they sell and who they sell to, *típica* vendors have greater access to information coming from tourism, the Guatemalan government, the Maya movement, and their hometowns about different concepts of who Mayas are and what constitutes Mayanness than do most Mayas living in Guatemala today. Vendors use these concepts for social and economic gain. Although these vendors participate in the tourism system and deal with the Guatemalan government, their identity choices are limited by and are not detached from local concerns. Kaqchikel Maya *típica* vendors navigate between these different concepts of what it means to be Maya by grounding themselves in pragmatic social and economic concerns. They avoid committing to rigid, monodimensional concepts of identity. When asked explicitly what their identities are, they answered, "We know who we are." As argued in this book, their answer suggests that they know how to use identity concepts and what the political and economic implications of that use are for them.

Social difference and hierarchy have been among the topics most studied by anthropologists working in Guatemala, beginning with Sol Tax's (1937) article, "The *Municipios* of the Midwestern Highlands of Guatemala." This tradition continues with recent ethnographies by Robert Carlsen (1997), Edward Fischer (2001), Diane Nelson (1999), and Kay Warren (1998a). To contribute to this body of work, I draw inspiration from Watanabe's (1992) ethnography to recontextualize difference and hierarchy in Guatemala by looking primarily at the existential social and economic practices of Kaqchikel Maya *típica* vendors who sell in Antigua Guatemala to show how the practices and identities of Kaqchikel Mayas have modified because of the international and transnational tourism setting in which they work.

Tourism reconstructs difference in concrete, observable ways. Both tourists and their Others mutually participate in this construction. The convergence of observers and observed, consumers and producers, spectators and performers has created new sociocultural and socioeconomic spaces of interaction that are part of local and transnational communities but are increasingly less limited by nation-states. This contributes to the new ways that Mayas live in and conceptualize the world. Vendors are still embedded in the nation in the ways they are subjected to political violence and co-opted to promote tourism. Nation, however, gets in their way. Because their economic connections are with their respective hometowns and with foreign tourists and businesspersons, they treat local-level to national-level institutions as obstacles to their economic and social autonomy. In contrast to Pan-Maya activists who are concerned with remaking the state and reconceptualizing the nation, handicraft vendors want to cut out the state and do away with the concept of nation, using community- and transnational-based identities, among others, rather than national identity.

As is illustrated in this book, international tourism (tourists, policies, institutions, etc.) affects how Kaqchikel Maya vendors organize and practice their lives. In relation to this, the following chapters deal with three major themes: (1) global and transnational flows of people and commodities, with particular attention to the conflation of global/local distinctions in some socioeconomic contexts; (2) tourism marketplaces and tourism routes as borderzones, where national and international, developed and underdeveloped, indigenous and nonindigenous come together; and (3) marketing to tourists as a significant socioeconomic practice that contributes to changing social roles, relationships, and identity in nonmarketplace contexts. As can be seen in the opening examples of this chapter, these themes relate to real concerns of Maya *típica* vendors.

Chapters 1 and 2 provide overviews of Maya *típica* vendors' practices and show how vendors are located within transnational economic spaces, international tourism structures, and debates about who Mayas are. Chapter 1 focuses on tourism structures and disjunctures between tourists and Mayas. Chapter 2 looks in greater detail at touristic constructions of Antigua and *típica* marketplaces and the contradictions between these constructs and actually living in the city.

Chapters 3 and 4 look at the handicraft market that is aimed primarily at foreign tourists who visit Antigua. Chapter 3 provides an overview of the market, the various places *típica* is sold throughout the city, and who is selling it. Chapter 4 concentrates on the Compañía de Jesús Artisan Marketplace, the largest *típica* marketplace in Antigua, by discussing the historical and political contexts in which these vendors are embedded. .

Chapters 5 through 8 look at the connections between the marketplaces in Antigua and the hometowns of the vendors. Chapter 5 discusses how vendors' concepts of identity and ideologies about gender roles are shaped by the social relations and particular activities in which they partake in the marketplace. Chapter 6 explains why community origins are of continuing significance to vendors who spend more of their time away from their hometowns. Chapter 7 describes how steep competition for customers among vendors has led to new selling strategies that directly incorporate households into global touristic processes. These economic strategies, among others (such as the formation of cooperative marketing groups [Grimes and Milgram 2000; Nash 1993a]), are used by handicraft makers and vendors selling in the global market. Chapter 8 examines how tourism can increase women's economic opportunities, which in turn contribute to greater prestige when they reinvest their earnings in community traditions.

Tourism takes the social, economic, and political concerns of some Mayas and places them into transnational and global arenas that, in certain instances, effectively circumvent the Guatemalan nation-state. The context of tourism in Guatemala is global and transnational, but the activities of the nation-state, both good and bad, temper how Mayas participate in tourism and how international tourists regard Guatemala as a destination for trips. This book focuses on the contradictions that arise when vendors negotiate economic transactions and social relationships within the marketplace, with their hometowns, with foreign tourists and businesspersons, and with the local and national governments. For Maya *típica* vendors in Guatemala, work and cultural identity are intertwined and set within these political, social, and national/transnational economic spaces.

Chapter 1

Guatemala as a Living History Museum

Day 2: Archaeology of the Maya Tour, July 1992

My first full day in Guatemala as a tour guide was spent showing the group Spanish colonial buildings in Antigua. The Guatemalan co-guide assumed the responsibility of explaining the various buildings that we passed in the tour bus, leaving me time to listen to the tourists. One commented that Antigua reminded him of Colonial Williamsburg, Virginia. The others agreed, then a small discussion began comparing the two places. They liked that Antigua was filled not with actors but with "real people" carrying on their "traditions," unlike Williamsburg.

Subjects and Places in Motion

Over the course of my fieldwork in Guatemala, both Maya handicraft vendors and tourists called to my attention that the tourism industry in Guatemala appears to share some structural similarities with institutions like Disney amusement parks and living history museums. The living history museum perspective is one of the ways that tourists and Mayas order (and are ordered by) tourism structures. This view serves to temporally separate tourists from Others, similar to how anthropologists of the past denied the coevalness of their subjects (Fabian 1983: 31).

Johannes Fabian (1983: 37–69) argues that anthropology circumvented coevalness through cultural relativity and preempted it by eliminating the "time of others as a significant dimension of either cultural integration or ethnography." The denial of coevalness in tourism facilitates conceptions of a different, unchanging "culture." How Mayas and tourists conceive of Others in relation to temporal, social, and geographic spaces is often unsettled because of the contradictions between tourism structures and Guatemala's social and political realities.

In this chapter I consider why tourists made reference to living history museums, even though they did not think Guatemala was actually a living history museum, and then relate these comments to Mayas. These often offhand remarks demonstrate one of the ways that tourists conceptualize their experiences in Guatemala and suggest that they think about the representation and order of places, people, and things. Prior knowledge of and experience with living history museums and Disney parks helps set up certain expectations that play into their reactions and responses when those expectations are violated. These places provide methods for them to frame their international travel experiences and contribute to the types of socioeconomic relationships they have with Mayas and Ladinos.

Akhil Gupta and James Ferguson (1992: 7) critique the failure to problematize the concept of space that functions to imprint "cultural difference, historical memory, and societal organization." Their research[1] brings out problems of linking place, space, and culture uncritically. Like Arjun Appadurai (1990, 1991), they are interested in the movements of persons and things from place to place.

Living history museums and tourism sites are spaces that are practiced places.[2] As people move through these places, interacting with them and being acted on by them, the places are in process of being defined. Edward Bruner (1996b) explains, "Tourism occurs in a zone physically located in an ever shifting strip or border on the edges of Third World destination countries. This border is not natural, just there, waiting for tourists to discover it, for all touristic borderzones are constructed." Gupta and Ferguson (1992) call for the concept of culture to be refashioned because of movements of people throughout the world, the multiplicity of ethnic groups within a single locale, and various types of cultural mixing. It should also be located within a conceptual frame that acknowledges how the meanings of places are reconfigured and in process too.

For example, tours offered in Guatemala by Clark Tours, Maya Trails, and Jordan Tours in the late 1930s focused on contemporary Maya villages (described as "Indian villages") and Spanish colonial architecture (Muñoz 1940). They went to Guatemala City, Antigua, Panajachel (Lake Atitlán), Tecpán, and Chichicastenango. Depending on the tour, brief stops were also made at Palín, Lake Amatitlán, Cobán, and the highland towns of Santa María de Jesús, Patzún, Sololá, Utatlán, and Sacapulus. In a 1947 development report (Robbins 1947), recommendations were made by the Inter-American Development Commission in Washington, D.C., to the Guatemalan government to expand tourism to other villages on Lake Atitlán, aside from Panajachel, and to restore pre-Columbian cities, such as Tikal and Quiriguá.

Over the past fifty years, the tourism borderzone in Guatemala has changed, and now emphasizes more archaeological sites. Today, Tikal is a required tourism stop. Tourists have nearly lost interest in Palín, Amatitlán, and Sacapulus. Sololá, Santa María de Jesús, Cobán, and Tecpán are minor stops today. Guatemala City is usually skipped by tourists traveling independently and by guided tours. In Zones 1, 9, and 10, Guatemala City persists as an important location for meetings and conferences for foreign diplomats, international businesspersons, academics, and political activists. Many of these people take some time from their meetings and work to experience Guatemala City and other locations as tourists.

This chapter, however, focuses on those tourists who visit Guatemala with the singular interest of taking a vacation. These tourists are a heterogeneous group, some participating in multiple types of tourism (ecotourism, adventure tourism, New Age spiritualism tourism, ethnic tourism, historical tourism) and combining their tourism activities with language study and volunteer work for grassroots development organizations. Such tourists are difficult to place into singular categories that capture who they are and what to expect of them as individual travelers and consumers. This is not to imply that this diverse group of people does not frame Guatemala as a living history museum or at least acknowledge that it is one way in which to conceptualize Guatemala.

Living History Theme Parks

Tourists in Guatemala commonly commented that their experiences in places such as Williamsburg and Disney World stimulated their interest in ethnic tourism. One family (parents and two children) from Illinois, on the 1992 International Journeys[3] tour, explained:

> We'd seen Williamsburg and been to the [Chicago] Field Museum [of Natural History] many times, but our favorite place to take a trip

is Disney World. We go there every year. Last year, we decided to start taking trips to other countries, to see in person the places we learned about. . . . We took a trip to the rain forest in the Amazon and saw animals, plants, and Indian tribes in the jungle. This year we decided to go to Guatemala to see Maya ruins and Indians.

This family was inspired to visit Guatemala after trips to the Field Museum of Natural History in Chicago and Disney World and Epcot Center in Florida, as well as from reading *National Geographic* magazine, which has been significant in shaping U.S. perceptions of people and places (Lutz and Collins 1993). Family trips to Guatemala may be motivated by multiple concerns, such as learning Spanish and gaining first-hand knowledge of pre-Columbian and contemporary Maya culture. Schools in Illinois, Massachusetts, and other areas of the United States include sections about Maya history and culture in their curricula (Kay Warren, personal communication 7/17/02). That some tourists first learn about Others in living history museums and Disney parks is not to imply that they mistook their tours for these places. In part, these institutions organize and represent culture to be consumed (see Bennett 1995; Karp and Lavine 1991; and MacCannell 1976), but they can also teach visitors how to consume (see Fjellman 1992 on Disney World).

According to Tony Bennett (1995: 59–88), living history museums are part of an "exhibitionary complex" that helps homogenize audiences and constructs exotic Others. This complex also includes art galleries, media, the state, sciences such as anthropology, and other settings and institutions. Similarly, Eileen Hooper-Greenhill (1989) and Timothy Mitchell (1988) explain how cultural exhibitions help shape patrons' "reality." The world becomes an exhibit.[4] The exhibit marks what is considered "real" and provides ways to comprehend and order the world. James Boon (1991: 265) argues, "Museums, then, or things or processes museum like, may be said to occur whenever viewers (or their equivalent) are guided, not always willingly, among artifacts . . . and . . . other goers." Thus framed, the distinctions between living history museums and guided tours are less clear. Tourists may not always distinguish between them in their attitudes and practices, as in the cases of the International Journeys tourists and others to be discussed in this and subsequent chapters.

The world viewed as an exhibition renders culture, place, and people as controlled, contained, organized, and unchanging. Because most museums are the constructions of dominant groups, they present history in ways that support their perspectives.[5] Guatemala as an exhibition obscures relations of power as well as social, political, and economic problems.

Disney theme parks are comparable to Guatemalan tours because in both the past is reconstructed for the present, and culture is consumed[6] in a context where people may be indoctrinated with the ideology of the dominant classes (Wallace 1989: 173). Though it is not a living history museum, Disney World participates in the commodification of the past that does not always make distinctions between fact and fiction (Fjellman 1992).

The construction of living history museum–type places and the consumption of Otherness, of course, is a far more complicated process than corporations and governments creating particular types of consumers or instilling dominant ideologies into the masses. Taking in mind Michel Foucault's (2000: 326) perspectives on power and on the "modes of objectification that transform human beings into subjects" can suggest why tourists and vendors behave in certain ways within the living history museum in Guatemala. Foucault (2000: 345) explains that "power relations within a society cannot be reduced . . . to a study of all those institutions that would merit the name 'political.' Power relations are rooted in the whole network of the social." It should not be misconstrued, however, that power is some amorphous concept that any and all exercise equally, or that tourist-consumers buy what is presented to them by tourism promoters. Indeed, the consumption of a tour to Guatemala does not mean tourists, or for that matter handicraft vendors who sell to those tourists, accept the dominant discourses. As indicated in the following chapters, tourists and vendors reinterpret and resist dominant touristic discourses. At the same time, tourists to Guatemala do behave in ways that appear to embrace dominant tourism ideologies. Why they view and consume Otherness in such an unproblematic way is an important question, which is not to imply that tourists themselves are simple, uncomplicated subjects.

Jean Baudrillard (1988) and Umberto Eco (1986) argue that Disney's reproductions of the past are better than the originals. By interacting with Disney World, tourists potentially view the world as unproblematic, not to be questioned.[7] The ways that the past and Others are reconstructed in Disney World and living history museums can lead to disappointment for some visitors when they travel to those other places as tourists. Knowledgeable visitors and experienced world travelers may have problems with the constructions of past and Others that are presented to them (Fjellman 1992: 232–233). In other words, tension exists between sites (living history museum–type spaces that tourists visit) and the experience and knowledge of the traveler.

All types of tourists, however, may choose to play along with the construction of space and people with which they are presented. Play, in fact, is instrumental to the Disney and living history museum experience and can take many forms. Some Disneyland exhibits place guests "in the domain of dangerous opponents: Indians, pygmy headhunters, pirates" (Wallace 1989: 163). The danger and excitement is staged, and visitors/participants are not put in jeopardy. Compared to the "hyperreal" world of Disney, the "real" world can be boring. In Guatemala, the problem for tourists is the potential unpredictability of ethnic tourism. If the tour gets dangerous, it is because something truly dangerous happens, such as a robbery, assault, or police/military search.

Of course, tourists visiting Guatemala know the difference between staged adventure and life-threatening danger. Tourists do not generally go to Guatemala looking for trouble. They also know that all the world is not an exhibit and that everything is not for sale. However, they tend to treat the places they have the most access to as exhibits and gift shops. Part of the reason they do this has to do with the contexts of and reasons for their travel. These reasons are linked to how they learned about Others and the past through a matrix of media, living history museums, Disney World, education, and personal experience.

Tourists in the International Journeys group and others are not necessarily unaware of problems, such as the ethnocide of Mayas by the military in the 1980s, the extreme poverty, and the high crime rates. Most realize that guerrillas and the military were waging war into the 1990s, that there have been thousands of victims from that fighting, and that Guatemala is one of the poorest countries in Latin America.[8] This is not what they visit. That place is different from touristic Guatemala.

Tourists tended to visit Guatemala in order to see Maya civilization, Spanish colonial architecture, and holdovers of that past in the people (Mayas and Ladinos) living there. Many pointed out that touring Guatemala is similar to a trip to Disney World because they could "be in the past and the present at once," and they can play with and in these constructions of past, present, and culture.

Despite the seemingly organized, ordered, and powerful effects of living history museums and Disney World on the behavior of visitors, the spaces for viewing the past, other societies, and material cultures are far from seamless. Some exhibitions and performances enter and exit the physical structure of the museum in ways that complement, contradict, or rupture the museum or the living history museum. Guillermo Gómez-Peña (1993) and Coco Fusco (1995) have contested the boundaries of the museum, with performances/exhibitions such as "Two Undiscovered Amerindians." In this performance, they portray indigenous people who are dressed as fictitious, undiscovered Amerindians, placed in a cage, and put on display in natural history museums. Audiences were then invited to touch the figures, pose for pictures with the "Indians," and look at the male's genitals for an extra fee. The presenters played with cultural boundaries by incorporating items such as boomboxes into the exhibition. The piece toured the United States and Europe around and during the quincentennial celebrations of Columbus's landing in the Americas.

Research on tourism and living history museums illuminates the ways that museum-like spaces are constructed (Bruner 1994, 1996a; Bruner and Kirshenblatt-Gimblett 1994; Castañeda 1996; Gable, Handler, and Lawson 1992; Handler and Saxton 1988; Kirshenblatt-Gimblett 1998; and Wallace, 1981, 1987, 1989). This scholarship shows how processes of museumification (see Graburn 1984) that seem to be totalizing and all encompassing are really full of rifts and ruptures. Tourists may see beyond the construction, play with it, deny it, and offer counterexplanations based on gender, class, ethnic, and other subject positions. Because of this, constructing exhibitions and performances is complicated, since the representation of culture and the use of sites are sometimes difficult to control.

For example, "authenticity," seemingly essential for living history museum and tourism sites, can be a nemesis for curators, performers, and tourists. For a site to be credible, it must be "authentic." It has to "*have the right stuff*" (Anderson 1984: 192; italics in original), but one has to be able to get it, or at least create an acceptable simulacrum of it. Authenticity is disrupted when the modern world intrudes on the site. For example, Maasai dancers at Mayer's Ranch in Kenya are instructed to hide radios and other "non-primitive" items (Bruner and Kirshenblatt-Gimblett 1994) so the tourists won't see them. At New Salem, Illinois, where Abraham Lincoln lived at the beginning of his law career, Bruner (1994) illustrates how authenticity is constructed from contemporary projections into the past at this living history museum. The practical business of operating and maintaining the site can compromise the reconstruction. A gasoline can "exposed to public view in the cooper shop" threatens the site's authenticity (Bruner 1994: 401) because it collapses the past into the present.[9]

Most tourists on ethnic tours or on trips to living history museums and Disney World know that much of what they see exhibited is constructed for them. Although seeing and participating in "real life" is usually out of the question, especially if the reconstruction is of the past, they have high standards for how the past, place, and people should be represented.

THE COLLAPSE OF TOURIST/OTHER DICHOTOMIES

Dean MacCannell (1992) explains that tourism can throw into turmoil primitive/modern, uncivilized/civilized, and folk/urban dichotomous representations and explanations of social reality because it places the supposedly primitive, uncivilized folk into a dialectical and dialogical relationship with the modern, civilized, and urban. For the dichotomy to collapse, it is not enough that tourism places tourists in direct contact with Others. Both tourists and hosts play prescribed roles, but these break down when either group does something outside of those roles.

Ironically, some tourists revel in the imperfections of the construction. However, most tourists react in three principal ways to Mayas who drive cars, work in offices, fax messages around the world, and attempt to draw tourists into conversations about international politics. First, some tourists are already aware of such developments and do not find them problematic. Second, some deny that these people are truly Mayas. Third, some reevaluate touristic discourse, which locates Mayas in the past (usually as degenerate heirs of a magnificent past; see Kratz and Karp 1993) or as contemporary exotic Others. If the second reaction happens, they continue their trip, unbothered by the contradiction because they do not acknowledge it. If the third one occurs, they rethink who Mayas are. They do not go back to the "age of the Maya"; instead, Mayas become part of the tourists' world. When the dichotomy between tourists and Others collapses, the conceptual framework—the traveling space of the living history museum—fails to reconstruct Guatemala and its inhabit-

Mayas in the Marketplace

ants in benign ways that facilitate uncomplicated consumption by tourists. As contemporaries, Mayas, Ladinos, and tourists treat each other differently, asking questions about family, poverty, politics, popular culture, and other aspects of "real" life.

For instance, at the outset of the 1992 International Journeys' trip, which comprised a diverse group of people—professionals, housewives, newlyweds, one family of four, one Spanish teacher—with no prior experience in Guatemala, the Guatemalan guide tried to talk about contemporary issues, focusing on the oligarchy's political and economic hegemony, poverty, the country's industries, and increasing crime rates. Most of the group ignored him, and others asked him to talk about folk traditions, Maya prehistory, and the Spanish colonial period. Midway through the tour they were jolted out of the tourist-Other dichotomy when they were robbed at gunpoint en route to Quiriguá. Afterward, they wanted to know about contemporary Guatemala.

The conceptual spaces of living history museums travel when they are internalized by tourists. Living history museums also travel when their conceptualizations are overlaid onto tourism destinations by promoters of tourism. Neither challenges relations of power because tourists' roles and tourism structures are not called into question. The third way living history museums and ethnic tours travel is when someone or something that is not part of the reconstruction collapses the distinction between, or illusion of, past and present, host and tourist. This can disrupt relations of power and expose the structure, as implied in Bruner's analyses of Mayer's Ranch and New Salem and explained later in this chapter.

Ethnic Tourism in Guatemala

Ethnic tourism links the United States to Guatemala through a number of border crossings: U.S. tourists travel to Guatemala, Guatemalan and U.S. businesspersons commute between the two countries, and Mayan handicrafts and artistic products flow to the United States. A substantial amount of research addresses these types of movements to and from other regions of the world. Some researchers have focused on the movement of artisan and artistic items from "pre-modern" producers to "modern" consumers (Clifford 1988, 1991; García Canclini 1993; Graburn 1976, 1993; and Price 1989). Other scholars have studied tourists' trips (Lanfant, Allcock, and Bruner 1995; Smith 1989; Urry 1990; van den Berghe 1995) and plotted flows of artisan products that are in the opposite direction of tourist flows (Nash 1993a;Tice 1995).

Tourists to Guatemala traverse a series of borders: state geopolitical borders, cultural borders (American-Guatemalan-Mayan), temporal borders from present to past to present again (contemporary United States and Guatemala to colonial Guatemala to Classic Maya Mesoamerica), and urban-rural borders. Tourists move from relatively known spaces to relatively unknown spaces, from familiar marked sites to unfamiliar marked sites. As they travel farther into the unknown, they are more dependent on a "guide"—in book or human form—that helps construct touristic Guatemala in culturally understandable terms.

Tourists on the 1992 International Journeys tour, those who studied Spanish and lived in the same boarding house in Antigua as I did periodically from 1994 to 1997, and other tourists (independent and guided) talked to me about their travel experiences, usually including frequent references to museums; media, especially *National Geographic* magazine (see Lutz and Collins 1993) and its documentaries; guidebooks (overwhelmingly the Lonely Planet guidebook *Guatemala, Belize, and Yucatan: La Ruta Maya*); and Disney World. During mealtime conversations, tourists used these types of media to help them comprehend Guatemala. Aside from providing neutral topics to talk about, they also allowed tourists to rank themselves in terms of experience and knowledge. For independent tourists, these exchanges of information are practical because they make it easier to get to sites and to know in advance what to expect.

One evening at the boarding house, an independent tourist asked about traveling in Guatemala and, specifically, about Lake Atitlán. The other guests deferred to me, saying that I was the "expert." However, after a few minutes into my description, another guest interrupted. "Lake Atitlán is like Epcot Center. Each of the towns is like a separate culture. You've got Panajachel, which has lots of gringos and hippies. You've got all these Indian towns that have different languages and clothes. You even have New Age-ers who give massages and sit under pyramids for spiritual power." Such descriptions function as shorthand ways to describe and understand places. By using a living history museum or Disney World model to order their touristic experiences, they make their tourism experience understandable.

Additionally, the tourism structure in Guatemala is pervasive and appears permanent because tourism operators have been taking foreign tourists to some of the same places for over fifty years. International

Mayas in the Marketplace

Journeys' "Archaeology of the Maya" tour made stops in Antigua, Chichicastenango, Lake Atitlán/Panajachel, Tikal, and Quiriguá. Tara Tours' "On the Mayan Path" tour follows the same path, except it makes an additional stop in Quetzaltenango and skips Quiriguá. Some tours offered by Mena Tours, Aviateca Tours, and Clark Tours let tourists construct their own packages, but their brochures offer similar destinations to those of International Journeys and Tara Tours. Many of the tourists who participate in these types of tours are first-time visitors to Guatemala on a fairly strict time schedule. Although the visitors are of diverse ages, economic circumstances, and occupational groups, the set patterns and routes of these standard tours make it possible for handicraft vendors to better predict where to find tourists and when the optimal times to sell to them might be.

This organized structure helps distinguish tourist Guatemala from nontourist Guatemala, but it also helps mark what is significant to be viewed. Although the Guatemalan tourism borderzone includes familiar elements to U.S. tourists, such as Domino's Pizza, Burger King, and television stations[10] from the United States in their hotel rooms, tourists know that they are not in the United States. They comprehend Guatemala (even though there are some familiar things) as different. Differences are constructed and maintained by spatializing practices that separate and contain the Other.

Spatially Delineating Difference

The process of the cultural and spatial demarcation of Guatemala by tourists begins with their study of the maps of the country and of the tourism routes that are included in the guidebooks and brochures they read in preparation for their trip. Tourists I talked with carried at least one map of Guatemala, but many carried more than one. Maps are important because they work with other spatializing and temporalizing elements to make distinct and special places. For example, according to Louis Marin (1984: 240), the map that helps visitors to Disneyland explore the park "can play the role of description; it performs the part of the representational picture." Maps can also help delineate spatial and temporal dimensions between reality and utopia, which Marin categorizes as the *limit*. This neutral space helps remove tourists from the mundane world of everyday existence to a fantastic utopia or dystopia. According to Marin (1984: 242), "This limit is thus an index and zero-point; it is also the bridge to the 'other.'" When tourists enter Disneyland, after driving through the main gate, parking their car, crossing the ticket booths, and entering the park, they know that they are in a different place.

The processes of delineating tourist Guatemala from tourists' respective home countries are similar to those that Marin describes. When tourists fly to Guatemala from the United States, the limit is defined by the airport in the United States, the plane ride itself, and crossing through immigration in Guatemala. Both the border crossings and the plane ride reinforce to tourists that they are going someplace different. Unlike the limit between the mundane world and Disneyland, which can be crossed fairly quickly, the limit between the United States and Guatemala takes hours to cross. On the flight, tourists study guidebooks and read itineraries. They strike up conversations with each other about their destination and compare information they had gathered previously. Once they are in Guatemala, there is no way to literally look back. They enter the Guatemalan living history museum when they exit the airport.[11]

STRUCTURAL CHARACTERISTICS
OF MUSEUMS AND LIVING HISTORY PARKS

A living history museum can be conceptualized as a system. The physical structure of museum-like spaces contains the following components: an entrance, a contained space, sites within the space, safe havens, and an exit. The *entrance* separates the known from the unknown. The *contained space* is delineated by walls, fences, and security guards that bind together the universe of the museum, preventing intrusions from the outside. Paths within the museum join exhibitions into a "rational" order. *Sites* exemplify, demonstrate, and express ideas of culture, society, and history from the perspectives of internal or external Others, and they are presented in ways that allow the visitor to consume the Other.

Certain viewpoints permit visitors to see order in the materials and people that they learn about. Glass cases and metal bars protect visitors and objects from each other but also function to symbolically order and control the Other. Interactive displays allow visitors to play with the Other. *Safe havens* are the hotels, gift shops, restaurants, and bathrooms found within living history museum spaces. These places give visitors some respite from the differences with which they contend and allow them to possess a piece of the past or digest it in a meal. The *exit,* which often doubles as the entrance, marks the spot where visitors travel forward in time or to their original culture.

Ethnic tours in Guatemala (and possibly in other destinations) impose a museum-like order that is not necessarily inherent in the lives of Guatemalans. Although I can make no claims that there was a concerted effort to organize tourism in Guatemala like a living history museum, there are similarities between these models. Unlike the living history museum, the guided ethnic tour operates within a transnational context. It positions Guatemala in contrast to other countries and occupies a cultural space between them.

In contrast to the Mexican-U.S. border, which Gloria Anzaldúa (1987) characterizes as fragmented and a space of contestation, the Guatemalan ethnic tour occupies a culture space where there is a myth of order and comprehensibility. Most tourists expect to leave behind their daily activities and problems in the United States. Mary and Alice, two college-educated but self-professed housewives from Texas, were given the International Journeys tour as a gift from their husbands to provide a break from housework and childcare. Steve, an independent traveler and schoolteacher from California, decided to visit Guatemala for a couple of months in 1994 to help him forget a recent mugging and robbery. Other tourists explained that they just wanted a break from work and thought going to a beach or a resort would be boring.

Although an ethnic tour in Guatemala can be experienced as a type of living history museum, there is a difference in scale. Living history museums do not occupy territories the size of Ohio. There are no walls or fences containing the tour space, as there are in living history museums, but ethnic tours are organized around specific features that can be experienced by tourists.

The entrance to Guatemala is Guatemala City. Guidebooks (Bereskey 1991; Brosnahan 1994; Crowther 1986; Glassman 1988; Greenberg and Wells 1990; Solares 1964; Whatmore and Eltringham 1993) typically begin with the capital city, and it is an appropriate entrance. It contains a mixture of modern, colonial, and pre-Columbian attributes. Some areas of the city, such as the Calzada Roosevelt and Zone 10 where the Camino

Real Hotel is located, have shopping centers, international chain restaurants, and office buildings similar to those found in cities in the United States. Positioned in the entrance, tourists glimpse the past—colonial architecture—and the Other—Maya women dressed in colorful *huipiles*—that they will see in closer detail on their trip. Like the living history museum's entrance, Guatemala City is presented as the gateway to all other places in Guatemala.

The contained space is that of Guatemala itself. The wall containing it is the air space between Guatemala and tourists' homes. Guidebooks, package tour brochures, and maps also contribute to the construction of Guatemala as a contained space. However, tourists differed in the degree that they used these. Independent tourists were rarely without a guidebook and map, while guided tourists primarily relied on their brochure and itinerary. The International Journeys tourists did not read about any places not covered in the brochure. Each was given a copy of Michael Coe's (1987) book, *The Maya,* but most put the book in their luggage for the duration of the trip. A couple of them gave the book to independent tourists they met in Antigua. A few read only the sections on the pre-Columbian sites they visited: Tikal and Quiriguá. All of them told me they did not need it because they had me and the brochure. They knew where they were going and when—nothing else mattered.

In 1997, while trying to interview tourists taking a "Panama Canal" vacation with Holland America Cruises, which included a two-day stop in Guatemala, I could not convince one to part with her brochure/itinerary because she "needed it." Likewise, others with her shook their heads negatively when I asked to photocopy one of their brochures.[12]

Similar to the living history museum, pre-established paths join together the sites—Antigua, Chichicastenango, Panajachel, and others—in a rational order. The order of the sites moves tourists back into time and away from the modern and known toward the past and the unknown Other. Guatemala City is an outpost of modernity. One can now eat a meal there at McDonald's or Pizza Hut. The short ride to Antigua takes the traveler back into Spanish colonial times, where the tour focuses on colonial exhibitions: La Merced (a convent and church), Capuchinas Convent, and San Francisco el Grande (church), and others. From Antigua to Chichicastenango, tourists travel farther into the past. It becomes less urban and more rural, more "Indian." By the time they reach Lake Atitlán, they leave behind the modern and the colonial. Only Indians and nature remain. According to Tara Tours' brochure, one can "visit the handicraft market for terrific bargains . . . [then take] a motor launch trip to one of the interesting Indian lake shore villages. . . ." International Journeys describes nature as ". . . a visit to picturesque Lake Atitlán, nestled amidst towering volcanoes. Enjoy the afternoon shopping and lounging in Panajachel surrounded by the beautiful scenery of natural colors."

Panoptical-type views (Foucault 1979),[13] such as those from the tourists' plane, from their hotel window at the Camino Real and other multistoried hotels, from the road leading down from Sololá to Lake Atitlán, and generally from the elevated and private position of the tour bus, give tourists a vantage point from which to order and "understand" the people and places they visit. The easiest way for the tour to maintain control is through chartered-bus travel. From the constantly moving space of the bus, the countryside and people pass quickly before the eyes of the tourists, making second looks difficult. The bus stops only at sites that are described in the brochure—places that are secure.

Unlike some living history museums, sites in Guatemala are not covered in glass or protected behind bars. Instead, the bus protects the tourists from the weather, other people, insects, and fatigue. From behind the glass windows, tourists watch Maya farmers in their milpas (cornfields); see the "natural" terrain, coffee plantations, and colonial buildings; and get their first views of the market before they buy anything.

Tour brochures emphasized the shopping bargains that could be found in Guatemala. Two of the International Journeys tourists decided to take the trip because of the handicrafts. Shopping in Guatemala is a well-established tourist activity that military repression temporarily slowed in the 1980s but did not stop.[14] Some tourists are under the impression that literally everything in Guatemala is for sale. They believe that they can purchase anything or take a picture of anyone. Many times I watched Mayas turn away from tourists' cameras and Maya women refuse to sell the *huipiles* off their backs.[15]

In the summer of 1995 I understood the offense Mayas can suffer at the hands of consuming tourists. While I was talking to my wife and some Maya friends in the plaza in Antigua, a tourist began to film my daughter, who was dressed in *traje* (indigenous clothing), and the two Maya girls she was playing with. The girls and I noticed the tourist at about the same time. When they tried to move out of view, she chased them. I asked her to stop. She ignored me. I stepped in front of her camera and she swore at me. They do not want to be filmed, I appealed. She said that it was her "right" to film them. Frustrated by her persistence, I pulled out my camera and took a picture of her. She stopped filming. Afterward, my Maya friends joked about using cameras to scare tourists.

The other similarities between living history museums and ethnic tours are the safe havens and the exit. Hotels serve as the primary places where tourists can get away from the barrage of difference they contend with during the tour. In their room they can watch cable TV with programs from the United States, take hot showers, and get an "American" meal or a safe, Americanized Guatemalan meal. The exit through which they can return home is Guatemala City, the modern outpost that partially holds back Maya and colonial Guatemala.

Confrontations and Ruptures in the Guatemalan Tourism Structure

Ethnic tourism is organized in Guatemala in ways that (1) bring economic benefits to the Guatemalan middle and upper classes while maintaining the current social stratification of Guatemala; (2) separate tourists from the internal social and political problems of Guatemala; and (3) offer opportunities for play, recreation, and adventure for tourists. These can be disrupted by the sociocultural misunderstandings between Guatemalans (Maya and non-Maya) and tourists who meet in the tourism zone, by a host of undesirable persons the tourism structure promises to shut out but does not, and by the ways some foreign tourists and Guatemalans interact with and act on the tourism structure.

SOCIAL STRATIFICATION IN TOURISM

Robert Hinshaw's (1975, 1988) research at Panajachel and mine (Little 1995) for Antigua and San Antonio Aguas Calientes suggest that the tourist industry is run by wealthier Guatemalans and foreigners. In 1929, an American, Alfred S. Clark, started Clark Tours, the first travel company in Guatemala, which is still run by his descendants. It is the largest tour company currently operating there. International Journeys was founded in the 1980s by Charlie Strader from Florida, who worked with an upper-middle-class non-Maya Guatemalan woman, Estela Jeanette Rosales, who subsequently founded Tessa Travel in 1992. There are dozens of these smaller tour companies in Guatemala. Successful operators have sufficient capital to easily travel between the United States and Guatemala in order to make business contacts, attract investors, and promote their company.

There are no Maya-owned tour companies, small or large. The reasons for this are multiple. Few Mayas have the economic resources and business contacts to get started. Ladinos and foreigners control businesses that are part of the tourism industry (hotels, restaurants, and Spanish schools) and, generally, will not work for, or as partners with, Mayas. Most Mayas directly involved in the tourism industry work as vendors of handicraft products or domestic servants and unskilled maintenance personnel for hotels. These are socially and structurally acceptable roles for Mayas that do not challenge the Ladino- and foreign-run tourism industry.

Multinational hotel chains, such as Best Western, Camino Real, Ramada, and Radisson, and tour companies, such as Clark Tours and Mena Tours, are the most visible to tourists planning trips. Not only do these hotels and tour companies advertise in U.S. newspapers, they are interconnected in the package tour. The International Journeys tourists stay in a Camino Real, a Ramada Inn, and a Best Western Hotel. Clark and Mena Tours book reservations in these same hotels. In Chicago, travel agencies sell package tours that include stays at these hotels. This tends to consolidate tourist dollars coming into Guatemala and fortify economically and politically dominant Ladinos and whites, who locate Mayas as relics of the past who are suited to pose for pictures, make crafts, clean floors, and take out the garbage. Publications aimed at businesspersons portray Mayas in a dualistic fashion: persons trapped in the past and a low-skill labor pool.[16] The link between multinational hotel chains and large tour companies strengthens the myth that Guatemala can be controlled like a living history museum.

Tourists explained that one of the reasons they visit Guatemala is because it is not as developed as their home country, but many do not realize the extent of the poverty there. In a country with 46 percent unemployment (*Crónica,* August 1998: 27), where up to half the population lives on less than one U.S. dollar per day, according to a United Nations report published in a local newspaper (*Siglo XXI,* April 19, 1998), and minimum daily wages for farm laborers and construction workers in 1997 were $2.65 and $3.04 respectively, most *típica* (handicraft) vendors are better off than the majority of the population. On bad days, vendors made between $4 and $8. Those vendors who answered my questions about annual income claimed to make between $2,000 and $7,000. One couple from San Antonio Aguas Calientes gave me their written (few keep records) financial records for three months, from December 1996 to February 1997. They averaged around $700 per month, which, judging by my observations of other vendors' sales, is high. Only 54 percent of the adult population is actively employed (including part-time and seasonal workers). Although 57 percent of the population has access to health services, there are four thousand persons to each doctor. Sixty-four percent has access to potable water. Thirty-seven percent of adult men and 52 percent of adult women are illiterate. Only 9.2 per ten thousand Guatemalans have access to the Internet, and 2.8 persons per one thousand have personal computers.[17]

CRIME IN THE TOURISM ZONE

Tourism brochures and guidebooks do not begin by explaining Guatemala's potential dangers, be they theft, assault, or health related. Instead, Guatemala tends to be described in idyllic terms: "The lake [Atitlán] is surrounded by three towering volcanoes and majestic mountains[,] and its shores are lined with colorful Indian villages" (Clark Tours). Only on the final page of the International Journeys' brochure are tourists warned of potential problems. They are advised to guard themselves against pickpockets in Guatemala City and dietary/health risks.

My point is not that the tourism industry should portray Guatemala as a dangerous country. Tourists, however, do not imagine themselves as potential victims of violent crime because of the ways they read and interpret guidebooks and brochures. The International Journeys tourists thought part of my job was to protect them. Because guidebooks emphasize the dangers of Guatemala City, not other parts of Guatemala, many tourists that I interviewed felt safe except when in Guatemala City. Once tourists exit the capital, many leave behind their fears and consequently become careless.

This behavior fits with the utopic vision of Guatemala as portrayed by the tourism industry. Nevertheless, the tour (guided or independent) occurs in a potentially unpredictable borderzone. When tourists begin their tour, they soon realize that they have entered not a utopia but a country with problems. But as long as they are shielded from those problems, tourists are not concerned.

For example, in 1992 when the International Journeys tour was robbed by thieves with automatic weapons in two pickup trucks while en route

Mayas in the Marketplace

to a hotel near the Quiriguá ruins, tour participants were violently jolted out of their idyllic illusion of Guatemala. The Guatemalan guide and I had advised them numerous times to split up their valuables, hide credit cards and cash, and not to wear prized jewelry when traveling or in crowded public areas. Because they had not witnessed or experienced anything threatening, all but one couple decided that we had overemphasized the danger. The thieves quickly took all their money and sped away into the night. Later, when we arrived at the hotel, all members of the tour group, aside from the one couple that had lost only a few dollars, met and decided to fire the bus driver, the Guatemalan guide, and me. Two female psychology professors represented the group and declared that we had "to be in league with the thieves because [we] didn't lose anything." Both the bus driver and the Guatemalan guide had been hit with gun butts. They, too, lost small amounts of cash. We spent the morning canceling the tourists' credit cards; arranging to have emergency money wired to them from International Journeys' Miami, Florida, office; and convincing the hotel owner to fix them a special lunch to help calm them. By lunchtime they realized that they needed our help and asked us to resume our roles. Although we reported the crime to the police, the robbery did not make the newspapers in Guatemala or the United States. One year later, however, in a similar incident, a group of high school students from Geneva, Illinois, were robbed when thieves boarded their tour bus (*Chicago Tribune,* July 12, 1993).

In general, crime in Guatemala has increased in the years leading up to and following the signing of the Peace Accords between the government and guerrilla forces (Guatemalan National Revolutionary Unity) on December 29, 1996. A United Nations report that included statistics on violent crime reported an increase of total offenses from 11,711 crimes in 1992 to over 19,094 crimes in 1996 (SNUG 1998). According to one of Guatemala's daily newspapers, only Colombia surpassed Guatemala in raw numbers of criminal offenses in 1997 (*Siglo XXI,* December 11, 1997).

Since my first trip to Guatemala in 1987, most Maya handicraft vendors and tourism guides now have personal anecdotes about being robbed. In their monthly meetings, vendors discussed ways to protect themselves and their clients from theft and scams. However, in 1992, when I led the International Journeys tour, few people working in tourism were worried about crime directed at them. Between 1994 and 1999 a number of crimes against tourists received high-profile coverage in the Guatemalan and international media. In 1994, three North American women were attacked by angry mobs, worried about foreign women as kidnappers, in three separate incidences: Melissa Larson on March 7, June Weinstock on March 29, and Janice Wogel on May 16.[18] In January 1996, an American woman and an English woman were murdered during a robbery at a resort on Lake Atitlán (*Boston Globe,* January 9, 1996).

In November 1996, a Spanish teacher was murdered and his sixteen students robbed at Cerro de la Cruz (*Guatemalan Weekly,* November 23–29, 1996). This hill overlooking Antigua has long been dangerous for tourists, Spanish school students, and local Guatemalans. The Proyecto Lingüístico Francisco Marroquín, the oldest Spanish and Maya language school in Antigua (see Warren 1998a), advises new students to avoid the Cerro de la Cruz, as do Maya handicraft vendors, who view money lost to thieves as a direct assault on their earning potential.

In January 1998, five Saint Mary's College students were raped, and others in the tour group were robbed, near Santa Lucía Cotzumalguapa (*The Siglo News,* January 21, 1998). In June 1998, a Chilean tourist was murdered during a robbery attempt in the middle of the day in La Merced church in Antigua (*La Prensa Libre,* June 14, 1998).

Between November 1996 and August 1998, I collected sixty-seven articles published in Guatemala's widest-circulating newspaper, *La Prensa Libre,* that dealt specifically with crimes against tourists that included robbery, assault, rape, murder, and fraud. The tourism magazine *The Revue* (July 1997) reported that the special tourism police[19] in Antigua apprehended forty-seven people between August 1996 and June 1997 for committing crimes against tourists. In a report from the Consular Section of the U.S. Embassy, eleven serious offenses—such as rape, physical assault, and gun wounds—and daily accounts of theft and scams were reported by U.S. citizens to the embassy between May and July 1997.

Despite the increase in crime, guidebooks underestimate crime directed at tourists, who generally do not worry about it. In a survey that Sergio García, Shana Walton, and I conducted in 1997 of 242 tourists in Antigua, 79 percent of them felt fairly safe in the marketplace and on the streets during the day. Only 14 percent of them felt that they could easily be hurt or robbed. In conversations with tourists, I learned that most feel impervious to crime. According to a male independent traveler, "Yeah, I know Guatemala has political problems, but the people here like Americans." And a woman on a guided tour related, "No, I'm not worried about crime. I took a tour because it's safer than going on your own. You're protected." When I gave several examples of crime against tourists, neither person thought that the information was relevant to them. The independent traveler commented that "those tourists must not have known what they were doing."

Following the January 1998 rape and robbery of the Saint Mary's College students, I informally asked tourists whether they were preoccupied about tourism crime. Among the dozens of tourists I spoke to, not one felt safe. Many were cutting short their trip because of the Saint Mary's incident. Being the victim of a crime, as well as merely becoming aware of crime, changes the ways that tourists imagine Guatemala. It forces them out of the living history museum perspective of culture because they cannot pretend to be outside of and apart from Guatemalan life. They realize that they cannot control which aspects of Guatemala penetrate the tour.

BENIGN RUPTURES

Simple things, such as listening to Spanish, which most tourists prepare themselves for, can be disruptive. My conversations in Spanish with the Guatemalan guide I worked with for International Journeys were considered conspiratorial by members of the tour group. Even those who had some Spanish lessons panicked at mealtimes and demanded that I translate simple phrases such as "What would you like to eat?" and "Do you want something more to drink?" Tourists who comprehended Spanish fairly well commented that Guatemalans intentionally spoke in ways to confound foreigners. One explained, "When Guatemalans do not want you to understand them, they speak in some kind of code."

In some contexts, Guatemalans spoke in ways that made it difficult for non-native speakers to understand them. Most Ladinos and Mayas assumed that tourists knew some Spanish. In order to prevent eavesdropping, Ladinos altered their dialect (or accent) and sped up the cadence of their speech. Mayas spoke in their own languages. All of the four-hundred-odd handicraft vendors that I worked with used these strategies to have private conversations. Although vendors used such linguistic maneuvers to set prices and discuss sales in progress, they also used them to keep tourists from learning details about their private lives. Most tourists in handicraft markets felt that vendors were discussing them and trying to take advantage of them.

Tourists also have preconceived ideas of linguistic boundaries. They expect non–Maya Guatemalans to speak Spanish, Mayas to speak Mayan languages and some Spanish, and tour guides to speak Spanish and English (or French, German, or Japanese). These ideas are confounded, however, when they travel to Lake Atitlán, Chichicastenango, and the artisan markets in Antigua, where they are surprised to hear Maya handicraft vendors switch from Spanish or a Maya language to English, French, or German.

My presence and language abilities also disrupted tourists' perceptions because I conversed with vendors in Kaqchikel and K'iche' Maya. Tourists rarely stopped to ask me what language I was speaking, but they often stood for several minutes listening. Most of the time, when I asked them if I could satisfy their curiosity about the language the vendor and I were speaking, they would hurry off without answering. Vendors who paused in their conversations to greet tourists in their own language (English, French, Italian, German, and others) were often regarded with suspicion, as is explained below.[20] They worked hard to learn the languages of tourists because they wanted to communicate with them in order to explain their products and make sales.

Not only do tourists experience these blurred linguistic boundaries, but guidebooks promise tourists that "Spanish is a relatively easy language for an English speaker to learn" (Brosnahan 1994: 36). International Journeys sent its tourists a list of common Spanish phrases and a list of K'iche' words with English glosses. They were advised to "have fun" with the two languages by "trying them out on the Guatemalans and Indians they met." Rather than being an easy language to learn, Spanish proved to be impossible. If they pronounced a phrase correctly, they could not understand the response. When they tried K'iche' words from the list, vendors ignored them, laughed, or asked (in Spanish, sometimes in English) what language they were speaking. Tourists to handicraft marketplaces want to communicate in Spanish. When confronted by Maya vendors who initiate conversations in tourists' native languages, tourists related that "it seemed fake" and that "I didn't feel like the experience was authentic." Some were offended. One complained, "They just started talking to me in English. They assumed I couldn't even understand Spanish." When I asked if he could speak Spanish, he confessed that he could not. "That is not the point," he said. "I didn't come all the way here to listen to English."

Thus the utopic Guatemala of the tourism industry is disrupted by multiple sources, not just by poverty and language. Military and police checkpoints and searches disrupt the utopia, as do robbery and panhandling. The behavior of Mayas and non-Mayas can disturb tourists when that behavior does not fit tourism stereotypes. Preconceived notions of occupational, ethnic, and gender roles by both tourists and hosts (Maya and non-Maya) upset the utopia. Within the touristic literature, Mayas are portrayed as ritual specialists, farmers, weavers, and vendors, not bank tellers, waiters, cooks, carpenters, masons, university professors, lawyers, or doctors. These Mayas generally go unnoticed by tourists except in rare instances. In one of the hotels where the International Journeys tourists stayed, several tourists heard a couple of the maids conversing in Kaqchikel. One of them said to me, "Oh, it's just tragic they have to clean rooms. I know they probably need the money, but they should be doing something that's part of their culture."

Male Mayas who vend in the marketplace and do not wear *traje* and all Guatemalan women except Maya women dressed in *traje* in the marketplace or behind a backstrap loom upset tourist conceptions. Tourists can be disturbed by Mayas who act as their contemporaries, illustrating common interests in cable television programs, U.S. sports teams, and world politics. They find themselves confronting an alternative difference that is not described in tourism discourse, and they have difficulty classifying it. The Other becomes unnamable and uncontrollable.

POLITICAL PROBLEMS

The tourism utopia of Guatemala is also disrupted by social and political problems within the country. All guidebooks mention Guatemala's politically troubled past and present. According to the Lonely Planet guidebook (Brosnahan 1994: 63–64), "Adventurous travellers especially should be aware that certain areas have been and may still be the scene of political and military conflict, and even attacks on foreign tourists. These incidents occur at random and are not predictable." In other words, if tourists wander into an area of political or military conflict, they may be harmed. Almost all tourists interviewed after 1992, the year that Rigoberta Menchú won the Nobel Peace Prize, knew something about Guatemala's violent past. Even so, almost all of these tourists felt that it did not relate to their experience.

The number of tourists to Guatemala during the 1980s, when the military violently repressed Mayas and others in rural communities or any organization deemed subversive, declined from 466,041 in 1980 to a low of 191,934 in 1984,[21] despite generally positive portrayals in guidebooks, such as Fodor's, Lonely Planet, a report by UNESCO (Núñez de Rodas 1981), and a United States Department of State report in 1985. Since 1990, the number of tourists has exceeded 500,000 per year but has yet to surpass 600,000.

Despite increases in social and political problems in the 1990s, most tourists to Guatemala do not experience major problems that would cause them to end their trip. They succeed in seeing the colonial architecture, Maya Indians, and archaeological sites that guidebooks and tourism brochures promise. However, both Mayas' and Guatemala's social, economic, and political conditions can disrupt tourists' trips so that they are forced to enter the contemporary universe. The fictions about Mayas, which allow tourists to imagine they can enter pristine Maya culture, then become almost impossible to maintain.

Negotiated "Culture" in the Guatemalan Tourism Zone

Indigenous "culture" in Guatemala has been contrasted with notions of civilization and modernity for much of the twentieth century. Using evolutionary discourses to discuss difference, economic development reports in the 1940s stressed that "pure-blooded Indians" had "only a touch of civilization's veneer" (Coordinator of Inter-American Affairs 1944: 6). However, the report went on to say that unless protected from "civilization," the "Indians" would soon become like the civilized. According to one report, the Guatemalan government should take an active role in encouraging "Indian" villages to perform festivals, dress in *traje,* and maintain their crafts (weaving, basket making) because these activities would stimulate tourism (Robbins 1947). A UNESCO report (Núñez de Rodas 1991: 18) states that "rural culture is formed by the mosaic of Indian cultures and the Ladinos who have preserved the traditional culture practically unchanged down through the years. This culture is beginning to be distorted with positive benefit only for industry and commerce." The report recommends preserving this "traditional culture." As in the area of tourism, "culture" from the perspective of development agencies is a thing that can be controlled, preserved, and recovered by contrasting "pure" forms of Mayan or Indian culture with corrupt forms of U.S. and European culture.

In the Guatemala City airport in 1997, a U.S. couple returning home exclaimed that they had just finished taking a tour that "was absolutely wonderful." They had known nothing about Guatemala before the trip, other than what they had read in the travel brochures. Like others who did not experience a rupture in the tour, they were impressed by "the natural beauty of Guatemala and the colorful outfits of the Indians." They were fascinated that "Indians could live so long surrounded by the modern world and keep their own culture." And, like other tourists who had similar experiences, they vowed that they would return. They felt that taking a tour was a "better way to learn about Guatemala" than reading books. Taking a tour, they explained, allowed them to see into the "lives of Indians" and the "history of Guatemala."

The couple's only direct contact with "Indians," as was true for International Journeys tourists and others, was in artisan marketplaces in Chichicastenango and Antigua. From their bus, they saw "Indian homes," men working in the fields, women weaving, and children playing. The markets, like museum gift shops, allowed them to purchase something from and interact with that Other, as in the staged demonstrations in living history museums. Similar to visiting a living history museum, they were guided through a space that was organized thematically and permitted some forms of participation.

Figure 1.1. *Típica* vending area behind cathedral. Photograph by author.

Another example shows both the negotiation of culture and the similarities between living history museums and Guatemalan tourism. One stop on most guided tours is the cathedral, located in the block east of Antigua's central park. Tourists exit the church onto a courtyard nestled between the church and the archbishop's palace, which has been transformed into a combination of living history museum by tourists and marketplace by an extended family of Mayas from a nearby Kaqchikel town, San Antonio Aguas Calientes. María, who runs the family vending enterprise, explained that she has sold artisan products in that location for fifteen years. She is aided by her husband and dependent children. Her married children also sell in the courtyard, but they are primarily economically independent.

The square courtyard was divided into five display areas that tourists passed before entering the bishop's palace. The display nearest to the street consists of various items—clay and cloth figurines, tablecloths, wall hangings, and a collection of *huipiles* from towns and villages throughout highland Guatemala. Two of the other displays are located on opposite sides of the bishop's palace entrance. Next to one, women sometimes weave on backstrap handlooms. The distinguishing feature of another display is that the women braided colored thread into the hair of tourists for a small fee. The family sell mainly to tourists and Guatemalan schoolchildren who visit the cathedral and the San Carlos museum.

Although some tourists purchased items, they mainly watched the vendors and looked at the displays. In the courtyard, they glimpsed aspects of Maya life: women weaving, men and women vending, women and men taking care of small children, and "real Indian language" being spoken. They took pictures of the vendors and posed with them. They rarely entered the spaces behind the displays where vendors stood and the small children played. The spaces of the courtyard were clearly defined, and tourists stayed on paths that led through the displays.

With the courtyard organized in a museum-like fashion, tourists were led through a group of people and items defined as Mayan or "Indian" by their guides. Maya women were acknowledged as "Indian" or Maya, but their spouses, children, and brothers were often not considered "Indian" because they dressed similarly to the tourists. The males were frequently asked if they were real Mayas or "Indians," and they were questioned about the authenticity of the items they sold.

One morning, after interviewing María's husband, Emiliano, I watched three tourists show interest in the clay and fabric figurines he was selling.

Mayas in the Marketplace

He made the fabric figurines at home in San Antonio Aguas Calientes. He said to them, "Examples of native (*indígena*) weaving." They looked at him, then one of them pulled out a camera and took a picture of María, but not of Emiliano, before responding. "We are looking for something that looks pre-Columbian, very old. Something made by an Indian," one of them told him. When they left without the figurine, Emiliano called to them, "These are made by real Indians." And as an afterthought, pointing to María, he said, "My wife is an Indian."

As the tourists walked away, I asked them why they did not purchase anything. It was a combination of things, they said. They wanted something that was "antiquish," that was handmade that "took a while to make," that was "Indian that was made by an Indian." They were not convinced that Emiliano was really selling "Indian" stuff. They decided to wait and buy something from a "real Indian" later. What they liked about the displays in the courtyard was the variety of items shown and being able to see Indian women and their children. It gave them some ideas about what they would purchase from "real Indians" in the artisan marketplace there in Antigua or Chichicastenango.

In the exchange between Emiliano and the tourists, culture was negotiated when he and they started laying out the conditions of Indianness. For the tourists, the authenticity of the items depended on the person selling it, that it was handmade, and, preferably, that it appeared old and somewhat used. They did not want something that was made just for tourists. The fabric figurines, which they accepted as representations of Indians, were new and made for tourists, so they did not regard them as part of organic Maya (Indian) culture. Emiliano's authenticity was also questioned. They did not doubt that he was María's husband, but they wondered what he was. To complicate matters, Emiliano did not present the figurines as something that he had made nor did he say that he was Maya or Indian. In fact, when we talked in Kaqchikel Maya, he did not describe himself as Maya or Indian or Kaqchikel. He was a farmer, a vendor, and a maker of figurines from San Antonio. Mayas and Indians, he was aware, were what tourists wanted to see. He tried to make figurines that captured what he thought tourists wanted to see about Indians. When tourists looked as if they were interested in something that he was selling, he told them it was made by Indians and, in the case of *huipiles* and other items of clothing, that Indians had worn it. If something did not sell, then María and he took it off the market.

This example draws on the interactions of a limited number of tourists and Maya handicraft vendors. It is not meant to explain the full range of tourists' motivations for purchasing souvenirs.[22] Instead, it is meant to capture how certain aspects of Maya culture are negotiated. Ultimately what sold became what was considered Maya material culture. What sold one day but later did not would cease to be considered part of Maya culture. The primary vendors tended to be females dressed in colorful *huipiles*. They were considered the practitioners of Indian or Maya culture. Hence, females, weaving, and handwoven fabric were recognized as Indian or Maya by the numerous tourists who passed through the displays in the courtyard.

Conclusions

Guatemalan tourism is similar to living history museums, where culture is both constructed and negotiated by agents of the tourism industry, tourists, and hosts. Guatemalan tourism can be conceived as a borderzone that is changing, moving, being forgotten, and remembered. As presented in tourism brochures and guidebooks, Guatemala as a living history museum is utopic, but the tour can be full of ruptures in the fabric of this ideal. Instead of being timeless and pristine, culture is constructed, and tourism discourses merely maintain myths of order.

Although this chapter only hints at the diversity of tourists visiting Guatemala, many are consistent in their expectations of what and who they will see. For tourists who discover that Mayas are not isolated, insulated, or ignorant of the so-called modern and postmodern world, the way they imagine Guatemala and Mayas can be challenged. Fantasies of "Indian," the past, and the present collapse. The construction of Guatemala as a tourist site becomes too obvious to ignore. In the words of one frustrated tourist, who echoed others I encountered, "I didn't pay to see Indians like these!"

When Guatemala is viewed as a living history museum by tourists, "Indians" seem like fakes, and travel into the past or to see the exotic Others appears to be a farce. Cynthia Enloe (1989) points out that socially conscious women who travel, and the women they encounter on those travels (and I presume other tourists, too), can use disjunctures and ruptures in the tourism structure as a way to transform politics. In other words, the preconceptions tourists have about a tourism destination may be unsettled by the actual conditions they encounter. This can lead them to reevaluate their politics, which, in the case of Guatemala, may inspire them to address issues of poverty through volunteerism or protest the U.S. government's foreign policy.

Ironically, the moments that made tourists aware of class, racial, and gender hierarchies and of the exploitation of Maya labor for tourism did not cause many of them to ask why Mayas participate, willingly and unwillingly, in tourism. Few of the tourists that I have met over the years felt any compulsion to try to change those inequalities of which they had been made aware, even though tourists do return, volunteering to build houses and to work in health clinics, among other activities. I can only surmise that this may have to do with the reasons that tourists go to Guatemala and how they conceptualize the place and their trip as vacation, play, and a visit to the past. Although tourists may learn of social and political problems in Guatemala, the living history museum perspective is pervasive and maintained through the combined practices of Ladinos, Mayas, the tourist industry, and foreign tourists.

Chapter 2

Place and People in a Transnational Borderzone City

Introduction

Antigua Guatemala is a place of contradictions: colonial, modern, and post-modern; Ladino, Maya, and foreign; a tourism site and a place for tourists to rest; an expensive suburb of and playground for elites from Guatemala City; the administrative and economic center of the department of Sacatepéquez. *Antigüeños* (residents of Antigua) view it as a preserved-in-time Spanish colonial city, a modern cosmopolitan city, or a combination of these. To tourists, Antigua is both inauthentic, corrupted by tourism and tourists themselves, and authentic, a place where "Indians," colonial architecture, and Western conveniences blend together. Some Mayas view it as their Ladino enemies' town, but others claim it as theirs, the place where they buy needed items and earn a living.

This chapter describes why Antigua is a heterotopia, a space that juxtaposes "in a single real place several spaces, several sites that are themselves incompatible" (Foucault 1986). It refers to tourists who travel independent of guided tours and who also visit Antigua to study Spanish. Comprehending the multiple meanings of Antigua depends on learning how people live, work, and survive in this heterotopia. Meanings are linked to the ways that people conceive of time, place, other people, and themselves. What Antigua is and what it means to those who live and work in it also relates to the specific ways that people use it. By paying attention to the heterotopic dimensions of the city, it is possible to draw out the contradictions between touristic constructions of Antigua and how people live in it. Drawing on specific cases of how people use Antigua can illuminate the city's unique social dimensions.

This chapter is framed by two concerns: first, how to describe Antigua and the people who live and work there, and second, heeding Alejandro Lugo's (1997: 61) call to make the study of borderzones "*anti*disciplinary" where their dimensions are framed within Foucaldian "terrains of Power" and nation-making. In other words, time, place, and people intersect, both with national and international tourism and with the local government and the nation-state. To address these issues, three different scenarios are described and discussed. These fragments illustrate particular aspects of the city and basic ways to engage it methodologically and theoretically.

Hence, this chapter looks at how Guatemalans and tourists use Antigua and the types of contradictions that arise from that use. Bruner (1996b) explains that some tourism spaces between First and Third Worlds are borderzones. But this chapter is concerned with how one such borderzone, Antigua, is made significant by local governments and people, then used by the Mayas, Ladinos, and tourists who inhabit or visit it.

First Scenario: Viewing Maps / Viewing the City

Antigua is manageable for local residents and visitors alike. They can imagine its limits. Tourists walk unimpeded from one corner of the city to the other. There are no ghettos, no mean streets with suspicious-looking characters. Maya vendors, laborers, housekeepers, nannies, gardeners, construction workers, security guards, and bank tellers, who come from surrounding and quite distant towns, likewise comprehend the city as a whole.

These perceptions are tempered by tourists' practices of surveillance, which is a convention of tourism itself. In fact, tourism operators and handicraft vendors encouraged surveillance to help tourists conceive of Antigua as a contained, manageable place. Surveillance is done primarily by reading maps of the city and by viewing people from high places, such as second-floor balconies of hotels and restaurants, colonial ruins, and the Cerro de la Cruz, a hill with a cross monument that overlooks Antigua. Both forms of surveillance remove tourists from the immediacy of who and what they desire to see and to understand.

On buses entering Antigua, one can watch tourists studying maps in guidebooks, planning where they will sleep and eat and learning where the Post Office, the telephone company, and major attractions are located. No respectable guidebook is complete without a map of Antigua. These maps list hotels, churches, the municipal marketplace, the bus terminal, the Central Plaza, and the local INGUAT (Guatemalan National Tourism Institute) office. On the streets, tourists are barraged by even more maps, especially if they follow their guidebook's instructions and go to the INGUAT office, where they are given more maps—a map of the city and maps promoting museums, Spanish schools, restaurants, and tour companies, should the independent tourist want to participate in some guided sightseeing. In hotels, restaurants, bookstores, and Spanish schools, even more maps are available.

Those who work in the tourism industry are self-conscious about maps. INGUAT publishes two different Antigua maps, one printed in color on glossy paper and the other printed in black and white on inexpensive paper. The former is free but harder to find. On the opposite side of this map, hotels, cultural centers, artisan products, restaurants, Spanish schools, banks, travel agencies, bus companies, and car rental companies are listed. The other map, which costs US$0.04, is a simple one showing the churches, the Central Plaza, and museums. Businesspeople want to be included on the glossy INGUAT map, since it indicates which businesses the Guatemalan government endorses.

Businesspersons also purchase advertising on other maps or collectively publish maps themselves, with their advertisements in the margins and on the opposite side. Maps produced by Cartoon's Advertising, Gare de Creación, and Agencia Publicitaria contain information about festivals, folklore, and brief histories of Antigua. Agencia Publicitaria publishes a monthly map, which includes a calendar of events. These maps cater to businesses owned by Ladinos and foreign expatriates.

Maps are important to Maya *típica* vendors and other merchants in tourism because they know that tourists read them. The vendors who sell in the Compañía de Jesús Artisan Marketplace have been particularly distressed about their relationship to the maps published by INGUAT, as well as those published by local Antigua businesspersons. Not only do the INGUAT maps *not* list the Compañía de Jesús Artisan Marketplace, but the more commonly distributed black-and-white map indicates that the municipal bathrooms are located along the southeast side of the Compañía de Jesús ruins where the marketplace is located. This is problematic to vendors because tourists do not frequent municipal/public bathrooms. To no avail, vendors have tried to get local INGUAT officials either to remove the reference to the bathrooms or, better yet, to list the

Mayas in the Marketplace

location of the marketplace on the map. Marketplace vendors also have been refused advertising space on the other above-mentioned maps. This is an example of the exclusionary practices of the Guatemalan government and of non-Maya Antigua businesspersons that have caused concern among vendors, who worry about tourists not knowing that they exist or, if tourists do learn that the marketplace exists, about them not frequenting it because it is not supported by the government.

The power of the state (INGUAT) or of non-Maya businesspeople, however, is not complete or consistent. Vendors learned that an expensive map (US$10–$15), "Modern & Colonial: Guatemala City & La Antigua Guatemala," with detailed illustrations and artwork, does include the Compañía de Jesús Artisan Marketplace and was sold by Colección Verás. The map was made for the Maya World (Mundo Maya) promotion organized by the governments of Mexico, Belize, Guatemala, Honduras, and El Salvador. A free map distributed by Burger King is the other map to include the marketplace, which surprised vendors because they had not asked to be represented in it. The limited distribution of these maps, compared to those published by INGUAT and Agencia Publicitaria, led vendors to figure that the maps would not bring many shoppers to the Compañía de Jesús Artisan Marketplace. They did not feel, therefore, that they were quite within the tourist gaze.

Drawing on Foucault, James Urry (1990, 1992), who has discussed various aspects of "tourist gazes," argues that "there are ways of being a tourist that do challenge and disturb dominant constructions of the spaces of a town or city — heterotopias, in other words" (1992: 178). In the case of Antigua, tourists comprehend the city first by studying maps and then by looking out over Antigua from the tops of Spanish colonial church ruins like Santa Clara, San Francisco el Grande, and the Capuchinas Convent. The effects of such gazing, or surveillance, can lead to a "process of interiorization as implied by the panopticon," where the subjects of the gaze "may believe that they are always about to be gazed upon, even if they are not" (Urry 1992: 177).

These panoptic effects are double edged. Mayas and Ladinos are aware of the tourists' gazes. In fact, for *antigüeños* who are involved in tourism, not being within the tourist gaze, such as not being shown on a map, worries them, even though being within the gaze may result in forms of self-discipline. For instance, Maya vendors advise each other to watch their behavior because tourists will see them acting up and then not visit the marketplace.

Tourists also find themselves being gazed upon by Maya and Ladino businesspersons, as well as by other tourists. Although only some people and things in Antigua warrant being gazed at by tourists, tourists are markedly different enough from locals that they, in turn, are the subjects of gazes. Castañeda (1996: 232–258) discusses how in the marketplace at Chichén Itzá both he and vendors were busy watching each other. Mutual watching is common in tourism places, but unlike Castañeda's self-example, being watched is not what tourists in Antigua expected or desired. In fact, they expected to be invisible while viewing their maps and standing on the upper balcony of the town hall (Ayuntamiento) and gazing down on the Maya street vendors, Ladino schoolchildren, and other tourists in the Central Plaza. Some felt that they should decide if and when to "reveal" themselves to the subjects of their gaze.

The incongruity between the map, which helps tourists conceptualize Antigua as colonial, and self-conscious subjects who want to be gazed upon disrupts and undermines the ways tourists imagine Antigua and its inhabitants. Because there are so many tourists in Antigua most of the year, they cannot ignore each other. For those who are in Antigua to regroup with fellow travelers, to rest, to send e-mails, and to eat non-Guatemalan foods, the city is a welcome stop where they can seek out other like-minded people with whom to compare travel notes and experiences. Some, however, are bothered by other tourists, who remind them that Antigua is touristic and that residents there expect and anticipate tourists' gazes.

The preponderance of maps undermines the touristic experience. It is one thing to read a map that was included in a guidebook purchased in a bookstore at home, yet quite another to be confronted everywhere one turns with another map suggesting what she or he should see and do. Sometimes, maps themselves undermine tourists' conceptions of Antigua's contained wholeness by revealing ways that the borders of the city are not contained—historically, economically, or culturally. For example, the cover of the Cartoon's Advertising map features Coca-Cola symbols. The Burger King map combines company advertising and information about Antigua. The brochure/map for the art exhibit "Painted Bodies: Forty-five Chilean Artists" that was displayed in the reconstructed parts of the Compañía de Jesús Monastery, which are occupied by the Spanish Agency of International Cooperation (Agencia Española de Cooperación Internacional), places Antigua in an international art scene. These maps remind tourists that Antigua is an international city with transnational companies, as well as one that is self-consciously maintained as a Spanish colonial time capsule.

Anzaldúa (1987: 3) writes, "Borders are set up to define the places that are safe and unsafe, to distinguish *us* from *them*. A border is a dividing line, a narrow strip along a steep edge. A borderland is a vague and undetermined place created by the emotional residue of an unnatural boundary." The dividing line between tourists and Others and between colonial city and transnational city is not clearly marked. Maps, then, ultimately fail to delineate the boundaries between tourists and others, and instead reveal to them, like seeing other tourists, the heterotopic dimensions of Antigua. Tourists, Ladinos, Mayas, and all others living in and visiting Antigua find themselves in a borderzone where the historical city of cobblestone streets and colonial buildings coexists with and contradicts the transnational city of Burger King and Radisson International resorts.

Second Scenario: Remaking a Colonial City

The Guatemalan historian Jorge Luján Muñoz wrote that during the first decades of the twentieth century Antigua remained a quiet, forgotten place. Interest in it returned when, "with the motive of its 400th anniversary [1941], . . . the rubbish was removed, the ruins were made adequate *without irrelevant restorations* [emphasis in original], and flowers were planted in the cloisters and atriums. Thanks to its tranquil life as a large town, hardly any new buildings had been constructed. Then it was rediscovered by many Guatemalans and it began to be enjoyed as a cultural and touristic center" (Pardo 1944: 259, quoted in Luján Muñoz 1966: 17).

RE/CONSTRUCTING COLONIAL ARCHITECTURE

The single defining characteristic of Antigua, and the one especially described in national and touristic discourses, is its colonial architecture. From its establishment in 1541 until it was shaken by a series of earthquakes in 1773, it was one of Central America's prominent cities. Not only a Catholic religious center, where Dominicans, Franciscans, Jesuits, and others were represented, it was an important administrative, political, and educational hub. Christopher Lutz (1994: 168) explains that Antigua was composed equally of Spanish, indigenous, and African populations, making it one of the most diverse Central American cities in the 1700s. Over time, the city became increasingly more Ladino, less overtly indigenous and Spanish, with few surviving traces of the African slave population. Today, Ladino residents, government officials, and Mayas conceptualize Antigua as a Ladino town, despite the fact that Mayas work there

Figure 2.1. Antigua, looking through the Arc of Santa Catalina on 5ª Avenida Norte, facing south toward the volcano Fuego. This view is commonly reproduced in guidebooks and on postcards. Photograph by author.

Mayas in the Marketplace

and participate in Catholic and Protestant church services and activities.

When Guatemala's capital was moved forty-five kilometers east to its present-day location of Guatemala City, following the 1773 earthquakes, Antigua practically languished in oblivion until the development of tourism early in the twentieth century. By the 1940s, Antigua was firmly on the tourism circuit, appealing to tourists because it appeared to be stuck in time, with its Spanish colonial buildings, cobblestone streets, and a large number of artisans who produced cotton textiles, ceramics, baskets, nets, furniture, musical instruments, jewelry, forged iron, and candles (see Subcentro Regional de Artesanías y Artes Populares 1990). Joaquín Muñoz (1940: 83) wrote, "It is the most impressive monument of Spanish Colonial magnificence and grandeur that exists in the world. Guatemala proudly shows their visitors this Jewel City with its ruins, history, and legend that very few cities in the world perhaps can equal." Although Muñoz's (1940) guidebook was the most widely distributed in the 1940s (it is still available in bookstores in Guatemala as well as in used bookstores in the United States), other guidebooks from this time praised Antigua's colonial features.[1]

Antigua's importance as a tourism center and its fame as a well-preserved colonial city grew after it was named a National Monument on March 30, 1944, by governmental decree. In 1965, the Eighth Assem-

Figure 2.2. Tanque de la Unión Park. Photograph by author.

bly of the Pan-American Institute of History and Geography named it a Monumental City of the Americas. Then in 1979, UNESCO included it in its World Heritage Site List. Despite these honors, little was done to restore or maintain Antigua's colonial buildings, although a national law was passed in 1969 to protect the colonial architecture. The Tanque de la Unión—a rectangular park with two rows of palm trees and a large community *pila* on its eastern side—although not a relic of the colonial period, was restored, since it was dedicated in the 1930s to dictator Jorge Ubico. The church of San Francisco el Grande and Fifth Avenue North were renovated and made more colonial. By 1972 the National Council for the Protection of Antigua was formed to regulate restoration projects. According to two of Antigua's prominent amateur historians, Elizabeth Bell and Trevor Long (1993: 15), "Tons of dirt and rubble covered fountains and courtyards. The city streets were a jumble of neon signs, billboards and other trappings of a contemporary 20th century."

Following the 1976 earthquake, the city fell into greater disrepair, but that natural disaster provided an opportunity for city officials and private citizens to ensure that the city would retain its colonial-style architecture. The National Council for the Protection of Antigua regularly published reports announcing the progress of renovations and the rehabilitation of the city. Both the municipal and the national governments were self-conscious about Antigua's look and were adamant about enforcing building codes.

Residents and merchants discuss building codes with mixed feelings. For some, the codes are too strict. While all agree that prominent historic buildings should be restored in colonial style, many argue that the codes inhibit the modernization of private buildings. Tensions between conservators and private citizens play out as individuals construct the buildings they desire, attending to the codes as they see fit. One debate that predominates in local newspapers is building height. Preservationists argue that with the exception of municipal and church buildings, few were two or more stories high in colonial times. To maintain the colonial integrity of the city, no buildings should be built over one story. However, for *antigüeños* with growing families or small businesses, building up is the only way they can gain extra needed space.

On June 10, 1997, the newspaper *Siglo XXI* reported that Mayor Víctor Hugo del Pozo granted construction licenses that violated building codes. Further denouncements were made against the mayor in the same newspaper on August 1, 1997, because of the incorrect renovations

Mayas in the Marketplace

that were made on the Convent of La Merced, the Arc of Santa Catalina, and office spaces in the Municipal Treasury building. By the end of August, as reported in the newspaper *La Prensa Libre,* the mayor was in search of a new conservator for the city. Three months after his appointment, the new conservator, Ramsés López, resigned under controversy about his lack of experience in historical conservation and restoration (*La Prensa Libre,* March 6, 1998).

Typical building violations included demolishing colonial-period walls, displaying signs that protruded into the street, constructing buildings greater than one story, using roofing materials that did not appear to be tile, installing doorways that did not reflect a colonial aesthetic, and painting buildings in bright color combinations like purple, yellow, and green.

In January 1998, in order to curb construction violations and better regulate restoration projects, the Guatemalan National Congress considered revamping the heritage protection laws, but in the end did not. Failure to comply with the new laws would have resulted in a maximum fine of Q100,000 compared to the current maximum fine of Q500 for similar violations. During the same month, under Mayor del Pozo's direction, concrete barricades were installed on some streets to block the passage of large commercial trucks and buses that were destroying the

Figure 2.3. La Merced Church and *típica* vendors. Photograph by author.

cobblestone streets because of their weight and ruining the paint on buildings because of their exhaust (*La Prensa Libre,* January 16, 1998). *Antigüeños* petitioned the mayor to be even more rigorous and diligent in the enforcement of traffic.

RE/CONSTRUCTING PEOPLE

At work in Antigua since the 1930s is the social construction of people living and working in the city. As both Christopher Lutz (1994) and John Swetnam (1975) have documented, Mayas have always been an integral and important part of the city's history. In part, the continuing practice of reconstructing and conceptualizing Antigua as a Spanish colonial city relates to how Mayas are represented touristically and allowed to present themselves culturally. Subsequent chapters deal with the problems Maya vendors have working in Antigua. Suffice it to say, in order to make a living, Maya vendors of products in the utilitarian marketplace and of handicrafts and other items for tourists accept the roles they play in re-constructed colonial Antigua.

At the same time, tourism representations re/construct Antigua as a colonial space and re/construct its inhabitants to fit the space. References to Mayas in guidebooks frequently locate them in historic terms or in particular roles, such as vending agricultural produce and handicrafts, which have been practiced since the colonial period. Thus touristic views of what is authentic are reinforced. For example, Víctor Díaz (1927: 18) described the process of erasing Mayas from Antigua and condemned Spanish colonial practices. He wrote of the early colonial period that "the unfortunate indigenous race from nearby towns . . . commenced to diminish . . . because of the hard work . . . , living in oppressive servitude, and laboring on the construction of buildings . . . , in order to enrich the families of the conquistadors." The passage indirectly inscribes Antigua as a Ladino place, since it infers that neither Mayas nor Spaniards exist in the city. Díaz's guidebook advised its readers that in order to see Mayas, or rather "*indios* [Indians]," one had to leave Antigua and visit nearby towns like San Antonio Aguas Calientes.

Similarly, Pedro Zamora (1943: 24) locates Mayas historically but does not deal with them as contemporary social actors. He described how the Central Plaza, "where women and *indios* who sold products met," served as the city's marketplace prior to the 1773 earthquake. A later guidebook that was published and distributed to tourists in the 1960s and early 1970s by the Sacatepéquez Departmental Body of Tourism firmly places Mayas in the marketplace: "Antigua's market is one of the best in the country, because of the great variety of products offered by the Indians from the nearby villages."

Today, Mayas who perform economic roles as vendors occupy a well-defined social space in Antigua that corresponds to the physical reconstruction of buildings. Not only do buildings need to be made in colonial style, but some people need to be located within the city as colonial subjects. Since the city's founding, Mayas have been the manual laborers, gardeners, and vendors of handicrafts and produce. Tourism practices continue to perpetuate these roles. Mayas who do not conform to them are out of place and out of time. Maya *típica* vendors use this legacy to argue that they "naturally belong" in Antigua. Whenever the municipal government or police tried to regulate the numbers of vendors and the places where they sell, vendors in the Compañía de Jesús Artisan Marketplace and peddlers in the Central Plaza explain their rights in terms of primordial origins. One Kaqchikel Maya vendor expressed the general sentiments of all: "We've always come here, bringing and selling farm products and handicrafts. Tourists want to see us."

Mayas who are not vendors or manual laborers are culturally silenced in their occupations. Maya scholars working in Antigua are invisible to tourists, even though they are openly promoting and living their Mayanness. Maya linguists and scholars working with the Francisco Marroquín Linguistic Project; a library and research center, CIRMA (Centro de Investigaciones Regionales de Mesoamérica); and a Maya linguistic research team, OKMA (Oxlajuuj Keej Maya' Ajtz'iib'; 1993), do not deny their culture, and, in general, they are not denied it by Ladino businesspersons and institutions of tourism. These Mayas occupy social spaces and physical places that are, at best, at the margins of Antigua tourism. A few Spanish students at Francisco Marroquín Linguistic Project are aware that they can study Maya languages, but the school is internationally known for its Spanish language classes.

Usually, Mayas must conform to Ladino norms if they get work in occupations other than vending or labor. Mayas who work in better-paying jobs, including positions in tourism, security, banks, restaurants, and hotels, must, according to them, act like Ladinos—wear Ladino-style clothing and not speak a Maya language—in order to keep their jobs. To illustrate how Mayas working in Ladino socioeconomic spheres are dominated by and coerced to conform to Ladino culture in order to get and keep their jobs, I present two examples: a security guard for GUATEL (previously the name of the national telephone company) and a bank teller.

For several years, 1994 through 1997, I used the telephones in the main GUATEL office, sometimes accompanied by Maya vendor friends. One day late in 1997, a GUATEL security guard approached me in the Central Plaza, telling me that he was a Kaqchikel Maya from San Juan de Comalapa. He had been hesitant to identify himself and his corresponding cultural identity because he feared repercussions from Ladino clients of the telephone company and from his Ladino supervisors.

In the other case, the bank teller and I crossed paths at a wedding in San Antonio Aguas Calientes, his hometown. He had served me at the bank and knew that I was working with *típica* vendors and Kaqchikel Mayas, teaching their own language. He began talking to me as if we knew each other, but I could not place him. When he explained where he worked, I realized who he was. On the job, he had to be Ladino, which was difficult for him when he had to help Maya clients of the bank. He spoke of how liberating it must be for the Kaqchikel teachers to have visible, prestigious work in Antigua that did not require them to "deny their language and culture." Of course, by passing as a Ladino, he has a better job than many of his peers.

EFFECTS OF RE/CONSTRUCTION AND GLOBALIZATION

In Antigua, few people would disagree about the economic benefits of maintaining, conserving, and constructing buildings in the Spanish colonial style for the promotion of tourism. Mayas also find themselves complying with a colonial legacy that assigns to them particular occupational roles when they retain their cultural identities, or negates those identities when they secure other types of jobs. Architecture and occupational roles articulate together to give visitors (not just U.S. and European visitors but also Guatemalans and other Latin Americans) the impression of a timeless, colonial city. It was because of the articulation of "Indians" with the Spanish colonial buildings that foreign tourists visited Antigua.

Baudrillard's (1983) theories on simulacra and Saskia Sassen's (1996) thoughts on the globalization of cities can be used to think about the re/construction of Antigua. Baudrillard (1983: 11) writes of the final phase of an image that "it bears no relation to any reality whatever: it is its own pure simulacrum." Later, he explains that simulation is based "on the structural law of value" (Baudrillard 1983: 83). In other words, the simulation operates at the level of signs for the sake of signs themselves, divorced from, yet based upon, the original and somehow better than it. He uses Disneyland as the ideal example of a simulacrum. And, it is ironic that some tourists to Antigua characterize it as a "Disneyland."

It is important to think about the image, or representation, of Antigua and what that representation means. More precisely, how Antigua is decoded by tourists who visit and how it is used by Mayas and Ladinos who live and work there reveal the unique characteristics of the city—part simulacrum of a colonial city and part actual colonial city. Those persons rebuilding and working in the shadow of colonial Antigua are clearly aware that Antigua today is a representation of a colonial city from a previous historical period. The politics of how Antigua is remade into a new colonial image of its former real colonial self is at the heart of debates among residents and those who work there.

Unlike Disneyland, which was constructed from scratch to entertain, Antigua's history has been one of constant rebuilding and change, primarily because of earthquakes, although in the twentieth century much of the rebuilding related to tourism. Building owners and government officials debated about what is colonial, which type of colonial style is to be used, and should only the façades of buildings be colonial or whole buildings from the ground up. According to an *antigüeño* friend who has worked on restoration projects, there is no one recommended colonial style. Residents and builders have their own particular visions about what Spanish colonial style consists of and how much a building should conform to it. Often, debates revolve around appropriate colors of paint, building heights, and the correct use of signs. The simulacrum always threatens to be unmade because of these debates. The internal tensions at work, related to how buildings are constructed and who occupies the city, are so great and so overtly contradictory that most tourists, especially those who spend more than a couple of hours there, see Antigua as a re-creation and representation of a colonial city.

Disneyland, unlike Antigua, does not have the problem of being more than what it is. Antigua, on the other hand, is something that signifies meaning and refers to both the real and the imaginary. Disneyland does not refer directly to the real, the authentic. Of course, Disneyland is physical and it can and does refer back to itself. It is a thing, too. However, Antigua is different. Some buildings, streets, and artifacts are actually from the colonial period, but at the same time, the city is a reconstruction of itself.

Antigüeños' debates about how to remake Antigua also relate to those who visit. Although the tourism industry promotes it as a colonial city, *antigüeños* know that foreign and national tourists would not stay and spend money if it really were a colonial city. Visitors expect both a colonial city and numerous amenities that will make their stay comfortable. In Disneyland no one is surprised to see fast-food restaurants, hotels with air-conditioning, and places that send faxes and e-mail messages, but in Antigua, these can threaten the authenticity of the city. Guided tour companies are careful to avoid these problematic places. Frequently, they will not pass by fast-food restaurants, like Burger King and the popular fried chicken restaurant Pollo Campero. They avoid bars and computer cafés, weaving through the city and selecting sites thought to exemplify the colonial period. To further safeguard against rupturing the colonial image, tourists are kept so busy, so overwhelmed with facts and activities, that they do not have the time to explore Antigua on their own. In their hotel, which is not marked as colonial, especially the guest rooms, tourists are not in colonial Antigua.

The majority of independent American tourists who visit Antigua go there to see a Spanish colonial city and to study Spanish. They look at colonial buildings and artifacts, gaze at and converse with "real Indians" (identified by their clothing and occupations) in the marketplace and streets, and eat dinner at the Fondo de la Calle Real restaurant, which serves typical Guatemalan food. If they are not disappointed by or want some of the conveniences of home, they can read and send e-mail messages, eat pizza for lunch, watch programs in English on cable television, and go to a sports bar to watch U.S. basketball games with other tourists. The interests of *antigüeños* are split between efforts to rebuild a colonial city and trying to serve their tourist guests.

Sassen (1996: 221) holds that "globalization is a process that generates contradictory spaces, characterized by contestation, internal differentiation, continuous border crossings." According to her, this disarticulates local interests from those of the nation, connecting them more to global political, economic, and social arenas. Antigua is one of these places. Mayas, Ladinos, and tourists meet in this borderzone, disrupting the notions that Antigua is singularly a Ladino place and the Maya towns in the highlands are singularly Indian places.

Third Scenario: A Typical Tuesday in Antigua

Another way of comprehending Antigua is by walking through it and living in it. This, of course, is a process of getting to know a city that differs from panoptic forms of gazing from the top of a tall building or at a map. To practice these latter forms of viewing, explains Michel de Certeau (1984: 92), "is to be lifted out of the city's grasp. . . . When one goes up there, he leaves behind the mass that carries off and mixes up in itself any identity of authors and spectators." However, he advises that in order to get at every-day practices, to know how the city is lived, it is important "to [begin] on the ground level, with footsteps" (de Certeau 1984: 97).

The following description of how I tended to spend Tuesdays in Antigua illustrates one way to understand the city. My interaction with the city helps demonstrate, according to de Certeau's theories of "spatial practice," the "contradiction between the collective mode of administration and an individual mode of reappropriation . . . [in which] . . . spatial practices in fact secretly structure the determining conditions of social life" (1984: 96). In other words, this section shows how an "everyday practice" can contra-dict the ways a place is constructed officially by the nation-state as well as by the economically and politically dominant participants.

EVERYDAY SOCIOSPATIAL PRACTICES OF AN ANTHROPOLOGIST

On most Tuesdays, for nearly one year, my day followed the same basic routine. From 5:30 AM until roughly 7:30 AM, I entered fieldnotes in my computer, watched CNN, and thought about the previous day. Aside from the occasional crow of a rooster or the calls of bus *ayudantes* (help-ers), Antigua's brisk mornings were quiet. By 7:30 AM, joining the hun-dreds of schoolchildren rushing to school, I left my apartment on Segunda Calle Oriente to eat breakfast at Café Condesa, located on the south side of the Central Plaza. En route, I purchased two daily newspapers, *Siglo XXI* and *La Prensa Libre,* and talked to vendors who were going to break-fast or to get their merchandise out of storage.

Owned by an American woman, the Café Condesa is one of the restaurants in Antigua that will serve anyone—provided they can afford the prices and want to eat U.S.-inspired food. Daily, it fills with a mixture of tourists and locals—foreign expatriates, retirees from the United States,

Antigua businesspersons, and others—intent on eating pancakes, scones, and American fried potatoes. Few Mayas go there to eat, which is not true for the many pizza restaurants located throughout Antigua. However, it was one of the few restaurants, other than those in the marketplace, where I did not have to worry about my Maya friends being refused service. We could meet, have conversations, and plan future projects. The backdrop of the restaurant—the U.S.-style food, the hushed mix of languages (Spanish, German, English, French, Hebrew, Japanese, and others), the colonial architecture with fountains and flowering plants—provided a perfect atmosphere for my Maya friends and me to make cultural comparisons.

The differences of the place and the food from the houses and meals of Mayas elicited descriptions of their own kitchens and thoughts on food and other topics that I could compare later when I was in their homes. It was a place where I could share a small part of my culture with friends whose chances of obtaining a visa from the U.S. government and saving enough money to visit me in Chicago were not likely. It was one of those places where my Maya friends and I could go unnoticed, where our presence did not matter to anyone, where we were not tourism spectacles. Café Condesa was also where I could find other anthropologists on leave from their research sites or en route to them.

After breakfast, around 10:00 AM, I usually went to the Compañía de Jesús Artisan Marketplace, located one city block from the Central Plaza. At this hour vendors were still unpacking merchandise and setting up their displays. They rushed to get their locales in order before tourists and Spanish students came to look at "Indians," practice Spanish, browse, and buy. I joined them by carrying bundles of clothes, bags, and other items; by sweeping and picking up trash left by tourists the previous day; and by relaying messages among friends and family members within the marketplace.

As in the Café Condesa, the sounds of the marketplace are a mixture of languages: Spanish, Kaqchikel, K'iche', Ixil. Vendors yelled instructions to each other in their respective languages, talked across language differences by using Spanish, and practiced phrases in English on me. Sometimes, I heard a voice a couple of aisles away yell, "*La at k'o,* Walter?" (Are you there, Walter?).

"*Ja*" (Yes), I would reply.

"*Tab'ana' utzil. Achike nab'ij chaleco pa ingles?*" (Do me a favor. How do you say *chaleco* in English?), the vendor might question me.

"Vest," I would yell back.

"Vest," the vendor would say. "*La ütz, xinb'ij?*" (Did I say it right?)

"*Ja,*" I would answer.

K'iche' speakers frequently interrupted my discussions in Kaqchikel by teasing me with comments like "When are you going to learn a real Maya language?" and "You'll never speak correctly unless you learn K'iche'." To kid me, other vendors would ask questions such as "*Walter, ¿puede decir 'buenos días' en koreano?*" (Can you say "good morning" in Korean?) or "*¿Sabe los números en japonés?*" (Do you know the numbers in Japanese?), knowing that I did not know the answers. By the time tourists started coming in larger numbers to the marketplace, around 11:00 AM, the linguistic terrain of the marketplace was even more complex: vendors talking to each other in their respective Maya languages, tourists speaking to each other in their own languages, each group trying to figure out what the other group was saying, and finally negotiating business transactions in mixtures of Spanish and English, or Spanish and Italian, or Spanish and German, or Spanish and Japanese, or Spanish and any other language.

The morning setup routines in the Compañía de Jesús were the times when vendors talked about the daily news, spread gossip, and thought about home. They discussed newspaper articles about the thieves, drug dealers, and murderers that were making Antigua a dangerous city. They fretted over articles that described violence that was increasing throughout Guatemala (murders, kidnappings, and robberies) and speculated how it would affect tourism and sales in the marketplace. Gossip topics ranged from wondering if the mayor of Antigua would kick all *típica* vendors out of the city to rumors about the amorous relations of other vendors. Despite the vendors' preoccupations about crime and the mayor, conversations always returned to home—to that place that made sense, that was comforting. Even those vendors from the departments of Chimaltenango, Sololá, and Quiché who suffered from Guatemalan military campaigns and guerrilla tactics in the 1980s thought of home in positive ways.

By 12:30 PM, I was often eating lunch with a group of male vendors (Kaqchikel, K'iche', Ixil, Ladino) in one corner of the marketplace. We purchased our meals from Oralia, a Kaqchikel woman from San Antonio Aguas Calientes. Typically, she made different main courses—fried chicken, chow mein, spaghetti with tomato sauce, beef stew, and occasionally seafood soup and *pepián*—all of which were served with tortillas, rice, potatoes, and a vegetable. Vendors ate lunch quickly, keeping an eye on potential customers. When interrupted by a group of tourists passing through the marketplace, they cut short their conversations about soccer teams and television programs they had watched the night before, stashed their meal out of sight, and greeted their customers.

Around 1:30 or 2:00 PM, I left the Compañía de Jesús Artisan Marketplace and walked to the Central Plaza to observe and have conversations with tourists and ambulatory vendors. In the late afternoon, I ran errands, checked my e-mail, and interviewed a vendor in one of the other marketplaces, such as in the courtyard of the Catholic church, San Francisco el Grande, or in the palm-tree-lined park, Tanque de la Unión. Occasionally, I sat in the park talking to tourists, where I was constantly being interrupted and teased by ambulatory vendors from Kaqchikel towns such as San Antonio Aguas Calientes, Sololá, and Santa Catarina Palopó, and K'iche' towns such as Momostenango and Chichicastenango. Vendors used this good-natured teasing to get me to introduce them to tourists or as a form of entertainment when business was slow.

By 6:00 PM, I returned to Compañía de Jesús to help some of my friends pack up and store their merchandise, always stopping at Antonio's vending locale. He is a Kaqchikel vendor from the town of San Juan de Comalapa. He and his children were among the first of my Kaqchikel teachers. Their home was one of my refuges from Antigua, where I could listen to and speak in one language, Kaqchikel, where I could sit at a warm hearth and listen to stories, and where I was not treated as a tourist—because in Antigua, if you are a white-skinned American, you're a tourist. Tuesday night, however, was our night to eat hamburgers and French fries from Burger King and watch professional boxing matches on cable television. We sat on the couch, eating our burgers, with me interpreting the English-language commentaries of the announcers into Kaqchikel and Antonio, who knows far more about boxing than I, explaining moves and strategies and telling me about learning how to fight when he was in the Guatemalan army in the early 1960s.

My paths and interactions with the places, people, and institutions of Antigua illustrate but a tiny fragment of the total ways that residents, workers, and visitors use the city. Tourists walk well-established routes, following instructions from maps, guidebooks, and guides, as they visit sites that are designated culturally and historically significant. The paths of handicraft vendors in Antigua (examined in depth in the next chapters) intersect with those of the tourists, but there are divergences in the ways that they use the city. Other Mayas who are laborers, cooks, gardeners, housekeepers, and clerks working in the city follow another set of paths that usually go unnoticed by tourists but are well known to Ladinos and crucial to the local economy. Ladinos follow yet different paths through the city that take them to the marketplace where they purchase food to serve their student/tourist guests, to local churches to participate in services, and to the homes of friends and family members. Each of these paths intersects one another, is trodden and retrodden by multiple users, constructing a living map of the city that contradicts the formal maps produced in the guidebook descriptions and the reconstruction of colonial buildings in Antigua.

A Transnational Borderzone City

Antigua's links to the global economy can be seen and experienced through the flows of commodities, people, and media that enter the city, pause, and then move on to somewhere else. Transnationality operates concretely according to the ways that people use the city and how spaces are defined by those people. My personal interaction with the place and people who populate it, like the interactions of other individuals, was continually entwined with transnational institutions, products, and individuals.

According to James Holston and Arjun Appadurai (1996: 199), the global marketplace "contradict[s] national boundaries." *Antigüeños* eat at Burger King and Domino's Pizza. They buy apples from Seattle, dates from the Middle East, padlocks from China, and cars from Japan. They use electronic mail accounts and watch cable television, which broadcasts stations from the United States, Mexico, Germany, and other countries. They host, entertain, and teach foreigners from different countries how to speak Spanish. They sell handicrafts to tourists and exporters, who take their purchases home, give them away, or resell them. The Guatemalan nation-state is of little import until it gets in the way economically, by restricting commerce and taxing or fining merchants, and politically, by not controlling crime.

Mayas, Ladinos, and tourists are all part of an intricate late-capitalist global system in which cultural differences come together in Antigua. The colonial architecture; the Maya Indians in costume; the mixture of Spanish, K'iche', Kaqchikel, and other Maya languages; and the two volcanoes, Agua and Fuego, distinguish Antigua from other global cities.

Mayas come from towns throughout the highlands of Guatemala to sell handicrafts, vegetables, and utilitarian items. Ladinos from Antigua itself provide Spanish lessons, operate restaurants, and rent rooms to foreign guests. Tourists, be they Guatemalan or foreign, come to eat, relax, and experience Antigua's Maya and Ladino cultural mix, its colonial and modern cultural mix. For foreign tourists, these are particularly significant in order to have an authentic and enjoyable experience.

Rosaldo (1989: 217) points out that ethnographers now "look less for homogeneous communities than for the border zones between them. Such cultural border zones are always in motion, not frozen for inspection." What the ethnographer strives to observe is quite different from what the tourist is promised. Tourists usually visit a designated site because it is perceived to have some enduring quality. Tour company owners and guides are aware of this as they whisk their tourists through Antigua before they realize how Mayas and Ladinos use the city. Usually, they tour the city in motor buses, making strategic stops at historically and culturally significant sites. Between stops, guides fill the time by telling stories, providing practical information, and explaining the next stop. These can be considered maneuvers of distraction, which, like sleight of hand tricks, take the tourists' attention away from what the guides do not wish them to see.

When one walks through the city; engages it by choosing a place to eat or somewhere to sleep; wanders through its marketplaces and shops; and finds postal, computer, and telephone services, Antigua as a borderzone becomes obvious. Here, the issue for tourists is not whether one has or does not have culture or even history;[2] rather, it is the breakdown of boundaries. A simple walk through Antigua reveals how boundaries between colonial and modern Antigua, Ladino and Maya Antigua, and "the West" and Guatemala are not always well defined.

Through the juxtaposition of the Ladino homeowners, the student/tourists, and the Maya vendors, distinct but conventional cultural boundaries in Antigua emerge. In one case, the cultural barriers between Ladinos and Mayas faded. The Ladina hostess from whom I periodically rented a room from 1994 to 1997 attended equally to her family and all her guests (anthropologists, students, and Mayas). Her behavior contrasted with the manner in which Ladinos treated Maya vendors in Antigua. The latter are accustomed to hearing derogatory and condescending comments, being denied service in some stores and restaurants, and even serving as convenient scapegoats for the police when they are looking for criminals. For

Mayas, being waited on and served a meal by a Ladina and then having her sit and converse with them as equals upset the order of Guatemalan society they were familiar with.

Living in this house allowed me to meet Spanish students and independent tourists, a group of boarders who represented a relatively narrow segment of the tourist population. Rarely did anyone older than thirty years of age stay in the house. Most of the guests were Northern Europeans and North Americans, but students and tourists from Australia, Japan, Korea, and Israel also stayed there. Although roughly equal numbers of men and women stayed in the house, relatively few U.S. women were among the boarders. Independent tourists stayed the shortest length of time, one week, which was longer than most tourists, but they used that week to take Spanish classes before continuing their trip. One group of American surfers spent their mornings surfing on the Pacific coast a few hours away and their afternoons studying Spanish for a week. Most dedicated a week to learning Spanish during the day and drinking and dancing in the clubs at night. The Spanish students were primarily motivated to study Spanish and usually stayed one or more months, occasionally up to six months. Most often those staying in the country longer than a month combined their Spanish learning with volunteer work in local Antigua clinics and nongovernment organizations or in other places of the country after completing their studies.

The Spanish students and tourists, however, reacted quite differently to my Maya visitors. After listening to them speculate about who the "Indians" were, wonder whether or not they could be considered Mayas, and question the authenticity and quality of their handicrafts, I thought they might not mind having the persons they were so curious about visit. The foreign guests tended to react negatively to the Maya visitors. They defined the interior spaces of the house as an English, then Spanish, language domain, since these were their common languages. Maya guests upset this order. I spoke to them in Kaqchikel and then in Spanish, the hostess and her granddaughter quizzed them about how to say words in Kaqchikel, and conversations switched with difficulty between Spanish and Kaqchikel and English. During dinner one evening a student said in outrage in English, "I didn't come all the way to Guatemala to listen to some language I can't understand and don't want to learn. Speak English! I'm tired." Concerned about the happiness of her guests, the hostess inquired what was wrong. Before I could reply, the Maya guest told her that the student was tired and wanted us to speak English.

My Maya friends were seen by the students and tourists as not only invading their "home" space but also disrupting their concepts of who Indians and Mayas could be. Not understanding Kaqchikel or K'iche' was really of minor concern to tourists when compared to their resistance to conversing with the Mayas. As more than one student or tourist reminded me, they did not want to know that "Indians" have cable television, follow U.S. sports like basketball and football, buy Jansport backpacks, and eat pizza and hamburgers. The student and tourist guests repeatedly asked me not to bring Mayas home, preferring distant observations of them and limited personal contact with them in spaces defined as "Indian," such as marketplaces.

These student and tourist reactions to the Maya guests were precipitated by several factors that did not necessarily have to do with Mayas themselves, such as exhaustion from studies and late nights at bars; illnesses related to altitude and food; and a general unfamiliarity with the place, food, people, and language. Immersion in a new cultural setting is difficult and unsettling, and finding a place and time to reenergize oneself in a Spanish-speaking household can be a challenge. Most often their solution was to go on the weekends to Panajachel, San Pedro La Laguna, or Monterrico; stay in a hotel; and associate with other travelers.

Bruner (1996b) argues that Westerners do not want to see impoverished Others at home, but when viewed in faraway places, that Other is exotic and a "pleasure." He explains that "there is a racialization at home and a primitivization over there, in exotica." This certainly applies to the general tourists visiting Antigua. However, the students and tourists who lived in the house with me desperately tried not to notice that the "Indians" whom they had come so far to see shared some of their same interests and were in some ways like them.

Foreigners are haunted by "Indians" who don't behave in ways that match their portrayal in the tourism literature, as discussed in the previous chapter. Certainly, Maya vendors are concerned with marketing themselves and their products to tourists by making differences clear, particularly in language and clothing. But like others using Antigua, they send e-mail; eat at their favorite Italian-style restaurants; and ponder political, economic, and entertainment events in other areas of the world. By observing how Mayas use Antigua, tourists learn that the boundaries between their culture and that of Mayas are not rigid or clearly defined. One of the effects of this contact, as well as the realization that built into the colonial architecture are modern conveniences, is that some tourists question the authenticity of Antigua, its Ladino residents, and its Maya workers because the roles and activities of each, including the supposed functions of buildings, are not contained by clearly marked boundary lines.

Conclusions

As visualized by Bruner (1996b), the tourism borderzone is where "the natives have to break out of their normal routines to meet the tourists. . . . The tourism borderzone is like an empty space, an empty stage waiting for performance time." As Bruner also notes, it is, of course, also a place of work and income. In contrast to Bruner's definition, in Antigua the normal routine of local people *is* tourism. Because of how Antigua is displayed and used by tourists and locals, especially when tourists rent rooms from Ladinos, the lines between home and work, tourist and local, blur.

The socioeconomic spaces in Antigua that have been opened by tourism and are enjoyed by Ladinos and Mayas have unmoored these citizens in some ways from the nation-state. Some Maya vendors go to the city to sell handicrafts, the sale of which the local government and police forces cannot regulate. The money they make from these sales goes untaxed, which is lost revenue known to exist by the local and national governments, yet out of their reach and control. Ladino families hosting Spanish students and tourists are also unregulated. Mayas and Ladinos are more concerned with foreign capital and commodities than with national policies and concepts of who is Guatemalan. Money earned from foreigners, especially if it is not in Guatemalan currency, is hidden from authorities and kept out of banks. In a country that has historically been plagued by violence, in addition to extreme social, economic, and political inequalities (see Montejo 1999 for a recent synthesis of this), hoarding foreign currency is a form of insurance.

For those working in Antigua, the concern about rebuilding Antigua's colonial buildings and mapping the city relates more to appealing to international tourists than to any sense of national sentiment or patriotism. State and local governments become an impediment to merchants, tour guides, handicraft vendors, and families who rent out rooms. War and military service, trade regulations, and taxes impinge on those who make a living in Antigua and remind them of the nation that they otherwise try to ignore. In other words, mechanisms such as INGUAT, maps, brochures, guidebooks, guides, and legal apparatuses used for policing the boundary lines and keeping colonial, Ladino, Maya, and tourist roles separate and distinct are inadequate and usually ineffective.

Although mapmakers and municipal planners attempted to construct a whole, contained city with identifiable boundaries, walking and living within Antigua calls attention to its borderzone and transnational qualities. The intended methods of containment through mapping and reconstructing colonialism are exposed when one walks, lives, and works in Antigua.

I tried to follow Lugo's (1997: 60) strategy "to juxtapose the analysis of" Antigua as a tourism site "with the analysis of the fragmented lives of" Ladinos and Mayas who live and work there, "both in the larger contexts of history and the present, the global economy and the local strategies of survival, and, finally, in the more intricate, micro contexts of culture and power." Conceptualizing Antigua as a borderzone not only allows its heterotopic characteristics to be described but also shows how Mayas, Ladinos, and tourists are located within structures of power related to tourism, the local municipal government, and the state. The next chapters, relating first to vendors and markets and then to community, continue to examine these juxtapositions.

Chapter 3   Antigua *Típica* Markets and Identity Interaction

Introduction

W hen Ma Xuan[1] and his fellow *cargadores* (porters) go to work at 6:00 AM, the streets of Antigua are quiet. Most mornings are cool and brisk. It is possible to spot a few tourists with cameras, taking advantage of the empty streets and the clear morning sky to snap some pictures of unobstructed colonial buildings and of Agua, the quiet cone-shaped volcano that dominates the southerly view, but most tourists are still in bed. It is too early to see schoolchildren, who fill the streets between 7:00 and 8:00 AM. Shopkeepers are still in their homes, just rising and eating their breakfast. For most people, locals and tourists alike, Antigua is a town that gets up late. Its rhythms often follow those of Spanish students and tourists who do not have to be anywhere until 8:00 AM, but usually later. But for Ma Xuan and other *cargadores,* the day begins early.

This chapter begins with a description of *cargadores'* work because a day in the marketplace starts when they take *típica* bundles out of storage and ends when they return the bundles to storage. Hiring *cargadores* is something that most *típica* vendors do in common.

The chapter looks first at marketplace locations and vendor locales from a closer perspective than in the two previous chapters, which dealt more generally with the spatial-temporal than with the social interactions in Antigua between vendors and Ladinos and tourists. It also provides an overview of the participants in the tourism market, who are discussed in greater depth in the next two chapters.

Second, it locates Guatemalan *típica* marketplaces within ethnographic studies of periodic marketplaces and examines various strategies and tactics that *típica* vendors use to make sales, deal with government officials, and co-exist with other vendors in a glutted handicraft market.

Overall, this chapter addresses how life and selling in a marketplace contributes to vendors' various expressions of collective identity. Although vendors in periodic/utilitarian marketplaces and tourism/*típica* market-places both sell products, how they sell and who they sell to differs. Furthermore, the social and economic conditions of the two types of marketplaces differ because utilitarian marketplaces are primarily locally oriented and repeatedly used by the same participants (buyers and sell-ers), whereas *típica* marketplaces are primarily globally oriented and used by buyers who rarely return. Recognizing distinctions between peri-odic/utilitarian marketplaces and tourism/*típica* marketplaces makes it possible to look at ways work and place help shape some aspects of col-lective identity. How issues of identity enter into and are part of the daily social relations and self-representations of vendors is discussed in depth in the coming chapters, which explore how marketing contributes to the identity concepts held by vendors, as well as how various identities are marketed by vendors.

The Work of a Cargador

Every morning all over Antigua *cargadores* haul large *bultos* (bundles) stuffed with various *típica* items to sell to tourists. It is hard work, since some *bultos* weigh over two hundred pounds. A few of the *cargadores* can heft the *bultos* with ease to their backs, but they, like Ma Xuan, are massive, nearly the size of an American football player. Most are small men whose bodies seem permanently bent and compacted from the arduous work. The more fortunate carry their *bultos* from *bodegas* (warehouses) just across the street from the various marketplaces scattered throughout the city. Or they use hand-drawn carts if they are bringing the bundles from more than a block away. The less fortunate walk several blocks, relying only on their bodies, grimacing under the weight of the *bultos,* sweating, and resting frequently. For their efforts, they earn a mere one or two quetzales (US$0.17–$0.34) per *bulto*.[2]

Because few of the vendors selling in the various marketplaces around Antigua have locales where they can safely store merchandise overnight, they put it in *bodegas* located throughout the city. These warehouses are often the spare rooms of small businesses or private residences. Vendors pay from Q10 or Q15 to Q30 (US$1.70–$5.00) per month to store their merchandise. Although some vendors haul all or some of their *bultos* to the marketplace themselves, most contract a *cargador* to do the work.

Figure 3.1. A *cargador* unloads *bultos* at the Compañía de Jesús Artisan Marketplace. Photograph by author.

Since it is rare for a vendor to have more than two *bultos* that will be displayed on any given day, *cargadores* try to make arrangements with a number of vendors. A few, like Ma Xuan, may make anywhere from Q50 to Q100 (US$8.33–$17.00) per day. The majority make only Q10–Q20 (US$1.70–$3.33) per day. How much a *cargador* makes ultimately depends on the business of the vendors. When business is slow, vendors haul their own *bultos*.

By eleven o'clock, most *cargadores* leave the marketplace, though some remain to run errands for vendors. In the case of Ma Xuan, he periodically stays to assist his wife at her locale, but he never sells. Some of the *cargadores* return home to the neighboring Kaqchikel towns of San Antonio Aguas Calientes, Santa Catarina Barahona, and Santa María de Jesús to work in their fields or homes the rest of the day, returning in the early evening to stow away the *bultos* in their respective *bodegas*. By the time they finish returning all the bundles to storage, it is dark, and most vendors are already at home eating their evening meal and relaxing in front of the television or by the radio.

Most days, *cargadores* look unkempt, frazzled, and exhausted. Many have drunk too much, are drinking too much, or are trying not to drink too much. Ma Xuan told me in Kaqchikel that alcoholism is a big problem among *cargadores*. It cost him his first marriage. "Because of moonshine, I lost my first wife. She left. We split, then she hooked up with another man." He said he spent too much time drinking and fighting, which defined him as a youth and made him a man. He watches the younger *cargadores,* who, he says, will eventually learn that drinking too much only proves that they are fools. He knows this because his fighting and drinking landed him in jail on numerous occasions. Now, he would rather be known for his hard work and dedication to his family.

Usually, *cargadores* serving the vendors in Antigua go unnoticed by the city's visitors. They are like the men who sweep streets, clean weeds from the cobblestone streets, and remove trash from the Central Plaza. As *indígenas,* Mayas, or Kaqchikeles, they are invisible to most tourists. When tourists glimpse *cargadores* in the Compañía de Jesús Artisan Marketplace, they tend to mistake their identities.

Tourists who browsed in the *típica* marketplace usually did not identify *cargadores* or male vendors as *indígenas,* much less as Mayas. Tourists from the United States and Europe frequently commented that it was easier to identify as Indians the female peddlers they encountered in the Central Plaza and at colonial ruins. One woman, a tourist from the United States, told me that she never shops in the marketplace—the municipal marketplace or the Compañía de Jesús Artisan Marketplace. "It's too dangerous, too many pickpockets and Ladinos. I only want to buy from real Indians, like Gladys. I just don't feel safe in the marketplace with those men around."

Gladys is a vendor who sells *típica* at the Tanque de la Unión, a park in front of the ruins of Santa Clara. She too hires a *cargador* to carry her *bultos* to and from a nearby *bodega.* She comes almost every day to the open-air mini-marketplace with some twenty to thirty other vendors. Dressed meticulously in her *po't* (*huipil,* or "blouse"), *uq* (*corte,* or "wraparound skirt"), and *pa's* (*faja,* or "belt"), Gladys typifies what contemporary Mayas should look like to tourists, even if the latter do not always agree that Mayas are living people.[3] On the other hand, *cargadores* and male vendors dress in jeans or chinos and T-shirts or old button-down work shirts, and thus do not fit into the visual stereotypes of who is Maya or Indian, which is why they are not recognized by tourists. Both male vendors and *cargadores* claim that the police take advantage of the fact that tourists fail to recognize *them*

Mayas in the Marketplace

as Mayas by accusing them of stealing legitimate vendors' products when they transport *bultos* to and from locales.

Overview of the Antigua Típica Market

From the 1940s through the 1980s, vendors peddled their merchandise on the cobblestone streets of Antigua and displayed it for sale on the weekends in the Central Plaza. According to vendors, by the mid-1980s the mayor of Antigua wanted them out of the plaza and off the streets. One city official explained that "there were too many vendors blocking the streets, especially on weekends." Two vendor sisters from San Antonio Aguas Calientes described that "the police seized the *bultos* and merchandise of vendors that they found on the street. If you had a lot of things, it was harder to get away." Vendors commonly referred to this as the period when the police started giving "*muchas multas*" (lots of fines).

Today, there are more than seventy locations where *típica* is sold in Antigua. These places range from strategic locations on streets where tourists congregate to boutiques and marketplaces. The boutiques are almost exclusively owned and run by foreigners and non-Maya Guatemalans. The discussion of these locations is limited to the ways that Maya

Figure 3.2. Vendor and tourists at Tanque de la Unión. Photograph by author.

Figure 3.3. Saturday *típica* market at La Fuente. Photograph by author.

típica vendors compete with these stores and deal with the attitudes of their employees and owners. Maya *típica* vendors sell in the Compañía de Jesús Artisan Marketplace (located in the courtyard of a Jesuit monastery ruin), in strategic locations in front of hotels and designated tourism sites, and in smaller marketplaces at the Tanque de la Unión, the San Francisco el Grande Church, and the Saturday *huipil* market in La Fuente (see Figures 3.2, 3.3).

The number of vendors in Antigua on a given day fluctuates greatly because of competition, tourists' itineraries, and vendors' out-of-market activities. Sometimes vendors sell in other cities. For instance, some sell to cruise ships that dock at Puerto Quetzal on the Pacific coast and Puerto Barrios on the Atlantic coast (see Figure 0.1). Other vendors from towns near Lake Atitlán return to their home communities to sell to tourists, who were arriving there in greater numbers. When vendors leave Antigua, new ones always take their places.

The greatest factor affecting how *típica* vendors sell in Antigua is the number of tourists who visit. Because most tour companies take groups to Chichicastenango on Thursdays, the *típica* marketplace is slow on that day. Some vendors, especially *ambulantes* (peddlers), take that day off. The greatest numbers of vendors are visible on Saturdays and Sundays because this is when the most national and foreign tourists visit. Despite

Mayas in the Marketplace

vendors' shifting locations and the changing attendance of vendors in the tourism/*típica* market, the four-hundred-odd vendors with whom I worked represent a relatively stable group. Some of them have spent twenty or more years selling *típica* in Antigua.

Traditional Marketplaces

The *típica* market within Antigua in particular and throughout Guatemala in general follows different patterns of social interaction, selling/marketing practices, and routines than periodic markets, which have been the focus of anthropological research not only in Guatemala but in other places in Latin America, Africa, and China. This research can roughly be divided into those that have emphasized the study of market systems (see Meillassoux 1971; Skinner 1967; and Smith 1976) and those that look at the particularities and peculiarities of distinctive marketplaces within the market system (see Babb 1998; Bohannan and Dalton 1962; Swetnam 1975; and Tax 1953). The differences between periodic marketplaces and *típica* market are discussed below.

PERIODIC MARKETPLACE ORGANIZATION

Most towns throughout the central and western highlands of Guatemala have one big market day and one or two additional smaller market days each week. These periodic marketplaces are part of a socioeconomic system that links smaller towns to larger cities through the trade of commodities (McBryde 1947; Smith 1976). Two types of vendors tend to be present in these marketplaces: those who are from (or live near) the municipality where the market is held, and those who come from more distant towns. The former sell products produced by them in their hometown marketplace at one or all of that town's market days. The latter, however, follow a circuit that takes them from their hometown marketplace to other marketplaces.

Sol Tax (1953) describes how Santa Catarina middlepersons and vendors purchased vegetables in Sololá, then sold them in marketplaces along the Pacific coast. They returned from the coast with food items that were unavailable in the towns around Lake Atitlán. Economic patterns such as these continue to this day. For example, vendors of greens (*ichaj*) from

San Antonio Aguas Calientes sell in San Juan de Comalapa (where the climate is too cold to grow some varieties of *ichaj*) on Tuesdays and Fridays, Antigua on Thursdays and Saturdays, and Guatemala City on Mondays, following the periodic market schedule in each of these towns.

Daniel and Flora, *típica* vendors from Comalapa who sell in Antigua's municipal marketplace, illustrate how some vendors continue to follow periodic market schedules. Originally, they sold *típica* to tourists, but they changed their vending routine when the marketplace grew around their *tienda* (store), making it difficult for tourists to find. They now travel to various marketplaces selling products to other *indígenas* rather than to tourists. Their vending route takes them to Antigua on Mondays, Guatemala City on Tuesdays, Comalapa on Wednesdays, Antigua on Thursdays, Sololá on Fridays, Antigua on Saturdays, and Sumpango on Sundays. Each of these days, with the exception of Wednesdays in Comalapa, corresponds with principal market days in those towns. The day in Comalapa is spent selling from their *tienda,* restocking and organizing inventory, and fabricating additional items.

Much of Daniel and Flora's inventory is purchased from middlepersons from Comalapa, Totonicapán, Quetzaltenango, and Cobán. Middlepersons may be producer-weavers too. Sometimes Daniel and Flora visit weavers in these towns to replenish stock, but more frequently the middlepersons go directly to them, either to their home in Comalapa or to one of the marketplaces they sell at throughout the week. According to Daniel, they had to change their business when their sales to tourists dropped in 1993. They decided to return to more traditional ways of vending. "We changed how we sell. We sell the same as in the past. Sales to tourists are low now. Almost only our people buy our things," explained Daniel.

Historically, the marketplace was located in the Central Plaza and market day was "*día de plaza*" (plaza day), a term that is still used in Antigua today, even though the marketplace has not been in the Central Plaza since the late nineteenth century. Periodic marketplaces tended to be organized according to town or ethnic group. Vendors from the same town sat together first, then divided again by item. Items and people were further divided according to gender (Bunzel 1959: 67–73; McBryde 1933, 1947: 82–83;). Women usually constituted the largest number of vendors in the marketplace, selling locally produced items such as fruit and vegetables (Bossen 1984: 62; McBryde 1947: 83; Tax 1953).

The regional and periodic marketplaces that Smith (1974, 1976) studied are part of a market system that is different from the tourism/*típica* market in Antigua. According to Smith, Mayas and Maya communities are linked horizontally through periodic marketplaces, where the goods they produce are redistributed among themselves.Vertically, they are linked to regional, state, and international markets when surpluses are sold to non-Mayas and industrial, non-Maya-produced goods are sold to them. Mayas, as consumers, traders, and producers, tend to find themselves at the bottom of the economic system.

Laurel Bossen (1989: 336–337) explains that in many regions of the world "market activities are . . . characterized by sexual divisions of labor." Women make, finish, and sell items out of their homes and in local marketplaces, but men make up the majority of long-distance traders. Drawing on her research, conducted in Guatemala in the early 1970s, she argues that even though women produce textiles, men distribute them, which is the more lucrative job and places control of the product in the hands of men (Bossen 1984).

Similarly, Tracy Ehlers (1991) argues that in Guatemalan society men are favored in such ways that women are excluded from occupations that produce the most income. In San Antonio Palopó, men composed all but 5 percent of the commercial weavers in the late 1980s. In 1978, however, no men wove (Ehlers 1991: 7) or marketed textiles to tourists. Most of the weaving was done for exportation, not for local consumption or tourist sales within Guatemala (Ehlers 1993). Both John Swetnam (1988) in Guatemala and Florence Babb (1998) in Peru also argue that in traditional utilitarian marketplaces, men control the distribution of commodities, which nets them the most income. June Nash's (2001, 1993c) research in Chiapas shows how Maya men have tried to wrest control of pottery making, distribution, and sales from women. Women have not stood by silently but have used political organizations, cooperatives, and gathering collectively as women to counteract the ways that the sexual division of labor is biased in favor of men.

Undoubtedly, more men than women control the distribution of commodities in Guatemalan marketplaces and the exportation of handicrafts and other merchandise. But within tourism/*típica* markets in Guatemala, women play more significant roles than men. According to Linda Asturias de Barrios (1994), women are not just producing textiles, they are also distributing them. The majority of the middlepersons selling to vendors in Antigua are women, or male-female (husband-and-wife) teams. In tourism marketplaces, women typically outsold their male counterparts. In fact, in most Kaqchikel vendor families that sold *típica* in Antigua, women were the primary retailers, and with regard to textiles, they controlled production, sales, and profits. In general, female vendors selling in Antigua made more money than men because most tourists tended to identify women, and only rarely men, as indigenous and as weavers themselves, thus connecting them to the products they were selling.

In the tourism/*típica* market, Maya weavers make goods that are consumed by non-Mayas but rarely used by Mayas themselves. Goods move outward from Maya producer households to urban marketplaces in Guatemala City, Panajachel, Chichicastenango, and Antigua, as well as to foreign markets.[4]

CONCEPTUALIZING MARKETPLACES

The periodic marketplace in Guatemala has changed over the past fifty years, according to Liliana Goldín (1987a). She explains that marketplaces in Guatemala have become more capitalistic, principally organized by products, not by ethnic group. She argues that marketplace relations have become less personal than they used to be; today, buyers and sellers may not know each other (Goldín 1987a: 243). Furthermore, city administrations moved marketplaces, originally located in the Central Plazas, from a few blocks of the city center, as in the case of Chichicastenango, to the city's edge, as in the case of Antigua. For K'iche' and Kaqchikel Maya vendors selling in these places, the Central Plaza was where the marketplace should ideally be located. K'iche' Mayas called it *ri u-c'ux cayb'al*. Kaqchikel Mayas called it *ruk'u'x tinamït*, which was where the *k'ayb'äl* (marketplace) was located. The plaza as *ri u-c'ux* in K'iche or *ruk'u'x* in Kaqchikel[5] is "center" or "heart" and is considered a privileged space (Goldín 1987a: 257).

The sociality of the plaza as a marketplace has been challenged and transformed by Ladinos in political power. During Dictator Jorge Ubico's (1931–1944) rule, permanent marketplaces were constructed in highland towns. The idea was to "introduce 'order' in the plaza by constructing market buildings and to insure that they were clean, just, and peaceful" (Goldín 1987a: 256–257). In the 1970s, construction of marketplace structures away from the town center was again a priority of city administrations with marketplace buildings being built in San Francisco el Alto, Momostenango, and Almolonga (all three in Goldín's study) and in Antigua (in Swetnam 1975). Goldín explains that this was a challenge to *indígena*

98

concepts of where it was best to sell, which was in the heart of the town in an open marketplace. But their idea contradicted the Ladino concept, which was that the market had to be a closed, clean, ordered place—free from dust, air, and foreigners (Goldín 1987a: 257). These differences in the ideology of where and how to market are present in the political relationships between Maya *típica* vendors and Ladinos.

Taking a symbolic interactionist position, Miles Richardson (1982) analyzes the differences between the marketplace and the plaza in a small Costa Rican town. Being-in-the-plaza and being-in-the-market correspond to distinct site-specific social realities, because the material conditions in each site are quite different. The marketplace is vibrant, loud, bustling, and full of smells and colors, but the plaza is "considerably more sedate" (Richardson 1982: 425). Looking dialectically at the social relations constituted in the plaza alongside those constituted in the market, it is possible to gain insight into "Spanish American" culture. Hence, argues Richardson (1982: 433), "cultures are composed of multiple realities, counterposed against one another like semantic domains and, through this juxtaposition, defining each other." In other words, these material realities (plaza, marketplace, church, cemetery, etc.), which are common arenas for Latin American social interactions, in juxtaposition with each other and in contrast with each other, serve as the domains that help Latin American culture become what it is.

Applying Richardson's perspective to that of Goldín's adds an additional layer of understanding to what it means to Mayas when the plaza is no longer also the marketplace. A specifically designated market day in *ruk'u'x tinamït* relates both vendors and buyers to each other in materially and socially distinct ways. Being-in-the-marketplace is different than being-in-the plaza. As illustrated earlier, tourists view and interact (socially and economically) with plaza vendors differently from those who sell in marketplaces like the Compañía de Jesús. Physically and socially, the plaza is the heart of Antigua, just as it is in other Latin American towns. To sell in a marketplace away from the town center is to remove Mayas from their most meaningful social and economic relationships. For them, cultural reality was partially constituted through the merging of marketplace and plaza on designated market days into one site for social and economic interactions. Hence, this contrasts with the Ladino (Goldín 1987a) or "Spanish American" (Richardson 1982) concept, which locates these two sites as socially and physically distinct.

Goldín's and Richardson's observations still apply. While conducting research in Antigua through the 1990s, I listened to the same types of debates between Maya *típica* vendors and Ladino government officials when the latter wanted to "clean up" and "bring order to" the streets of Antigua. Because *típica* vendors recognized differences in the ways they interacted with tourists while in the plaza compared to the marketplace, debates often arose among marketplace vendors about their right to sell in the plaza, which was in direct opposition to municipal policy. Some marketplace vendors in the Compañía de Jesús thought about siding with the municipality in order to curtail the marketing activities of plaza vendors who were believed to be undercutting marketplace vendors' sales. For some *típica* vendors, there is no place to be other than the plaza. They sell there despite municipal fines, police seizures of their merchandise, and tensions with marketplace vendors.

MARKETPLACE SOCIALITY

The marketplace, even if, according to Goldín, it is more capitalistic and separated from its ideological heart, is still social—a facet of marketplaces observed by other anthropologists (see Babb 1998; Castañeda 1996; Clark 1994; Mintz 1961, 1971; Swetnam 1975, 1978). The marketplace is an important arena where social, as well as economic, life takes place. It is the neutral locale where families can meet and exchange news. Here persons meet their future spouses, and men drink with friends and acquaintances (Babb 1998; Bunzel 1959: 67; Glittenberg 1994: 46; Reina 1966: 200). Although Tax (1941) did not consider most of the personal, noneconomic relations in the marketplace to be significant, other than for providing amusement and diversion from daily tasks, these types of relationships are tied to economic activities in the tourism/*típica* market that help vendors stay in the business.

Social relations in the marketplace are more complex than vendors meeting each other and consumers, and consumers meeting each other and vendors in simple interpersonal situations—visiting with friends and making economic exchanges. For example, Tax (1937) also argued that markets help to integrate the region socially because they place persons of different socioeconomic classes and ethnic groups together. Ladinos and Mayas meet there, as do different Mayan linguistic groups. Contact with other social groups through travel and commerce is essential, according to Tax, in establishing the particular ethnic identities of *municipios* (the administrative and territorial jurisdictions that include a town center and its outlying hamlets, similar to townships).[6] It is not by recognizing similarities or appropriating ideas and things from other communities that Mayas develop their ethnic identity. Rather, it is through constant contact with others that they recognize and maintain differences (Tax 1937: 427).

Goldín (1985) develops Tax's theoretical and ethnographic perspectives a bit further by drawing on the socioeconomic relations (bartering situations) between K'iche' Maya vegetable vendors and other K'iche' Maya buyers, Ladino buyers, other Maya vendors, and foreigners from the United States. These economic relationships reveal that the marketplace provides a context in which interethnic relationships can take place peacefully and repetitive meetings "allow people to learn their place in the region's sociological map" (Goldín 1985: 186; 1987b).

In the marketplaces that Goldín studied, U.S. tourists and Peace Corps volunteers, otherwise known as "gringos," are located "far enough in the cognitive and ethnic maps of the people . . . as to be of little significance to engage in any productive negotiation" (Goldín 1985: 195). Bargaining between K'iche' vegetable vendors and other K'iche' Mayas or Ladinos indicates the ethnic and general social relationships between these sellers and buyers. Gringos are categorically different and, I assume, rare enough to make socioeconomic relationships between the vendors and gringos of minor significance. In the context of tourism/*típica* marketplaces in Antigua, however, gringos are everything to the Maya vendors.

Although difference plays an important part for Mayas in framing their ethnic identities, it is but one component that factors into vendor identity construction and maintenance. Difference cannot simply be framed in terms of Maya versus Ladino or gringo, Kaqchikel versus K'iche, or San Antonio Aguas Calientes versus Santa Catarina Barahona, which have been the types of identity juxtapositions most frequently identified in the ethnographic literature for Guatemala (see Annis 1987; Colby and van den Berghe 1969; Hawkins 1984; Redfield 1956; Swetnam 1978; Tax 1941; Warren 1989). In the context of *típica* marketplaces, differences and similarities reconfigure according to context and are never universal or constant.

Marketplaces today certainly serve to regionally integrate Guatemala in social and economic terms, but, as Goldín (1987a) argues, the marketplace can also be the ground where Mayas contend with the contrasting opinions of the Ladinos running local and state governments, and, as Smith (1975) points out, marketplaces are part of an economically stratified system in which remote villages are poorer than larger cities because they do not have equal access to exchange systems (roads, transportation, markets). Difference, similarity, Ladino and state hegemony, tourists, and media work together to form the contexts in which the social relations of *típica* vendors operate.

Tourism/Típica *Market and Marketplaces*

Típica vendors are a strong presence in Antigua. Similarly, Panajachel (Villatoro 1988) and Chichicastenango boast strong *típica* marketplaces. Only the marketplace in Chichicastenango follows periodic marketplace rhythms in which the largest market and the best days to buy and sell are on the "*día de plaza*." In Antigua and Panajachel, the *típica* market has little to do with periodic marketplaces or even principal market days.

For both tourists and *típica* vendors, the periodic (or municipal) market and the *típica* market are different physical and conceptual domains. This relates to the ways that towns such as Antigua and Panajachel are occupied and used by Mayas, Ladinos, and tourists. The interrelation of tourism, periodic marketplace, and *típica* vending in Chichicastenango, and the separation of tourism and *típica* vending from the periodic marketplaces in Antigua and Panajachel, relates to the different ways that tourism developed in each of Guatemala's tourism sites and how these sites are placed into and associated with certain tourism routes.

Within touristic discourses, and initially through the promotions of Clark Tours in Guatemala in the late 1920s, Chichicastenango became a place specifically to see "Indians" and various aspects of their lives, such as religious rituals and selling in an indigenous marketplace. Panajachel became a place to embrace nature, where one could go fishing and boating and see, to paraphrase Aldous Huxley (1960), one of the most beautiful places on earth. Antigua was designated as the place where tourists could travel back in history, wander down cobblestone streets, and explore colonial buildings. Because tourists are promised Indians and Indian life, tour companies coordinate their schedules to take tourists to the Sunday or Thursday markets in Chichicastenango. For more than sixty years, it has been promoted as having the "most authentic Indian marketplace." Certainly, it is the most frequently mentioned marketplace in tourism literature and the one marketplace that most tourists mention visiting. Ironically, most tourists also visit the Compañía de Jesús Artisan Marketplace, even though it is not widely regarded as an authentic "Indian" marketplace.[7]

Although Mayas were (and still are) the main draw attracting tourists to Chichicastenango, they do not figure strongly in the touristic discourse about Antigua. Mayas have been present since the founding of the city, first as its builders and then as those responsible for providing food and labor to it (Annis 1987; Lutz 1994; Swetnam 1975). So Mayas were already there when Antigua developed into a tourism site. Vendors from San Antonio Aguas Calientes, Chichicastenango, and other towns with Maya populations who came to Antigua to sell utilitarian items in the municipal marketplace were familiar with foreign tourists' interest in indigenous culture, especially material aspects of it. According to older *típica* vendors, they wanted to participate in this developing market because foreign tourists paid more for handicrafts than Guatemalans did.

The tourism/*típica* market in Antigua represents a small segment of the total tourism/*típica* market system in which Maya handicrafts are sold. It is beyond the scope of this book, however, to explain all the economic and social intricacies of this system, which involve the movement of handicrafts, vendors, and tourists throughout and outside of Guatemala. Handicrafts move from home production centers to marketplaces in Guatemala and to boutiques and shopping malls in the United States and Europe (see Nash 1993a and García Canclini 1993). Some artisans and vendors travel back and forth between Guatemala and Mexico, other Central American countries, the United States, and Europe. Tourists from numerous countries converge on Guatemalan tourism sites, encountering vendors, handicrafts, and Maya and Spanish ruins (see Castañeda 1996 for Mexico). Wealthy collectors of Maya textiles come themselves, or send emissaries, to find and purchase antique handwoven Maya clothing that costs them hundreds of dollars. These prized items, as well as the trinkets and mementos that tourists purchase, travel from their places of origin to distant locations where both their utilitarian and aesthetic meanings change (García Canclini 1993). In a sense, these items take on social lives as they travel and as they are exchanged and passed from artisan to vendor to tourist or collector (see Appadurai 1986). Utilitarian items like handwoven blouses (*po't*) are sometimes transformed into slipcovers for pillows when they eventually arrive at their final destinations as gifts for friends or relatives of U.S., Japanese, or other tourists.

Antigua is one of many places throughout Latin America where artisans, vendors, and tourists converge and engage in socioeconomic relations (see Ariel de Vidas 1995 for South America; Castañeda 1996, García Canclini 1993, and Stephen 1991 for Mexico; and Tice 1995 for Panama). Although it is not promoted as a place for tourists to encounter Mayas or handicrafts, it has become that type of site in practice because the presence of Mayas challenges tourists to rethink the kind of place it is. Since female Maya *típica* vendors are the most recognizable Mayas in Antigua, tourists have come to associate them with the city.

With regard to the tourism market, the divisions between producers, middlepersons, and vendors are not always clearly defined. One family from Comalapa weaves and fabricates bags, vests, and other items, which they market to other Maya vendors, foreign exporters, and non-Maya shopowners in Guatemala City and Antigua. They also maintain three marketplace stalls in two different tourism marketplaces in Antigua. Although the men do not weave, both men and women in the family sew and vend. Another family from San Antonio Aguas Calientes produces table runners, small bags, and Christmas decorations, which are marketed to boutiques and other Maya vendors. The San Antonio family also maintains a couple of stalls in one of the tourism marketplaces. The women in this family weave, and the men sew. Both sell in the marketplace, but women are the primary vendors. Most vendors fabricate some of the handicrafts that they sell, and sizable portions of their inventory are provided by extended family members.

In Antigua, there are five marketplaces that exclusively sell handicrafts (See Figures 0.2, 0.3). There are also numerous vendors of handicrafts in the municipal marketplace. The largest marketplace is the Compañía de Jesús Artisan Marketplace. It and the vendors there are the subjects of Chapter 4. A new marketplace, called simply the Mercado de Artesanías (Handicrafts Marketplace), was completed by the municipality and officially opened on February 20, 1998. Because of numerous conflicts between Maya vendors and the municipality over who would be allowed to sell there and what types of products would be permitted for sale, it took over two years for all stalls in this marketplace to be occupied. In terms of vendors, it rivals the size of the Compañía de Jesús Artisan Marketplace. Both of these are daily marketplaces for which vendors pay rent—Q34 per square meter—to the city and, in theory, pay taxes. No one in the Compañía de Jesús Artisan Marketplace or in the city Artisan Marketplace paid taxes while I was in the field, but they did pay rent. The other three marketplaces—the courtyard of the San Francisco el Grande

Church, the plaza at the Tanque de la Unión, and the "traditional Maya *típica* marketplace" in La Fuente's courtyard—are much smaller, with an average of twenty to thirty-five vendors selling in each. Vendors in these locales also pay rent varying from Q20 to Q100.

Each of these marketplaces shares a number of differences and similarities with the *tianguis* (marketplaces) that Castañeda (1996) studied in Chichén Itzá and Pisté, Yucatán. Both the Antigua and the Pisté marketplaces operated through a combination of self-regulation and regulation by local governments, but the *tianguis* were more regulated by local government (Castañeda 1996: 245–258). Like the *tianguis,* all the tourism marketplaces in Antigua, with the exception of the city's Mercado de Artesanías, were formed by invasions of *típica* vendors. The Compañía de Jesús Artisan Marketplace was formally recognized by the Antigua municipality in 1992, at which time vendors had to pay rent, register their names and hometowns, pay taxes, and keep their locales and the marketplace clean. Like the *tianguis* vendors in Castañeda's study, those Kaqchikel vendors from the nearby towns of San Antonio Aguas Calientes and Santa Catarina Barahona have been economically linked to Antigua for generations. But unlike the residents of Pisté, who were contracted to work on the Carnegie Chichén Itzá project in 1923, Kaqchikel Mayas from towns neighboring Antigua and K'iche' Mayas from more distant towns

Figure 3.4. Handicraft vendors selling in a hotel entryway. Photograph by author.

have been linked economically and politically to Antigua from as early as 1528, the founding of the city. They provided agricultural products to the colonial capital as well as labor for construction projects (Lutz 1994).

The greatest difference between the *tianguis* at Chichén Itzá and any of the marketplaces in Antigua (or, for that matter, those in Guatemala City, Panajachel, and Chichicastenango, too) is the ethnic diversity of the vendors and their proximity to Guatemala's commercial and political center. Whereas the marketplace in Chichén Itzá is relatively new—it began with the invasion of around three hundred vendors from the nearby town of Pisté in 1982–1983 and was formally recognized in 1987 (Castañeda 1997)—*típica* sales, mainly in the form of a weekend plaza marketplace, have been held in Antigua since the 1930s, with vendors coming from numerous towns and representing different linguistic groups. Swetnam (1975) explained that Antigua's marketplace was also ethnically diverse during the colonial period, when it was located in the Central Plaza and was composed of vendors (*cajoneros*) who sold in semipermanent stands called *cajones*. According to Swetnam, the *cajoneros* could be classified as Indians, Mulattoes, and Ladinos. Hence, ethnic and community diversity has been a common feature of marketplaces in Antigua since the city's founding.

In the 1990s, the Compañía de Jesús tourism/*típica* market was served by *proveedores* (middlepersons who provide merchandise to vendors) from twenty-six different towns in nine different departments who spoke six different Maya languages and Spanish. Among the vendors selling there, only 13 of the 205 vendors identified themselves as Ladinos from Antigua. Other marketplaces are equally diverse, but in these places, excluding the new Handicrafts Marketplace, there are no Ladinos. This linguistic and community diversity distinguishes the tourism/*típica* market in Antigua from the *tianguis* in Chichén Itzá and influences the ways that vendors relate to each other socially and economically, interact with tourists, and deal with the Ladino-run municipality and police forces.

Surviving in the Market: Strategies and Tactics

By participating in the tourism/*típica* market in Antigua, vendors are part of a complex matrix of social relations. This market is made up of various social actors, not all of them willing or interested participants. These include vendors and consumers, who willingly enter into economic and social exchanges. Like vendors, consumers who enter marketplaces to buy *típica* or other souvenirs are diverse in terms of age, countries of origin, primary languages spoken, interests, and initial objectives for going into the marketplace, which may not always be to make purchases. For instance, numerous students of Spanish (who are a type of tourist) first visited with vendors in order to practice what they had learned in class. Later, they may decide to buy something. Other tourists (mainly those traveling independently of a guided tour group) entered the marketplace and spoke with vendors because it gave them an opportunity to talk to Mayas. This encounter with the Indian or the Maya Other enabled them to fulfill the experience described in the travel and tourism literature. Unlike hotels and the boardinghouse described in the previous chapter, the marketplace and other types of vending locales were culturally designated places to meet local indigenous people.

Other willing participants in the tourism/*típica* market include *proveedores, cargadores,* store/boutique owners, Ladinos who rent storage spaces and rooms to vendors, and thieves. Each of these actors has her or his own agenda and is, like vendors and consumers, part of diverse groups of people. Maya vendors, however, consistently described thieves uniformly. They were "lazy Ladinos whose parents never taught them how to work." For a Kaqchikel vendor to be called an *eleq'on* ("thief" in Kaqchikel) was the same as being called a Ladino. A person whose chosen profession was theft was Ladino, not *indígena,* Maya, or Kaqchikel, according to Maya vendors. The other participants in the market were not so uniformly regarded, even the *cargadores,* nearly all of whom were impoverished Ladinos (by their own self-descriptions). Although most boutique owners were of foreign and Ladino origins, Mayas from San Antonio Aguas Calientes (Kaqchikel), Santa Catarina Barahona (Kaqchikel), Santa María de Jesús (Kaqchikel), Chichicastenango (K'iche'), Momostenango (K'iche'), and Totonicapán (K'iche') owned a total of seven boutiques in Antigua.

Unwilling participants in the tourism/*típica* market include city government officials and police officers, who participate because of their official duties; most Ladino homeowners and businesspersons, who want tourists' business in other sectors; and some foreign tourists and Ladino tourists from Guatemala City, who visit only to eat at restaurants and see Spanish colonial architecture. These people do not reap any direct benefits from the market. They are unwilling participants because of how Antigua has been conceptually and spatially defined, as discussed in the previous two chapters. To them, Maya vendors are intrusive and out of place because Antigua is conceptualized as a non-Maya Spanish colonial city, and they are undisciplined because they do not follow the rules of the municipality. In other words, vendors resist the "*officializing strategies,*" to borrow from Pierre Bourdieu, of the Ladino-run municipality of Antigua, the Ladino residents of Antigua, and the weekend Ladino visitors from Guatemala City, all of whom seek to change vendors' personal and private interests "into disinterested, collective, publicly avowable, legitimate interests" (Bourdieu 1977: 40). This, however, is not to imply that Ladino merchants do not want Maya-produced handicrafts to be sold to Ladino elites and foreigners. Rather, it is the vendors themselves who are problematic.

One method the municipality of Antigua used to try to get Maya *típica* vendors to conform to its standards was to offer them spaces in the new Handicrafts Marketplace, located behind the fried chicken restaurant Pollo Campero on Alameda Santa Lucía and across from the utilitarian marketplace. It was presented as a place safe from thieves, bad weather, and dirt. It has running water and toilets. It is patrolled twenty-four hours a day by police officers and night watchmen. Major hotels and the municipality pledged to promote the new marketplace and convince large tour companies, such as Clark Tours, STP Tours, and others, to visit the marketplace. Despite these benefits, few Maya vendors moved into the new marketplace and most of the occupied stalls are held by Ladino retailers.

Maya vendors saw the new marketplace as a way for the municipality to control those who entered it and to politically divide those who did not enter it. Although there are over two hundred vendors in the Compañía de Jesús Artisan Marketplace, the municipality offered them only forty locations in the new marketplace. Maya vendors in other locations were not invited to rent stalls. Families were not allowed to occupy more than one locale, even if members could demonstrate that they were part of separate households. Additionally, vendors in the new marketplace were not to sell (either in person or through their agents) in other marketplaces or on the street. Even so, a couple of families moved into the new marketplace and are breaking all of these rules. One family, however, had been found out in 1999 and was apprehensive about being expelled.

Rumors circulated among vendors that if they accepted the new marketplace wholesale, all other vendors would be forcibly expelled from Antigua. Most did not believe the municipality had the power to do that,

Mayas in the Marketplace

but they did believe that it would crack down on vendors by levying more fines, seizing merchandise, imprisoning some vendors, and selectively expelling others. Most Maya vendors chose to continue selling in the same locations they had occupied prior to the construction of the new marketplace. The general feeling was that they were relatively secure if the new marketplace had a number of vacant stalls. Those Maya vendors who have rented stalls there redefine the rules of the space by selling in multiple locations around Antigua, lying about their kin relations so they can occupy more than one locale, weaving on backstrap looms in the corridors of the marketplace (also a flagrant disregard of marketplace rules), and allowing their children to play in the marketplace's two courtyards. Unlike the establishment of the marketplace within the confines of Chichén Itzá, which was considered well won by vendors from Pisté (Castañeda 1996, 1997), the new Handicrafts Marketplace in Antigua was considered a threat by Maya vendors, who saw it as an attempt by the municipality to curtail their economic independence and ability to sell in Antigua.

Surviving in the market, which is more than merely making a meager profit of at least Q20 (US$3.33) per day (which vendors claimed was the minimum amount they needed to stay in business), entails vendors successfully navigating through the political and social relationships of which they are a part. The example of the new Handicrafts Marketplace given above, the example opening this chapter, and others can be understood using Michel de Certeau's (1984) theory of "making do," which can be applied to the tourism/*típica* marketplace, especially as part of the structures of power. In particular, his definition of the concepts, strategies, and tactics enumerated below is productive for thinking about *típica* vendors' socioeconomic and political relationships. According to de Certeau (1984: 35–37):

> [A] *strategy* [is] the calculation . . . of power relationships that becomes possible as soon as a subject with will and power can be isolated. It postulates a *place* that can be delimited as its *own* and serve as the base from which relation with an *exteriority* composed of targets or threats . . . can be managed. . . .
>
> By contrast . . . , a *tactic* is a calculated action determined by the absence of a proper locus. The space of the tactic is the space of the other.

In the context of the tourism/*típica* market, strategies are not solely the techniques of persons and institutions that have the most political and economic power, but can be used as well by collectives, like vendors, who see themselves as a cohesive group with common economic and political goals, located within both a conceptual and a physical place. However, the places in which the municipality operates are politically and economically more powerful than the places in which vendors operate. Vendors employ strategies in order to achieve economic and political goals, but because of their precarious, relatively weak political and economic positions in relation to the municipality, foreign tourists, exporters, and others, they often resort to using tactics.

STRATEGIES IN THE MARKETPLACE

The most common strategies that vendors used collectively as political actors were protests and petition drives, which were organized to assert and protect their right to sell *típica* in Antigua. These were aimed at the municipality, and part of their strategy was to employ the support of tourists, Spanish students, and Ladinos who rent rooms and storage spaces to vendors. They organized these activities during the times of the year when large numbers of foreign tourists were in Antigua, knowing from past experience that the use of force by the police would drive tourists away from the city and the tourism businesses that the municipality considers legitimate, such as hotels, restaurants, and boutiques.

One such petition drive was organized the week of March 4, 1997, in response to the expulsion of all types of street vendors and in anticipation of Holy Week, which draws thousands of tourists from around the world. Organized by Maya street vendors who sell handicrafts and supported by those in the permanent marketplaces, vendors canvassed the city collecting the signatures of Spanish students and teachers, sympathetic Ladino residents, and any foreigner, tourist or otherwise. After hundreds of signatures were collected, the forms were presented to the mayor's office. One vendor commented with skepticism, "Nothing will come of this petition. The mayor will not change his position." Other vendors explained that the petitions were "necessary because they remind the mayor we are wanted by the tourists" and give us "a peaceful way to assert our rights." In this case, as in all others, the municipality did not make any policy changes in favor of the vendors. Officially, anyone with

Mayas in the Marketplace

the capital to rent retail space, keep records of transactions, and pay taxes can sell in Antigua. Depending on the size of the retail space, the two-hundred-dollar-or-more monthly rents are prohibitive to all but a few vendors.

The other types of strategies used by vendors did not relate to organized collective political actions, but were based on my observations of their activities, conversations, and meetings. These included economically oriented activities, such as expanding their customer base by selling to shopowners and extending invitations to Spanish schools to visit the places where they sell; questioning tourists about the types of items, colors, and fabrics they preferred; and developing friendships with *proveedores* and Ladinos. Sympathetic Ladinos can help them when sales are low and they cannot pay for new merchandise, their sleeping room, or storage. Like patron–client relations in other parts of Latin America (Wolf and Hansen 1972), economic relations are intermixed with personal relations and obligations. Making friends with tourists is another strategy employed by vendors, but the end is different than with *proveedores* and Ladinos because the goal of the vendors is to make a sale. Rarely do they see a "friendship" with a tourist becoming an enduring social relationship once the sale has been made or the tourist leaves the country.

TACTICS IN THE MARKETPLACE

According to de Certeau, the tactic, on the other hand, belongs to the politically and economically weak—those who do not control or command the place. Vendors resort to the use of tactics, which de Certeau equates with trickery (1984: 37), especially when their well-laid plans go awry because of their relatively weak positions of power. Vendors use tactics during times of insecurity and uncertainty, such as the contexts of some sales to tourists, encounters with police officers, and when presenting one's community affiliations to the municipality.

Most sales to tourists by Maya *típica* vendors are tactical. The goal is to sell, but how they do it is tactical, as they rely on trying to figure out ways to hook the tourist and outcompete each other. They attend to how long a potential buyer's eyes linger on an item, who is with the buyer, the age and the sex of the buyer, the way the buyer is dressed, and the buyer's level of Spanish. Saying the right words may result in the tourist stopping for a moment in the vendor's stall and could lead to a sale. Most vendors, all of whom recognized that tourists were a diverse group, believed that most tourists did not really know what it was they wanted to buy. The objective of the vendor, therefore, is to figure out what appeals to a particular tourist, then bring it to the attention of that person. In the clearly marked retail spaces of boutiques and marketplaces, assessing what item appeals to a tourist, or even convincing tourists that they should buy anything at all, is a difficult task, but it is even more challenging when the economic transaction takes place in the spaces that Maya vendors tend to occupy.

Maya *típica* vendors often occupy spaces that are ambiguous because of their multiple uses, as well as spaces that have well-defined, non-*típica* associated meanings. For instance, the Central Plaza is an ambiguous space because it is defined in multiple ways. In the tourism discourse of guidebooks, it is a place where one can relax, people-watch, and buy *típica;* a hub from which to geographically orient oneself in the city; an outdoor classroom for Spanish lessons; and the physical location of the city government. Other sites in Antigua are singularly defined, such as the ruins of Spanish colonial churches and other buildings. Tourists do not go to places such as churches (La Merced and San Francisco el Grande) to purchase souvenirs. To complicate matters further, some tourists enter recognized marketplaces and retail stores because they are interested in seeing "Indians" or "Mayas," not because they are interested in buying anything.

In each of these situations, vendors employ tactics to convince tourists that they also entered a particular site in order to make a purchase. Typical vendor sales lines, such as "*Cómpreme algo*" (Buy something from me), "*Hay telas y cosas bonitas*" (There are beautiful fabrics and things), and "*Solo tenemos cosas hechas a mano*" (We only have handmade things), do not work in these situations. Sales pitches are more subtle in cases where vendors try to become a natural part of the site and then appeal to tourists' aesthetics, ignorance, or sympathy. The item that will eventually be offered for sale remains in the background, but visible, while the vendor tells her personal hard-luck story, discusses the friendliness and beauty of Antigua and its residents, explains Maya life, or talks to the tourist about why he or she is visiting Guatemala. Only after establishing a friendly conversation do vendors appeal to tourists to buy, explaining how buying the item will help the vendor cover her child's education or medicine costs, how the purchase will help the tourist remember their conversation and the good time they had in Guatemala, how the tourist can take an authentic piece of Maya culture home with them, or how the tourist's mother, father, or significant other, who was mentioned in the conversation, would appreciate a colorful handcrafted item from Guatemala because it would demonstrate that the person was on the mind of the tourist.

These selling tactics, which are used in ambiguously defined *típica* sales spaces, require time and appeal only to types of tourists with certain interests and personalities. Tourists on guided tours represent some of the least-appealing customers because they do not have time to talk with vendors for more than a few seconds. There is little chance for vendor and tourist to develop a positive rapport with each other. This is frustrating to tourists on these tours because some feel that vendors intrude in their space and take their limited time from them. Others on guided tours would enjoy some time to converse, to meet an "Indian" or Maya, but it is not possible because of the time constraints of the tour and the guide's responsibilities to the group in regard to maintaining the schedule and keeping participants safe. Spanish students and individuals traveling independently represent the most promising tourists on whom vendors can practice these selling tactics.

Although vendors utilize some collective strategies, such as protests and petition drives, most of their dealings with the police force and the municipality are tactical. Street vendors, ambulatory and stationary, generally try to avoid police officers. When they do encounter them, they try to contextualize their presence in ways that deny that they are selling anything. Vendors in the plaza do not sell; they are resting or conversing with friends. Peddlers are not selling; they are going to worship in one of the churches, taking an ailing family member to the Brother Pedro Hospital, or running errands in Antigua for the day.

Vendors also put themselves in places where police jurisdiction is unclear, such as alongside entrances to museums, churches, and businesses. Some vendors get permission and sometimes pay rent in order to sell in these places. Other vendors occupy similar places when rumors circulate among them that police officers are seizing street vendors' merchandise. When vendors see police officers coming, they may move the display of their merchandise next to the entrance to a museum, church, restaurant, or hotel that is frequented by tourists, thereby subverting the municipality's attempts to remove the streets of unwanted vendors. Because these places are patronized by foreign tourists, the police avoid altercations with vendors.

Conclusions

The tourism/*típica* market system differs from that of the periodic market system in that goods are produced primarily for foreign consumption, not for other Maya households. Most of the items for sale have marginal, if any, use values for the producers, distributors, and vendors, whose common goal is to sell their products to tourists or exporters. This market system connects local Maya communities, where items are produced, to regional marketplaces, where they are distributed, to foreign consumers, who take them to wear and display in their countries of origin.

The socioeconomic relationships between the vendor and the consumer are fleeting and unequal in this system. Both Smith (1975) and Goldín (1985) demonstrate how social inequalities, economic stratification, and ethnicity are upheld and embedded in the socioeconomic relations of periodic market systems and marketplaces in Guatemala. The social distance between Maya vendors and foreign consumers is greater in the tourism/*típica* market than in the periodic market because of economic, cultural, and linguistic differences. Maya *típica* vendors participate regularly, but their foreign customers rarely return. For Maya participants, their work in the market is invested with meaning as the place where they provide for some of their basic subsistence needs. Tourists go to indigenous marketplaces mainly to experience Others and buy souvenirs.

Although Mayas and Ladinos, as Goldín (1985, 1987) points out, conceive of markets and marketplaces in different, sometimes conflicting ways, tourists do not necessarily conceive of indigenous marketplaces in ways similar to either Mayas or Ladinos. Tourists regard marketplaces in terms of authenticity. Marketplaces that were self-consciously constructed for tourists, such as the new Handicrafts Marketplace, are often regarded with suspicion by tourists. Almost uniformly, they did not think that these marketplaces were authentic, and they usually doubted that they would get the best prices in them, indicating that tourists, in general, assess these places accurately.

Maya *típica* vendors used a combination of strategies and tactics in order to attract tourists and deal with government officials and police officers. *Típica* vendors in Antigua had to maneuver between local government and tourists' concepts of them and the places where they should sell.

Chapter 4   Mercado de Artesanía Compañía de Jesús and the Politics of Vending

Introduction

As in marketplaces in other areas of the world, the social, economic, and political relationships of the vendors in the Compañía de Jesús Artisan Marketplace are framed by the daily life and historical contexts in which they are enmeshed. Understandably, these contexts vary from marketplace to marketplace. Previous studies of utilitarian marketplaces have illustrated the socioeconomic practices particular to vendors and consumers from the same localities and regions (Tax 1953), the ethnic relations between Mayas and Ladinos (Goldín 1985; Swetnam 1975; Tax 1937, 1941), the socioeconomic relations between urban and rural residents (Swetnam 1978), and the significant ways that women contribute productively to and become politicized within the marketplace (Babb 1987, 1998; Clark 1994). This research contrasts with other studies done in marketplaces oriented toward tourists, such as Castañeda's (1996, 1997) and this work. In Guatemala, the differences between utilitarian and tourism marketplaces give female vendors advantages over male vendors, in part, because Maya women are represented in touristic discourse as associated with the latter marketplaces. Transnational actors, such as international tourists and importer-exporters, seek out Maya women vendors over men. The roles that men and women vendors perform will be discussed in this and subsequent chapters.

The differences between these types of marketplaces have important theoretical implications related to ethnic relations and cultural identity because tourism marketplaces are set within a transnational context that is easily recognized by the vendors. They know that they are selling to foreigners and that most of the products sold are leaving the country.

Even if a utilitarian marketplace is connected to transnational economic processes (and most today are), the connection is indirect. Local people buy and sell in a local context. They know each other because their interactions are repeated weekly. They share cultural complexes, or they are familiar with each others' cultural complexes. This is not to imply that *típica* and tourism-related items are not sold in the utilitarian marketplace or that tourists do not enter it to purchase food, soap, and other products. Rather, the social and economic interactions in each respective type of marketplace affect how local persons (Mayas) think about ethnic difference and use their cultural identity.

Daily Life in the Marketplace

The day-to-day existence of vendors in the Compañía de Jesús Artisan Marketplace is shaped by their preoccupations: tourists' distrust and ignorance of prices, lack of protection from thieves and support from authorities, and insecurity about the future of the marketplace. Though not the preoccupations of utilitarian marketplace vendors, they are daily concerns for Compañía de Jesús vendors, who need to be able to recognize cultural differences between themselves and tourists and to navigate hostile political terrain.

Aside from these worries, a vendor's typical day consists of a series of mundane activities. Between 8:00 AM and 10:00 AM, vendors enter the marketplace and unpack *bultos* filled with merchandise. Each vendor arranges it in a fashion that she or he feels will attract buyers. Sometimes items are organized according to style. Sometimes they are grouped by color. Sometimes items that have sold well in the past are featured. Vendors also try to showcase unique items. By 11:00 AM, they finish putting merchandise on display. From noon to 1:30 PM, they eat lunch in their locales. Around 5:00 PM, they begin repacking *bultos,* which are returned to storage by *cargadores* between 6:30 PM and 8:00 PM.

From the time they arrive in the marketplace until the moment their merchandise is stored, vendors concentrate on making sales. As vendors unpack and repack their *bultos,* they sometimes call out the items that they are selling in the hope that passing tourists will stop to see the merchandise. Vendors sell until the time the *bultos* are actually put into storage, even if that means missing the bus to their hometown. On one occasion, a vendor had almost finished packing when three Italian tourists, who had visited his locale earlier in the day, returned and inquired about some handwoven bags. He unpacked the *bulto* and found the bags they wanted. When they left, they had spent a little over Q500 (roughly $83) on several of the bags. On another occasion, a vendor woman and her daughter sold over Q2,000 ($333) of *cortes* (wraparound skirts) to a customer. In both cases, the vendors missed the evening bus back to their towns and had to spend the night in Antigua.

The marketplace is busiest between 11:00 AM and 5:00 PM. Vendors complete their displays by 11:00 AM, then wait for tourists. One strategy they employ is to learn as much as possible about tourists. Provided there is a common language, they ask tourists where they are from; how long they are staying in Antigua; if they are married; and whether they have

Figure 4.1. Compañía de Jesús vendor bargains with tourists. Photograph by author.

siblings, children, and other kin. They conduct market research by asking tourists what colors they prefer, what types of thread they like, if sizes and styles are appropriate, and what they like in general. Jokingly, vendors say that they have these conversations merely to "kill time" and to keep from being bored, but the reasons are apparent. Vendors make new items or relay the information they collect to *proveedores,* who return weeks later with the modified products.

Depending on the hour of the day, the day of the week, and the time of the year, vendors may wait hours between clients. They complained that boredom was the most difficult aspect of their work. They do a number of things to alleviate it. Women and girls weave *tapetes* (throw cloths), table runners, and wall hangings. They do not weave clothing (*po't, uq, pa's*) because the posts to which they affix their backstrap looms are not sturdy enough to support the tight weave required for clothing. Young girls make bracelets, which they sell to tourists and local teenagers in the Central Plaza. Some men sew by hand—repairing damaged goods, inventing new styles of bags, vests, and hats. Four men from Nebaj and one from Todos Santos Cuchumatanes knit hats and bags. Some male and female vendors are reluctant to do this work in front of their peers because they feel that it allows others to see their ideas. Others think there is no good reason to create and add more merchandise to their inventories if they are not selling what they already have.

Quite a few vendors used their free time to read the newspaper and study. Most of the vendors younger than thirty were taking classes. Some were trying to get through grade school, but others were working toward undergraduate degrees in accounting, business, tourism, law, and other subjects. Vendors also assisted their children with homework. Productive and school-related activities were the ideal ways vendors said they occupied their time. However, they often used the downtime between customers to play cards, listen to soccer games on the radio, kick around Hacky Sacks, and tease each other. One of the big jokes among them was that I was there to keep them from getting bored.

Vendors preferred to have the marketplace brimming with foreign tourists. Although tourists are a diverse group in terms of personal histories, languages spoken, countries of origin, and interests, vendors said that tourists enter the marketplace either to look at Indians or to purchase something. Vendors call out the names of products and indicate specific items, pointing out the quality, utility, color, and versatility of items that tourists touch and hold. They also advise tourists to compare prices.

Mayas in the Marketplace

Tourists are especially encouraged to go to boutiques around the city to make price comparisons. "When you see that my prices are the best in Antigua, you will return," vendors tell them. On separate occasions, a vendor from Chichicastenango and one from San Antonio Aguas explained that they used this strategy because, in general, tourists seem to be ignorant of prices. The only way they can learn how good the marketplace prices are is to compare them with prices in boutiques. Vendors purchase *típica* from the same *proveedores* as the boutiques do and for the same prices, but they do not mark up their prices as much. *Proveedores* from San Juan de Comalapa, Chichicastenango, and Totonicapán have kin who sell in the Compañía de Jesús Artisan Marketplace, some of whom have helped in *típica* production. One of them said, "It is not difficult to learn that you can buy cheaper here. My rent is low. Also, I don't pay sales taxes, light, or water." Some tourists take vendors up on the suggestion to comparison shop, but others see it as a sign of good faith and make a purchase after a little bargaining.

Identity Conflicts in the Marketplace

The majority of tourists that I spoke to initially visited the marketplace to "see Indians" and "Indian culture." Some returned to socialize, practice Spanish, watch women weave, and learn about Maya life. Tourists who make return trips are relatively rare. For *típica* vendors, fostering these occasional relationships is worthwhile because these tourists may buy merchandise worth hundreds of quetzales.

Tourists who come to the marketplace once, only to see Indians, are the toughest customers. They are the most difficult to "hook" because they are not interested in products. Many have preconceived notions as to who is an "Indian" and who is not. Usually, to them an Indian is a woman dressed in *traje* who speaks a Maya language. These contact situations in relation to gender, as well as the general gender orientation and organization of the marketplace, are discussed in the next chapter. The other effect of these encounters is how vendors respond to these tourists in terms of cultural identity. Vendors want tourists to consider them Indians, Mayas, or Kaqchikeles. In other words, they want to be Others in relation to tourists and to Ladinos. It is this difference that they hope will induce tourists to buy.

Competition among vendors was the most obvious when tourists looked for "Indians." Ordinarily, vendors try to give tourists the impression that they are not in competition with each other. When vendors are treated as vendors, not Indians, they act as if the products speak for themselves. Unsuccessful vendors are jealous of successful vendors. They say derogatory things among themselves about those who consistently have high sales, and they try to copy successful designs. They do, however, accept the fact that tourists must choose from among hundreds of products being sold by hundreds of vendors in Antigua and thousands throughout Guatemala. Showing jealousy, trying to steal customers, and otherwise attempting to demean competing vendors in front of tourists is considered to be not only in poor taste but wrong. Vendors do tell tourists who have just made a purchase and left the seller, "Don't forget your other friends. Buy something small from me too" or "Please return with your friends to buy something from us."

When tourists come looking for Indians, vendors' attitudes about competition change. The context is no longer just economic; now it is also about authenticity and identity. Maya *típica* vendors use their indigenous identity to distinguish themselves from Ladinos for tourists and to convince the municipality that they attract tourists to Antigua. Even the few Ladino vendors in the Compañía de Jesús Artisan Marketplace emphasize to city officials that the marketplace is "*indígena.*" By selecting some vendors over others as being Indian, tourists' can draw out some of the ways that vendors think about their identities.

One example of how vendors react to this identification by tourists occurred when a Puerto Rican–American couple walked through the marketplace. Only in Antigua for a couple of days, they read their guidebook closely and "hoped to find some real Kaqchikel Indians" from nearby towns. They slowly looked at vendors and then at the merchandise. The man carried a video camera at his side, and a camera dangled from his wife's neck. With passing glances, they walked by vendors from San Antonio Aguas Calientes and Santa Catarina Barahona who were dressed in blouses because of the warm weather. They did not even look at male vendors dressed in "American-style" clothing. When they reached Elena, who was nursing her baby, they stopped. She was dressed in San Antonio–style *traje*. A small backstrap loom hung from one of the locale's support posts. "*Aquí hay una indígena*" (Here's an Indian), said the man to his wife. "*Usted es una indígena Kaqchikel, ¿no?*" (You are a Kaqchikel Indian, aren't you?), he asked Elena.

"*Sí, puro indígena Kaqchikel*" (Yes, pure Kaqchikel Indian), Elena answered.

At that moment, Karín, a Kaqchikel vendor from San Antonio Aguas Calientes, shoved me. "Did you hear what she said?" she asked me in Kaqchikel. While I nodded in affirmation, she directed her next comments to a couple of vendors in locales next to hers, "She is not Kaqchikel, she doesn't speak Kaqchikel well, nor is she from San Antonio. She lives in a Ladino town, and she is married to a Ladino."

While Karín explained that neither Elena nor her husband, Carlos, was an "*indígena maya*" and that Elena could not really weave, Elena had agreed to be videotaped. The tourist asked her to say some words in "her language," hold up some of the *típica* displayed, explain differences between textiles, demonstrate how to weave, and nurse her baby. When they finished videotaping, they spent only a few quetzales.

I asked Karín if she wanted to be videotaped. No, she didn't want a bunch of tourists taping her, but she didn't want non-Kaqchikeles claiming to be what she is. "Now they will return to the United States, and they didn't learn about the real *indígena* Kaqchikel," she explained.

Later, I spoke with Elena, who was born in San Antonio, and Carlos, who was born in Tecpán, both Kaqchikel towns. After all the time they had spent with the tourists, and even agreeing to be videotaped and photographed, they had made less than one dollar from the sale of the small change purse that the tourists bought. Although they had heard the other vendors comment about them not being *indígenas* Kaqchikeles, they were more bothered by the fact that the tourists had spent so little money. If they had spent a "couple of hundred quetzales," said Elena, that "would have humbled the other vendors."

Such encounters are commonplace. Tourists who ask vendors questions about what makes someone Indian, Maya, or Kaqchikel tend to draw the attention of nearby vendors, who then comment among themselves about the things that they feel disqualify the vendors questioned from claiming that category. Sometimes vendors say to tourists, "Now you have to get to know a real *indígena*." Or they ask, "Don't you want to buy something from an *indígena*?" Although vendors generally avoid telling tourists that they are Mayas because they feel tourists will not believe them,[1] they are particularly frustrated when tourists do not identify them as *indígenas*. If tourists cannot tell them apart from Ladinos, it makes their position as vendors in Antigua more precarious.

In 1994, vendors avoided my questions about what they thought their identity was. As soon as I brought up the topic, they changed it to something else. However, in 1996, the Compañía de Jesús Artisan Association endorsed my project on Maya concepts of identity, and subsequently vendors would speak to me on the topic.

From November through December 1996, I administered a survey/questionnaire in which vendors could choose more than one category of identity, including Ladino, Maya, *indígena*, Guatemalan, ethnolinguistic group (Kaqchikel, K'iche', and others), and town. Of the 205 vendors surveyed, 13 persons chose Ladino, 50 chose Maya, 136 chose *indígena*, 106 chose Guatemalan, 116 chose an ethnolinguistic group, and only one chose a hometown. These figures are significant for a number of reasons. Vendors tended to give me information that they felt could be used when they argued with the municipality about their rights to sell in Antigua. Next to no one chose a town identity because rumors were circulating that all non-Antiguan vendors would be expelled. When I talked to Kaqchikel and K'iche' speakers later, few claimed to be Guatemalan, but they had marked that category on the survey because they figured it would look good to the municipality. Follow-up conversations revealed that most vendors did not consider themselves Mayas but rather descendants of Mayas. They explained how they were taught in grammar school that Mayas were from the past, that tourists did not tend to identify them as Mayas, and that the municipal officials and police officers did not regard them as Mayas.

Although most vendors know about the Maya movement's[2] promotion of Maya as an identity label, they did not see any political, economic, or social advantages for adopting the term for themselves. They consider themselves to be *indígenas*. In later conversations and eavesdropping, only the thirteen vendors who originally chose the category Ladino did not use *indígena* to describe themselves. All others used it self-referentially and applied it to their peers and family members. As other chapters illustrate, vendors claim identity labels, including Maya, that help them economically and socially.

Historical Background of the Compañía de Jesús

The Compañía de Jesús Artisan Marketplace began in 1986, when about ten vendors from San Antonio Aguas Calientes moved into the courtyard in front of the church ruin's decaying façade. At that time, most *típica* sales took place in the Central Plaza on weekends, Sundays especially. According to vendors located there today, the church courtyard was chosen because of the location's historical significance, because of its proximity to the center of Antigua, and as a means to band together against abuses from the local police force, since being off the street meant less harassment.

Since the building named Compañía de Jesús was constructed, it has had four distinct lives. First, during the colonial period from 1608 to 1773, it was a Jesuit monastery, a grade school for boys, and a church until an earthquake shook Antigua in 1773, leveling much of the city (Lutz 1994: 63, 169). Second, from 1773 until 1912, and again from 1976 to 1986, the Compañía de Jesús building was abandoned. Third, from 1912 to 1976, it was the site of the municipal marketplace. Fourth, it became a tourism site by the 1930s and eventually evolved into Antigua's largest *típica* marketplace in 1992.

The Compañía de Jesús Artisan Marketplace that Swetnam (1975, 1978, 1988) studied in 1969 and the early 1970s was different from municipal and tourism marketplaces today. The municipal marketplace has grown tenfold, and though it is busiest on Monday, Thursday, and Saturday (the principal market days in the past), business thrives every day of the week, drawing hundreds of vendors and buyers from throughout Guatemala.

In the years when the municipal marketplace was held in the Compañía de Jesús, *antiguenos* generally viewed (and some still view) the municipal marketplace negatively because they and tourists supposedly felt that it detracted from the colonial charm of the city. As early as 1967, the municipality planned to move it to the city's west side. The ruins had also been marked for restoration by the municipality and the Spanish Agency for International Cooperation (AECI, Agencia Española para la Cooperación Internacional), as part of a larger project to help Antigua protect and maintain its colonial look. In 1974, Carlos Flores (1974: 5-14) wrote that in order to reduce the commercial traffic, which contributes to the "visual contamination" of Antigua, the "marketplace . . . will have to be moved because it is on the site of the ruins of the monastery and church of La Compañía de Jesús."

According to one woman whose mother sold chickens there in the 1950s through the 1970s, the marketplace was "smelly and chaotic." An "influential *antigüeño*" described "with distaste the clustering of bars, shops, and rooming houses around the present market. The removal of this commercial activity from the center of the city, he asserted, 'would make Antigua a purely colonial city'" (Swetnam 1975: 45). In the newspaper *La Verdad* (February 19, 1978), an article states that to improve Antigua, the municipal market "will be the object of our most immediate concern." La Pólvora was deemed the place best suited for the market, bus, and cargo terminal—their location today.

The plan to develop and improve Antigua's touristic image put the municipal marketplace on the margins of the city. Today, no tour companies visit it, and Spanish schools strongly advise their students to avoid it. Even so, some tourists, especially independent travelers and Spanish students, do venture into the marketplace, but compared to the thousands of tourists who visit Antigua weekly, they are few.

Despite the "distaste with which the government of Antigua views its market" (Swetnam 1975: 45), it was a regular stop for tours during Swetnam's research, even though some tourists found it unappealing. Earlier guidebooks mentioned it as a tourist-worthy site. In her 1933 travel book, Dorothy Popenoe (1973: 40) wrote that the "place is worth a visit, for Indians from nearby villages congregate here to sell the produce of their farms and gardens, and, equally important, to exchange gossip of the day." Two guidebooks from the 1940s (Muñoz 1940 and Zamora 1943) recommended that tourists visit the marketplace to find "Indians." Through the 1960s, other guidebooks[3] recommended it, and tours made it a regular stop. When the marketplace moved to La Pólvora, an area between the Alameda Santa Lucía and the cemetery, tour companies ceased visiting it.

Guidebooks used by tourists in the 1990s recommend visits to marketplaces, especially in the western highlands where the indigenous population is densest. The Knopf Guide (1995: 374–375) states, "Markets are an important part of Indian economic and social life. They provide an opportunity to meet friends and acquaintances. For many inhabitants it is the only time they come down from the mountains. . . . Unlike Mexican markets, the markets of the Guatemalan *altiplano* have retained their authenticity, remaining primarily Indian markets." Guidebooks also encourage tourists to visit utilitarian marketplaces because they are places to interact with "Indians."

When vendors opted for the modern reinforced cement block walls of the new marketplace and left Compañía de Jesús after the 1976 earthquake, it allowed the AECI to begin restorations. Today, the AECI occupies the first cloister on the northeast side of the block, the corner of Sexta Avenida Norte and Tercera Calle Poniente (Figure 4.2). The cloister is now used primarily as office space for the AECI and as a space to host art exhibitions. It was the merchant and vegetable sales area when the municipal market was located in Compañía de Jesús. The northwest corner of the monastery, a chapel, was restored and occupied by CIRMA, a research center, which used the space as a conference room and storage facility. Other parts are still being restored.

Growth of the Típica Market in Antigua

Following the 1976 earthquake, international development money poured into Guatemala to help rebuild the damaged areas of the country. Some of the complexities resulting from this money and the impact of development projects[4] have been addressed by Sheldon Annis (1987), mainly

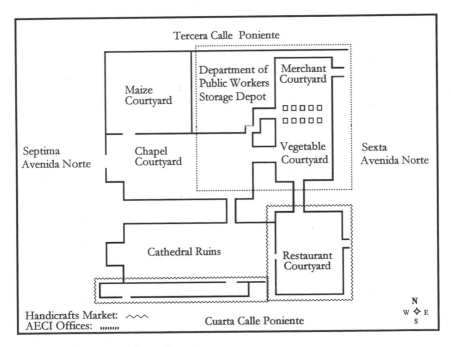

Figure 4.2. Map of the municipal marketplace in the early 1970s with current boundaries of the handicraft marketplace delineated. Floor plan of the Compañía de Jesús redrawn from John Swetnam (1975).

with respect to agriculture, and Virginia Garrard-Burnett (1998), primarily in reference to the Protestant church. Instead, I reflect on the effect that this development money has had on the *típica*/tourism market in Antigua.

Annis (1987: 160) reports that "'artisan recovery' funds from the International Development Bank were made available" in the form of loans to families in San Antonio Aguas Calientes, resulting in an increase in artisan production and *típica* vendors. Some development strategies used during this period included the formation of weaving cooperatives by the Peace Corps and entrepreneurial management training through the Agency for International Development.[5] Although the weaving cooperative in nearby San Antonio Aguas Calientes failed, cooperatives in Tecpán, Totonicapán, and San Juan de Comalapa did succeed and have provided *típica* to vendors in Antigua. For the most part, these cooperatives wove various items—decorative hangings, tablecloths, change purses, and bags—that incorporated design patterns associated with indigenous Guatemalan culture, such as *kumatzin* (zigzags), *chumila'* (stylized stars), quetzals (birds), and *jicha'n* (stylized combs).[6] As the market became flooded with textiles, vendors found themselves with more items than they could sell and more competition than they had anticipated.

In the late 1980s, when the most violent period had subsided, tourism began to recover and artisan production increased along with it.[7] However, tourism locales in San Antonio Aguas Calientes did not increase, "since a few entrepreneurial families . . . [held] a . . . monopolistic grip on the local tourist industry" (Annis 1987: 148). With most of the *típica* market cornered in their hometown, vendors from San Antonio Aguas Calientes went to Antigua, which was also attracting vendors from other regions.

By 1986 a few vendors from San Antonio Aguas Calientes had moved into Compañía de Jesús's abandoned courtyard and were displaying their merchandise on the ground. They explained that the decision to sell there related to several factors, not the least of which included reduced harassment from the police. The best places on the streets were already staked out by vendors who had been selling there since the 1970s. Some were tired of walking the streets with their merchandise. Over the next few years, vendors from other towns also settled in Compañía de Jesús.

One of the Ixil families from Nebaj selling in Compañía de Jesús explained that they left their hometown for Panajachel to escape military and guerrilla violence, figuring that they would be safer in a tourist town.

Mayas in the Marketplace

As tourism increased in the late 1980s, they began to sell *típica* in Panajachel. Later, because they wanted their children to go to good schools, they moved to Antigua. Vendor families from San Juan de Comalapa, Santo Tomás de Chichicastenango, and other towns also came with the dual purpose of selling *típica* to tourists and putting their children through Antigua's middle and high schools. They brought merchandise that they, their extended families, and producers from their hometowns had made, further contributing to the handicrafts entering the city.[8]

Regardless of the reasons given by vendors for going to Antigua and selling in Compañía de Jesús, tourist numbers were on the rise as violence in the countryside diminished, allowing Guatemalans greater freedom to travel and inspiring more vendors to go to Antigua, as well as Panajachel (Villatoro 1988) and Chichicastenango, to sell handicrafts.

Vendors frequently compared the late 1970s with the period from 1992 through 1998. As a group of vendors commented on a slow afternoon, the late 1990s are "worse than the armed conflict because there are more thieves and assailants." Their assessment of the two periods was similar: too many vendors, too few tourists, lack of cooperation from INGUAT and private travel companies, and too many political problems.

Indeed, May 28, 1978, was when over one hundred Q'eqchi' Mayas were massacred in Panzós, Alta Verapaz, heralding the Guatemalan military's violent siege on the countryside and the rapid decline in numbers of tourists, dropping from 466,041 in 1980 to a low of 191,934 in 1984. In a report by Mazariegos de León in *El Gráfico* that year, INGUAT officials believed that foreigners visiting Guatemala were probably businesspeople rather than tourists, whose numbers had diminished because of "the adverse conditions." At the end of the 1970s, fewer tourists arrived as the insecurity and violence grew, but development money increased, contributing to more vendors, artisans, and *típica*.

With the continuation of "adverse conditions" through the 1980s, some vendors and artisans got out of the tourism business—at least temporarily. A couple from Tecpán explained, "No one could make any money in those days. We made ours before then, bought some land, and started selling medicinal herbs here" (in the municipal market in Guatemala City, where they are today). Even though tourism shrank, other vendors who stayed in the business explained that they had no other employment options. They either lacked access to land or felt that it was unsafe to work it. As the 1970s closed, with the municipal marketplace in Compañía de Jesús destroyed by the 1976 earthquake and the violence in Maya areas of Guatemala increasing, *típica* vendors had two immediate options. One was to secure a place in the new municipal marketplace that was under construction, and the other was to sell on the streets and in the Central Plaza.

Típica vendors who moved into the new municipal marketplace explained that it was difficult for them to secure locales. Those who did get one chose locations on the perimeter of the marketplace, where they would be visible to tourists. When I visited several of these *tiendas* in July 1987, they were doing a modest but steady business. The two families I know the best, one from San Juan de Comalapa (discussed in the previous chapter) and the other from Chimaltenango, were pleased with their locales. They were free from police intimidation and had permanent stores. Over the next fourteen years, however, the marketplace grew. Now their *tiendas* are deep within its confines. Foreign tourists rarely venture into that area, as no tour company has led or directed tourists to it.

Today, a few vendors have *tiendas* visible to tourists on the outer edge of the marketplace along Calle Ayuntamiento, which leads to the bus terminal. They are aware that persons arriving in Antigua by bus, laden with luggage, are not likely to make purchases en route to a hotel or Spanish school. They also know that the Spanish schools warn their students that the marketplace is dangerous.

New Marketplaces: Tourism / Típica Marketplaces

Tourism/*típica* marketplaces are relatively recent phenomena that arose in response to the growth of international tourism following World War I (Fussell 1980). The largest increases followed World War II. From 1945 to 1990, international tourists worldwide increased from 24 million to 415 million (McLaren 1999: 29). Lynn Stephen (1993: 39–40) explains that in the 1940s tourists began visiting Oaxaca "in larger numbers than ever before. . . . To capture the interests of tourists, particular features of culture and material production were commoditized and packaged for sale by the federal government [of Mexico]. . . . Of primary import in this cultural package is the Mexican 'Indian.'"[9]

From tourists' perspectives, there is confusion about the prices of items in utilitarian marketplaces. Swetnam (1975) and Goldín (1985) discuss the cross-cultural encounters between Guatemalan vendors and

American tourists in these marketplaces. Prices are predictable for Guatemalan participants, but not for tourists. In addition to not knowing proper bargaining protocol, the "tourist is inevitably convinced that he is being cheated and acts the part" (Swetnam 1975: 234). According to Goldín (1985: 195), K'iche' vegetable vendors did not reduce their prices to Americans because of the "striking social (ethnic) distance between the vendor and buyer." Bargaining served as a way for vendors and consumers to forge a relationship and to identify each other socially. In the view of vendors, foreign tourists are not worth bargaining with because there is little chance of developing ongoing social or economic relationships.

Although only items for tourist consumption are found in the Compañía de Jesús Artisan Marketplace, tourists are skeptical about the prices they are quoted. Castañeda (1996: 221–224) explains why tourists distrust *típica* vendors at Chichén Itzá. In addition to ignorance about and fear of bargaining, tourists must surmount racial, language, and other cultural differences. They are advised by guides and guidebooks that they will be cheated or robbed. Tourists visiting Compañía de Jesús had similar preoccupations. Many were convinced that vendors overcharged them. However, some felt they got "good deals" relative to similar handmade items in their home country. In a survey of 243 tourists in Antigua (Little and Walton n.d.), 57 percent of them felt that they personally got a fair deal in their shopping, though they were not sure that everyone was getting a good deal. Thirty percent thought that vendors were charging too much. In general, foreign tourists commented that they did not really know if they received fair prices relative to Guatemalans.

Castañeda provides an example in which, unknown to the tourist, a vendor substituted one knife for another, which the vendor felt matched the amount of money the tourist was willing to spend. "The Tianguis was all smiles over this tactical coup," Castañeda writes (1996: 223–224). Such tactics horrify Compañía de Jesús vendors. They know that tourists are suspicious of prices. Consistently, vendors of similar items—T-shirts, table runners, and bags—reduce the opening price to the same base price after mild bargaining. Tricking tourists is discouraged, and they are always made aware of substitutions.

Frequently, vendors questioned me about how to gain tourists' trust and discussed how it was necessary to give fair prices. When there were differences in prices between two similar woven items, they explained why (if the language gap was not too great): differences in threads, intricacies of weaving, density of fabric, age of the textile. They also tried to explain how prices quoted in guidebooks tended to be out of date. Any activity that caused mistrust was discouraged.

Emergence of a Handicraft Marketplace

In 1986 and 1987, Compañía de Jesús was less a marketplace than a way station. All of the ten or so people selling at that time also sold in the Central Plaza. Those first few years in Compañía de Jesús were generally described by vendors as very difficult, "*Yalan k'ayew,*" because "few tourists came and there was no shelter from the rain." Guidebooks, INGUAT, and tourism companies did not identify it as a place to buy *típica,* and guides discouraged tourists from purchasing there. Regardless of this, vendors needed a place to sell handicrafts.

The first vendors recolonizing Compañía de Jesús hoped to make sales when tourists passed to look at the ruins. This, however, cannot be considered a dependable advantage—then or today. Although the Compañía de Jesús is mentioned in numerous guidebooks (Bell and Long 1993; Ramírez and Zúñiga 1996; Whatmore and Eltringham 1993) and listed on maps of Antigua, it is a church of minor touristic importance, which is not even listed in the section "Other Churches" of the popular Lonely Planet guidebook, *Guatemala, Belize, and Yucatan: La Ruta Maya* (Brosnahan 1994). The Consejo Nacional para la Protección de la Antigua Guatemala does not recommend it for tourism, and Guatemalan tour companies, such as Clark Tours and Kim' Arrim, do not lead tours there. Despite this lack of recognition or support from prominent tour companies, the marketplace grew steadily as tourists and Spanish students visited it by chance or were guided there by family members of the Compañía de Jesús vendors.

In 1992 the mayor ordered all vendors off the streets and out of the Central Plaza, officially ending the weekend *típica* market. Vendors were directed to rent rooms or move into one of the locations designated by the city, such as Compañía de Jesús or Tanque de la Unión. As they were forced off the streets and out of the plaza, some vendors chose to make arrangements with the Catholic church San Francisco el Grande rather than contend with the city.

Most vendors found themselves forced into Compañía de Jesús locales. At least one person works and runs each locale, although many locales are attended by additional people aside from the "owner." These

Mayas in the Marketplace

usually include spouses and children, but a few owners hire nonfamily members. Occupation of the site in 1992 rapidly filled to capacity, around two hundred locales. Since 1992 the marketplace has been recognized by the city but not promoted. Vendors pay monthly rent to the municipality, Q32 ($5.33) per locale, and receive trash removal and water from a single spigot.

In 1993 vendors organized themselves into the Compañía de Jesús Artisan Association (Asociación de Artesanos de la Compañía de Jesús) to regulate marketplace activities, make requests and present grievances to the municipality, and formulate strategies for self-promotion. The vendors' presence became more noticeable that year, as all vendors completed building structures to protect themselves and their merchandise from inclement weather. Membership in the marketplace stabilized, since there was no more room for additional vendors. Those present were committed to the artisan association by paying dues (modest amounts of Q5–Q15 per month), by contributing labor to keep common areas clean, and by policing the marketplace to keep it free of thieves.

In June 1994, the Compañía de Jesús Artisan Marketplace attracted a steady daily clientele, but business was especially good on weekends, when its crooked aisles filled with Spanish students and tourists from all over the world. Sales averages during the week were generally low, Q20–Q50 ($3.33–$8.33) per day, but on weekends some vendors made several hundred quetzales per day. Combined with these decent earnings, vendors talked about positive political changes occurring in the country, frequently mentioning 1992's Nobel Peace Prize winner, Rigoberta Menchú. They felt confident about their future and security as vendors.

Vendor Insecurity in the Marketplace

The positive attitudes of vendors between 1992 and 1994 came to an end in 1994 with a series of attacks on female tourists that year, mentioned in Chapter 1. Unlike the earlier period of violence in the 1980s, these attacks and general increases in crime were directed at tourists as well as Guatemalans. Mayas and tourists increasingly worried about safety, and tourists were particularly concerned about safety in marketplaces. Vendors mark 1994 as the beginning of a new period for the marketplace and relate it to increased crime (or their perceptions of it).

According to a 1998 United Nations report, violent crime in Guatemala rose from 11,711 offenses in 1992 to 19,094 offenses in 1996, which can partially be attributed to the declining economy of Central America and final guerrilla and military offensives before the December 1996 Peace Accords treaty. During this time, newspapers regularly reported crime statistics that indicated increases in kidnapping and robbery. Vendors commonly discussed crime among themselves as well as with tourists and Spanish students.

In 1996, vendors also felt insecure when construction of a new Handicrafts Marketplace began, and they were notified that the AECI and the municipality would continue renovations on the main church of Compañía de Jesús. By November of that year, with construction of the new marketplace under way, rumors about closing the Compañía de Jesús Artisan Marketplace intensified. Vendors feared the worst: that they would be expelled not only from Compañía de Jesús but from Antigua altogether. Few of them were confident that they would obtain places in the new marketplace, since it was rumored that those certain to get locales would be Ladinos and officers of the artisan association. Some vendors had heard that possibly up to forty spaces would be awarded to vendors from Compañía de Jesús, but few were confident that it would happen. Besides, there still would not be enough spaces to accommodate all vendors from Compañía de Jesús.

Vendors feared that the combination of the AECI renovations of Compañía de Jesús and the construction of a new government-approved Handicrafts Marketplace would result in the expulsion of *indígena* vendors throughout Antigua. "They want to throw us out of Antigua, but we won't go," declared vendors in November and December 1996. They were under the impression that the marketplace would be closed by Christmas of that year. However, when that date passed and work had stopped on the new Handicrafts Marketplace and the church in Compañía de Jesús, vendors' preoccupations temporarily abated.

A year later, in September 1997, Compañía de Jesús vendors' worries were renewed because the AECI and municipality planned to renovate additional parts of the monastery. Municipal officials told vendors that in order to stay in Compañía de Jesús they had to physically reorganize the marketplace. They were given five days to complete the task, September 8 through September 12. The first two days were spent tearing down their locales and marking the new measurements of the marketplace. In the current marketplace, the dimensions of vendors' stalls varied and the paths and spaces between them twisted and turned, but the reconstructed marketplace would have straight aisles and locale size would be standard, one meter by one meter. Wednesday and Thursday, vendors and their extended families worked to rebuild the marketplace according to the new specifications.

On Friday, they put the final touches on their locales, decorated the marketplace, and reopened with a celebration to mark the successful completion of their work. Mayor Víctor Hugo Pozas, Beatriz Juárez, the head of the Departamento de Catastro Municipal, the architect from the AECI, and other local government officials attended. Certificates of appreciation were presented by the vendors to officials. Food and drinks were served. Recorded music played on a loud public address system. Government officials and vendors gave speeches about how hard they had worked and what they could accomplish together.

Although vendors grumbled among themselves about having to occupy smaller locales, they felt that their successful efforts had demonstrated to the municipality their organization and strength. As the celebration ended, some government officials in attendance confessed that they were surprised that the vendors had completed the reconstruction within the allotted time.

Figure 4.3. Compañía de Jesús Artisan Marketplace reconstruction. Photograph by author.

Vendors in Compañía de Jesús continued to worry. Nearly every day I listened to speculations about when they would be expelled and the marketplace torn down. Construction on the new Handicrafts Marketplace and renovations in Compañía de Jesús resumed. The reconstruction of the marketplace may have demonstrated the cooperation and unity of vendors, but from that time on, they were nervous about their future in Antigua.[10] Vendors doubted that the municipality would provide stalls for "*vendedores indígenas*" to sell from legally once the new Handicrafts Marketplace was completed.

Artisan Association Meetings

If the marketplace was the place where vendors conducted economic transactions and contended with tourists, government officials, and anthropologists, association meetings were where vendors planned their collective political and economic strategies, self-critiqued their behavior, and disagreed with each other. Vendors met once a month on a Monday to discuss attracting customers to the marketplace, forming alliances with other organizations, cleaning details, disciplining vendors who were not following association rules, and gaining official recognition as an organization from the municipal government and INGUAT. The meetings were closed to all except association members.

The Compañía de Jesús Artisan Association is not recognized officially by the local government or the Antigua Chamber of Commerce. Nevertheless, like an official organization, the marketplace association drew up by-laws, elected officers, paid dues, kept minutes, enlisted the aid of a lawyer to register the association, and met with the Human Rights Officer of the United Nations on several occasions. The association joined CONMIGUAT, the Comité Nacional de Microempresarios de Guatemala (National Committee of Small Businesspersons of Guatemala), which included ten other artisan and vendor associations. At one time, a Compañía de Jesús vendor was CONMIGUAT's treasurer. Vendors hoped that official recognition would make it more difficult for them to be removed from Compañía de Jesús.

In 1996 vendors tried to be endorsed by INGUAT. When it became clear that endorsement meant giving up control of how the marketplace was run, they voted against it. They wanted INGUAT endorsement for pragmatic reasons: it advertises internationally, and it makes recommendations to tour companies. Large tour companies tend to go only to INGUAT-endorsed sites.

One of the preoccupations of vendors discussed during meetings was how to attract new customers. INGUAT endorsement was one avenue to get more customers. However, in addition to not giving up their autonomy, they also came to realize that even though the endorsement could potentially draw tour groups, guides would want to be tipped or given commissions on the items that were sold. Guides demanded tips or commissions from all retail outlets to which they took tourists, and these added 10 to 40 percent to the final cost of the item purchased. Commissions vary in relation to kinship or ethnic bonds that guides have with the outlet and the length of time they have taken tourists there. With only one relative working as a guide and no other Mayas working for tourism companies, the vendors refused to pay guides tips or commissions for bringing tourists into the marketplace.

Most artisan association meetings were dedicated to disciplining members and dealing with the Antigua municipality. Sometimes hours were spent as the president reprimanded vendors for playing card games, kicking Hacky Sacks, making sexual jokes, not keeping their stands clean, not participating in collective cleaning parties, and listening to loud radios. Most of the time the members of the association ignored him: They came late; they left in the middle of speeches to get something to drink; they conversed with each other about their days, tourists, and families. They explained that the president attempted to discipline them because he did not have anything important to say.

During one of his speeches, the president urged vendors to treat tourists with respect, not to give a bad impression of the marketplace, and always to act professionally. As the speech drew on, one of the vendors, an outspoken woman from San Antonio Aguas Calientes, stood up and asked him to finish, drawing laughter from the other vendors. I was perplexed by their behavior. Kaqchikel and K'iche' Maya vendors explained that the president does not really run the artisan association, and few of them had respect for him as an individual. They said that he did not understand them, not only linguistically but also culturally (*man junam ta qak'aslem* [our lives are not the same]). However, since he was Ladino, like the mayor, his cabinet, and the police officers, they felt that it was best to have a Ladino represent them. By using a Ladino as their representative, they could be more anonymous to the municipal government while having their ideas filtered through a Ladino whom they felt had more in common with other Ladinos than they did. They did not want dealings with the mayor and other officials to be about *indígenas* versus Ladinos. All presidents of the association have been Ladinos.

The agenda that concerned vendors the most was their relationship to the mayor's office. From November 1996 through June 1998, they debated each month, not only about how to gain official recognition, but how to get the city to provide lights, reliable security, and regular trash removal, since they paid a little over $1,000 collectively in monthly rent. They fretted over the future of the Compañía de Jesús Artisan Marketplace and discussed ways to secure places there or in other locations. They discussed protesting and picketing city hall, as well as refusing to leave the marketplace. They contacted the United Nations Office of Human Rights on numerous occasions to discuss their rights as vendors and Guatemalan citizens, but nothing came of these meetings. As discussed in the previous chapter, they also participated in petition-signing drives that *ambulantes* and other vendors organized against the municipality and the police.

AN ARTISAN ASSOCIATION MEETING

On September 30, 1997, the Compañía de Jesús Artisan Association convened in El Señorial, a small hall that was used for meetings, dances, weddings, and other celebrations. It was a particularly volatile meeting. Vendors were annoyed that they had to rent the hall for Q500, then pay an additional Q10 per person above the regular dues. It was the first meeting after the reorganization of the marketplace for the municipality earlier that month. They were unhappy about the redesigned vending spaces. They had less space, since they had to build their little stores three meters from the walls of the church, shrinking the total vending area.

The president began the meeting by castigating the vendors for their behavior in the marketplace and their lack of participation in the association. He and the vice president explained that their positions in Compañía de Jesús were far from secure. They urged vendors to stay united. "Within the association meetings, we are associates and independents who must work together and compete with each other," the vice president explained, "but outside the meetings we are friends and family."

Then, with the other directors of the association, they proceeded to list a number of rules that vendors were to follow, with the expectation of fines, suspensions, and expulsion from the marketplace if they did not comply. First, they recommended changes that they felt would make the marketplace more appealing to tourists and put them in favor with the AECI and the municipality. Vendors were not to display too much merchandise, not to sell in corridors, and to keep aisles clear for visitors.

As is customary in meetings, vendors break into subgroups corresponding to the municipality that they consider home. As groups formed to vote on rules and recommendations, discuss appropriate punishments for vendors who broke rules, and decide how to pay for the hall's rent, the meeting divided into Ladinos and Mayas, owners and workers, and across municipalities and families. Kaqchikel Mayas complained, "The Ladinos always do wrong" (literally "evil"—*Jantape nikib'an itzel ri mo'soi*). K'iche' Mayas threatened to leave the marketplace and sell in the streets. In the end, tired of arguing and ready to go home, they approved the rules and charged a portion of the hall's rent to the vendors who had not attended.

Although the idea behind the division of vendors according to municipality is to encourage all vendors to participate in the meetings, it encourages the division of vendors according to home community, which is often linked to ethnicity. Maya vendors feel that such divisions can weaken their position in Antigua and privilege the few Ladino vendors in the marketplace because of the general ethnic tensions between Mayas and Ladinos in Antigua, which is politically and juridically managed by Ladinos.

Identity Positioning in Meetings

In contrast to the marketplace, where they attempted to give the impression that they were all "friends and family" who cooperate, vendors frequently split during the meetings. Although within the artisan association committees were formed according to community affiliation for official business, most divisions related to the particular ways that vendors wanted to position themselves politically in relation to each other and the municipality. Identity positioning was most evident when vendors broke into community-based committees. Vendors used and chose certain identities and affiliations over others in meetings.

To understand the fluidity of identity concepts, it is important to discuss how Maya vendors organized themselves socially and physically during these meetings. Unlike the few Ladino vendors present, Mayas rarely stayed in one group or, for that matter, stayed in the same seat for the duration of a meeting. Typically, they came to meetings with other family members. Conversation is usually in Spanish when different Maya ethnolinguistic groups and Ladinos socialize with each other.

When the meetings were about to begin, the first division that Mayas made was according to gender. Males and females rarely sat together. This division has little to do with any form of political identity positioning, but more with the ways that Mayas traditionally and typically divide themselves in social situations. Division according to gender is common in the church, at fiestas, within *cofradía* (religious brotherhood) houses, during dinners, and at dances (until a couple dances). There were no other recognizable divisions. They did not sit according to language, community, or occupation (worker, owner, or craft).

Once the meeting started, Maya vendors first moved to sit near others of their linguistic group. Depending on the agenda, vendors would ignore or comment on it in their respective language: Ixil, K'iche', or Kaqchikel. Linguistic group, then, was the first way that vendors distinguished themselves during meetings. Incidentally, there was nothing private about their choice of language, but vendors felt that it was more appropriate to complain about or critique the proceedings in a language other than Spanish, which was the common language. A few of the Ladino vendors could understand some Kaqchikel words (but none could converse), and K'iche' and Kaqchikel vendors could generally understand each other.

Language choice was one way that vendors established difference. It was how Maya vendors reinforced that the meetings were *indígena,* not Ladino. An Ixil Maya vendor said once, "We're like Guatemala, a mixture of languages, cultures, and pueblos." To which a K'iche' speaker added, "Like Guatemala is not only Ladino, we're not Ladinos. That's why we speak *lengua*." A final example came following a meeting, when I asked a Kaqchikel speaker why he did not speak up during the meeting about an issue that was bothering him. "As they speak Spanish, I don't speak. In the group, we don't work, we just talk. Afterward, our people talk about what we will do." Such comments also suggest that some Maya vendors reject Spanish and that the meetings are not forums where they feel free to speak their minds or decide plans of action.

During the course of a meeting, the officers asked vendors to divide into committees organized by town or community to discuss particular items on the agenda before voting to accept or reject them. The groups included Momostenango, Chichicastenango, San Antonio Aguas Calientes, and Antigua. Sometimes, a fifth, generic committee would be used to include all other communities. According to association officers and members, the idea behind the division by community was that vendors would feel more comfortable discussing the meeting's business in their own language with others from their own community. The goal was to remove ethnic and linguistic differences so that they could speak freely and discuss the matters at hand. The problem for vendors was not ethnic, community, or language differences. Rather, they were preoccupied that what was said, or whatever plan or action they decided on, could be held against them if the local police, military, or municipality learned of it.

Rarely did vendors consistently go to the same committee based on hometown. During meetings, vendors from Momostenango joined vendors in the generic committee, the Antigua committee, and the San Antonio committee. Vendors from San Antonio often joined the Antigua committee, as did those from Chichicastenango and other areas of Guatemala. From meeting to meeting, vendors from Nebaj split up and went to any one of the committees. Vendors frequently joked about switching towns/committees. One vendor reasoned, "What difference does it make what town I go with?"

It did, however, make a difference. Ladino and Maya vendors felt that they were in a conundrum because of their different perspectives of the municipality's position on vendors. When rumors circulated about the city planning to allow only vendors originally from the department of Sacatepéquez, Maya vendors from other departments participated in the Antigua and San Antonio committees. When rumors spread that only vendors from Antigua would be allowed to sell in the city, vendors were from Antigua. When they felt that tourism companies, INGUAT, and the municipality were more interested in craft specialization and diversity, vendors demanded even finer divisions according to language. On the rare occasions when they felt secure, vendors said such things as, "Because we are individuals, it doesn't make sense that we divide by language or town," or "First, we are artisans."

Maya vendors from towns in the departments of Sololá, Quiché, and Chimaltenango, like other Mayas in Guatemala, came from places that were hit by the Guatemalan military's counterinsurgency offensive (see

Carmack 1988 and Green 1999). Most of them had family members who had been killed, tortured, or "disappeared" during La Violencia. Some of them, especially families from Nebaj and Chichicastenango, were motivated to sell in Antigua because of the violence. Giving out information, voicing one's opinion, and making oneself known were dangerous, potentially life-threatening activities.

To the few Ladino vendors in the marketplace, the shifting among community committees by Mayas was a major source of frustration and annoyance that operated on different levels. First, some felt that the Maya vendors should be forced to participate in the community where they were born. To Ladinos, it was there that language, community, and customs converged, so it was there that Mayas should orient their collective identities. Second, Ladinos were afraid that local government officials would become suspicious if they discovered Compañía de Jesús vendors' community affiliations were constantly changing. They felt that the municipality would see it as some sort of way to subvert real, potential, or imagined city policies regarding vendors. Third, the Ladinos vendors were not able to switch among community-oriented identities, linguistic-oriented identities, or ethnic identities because they were the minority group in the marketplace, were monolingual (though a few could understand some Kaqchikel), and in general made the lowest sales of all vendors.

Maya vendors related to Ladinos as fellow vendors but not as fellow artisans. Because most Ladino vendors had a better rapport with local law enforcement officers and with the officials in the mayor's office, Maya vendors did not trust them. During the course of my research, four Maya vendors were arrested on various fabricated charges (such as stealing merchandise, drunkenness, selling drugs, and disorderly conduct), which were later dropped after they spent some days in jail. In one case, the Maya vendor was with two Ladino vendors. The police singled him out and took him to jail for being drunk in public. Furthermore, the mayor tended to refuse to meet with Maya vendors. In public ceremonies involving the vendors, he rarely acknowledged the Mayas present. During the reopening of the Compañía de Jesús Artisan Marketplace in September 1997, the mayor pointedly walked through a group of Maya vendors waiting to talk to him without acknowledging them.

Given the lack of rapport with the local law enforcement and the mayor's office, as well as the violence levied historically on Mayas, it is not surprising that Maya vendors both refused to commit to one meeting committee and marked themselves differently from Ladino vendors. The only identity they ever committed to in meetings was that of artisan or vendor, but they never let the Ladino vendors forget that they were not like them.

Conclusions

The economic, social, and political contexts in which *típica* marketplaces such as the Compañía de Jesús Artisan Marketplace exist are different from those of utilitarian marketplaces that have been described throughout Latin America, Africa, and Asia. The economic role the marketplace plays at local and state levels, the types of participants in the marketplace, and the political contexts in which these marketplaces exist and participate help shape the social relations and expressions of collective identity present in new ways.

Economic transactions between vendors and consumers take atomized or embedded forms (Plattner 1989a: 210–214). In the former, there is no relationship beyond the transaction. In the latter, the relationship continues and may include noneconomic social relations. In utilitarian marketplaces, both types of transactions take place. Because of regular economic transactions among producers, middlepersons, vendors, and consumers in utilitarian marketplaces, participants form enduring economic and social relationships, as Tax (1937) pointed out. The foundation of these social relations is what is provided and available to the participants in the marketplace on a regular and reliable basis. Although surpluses of commodities may go from local to regional to national and even international markets, the local marketplace must satisfy the basic needs of the local population. In utilitarian marketplaces, producers, middlepersons, and vendors also double as consumers, which further integrates participants into the socioeconomic fabric of the marketplace.

In contrast, tourism/*típica* marketplaces, such as those in Pisté/Chichén Itzá, Mexico (Castañeda 1996); Otavalo, Ecuador (Ariel de Vidas 1995); and Antigua Guatemala, are not places where producers, middlepersons, vendors, and consumers satisfy basic utilitarian and subsistence needs. Consumers are neither part of the local population nor often part of the broader regional or national population. *Típica* vendors do not buy items in the tourism/*típica* marketplace for home use. Economic transactions tend to be atomized in *típica* marketplaces and can lead to different forms of social relations among marketplace participants and different expressions of collective identity.

Some transactions between *típica* vendors and tourists give the impression that they are personal. However, vendors use this selling strategy to develop situational friendships with tourists in hope of increasing sales. Tourists also promote this relationship to increase their contact with indigenous people. Inviting a tourist for lunch does not have the same connotations for a vendor as inviting a buyer to lunch who has purchased from her for years (and will for years to come). The personal nature of transactions between tourists and vendors lasts only while the tourist is visiting and should be considered part of the vendor's selling technique because as soon as the sale is made the relationship ends.

In the Compañía de Jesús Artisan Marketplace, vendors played on their cultural difference to attract tourists. The social and economic relationships that endure in *típica* marketplaces are those among vendors, middlepersons, and fabricators.

Tourism/*típica* marketplaces, as Ariel de Vidas (1995: 72) points out, can preserve ethnic distinctiveness. However, those distinctions can be slippery when set into historical and political contexts. The fluid uses of identity by vendors related to the contexts in which they were embedded. The well-documented history of violence against Mayas in Guatemala,[11] and the ways that *típica* vendors in Antigua have related to the local police and government, set the stage for how vendors manipulate common identity categories, such as community, language, ethnicity, and occupation.

Vendors evoke Indian, Maya, Kaqchikel, and other identities that mark them as different from tourists and distinguish themselves from Ladinos in economic transactions with tourists. At the same time, when dealing with government officials, police officers, and Ladinos, vendors avoid these classifications.

The artisan association meetings demonstrate how Maya vendors attempt to mask their identities and decision-making roles behind Ladino presidents to try to remain anonymous. By avoiding essentialized identities with respect to Ladino vendors and Antigua government officials, where place, language, and other customs converge, Maya vendors are able to choose among multiple identities for economic, social, and political gains.

Chapter 5   Gendered Marketplace and Household Reorganization

Scenario: Household Work Routines

For over a week my weaving lessons had been a source of ridicule, humor, and debate about the gendered division of labor in the Sotz household in the Kaqchikel town of San Juan de Comalapa. Chopping firewood with the young men in the family, as well as accompanying them to the milpa, did not assuage the chiding I received from the males in the household for doing women's work. After all, they reminded me, I was the man who learned how to make tortillas a few years earlier.

As I chatted with Antonio one Saturday morning while he washed clothes, it struck me that here was an older man (in his fifties) doing a traditionally female job. Jokingly, I asked him what he and his sons had been asking me since the weaving lessons started, "*La rat at achin*" (Are you a man)? He looked up and asked, "Why?" I ran down the various activities that he had done that morning: making breakfast, then washing dishes, and now washing clothes. "You know that my wife is in Antigua today," he said. Antonio and his wife, Antonieta, sell *típica* in the Compañía de Jesús Artisan Marketplace.

"But one of your [adult] daughters is here, and so is your daughter-in-law," I argued.

"Yes, but Ana has to help her aunt, and Rosa has a lot of work to do with her baby," he said and then added, "When there is work to be done, you do it."

Introduction

In the Compañía de Jesús Artisan Market-place, how vendors interact with each other in terms of gender, ethnicity, and class is tied to transnational and national socioeconomic contexts. The example above serves to show that the gender division of labor within Kaqchikel Maya vendors' households is changing as a result of their participation in tourism/*típica* marketplaces. Other examples will indicate that work and identity are related in terms of gender. Specifically, the socioeconomic interrelations of vendors and tourists in the Compañía de Jesús Artisan Marketplace have contributed to changes in Maya vendors' practice of gender roles in their households. Vendors organize the marketplace and household activities in ways that accommodate the association of women with the marketplace by touristic discourses and the practices of tourists. Of course, vendors are motivated to make changes in selling strategies and behavior to improve sales, but the emphasis here is on how these strategies reconfigure gender roles at home and generally lead to strategic identity changes. Finally, relating socioeconomic practices in the marketplace to the organization of households makes it possible to assess the interplay of established identities and types of political action, such as the petition drives, protests, and complaints lodged against the municipal government that were described in earlier chapters.

The incorporation of women and the products they make for domestic use into broader economic contexts can change household gender dynamics in unpredictable ways (Nash 1993c). In Amatenango, Mexico, women's cooperatives that took over the commercialization of pottery made by the women challenged male control over the earnings. This resulted in community-wide repression of successful, independent women. In contrast, Kaqchikel Maya women vendors have gained prestige and community-wide respect for economic success in the tourism marketplace, which has led to household reorganization. The reasons why Kaqchikel Maya vendor women have not experienced the problems of Maya women in Amatenango are complex, but they include, among other factors, longer participation in the tourism marketplace, changing political and economic roles for men and women during and after the violent 1980s, and the distinct ways the women reinvest in community traditional practices. These differences will be explored here and in the next three chapters.

Marketplaces as Feminine Social Spaces

My initial fieldwork as a tour guide in Guatemala in the summer of 1992 alerted me to the conception of the marketplace as a feminine social space. As the group toured marketplaces in Antigua, Panajachel, and Chichicastenango, the colorfully dressed Maya female vendors regularly drew their attention. Framed by their merchandise, they became the subjects of the tourists' photographs and commentaries. Men were rarely mentioned except for their supposed absence. Marketplace stalls with male vendors were often considered empty. One of the tourists enthusiastically described the picture he had just taken of a large display of masks used in traditional dances. He made certain that the "poor man" was not in the picture so as not to disrupt the scene's "exotic beauty." In subsequent years, I found that this attitude that Maya females are bearers of culture and Maya males are missing persisted among tourists.

Tourists' attitudes that marketplaces are feminine and Maya culture is demonstrated through female vendors are rooted in the types of texts tourists use, such as guidebooks, postcards, and tourism brochures, all of which highlight Maya women. Tourists rarely read ethnographies on Mayas or marketplaces in order to gain a more complex understanding of Guatemalan and Mayan life. Carol Hendrickson (1995), Diane Nelson (1994), and Carol Smith (1995) explain that Maya women are thought to maintain cultural traditions, in part, because of the roles they assume and are forced to assume with regard to rearing and educating offspring. At home, children, especially females, learn core Maya values, to speak Kaqchikel, to weave, and to prepare traditional meals. Anthropological explanations of why women have become bearers of culture and tradition have been given for a number of former colonies around the world that reflect women's resistance to men and their places within the broader economic and political spheres. Specific sites, such as the body (Babcock 1993; Shaw 1995), the home (Stoler 1991), and the community (Babcock 1993; Smith 1995) can be places where women organize politically and economically. Although women selling in the Compañía de Jesús Artisan Marketplace may be the primary decision makers and wage earners in their respective families, the place itself can be the site of resistance to dominant Ladino society through the adherence to traditions like weaving, speaking Maya languages, and wearing culturally marked clothing (see Hendrickson 1995; Otzoy 1996). This is not to argue, following Sherry Ortner (1995), that all everyday life is resistance, but to look at those aspects of everyday life that indicate resistance and complicity.

In tourism literature that describes and shows pictures of marketplaces, women are usually the most visible actors. For example, a *Chicago Tribune* article (September 23, 1990), "Heart of Maya beats in Guatemala," describes marketplaces in Panajachel and Chichicastenango without specific references to vendors. The Chichicastenango marketplace is represented by a list of items available for purchase: "Rich in the superbly woven textiles for which the Maya are famous, the market also displays cunning painted boxes, jade necklaces and the lurid masks the Maya use in their dances." A Maya woman seated at her loom is pictured in the corner of the page. A child plays near her. The caption reads: "While her youngster plays, a Maya mother completes a weaving for selling at a local market."

Guidebooks likewise include pictures and descriptions of Maya women in marketplaces. For example, the first picture in the Lonely Planet guidebook *Guatemala, Belize, and Yucatán: La Ruta Maya* (Brosnahan 1994) is of a Maya market woman from Sololá. An early guidebook, *Guatemala, from Where the Rainbow Takes Its Colors* (Muñoz 1940), primarily describes marketplaces in genderless terms. However, in the accompanying photographs, women are linked to the marketplace. Of the nine pictures of marketplace scenes, only one portrays male vendors. In *Guatemala Alive,* Arnold Greenberg and Diana Wells (1990: 198) describe the center of the Chichicastenango marketplace as populated by "Indian women of all ages, from very young girls, to mothers nursing their babies, to the very old and toothless." This guidebook has two pictures of the marketplace, one of a group of female vendors and one of a rack of ornamental and dance masks, which are almost always sold by male vendors. The women occupy the foreground of the former photograph and are clearly its subject, but the other picture does not include the vendor.

The Gender of the Tourism/Típica Marketplace

Many more vendors than the 205 who officially manage stalls participate in the Compañía de Jesús Artisan Marketplace. Of vendors managing stalls in the marketplace, 68 of them are men, and the majority of them are from the K'iche' towns of Momostenango and Chichicastenango. Thirty-one stalls are jointly run by men and women. Additionally, men who do not vend or manage stalls perform a number of services, such as carrying *bultos* from storage facilities to the marketplace, selling soda and snacks, repairing or improving stalls, and running errands for wives, daughters, and mothers. Although none of the men in the marketplace wear *traje* or clothing identified as indigenous, all Maya women in the marketplace do.

Among Kaqchikel Maya vendors (98 stalls), women controlled and ran the majority of *típica* stands. Only in four cases did men completely control the business. Of these men, one is a widower whose wife previously managed the stall, and one is older and has never married. Men primarily assisted women and followed their instructions. Most Kaqchikel men in the Compañía de Jesús Artisan Marketplace played subordinate roles in respect to women, and only a few women were without male assistants. Some Kaqchikel couples, four to be specific, are almost equal partners, but even in these cases the women decided what was to be purchased from middlepersons.

Even in the artisan association, described in the previous chapter, Kaqchikel male vendors participated the least, not holding official positions in the association, and some skipped the once-a-month meeting, humorously claiming that it was their "day off." As one man explained, "This is my wife's business. She knows the *proveedores,* the weavers, and the prices. She makes the decisions." The few Ladino vendors and males coming from K'iche' and Ixil regions of the country participated in the political organization of the marketplace, but it was Kaqchikel women who held officers posts such as vice president, treasurer, and secretary. They were most vociferous in regard to marketplace-related decisions. However, on the one or two mornings per month that the vendors cleaned the marketplace, the Kaqchikel men picked up trash, swept the stone floor of the marketplace, and repaired stalls. Their wives sometimes arrived later when the cleanup was completed—just in time to arrange the stall and greet customers.

Compared to other communities in Latin America, the control Kaqchikel Maya women have in the affairs of the marketplace, if not unique, is not common. In the central Peruvian Andes, a woman's access to agricultural land or commercial firms, including the degree to which they make key decisions regarding these types of economic enterprises, depends on her relationship to men (husbands and fathers), the marital relationship she has with the father of her children, and the wealth of the family. Women in the commercial community of Chiuchín, however, have more opportunities than those in the agricultural communities

(Bourque and Warren 1981). According to Babb (1998), although more women than men work in the utilitarian marketplaces in the Andean city of Huaraz, Peru, men control the commodities that bring the biggest profits, deal with larger volumes of merchandise than women, and dominate the political organizations associated with the marketplaces. Peruvian female vendors are not passive, though, and actively participate in the political and economic decisions of the marketplace. In Oaxaca, Mexico (Cohen 1999; Cook and Binford 1990; Stephen 1991), and Nicaragua (Field 1999), artisan production and marketplace relations indicate similar patterns.

Kaqchikel women vendors in the Compañía de Jesús Artisan Marketplace differ from businesswomen in other areas of Latin America with regard to access to resources, participation in organizations, and decision making because of the socioeconomic relationships in which they are embedded, their specialized knowledge related to weaving, changing household economic roles in relation to the broader national and global economies, and the specific ways that touristic discourse genders handicraft marketplaces.

Social Relations and Work in the Marketplace

The actual social composition of the Compañía de Jesús Artisan Marketplace, in which men are prevalent but generally subordinate to women, contradicts the ways marketplaces are represented in the tourism literature. Tourists usually enter the marketplace looking for female Maya vendors dressed in *traje*. Because Maya women wearing *traje* are commonly featured in tourism materials, tourists learn in advance who to look for. They do not look for men. The socioeconomic relationship is thus not just between buyer and seller, or tourist and exotic Other, but between the tourist/buyer and Other/woman/seller.

Sidney Mintz (1964: 3–4) observed, first, that to understand the marketplace, one needs to understand the relations of the people there. Second, "exchange is typified by important institutionalized personal economic relationships, through which small favors, concessions and credit are employed to protect the traders' competitive positions" (Mintz 1964: 4). Finally, he noted that primarily women participate in internal petty commodity markets (Mintz 1971).[1] He did not ask what happens when

Mayas in the Marketplace

males are part of petty commodity markets where women are the most prevalent vendors.

Swetnam (1988) and Bossen (1984: 76–78) reveal that marketplaces are sites of both class and gender stratification. Although more women than men trade in the marketplace, few have access to products and volumes that would net them better financial returns. According to Ehlers (1991: 5), it is "male dominance over economic and political institutions that limits female access to economic resources." Swetnam (1988: 334) agrees that gender relations are unequal between men and women in the marketplace. However, women who are relatively successful, which is not uncommon, form more egalitarian relationships with their spouses. Ehlers (1991) explains that women without the support of men are forced into low-earning weaving and marketing relationships, which only serve to further subject them to male dominance. In contrast, Swetnam (1988) offers evidence of female vendors and traders who, instead of being dominated by men, negotiate better relationships with their spouses or male partners.

Like all marketplaces, the Compañía de Jesús Artisan Marketplace is socially constructed through its participants (male and female), the roles that they perform, and the fact that some vendors are recognized as significant and others insignificant by the tourists/buyers who enter it. Tourism distinguishes the Compañía de Jesús Artisan Marketplace from the petty commodity marketplaces that are discussed by Mintz, Swetnam, Ehlers, and Bossen. Within touristic contexts, women are the dominant actors, not only in the marketplace, but often in their homes. Because Maya women are the most significant subjects of tourism, men cannot easily enter the marketplace and supplant women. Kaqchikel Maya vendor women, in addition to making the decisions about what inventory to purchase and how to spend the money they earn, purchased additional inventory from female *proveedores* (middlepersons) and weavers. Everything from production to final sales to tourists is often in the hands of women. Usually, the Kaqchikel Maya men that enter the marketplace find themselves assisting and supporting their spouses, mothers, and sisters, but they do not bring in the most money from sales.

Marketplace vendors engage in multiple identities and have others ascribed to them. They can be Kaqchikel, Guatemalan, a vendor, a buyer, a sales clerk, a small business entrepreneur, a spouse, and a tourist attraction all in the same day. The subject position that is ascribed to or assumed by the participant relates to the type of economic, social, kinship, gender, or touristic relation she or he is engaged in at the time. Through these relationships, class, ethnic, and gender consciousness is manifested. These consciousnesses may arise simultaneously and be given equal importance. By focusing on sets of personal interactions—tourist and vendor, vendor and consumer, vendor and vendor, and male and female—it is possible to understand concepts of political action held by vendors.

Vendors had regular socioeconomic relations with only a limited range of international tourist types. For example, low-budget backpackers, the majority of whom are males eighteen to thirty years old, rarely entered the marketplace. Tour groups, which tended to be gender balanced, older, and more affluent, did not enter the marketplace either. Though vendors have observed both of these tourist types, they are not as concerned with the budget travelers as they are with the tour groups. That tour groups do not enter the marketplace causes them a great deal of dismay. Most of the tourists who entered the marketplace were students studying Spanish and independent tourists who stayed in hotels above the budget level and usually traveled with the opposite sex. Both male and female Spanish student tourists often entered the marketplace alone in order to practice Spanish. Independent tourists tended to enter the marketplace with the person they traveled with and occasionally hired guides. Overall, these types of tourists, male and female, interacted with vendors in similar ways, which may have to do with the types of information they read and the structural characteristics of tourism in Guatemala. In fact, in a survey of 242 tourists (53 percent female), there was no significant difference between the ways males and females interacted with and thought about vendors (Little and Walton n.d.).

Most often, Spanish students and independent tourists sought out items for sale that embodied notions of pre-Columbian Mayas and Indians. Manufacturers tried to create products that were inspired by that past and played up to tourists' conceptions of pre-Columbian Maya society. Representatives of Maya culture and their representations were dynamically interrelated with consumers and consumers' concepts of Mayas through the marketplace.

Tourists tended to gravitate toward female vendors dressed in *traje*. Activities such as weaving, attending to small children, or braiding hair caused tourists to pause and attempt to take photographs. This form of "staged authenticity," which is similar to that discussed by Dean MacCannell (1974), is a common strategy to attract customers. In general, the women did not mind having their picture taken, provided the tourist asked first and bought something. On occasions when tourists took pictures of women and children in nonvending situations without asking, Mayas reacted with hostility by attempting to spoil the scene. Some yelled, made faces, or turned their backs. Tourists felt vendors were there to provide photographic opportunities. Some went so far as to pose or reposition their subjects in order to remove people or things that were not considered Maya or aesthetically pleasing. When their subjects reacted negatively or tried to take themselves out of the picture, tourists sometimes physically attempted to put their subject back into position. The behavior of tourists and vendors in these situations suggests the ambiguity of ethnic tourism.

Male vendors were of little interest to tourists, but sometimes the manner in which they displayed their products made good pictures. Like the photograph of the masks, described earlier, displays of traditional Maya blouses (*po't*), rugs, and bolts of multicolored fabric used for skirts (*uq*) caught tourists' eyes, not the male vendors who sold them. Male vendors emphasized their products, often removing themselves from the stall. When customers appeared interested in something, vendors returned and tried to finalize the sale.

The group of tourists that I guided in 1992 was suspicious of male vendors, but they did purchase some items from them. Other tourists that I interviewed between 1994 and 1998 refused to buy from the male vendors because some sort of social interaction with Mayas was considered an important part of their travel experience. Since Maya men in the marketplace do not wear clothing that identified them as Mayas or distinguished them from non-Maya males (tourists or Guatemalans), they could not be used by tourists to indicate or prove that they had seen "Indians" or "Mayas."

One tourist described an "incredible Maya woman" he had been visiting for a couple of weeks. He practiced Spanish with her and vowed to purchase from her. He suggested that I go see her because she "knew a lot about Maya life and was easy to talk to." He explained, however, that I had to wait to meet her because he had gone to the market and could not find her at the stall. "There was no one there; some man told me she'd be back in several days," he said. It turned out that the man was the woman's husband, and she was at home preparing her daughter's *quinceañera* celebration (fifteenth birthday coming-out party).

Female vendors' responses to tourists were far more varied than the opinions of male vendors, ranging from disgust to tolerance and even to genuine interest because tourists in Antigua tended to visit the same women several times. Rarely did they consider tourists friends, even though the majority of interactions between them were congenial and friendly. Female vendors acted out the confused ways tourists wandered through the marketplace, asked why many stopped and stared at them without even saying hello, and told me stories about the tourists they found unusual or interesting. They asked why someone who had the time and money to travel would wear the same dirty clothes day in and day out. Some spent hours talking to tourists (and Spanish students) about their respective countries, families, occupations, and interests. Tourists who could speak Spanish questioned the women about weaving, food, beliefs, and other aspects of their lives.

Male vendors viewed tourists from a more detached perspective. Since tourists did not seek them out as representatives of Maya culture, male vendors were more anonymous. Although it probably occurs, I have yet to meet a tourist who has visited the same male vendor on several occasions or a male vendor who has had an extended conversation with a tourist. Male vendors and tourists tended to have relationships that were limited to business transactions. Tourists who could speak Spanish asked male vendors questions about price, colorfastness of dyes, and care of fabrics that they also asked women, but they did not engage male vendors in conversations about Maya life. Some were concerned about the authenticity of the items for sale. Although tourists commonly asked male vendors "Was it made by Indians?" and "Did Mayas use it?" they did not ask female vendors such questions.

Generally, male vendors treated tourists only as customers instead of trying to establish a rapport with them. Whereas female vendors tended to form opinions about individual tourists, male vendors tended to form more general, impersonal opinions of tourists. One day in the marketplace, I sat with a group of male vendors (a couple of K'iche' speakers, a couple of Kaqchikel speakers, and an Ixil speaker). One of the K'iche' speakers said, "You know you can tell how tourists are going to act by the country they are from." He then explained how French are "hot-tempered bargainers." Another volunteered that U.S. "tourists were loud, cheap, and confused." Italians were "tough" bargainers; Germans were "cold"; Japanese and Ko-

Mayas in the Marketplace

rean tourists were "mysterious" or "tight" with their money; and Central American tourists were "sympathetic, but had little money." Only a few male vendors knew tourists on personal levels, and this was usually because their wife, daughter, or mother had met them first.

Carol Smith (1995) explains how social relations between Mayas and Ladinos are played out within the contexts of nation building, where each group has distinct notions about what constitutes the nation. Some of the differences between Ladino and Maya concepts of nation relate to the specific gender relations operative within each group and between them, but each concept of what makes a nation is rooted in ideas of blood and descent. The concern here is not to offer a counterexplanation, but to elaborate on Smith's work by placing Ladino and Maya social relations within transnational contexts.

The social relations between Maya vendors and non-Maya Guatemalans (primarily Ladinos) differ from those between Maya vendors and foreign tourists. Ladinos who enter the marketplace are not interested in making contact with "Indians." They go there to look for particular kinds of items to buy: caps, key chains, and small change purses. These items rarely exceed Q10 ($1.66) each. In contrast, although tourists primarily go to look at "Indians" in the marketplace, they tend to purchase higher-priced items ranging from Q50 ($8.33) to Q600 ($100), such as place mats, vests, and sometimes *traje.*

Though my conversations with Maya vendors in their own language frequently caused Ladinos to stop and watch, it was more the novelty of a gringo speaking a *"lengua indita"* (little Indian dialect) than any interest in Mayas. Some asked why I was interested in *"inditas"* (little Indians) and how it was possible to learn their dialect, because it sounds like animal sounds. Such pejorative comments, in which Maya languages are frequently regarded as less than a real language or just a collection of sounds but not really a language, and that Mayas are *"inditas,"* reveal some of the insulting ways that Mayas are regarded by many Ladinos.

Maya vendors are particularly problematic for Ladinos, since Mayas have simultaneously and perhaps contradictorily been viewed as both impediments to progress and producers of traditional Maya culture, aspects of which are not considered to be exclusively Maya by some European (Huxley 1960) and Ladino intellectuals (Asturias 1923; Morales 1998), including some weaving techniques and certain handicraft production (Cojtí Cuxil 1991). Mayas in *típica* marketplaces also cause Ladinos to wonder about their identity, because the Mayas produce and sell items that have come to symbolize Guatemala internationally. Similarly, because it is also linked to national and global economics and politics (Fischer 2001), "the Maya movement sends a powerful message to Ladinos, beginning with a searing critique of Ladino identity itself" (Hale 1996: 43). Charles Hale (1996) discusses some of the social agendas of Ladino elites to delegitimate the Maya ethnic revitalization movement (also see Cojtí Cuxil 1997; Fischer and Brown 1996b; Warren 1998a) and the specific worries of Ladinos who feel their own cultural identity is weak or, according to a Ladino physician, is "disappearing, because it lacks a historical and spiritual grounding" (quoted in Hale 1996: 34). When Ladinos enter the *típica* marketplace to buy items for their homes and gifts for foreign friends that symbolize Guatemala, they come face-to-face with vendors who are promoting their indigenous Maya heritage and foreign tourists who are there because of their interest in Mayas or Indians. In other words, Mayanness, or Indianness, holds more value in the transnational contexts of tourism than Ladinoness.

My presence was disruptive to Ladinos because it also called attention to the vendors. Some wanted to know why I thought the lives of vendors were worthy of study, suggesting that there are more interesting people and things in Guatemala. Ironically, their suggestions related to studying Maya religion, pre-Columbian society, and weaving rather than Ladinos. Others, on the contrary, said that it is not surprising that anthropologists and foreign tourists are interested in "*indígenas*" because they have "culture and history." One Ladino couple who were showing a U.S. businessman tourism sites commented inside the Compañía de Jesús Artisan Marketplace, "It makes sense that foreigners are not interested in us. What do we have to offer them that is different? We have taken our history and culture from Europe and the United States."

From the perspective of Ladinos, some concepts of Guatemalan national identity are related to material items, such as pre-Columbian cities and contemporary weaving patterns. In national discourses, Maya women become objectified as some of the icons of national identity (Hendrickson 1995; Little 1995; Nelson 1994). Although foreign tourists go to the marketplace to have contact with Maya women, Ladinos do not. As Nelson (1999: 170–205) notes, whereas Maya men are unproblematic,

Mayas in the Marketplace

"disempowered along national, ethnic, and gender lines," Maya women are problematic because they call into question Ladino concepts of identity and nation.

Maya vendors' comments about Ladinos were far more guarded than their comments about tourists, but some general observations can be made. On weekends, Ladinos from Guatemala City visit Antigua. The cobblestone streets fill with cars and people. When asked if the additional people helped increase sales, most vendors emphatically stated that they did not. According to vendors, large numbers of Ladinos made it more difficult to sell to foreign tourists because vendors felt tourists were intimidated by the Ladinos' presence. Ladinos were described as pushy, cheap, and sometimes thieving.

Not all Ladinos were regarded in these ways. Those who worked as tour guides, provided they did not demand commissions, were welcome because they brought tourists to the marketplace. The sociostructural position of the guide, however, brings Ladino-Maya differences to the foreground. The guide's social position is located hierarchically above that of the vendor because the guide is the one who introduces, explains, and translates Maya culture to the tourist. Guides tend to both pacify and exoticize Mayas. They provide descriptions and explanations of who and what is Maya by contrasting Ladino to Maya culture. Female vendors seated at a backstrap loom or nursing an infant elicit commentaries about the timeless traditions of weaving and the central role women play in reproducing Maya culture. Tourists are told to observe differences in clothing (that indicate village origins) or to note women's bare feet. They do not explain that women take off their shoes to weave.

Both Ladino tour guides and Ladino consumers of Mayan handicrafts recognize male and female vendors in the artisan marketplace equally. They may purchase items from either. Although the artisan marketplace is open to male and female vendors, including a small number of Ladino vendors, Ladino guides and consumers identified the marketplace as "*indígena*" because of the Maya women dressed in *traje* and the types of items being sold, primarily handwoven items.

A third socioeconomic relationship is between vendors and the Ladinos who rent rooms and storage spaces to them. Unlike consumer-vendor economic relations in the marketplace, which can be framed in ethnic, gender, or national terms, vendors described their relation to Ladinos who leased living and storage spaces in class terms. Even vendors that were economically successful referred to themselves as working persons (*samajela'*), farmers (*tikonela'*), or simply vendors (*k'ayinela'*) who did not have the leisure time that their Ladino lessors and foreign and Guatemalan tourists had.

Ironically, some Maya vendors had traveled to other countries, but the Ladinos they rented from had not. Sometimes Mayas brought them gifts from the United States and Europe. These trips were not for leisure but for work. Female vendors from several families that I worked with sold textiles and demonstrated backstrap weaving on these trips. Regardless of this, vendors often described their Ladino lessor as their *patrón* (boss) rather than a friend or *compadre* (co-parent, companion). Such sentiments can also be viewed from a Ladino perspective. Smith (1995: 734) argues that the "class position of most Ladinos is that of salaried workers and petty bureaucrats, which . . . puts them in the middle, rather than lower, class rungs of the system. Lower positions are reserved for Indian peasants and artisans who bear the burden of absolute, rather than relative, class exploitation." Within this conceptualization, no matter how economically successful a Maya vendor becomes, in the racial and class system of Guatemala, he or she will always be socially and structurally positioned in the lowest class. This perspective is similar to Judith Friedlander's (1975) argument in her Hueyapan, Mexico, research, which suggested that indigenous culture is tied to lower-class status rather than to distinct cosmological, material, and value systems.

VENDOR–VENDOR RELATIONS

In the marketplace, Maya vendors interacted among themselves with both similarities and differences in the performance of some roles in relation to gender. Both Maya men and women operate stalls in the artisan marketplace, but rarely does one run the business without the aid of other family members, usually the spouse. Maya males play roles as salesmen and in support of their wives' vending activities, but men usually occupy less visible positions in the marketplace. They will, however, take over the vending stall if their wife cannot run it. A number of Kaqchikel vendors split the marketing duties. Husbands worked during the week and slow tourism seasons, and wives worked on weekends and during high tourism seasons (June through August, December, and Easter week).

Families worked together in the marketplace at least part of the time. On Sundays, husbands, wives, and sometimes children were in the marketplace. Any one of those present will meet customers, display merchandise, and deal with middlepersons and weavers to replenish their stock. Even when the stall was considered exclusively the woman's business, the family divided tasks among themselves. The husband and male children ran errands and communicated with other vendors over inventory needs or made change for customers' purchases. The wife and older daughters set up their looms, talked with potential customers, and finalized sales. Though it was widely acknowledged among vendors that women wearing *traje* and weaving attracted foreign tourists, both male and female vendors thought either gender could finalize sales equally well.

Generally, women ran the stalls, and their husbands supported them by replenishing stock and filling in when their wives had other business. When I asked one man how long he had worked in the market, he replied that the stall was his wife's. She decided to pursue a teaching degree and asked him to keep shop when she was in class. He suggested that I return when she was there, since she knew more about the marketing business than he did. Other men took more active roles, even though they were not always visible participants. Some worked for their wives as artisans but without pay (or they were not directly paid for their work because the money from sales was used for household expenses). Men played central roles when it came to setting up and taking down the merchandise that is displayed in the stalls each day. Those men who were farmers or artisans arranged their schedules to help out with childcare and bring their wives and daughters their lunches. Maya males working as wage laborers spent less time in the marketplace assisting the females of their family, but most tried to help sometimes and to do physically taxing activities, such as rebuilding the stall and carrying *bultos*.

Aside from these gender-oriented ways of intrasocial relations, Maya vendors organized themselves in ways that reflect intraclass differences. Because class is to some extent a cultural construct (Nash 2001: 18), most Mayas are located at the bottom of the Guatemalan class system regardless of how much money they make (Smith 1995). According to one Ladino vendor, "persons with high political and social positions are not Mayas." In general, both Maya and Ladino vendors in the *típica* marketplace indicated that they regarded themselves as a type of occupational group, like farmers, teachers, or artisans. They noted that in the *típica* market (the system of peddlers, marketplaces, and stores selling handicrafts), they are "not all alike" and that the economic distinctions among them can be great: "There are those with money and there are those without money."

At the bottom are persons who work for wages or commissions. Rarely did Mayas work as salespersons more than a few months before attempting to find some other job or establish themselves as a producer or vendor in their own right. In contrast, one Ladina woman has worked for another Ladina woman selling jewelry for five years. Even though Maya husbands and sons worked for and assisted their female relatives and spouses, they were not paid and they did not consider themselves to be hired salespersons. The few Maya salespersons in the Compañía de Jesús Artisan Marketplace make between nothing—if they don't sell anything—and Q20 ($3.33) per day. For example, one woman and her mother worked as salespersons for one of the wealthier Kaqchikel Maya families in the Compañía de Jesús Artisan Marketplace for a daily wage of Q20. When they learned that if business was slow they would make less money, or even no money if nothing was sold during the day, they went back to doing agricultural labor, such as weeding and commercial flower picking, for Q15 ($2.50) per day. The two female Ladino salespersons did not fare any better and sometimes even worse, since they did not have access to agricultural jobs.

In 1997, one Kaqchikel family of vendors gave me several hundred dollars to purchase replacement parts for their computers when I visited my home in the United States. This family and others like it (selling over $5,000 per year in merchandise of handwoven *típica*—decorative weavings, tablecloths, vests, bags, and shirts) attempted to function as a self-contained and self-sufficient production unit, making items and then selling them. Often these vendors were part of extended families that included weavers, middlepersons, marketplace vendors, and exporters with land, material possessions, and cash totaling thousands of dollars. Although they made more money than those who worked for wages, they did not hire salespersons or wage laborers to assist them. Of all the Kaqchikel vendors controlling stalls in the Compañía de Jesús Artisan Marketplace, only two (including the previously mentioned one) hired salespersons. In fact, vendors criticized these two families by saying that "they were acting like Ladinos" because nonfamily members were working for them.

Vendors describe themselves as being a single class, despite sometimes large differences in wealth. Social and economic class, as conceived of by Maya vendors, is in relation to Ladinos. In the marketplace, as in other social, economic, and political settings, Mayas positioned themselves as subordinate to Ladinos. Not once did Maya vendors claim to be of different socioeconomic classes or to have the ability to rise to socioeconomic classes equal to or higher than those classes accessible to Ladinos if they continued to work as vendors. Weberian (see Weber 1946) concepts of class stratification and mobility, which are tied to a combination of wealth and prestige, are applicable to Guatemalan contexts to a certain degree. According to Ladinos I interviewed, Maya vendors will always be "Indians" and "beneath Ladinos" socially, regardless of the amount of money they make, because class is more than money; it is "culture and education."

Issues related to class are complex in Guatemala. Maya communities themselves may be stratified along class lines that do not relate to ethnicity. For example, John Watanabe (1992: 148–156) shows that despite vast differences in wealth and occupation—landless, unskilled laborers to landowners and merchants—Mayas in Chimbal do not aspire to become Ladinos or embrace what they consider Ladino values. This is not to argue that class differences within Maya communities cannot cause rifts between peasants and elites, as Greg Grandin (2000) adeptly shows for Quetzaltenango, where Mayas developed new concepts of race and nation that differed from those of Ladinos. Vendors recognized distinct differences between themselves and other Mayas working in factories and in professional occupations. Vendors commonly aspired for their children to pursue careers that would increase their children's social mobility, wealth, and overall economic security beyond what their parents had achieved. The children of vendors can be found working as educators in grade schools and high schools, as social workers for international development projects, as book publishers for national presses, and as professionals in human rights organizations. Outside the marketplace, in their hometowns, wealthier vendors, including the example of the family that introduces this chapter, will hire poorer Mayas to help with housework. Vendors have no qualms about themselves or others, such as landowners, hiring workers. A couple of vendor families from San Antonio Aguas Calientes hire poor Ladino women to do menial housework, which inverts the historical subordination of Mayas by Ladinos.

Although the domination of Mayas by Ladinos is well documented by anthropologists (Ehlers 1990; Hawkins 1984; Nash 1993a, 2001; Nelson 1999; Plattner 1975; C. Smith 1990b, 1995; W. Smith 1977; Warren 1989; Watanabe 1992; and others), Mayas do not passively accept this position. As Tracy Ehlers (1990) illustrates, Mayas in San Pedro Sacatepéquez may change their class designation by learning and adopting cultural values and acquiring material items associated with Ladinos as well as developing businesses to increase wealth. However, in San Andrés Semetabaj, Kay Warren (1989) shows that although Ladinos dominate Mayas in social and economic spheres, Mayas strive to become self-sufficient and do not associate wealth and higher class position with being Ladino, which is also argued by Pan-Maya activists (Warren 1998a). Likewise, Maya handicraft vendors do not accept the conceptualization that class and ethnicity are tied together; rather, they recognize that in their social and economic relations with Ladinos, both come into play. Some revel in telling Ladinos about trips abroad because it suggests that they are members of a higher socioeconomic class.

Similar to Mayas in San Andrés Semetabaj (Warren 1989), Maya vendors describe themselves as different from Ladinos in terms of values, lifestyle, and personhood: "*Man junam ta qana'oj*" (Our thoughts/beliefs/values are not the same); "*Man yojkoje' ta; man yojsamaj ta junam. Man keteman ta yesamaj ri mo'si*" (We don't live the same; we don't work the same. Ladinos don't know how to work); "*Ri indígena man junam ta ri mo's*" (The *indígena* is not the same as the Ladino).

As vendors interact with foreign tourists, Ladinos, and each other in order to earn money, marketplace socioeconomic relations influence other social and economic spheres. In other words, the gendered nature of the marketplace, set within the dual contexts of transnational tourism and the Guatemala nation, contributes to changes in the ways Maya vendors organize their households and participate in the social, economic, and political institutions of their respective communities.

Household Organization and Change

There is a great deal of variability in the ways Kaqchikel Maya *típica* vendors' households are organized in terms of work and decision making. Rather than conceptualize Maya households as ideal types, traditional or modern, which do not capture their heterogeneity or the ways Mayas live within and reproduce their households, it is more productive to think about households as performative in the same way that Judith Butler (1990, 1993) argues about gender. According to Butler (1990: 173), the "acts and gestures, articulated and enacted desires create the illusion of an interior and organizing gender [substitute "household"] core, an illusion discursively maintained for the purposes of the regulation" of individuals. Performativity is not a "singular or the deliberate 'act,' but . . . the reiterative and citational practice by which discourse produces the effects that it names" (Butler 1993: 2). Part of this discourse relates to the relatively consistent ideas that vendors have about what constitutes a traditional Maya household, even if their own households do not operate in such a fashion. Vendors' notions of traditional households, however, often conflict with the ways they organize their households because of the socioeconomic contexts of the marketplace. The tension that results from this conflict is instrumental in mobilizing them, especially women, to political action. Butler (1993: 188) explains that "the failure of discursive performativity to finally and fully establish the identity to which it refers" is politically problematic because the formulation of politics assumes particular categories. In the case of vendors, this includes, among others, categories of marketplace, household, woman, Maya, *indígena,* Ladino, tourist, and vendor that are always in formation and may conflict with each other.

TRADITIONAL HOUSEHOLD IDEALS AND PROBLEMS

According to vendors, the traditional Maya household is divided according to gender with neither the male nor the female domain being more important than the other but rather hierarchical in terms of age and gender, with the eldest male having the most prestige and decision-making power. Kaqchikel households tend to consist of one to three generations revolving around a core made up of father, sons, and grandsons. Daughters move out when they marry, and daughters-in-law move into the household. This group works as a unit to provide the subsistence needs and luxury desires of the family. Men, assisted by sons, work out of the household as laborers, long-distance traders, and farmers (the ideal). They provide for the household's basic subsistence needs by farming maize, beans, and squash while bringing in cash through wage labor or market sales of surplus maize. Women, assisted by unmarried daughters and daughters-in-law, maintain the household by taking care of small children, cooking, cleaning, and making clothing. They may make small amounts of money by selling handwoven blouses (*po't*) and belts (*pa's*) to others in their village, as well as vending at local periodic marketplaces small amounts of garden vegetables (tomatoes and peppers) and fruit (*jocotes,* avocados, and limes) grown in their courtyards. They maintain that the only overt gender hierarchy relates to meals. Women and girls prepare and serve men and boys their meals, and then they eat after and separately from the males.

In terms of this ideal household, three aspects that stand out have been demonstrated ethnographically (for example, see Nash 1970; Ehlers 1990): the division of labor according to gender, the mutual dependence and support of household members, and the respect and obedience toward elders. Men and women performed complementary but separate tasks and mutually relied on each other (Ehlers 1990: 6). However, according to Nash (1970: 70–71), who worked in the Maya town of Amatenango, Mexico, where women produced pottery for domestic and commercial use:

> Women can live without men in the household economy of the town, but men cannot live without women. . . . A widow can hire a man to work in her fields, but a man cannot hire a cook. If he is widowed, he must remarry, move into his mother's house, find a wife for a grown son, or find an unattached female relative to live with him.[2]

In both cases, male and female labor is separate. Males do not do women's work, and women do not do men's work. Ehlers (1990: 70) explains that "since a woman's income is usually separate from what her husband produces or earns, there are clear-cut domestic responsibilities for each sex. The husband supplies corn and firewood . . . and the wife must meet the remaining household expenses from her business profits." Aside from men growing maize and women making tortillas, *típica* vendors maintain few of these gendered divisions. Similar to most Maya households (Hendrickson 1995; Warren 1989; Watanabe 1992), not one vendor family that I worked with regularly maintained or kept their household according to the "traditional" ideal. Only during formal dinners were traditional ideals usually standard; daily meals, on the other hand, were characterized by families eating together and men helping with meal preparation and cleanup.

Ehlers (1990), like Bossen (1984), demonstrates how economic development in Guatemala can change the organization of Maya households. Male and female work domains remain divided, but women become increasingly dependent on their spouses. Maya women sacrificed

Mayas in the Marketplace

their own businesses and decision-making power when their husbands became economically successful. Men demonstrated their success by requiring that their wives not work in money-earning activities outside of the household. When women did work, it was "as unpaid employees in their husbands' businesses." As families "become more affluent, [they] abandon separate monies and responsibilities and instead adopt the Ladino habit of male control of domestic resources" (Ehlers 1990: 70). This is a class issue that has been documented in other parts of Latin America, such as Andean Peru (Bourque and Warren 1981), Oaxaca, Mexico (Stephen 1991), and elsewhere (Nash and Safa 1976), and theorized earlier by Engels (1972).

The increased dependency on men affects women in several ways. First, it isolates them from broader social and economic networks. Second, it takes away their ability to earn their own money. Third, it diminishes their power to make decisions in the household and privileges males over females with regard to providing education and future employment opportunities. Overall, women lose their economic and social autonomy. This dependency, as Engels similarly argued, is especially problematic when men leave their spouses or spend their wages on mistresses, because women have a difficult time entering the market economy as wage laborers, vendors, artisans, or small shopkeepers.

In her restudy of Amatenango, Nash (1993c) describes how the town's interrelations with national and global economies have resulted in different patterns of household organization. As men in Amatenango leave to pursue jobs in Mexican cities and even the United States, there is no guarantee that they will send money home to maintain their households. At the same time, because of the proximity of the town to the Pan-American Highway and tourism routes, women have intensified pottery production for commercial sale to tourists. In the past, pottery production was primarily for domestic use. Making money has permitted women to make decisions about who they marry (formerly arranged by parents) and how wealth is redistributed within the family. Some men responded by becoming more involved with pottery production and vending processes, appropriating women's wealth-generating activities. Men have turned pottery profits into trucking businesses, further improving their abilities to make money. Those women who are economically successful and independent, however, face community-wide condemnation for disrupting male authority and altering household divisions of labor. Despite these problems, Nash (1993c: 148–149) predicts that women may eventually have more political power because of trends toward more female-headed households and greater economic autonomy.

In contrast to Ehlers and Nash, I observed different trends among vendors. Men did not attempt to appropriate women's wealth or castigate women for diverging from traditional community norms. Although tourism intensified over the last fifteen years of the twentieth century, economic participation in tourism is not new. If Kaqchikel vendors themselves had not been involved in sales to tourists for a couple of generations, they were from towns (especially San Antonio Aguas Calientes, Santa Catarina Barahona, and Santa Catarina Palopó) where people have been involved in tourism that has promoted Maya women and textiles for most of the twentieth century.

The social isolation of women and their economic dependency on men that characterizes the upwardly mobile households described by Ehlers (1990) follows trends observed in many other places (Moore 1988) and documented by feminist scholars (Bourque and Warren 1981; Deere and León de Leal 1981; Nash and Safa 1976, among others) conducting research in other parts of Latin America. In these cases, by giving up economic and social autonomy, women may accept their subordination to men as a way of demonstrating that they are not part of the lower classes. It is widely recognized by Latin Americans and scholars of Latin America that poor women have to work.

In the case of some Kaqchikel vendor families, it is men, not women, who are giving up some of their economic and personal autonomy because of the ways international tourism has favored Maya women over men as subjects. Looking specifically at intrahousehold dynamics can help explain why this is happening and how it can lead to political action. Ehlers (1990) explains how, in the national context of the 1980s, Maya women gave up the economic and social autonomy they had established from tending shops, selling in the marketplace, and weaving when their families adopted Ladino forms of household organization, which affect women politically by making them more dependent. Nash (1993c) demonstrates that within the context of the globalization of the handicraft trade, Maya women's autonomy can increase and contribute to new concepts about women's economic and political roles in the family, the community, and the state, even if women's autonomy is not sanctioned by the community. In other words, changing economic opportunities, set within specific sociopolitical contexts, can lead to changes in both household organization and political action.

KAQCHIKEL MAYA VENDOR HOUSEHOLDS

Kaqchikel Maya vendors organized their households in a number of ways that complement and contradict their traditional ideals and also indicate changes in who performs household tasks and makes decisions. Because there is no general type of household organization among Kaqchikel Maya *típica* vendors, it is productive to look at different households and discuss what it is common among them.

I return to the description of the family that was used to introduce this chapter. Antonio and Antonieta, the heads of the household, live with nine of their ten offspring of six boys and four girls. To varying degrees, all of their children have helped with the fabrication of items for sale in the marketplace by sewing and weaving. They have also taken turns selling in the Compañía de Jesús Artisan Marketplace when not taking high school and university classes in business, accounting, history, and other subjects in Antigua, Chimaltenango, and Guatemala City. Antonieta buys used *traje* from women from Comalapa and its neighboring hamlets, as well as women from nearby towns such as San José Poaquil and San Martín Jilotepeque, who come to her house between Tuesdays and Thursdays. On Saturdays, she buys used *traje* and items manufactured solely for sale to tourists from middlepersons and individual weavers. Although Antonio sells in the marketplace four to five days per week, he defers most decisions regarding buying to his wife. Their children also give the proceeds of all sales to her. In effect, the *típica* business is in Antonieta's control, and it provides the basis for bringing in cash.

The adult children (of the nine at home, only one is considered a minor) of the couple also contribute to the household by giving a portion of their wages from their other jobs (teaching grade school, running a computer training school, repairing appliances, welding, and constructing buildings). This economic contribution is considered mandatory for children living at home, and their parents openly criticized those who did not make it. The amount contributed changes over time, because children are expected to assume more responsibility for household expenses and care of the infirm and elderly as they become more economically successful. Antonio complained one evening at dinner, "Bryon is my worst child. He doesn't contribute any money from his teaching job, and he doesn't help in the milpa. He doesn't do anything to help in our house." Ideally, everyone gave some of their wages toward the maintenance of the household. Members of the household could expect food, a place to sleep, and assistance with school expenses—even when they were not putting money into the household budget.

The family divides some household work according to traditional standards. Men plant maize, growing only enough for household consumption, and cut firewood. Women weave some of the *po't* they wear, and they make tortillas, which the males will reheat but not make from scratch. Women tend to do the food shopping in the marketplace, but men purchase food and other items in stores. Although women cooked more elaborate and complex meals, the men cooked regularly during the week, giving the women time to pursue work and education interests. All other housework, such as sweeping and mopping floors, removing trash, taking care of small children, washing clothes and dishes, feeding animals, and taking care of elderly kin, are performed by both males and females.

This reflects a different pattern than that described by Ehlers (1990), in which Maya women's and men's work is not only separate, but women must rely on support from other female kin (especially daughters) to fulfill household duties and pursue money-making activities. Men in the Sotz family help with domestic tasks and contribute wages to domestic expenses. When they and the women have too much work to do in the marketplace and other occupations, a domestic servant—a girl or young woman—will be hired to help. Women in this economically successful household do not bear the burden of housework alone, and they do not have to assume most of the domestic expenses. At the same time, they make major decisions about household expenditures. In fact, Antonieta has final say on all major purchases. When Antonio wanted to purchase a truck and visit friends in the United States, Antonieta vetoed the trip, telling him: "It would be a waste of time for you to go, since you are too old to learn English and we've done just fine without a truck. It would be better to send one of the children who could study."[3]

In a Kaqchikel Maya household from San Antonio Aguas Calientes, domestic and marketplace responsibilities were divided in other ways. This household consists of a married couple with five children (three daughters and two sons). Although the couple lives separately from their respective parents, they and their children, ages nine to sixteen, regularly

Mayas in the Marketplace

assist the two sets of parents with housework and subsistence needs. Frequently, the grandparents eat with their children and grandchildren but do not contribute to cooking. Celia maintains a stall in the Compañia de Jesús Artisan Marketplace, which, until recently, she managed with her second oldest daughter, Myra, who now has her own stall in the same marketplace. When the women worked together, Celia controlled the finances of the stall, bought from middlepersons and weavers, and decided how to spend money earned from sales. Both women wove and contributed earnings from the sale of their textiles to the general household expenditures. Myra retained some of her profits for personal use. The oldest daughter, Magda, devotes herself to school and hopes to graduate with a university degree. She helps in the marketplace only in cases of emergency. The youngest daughter, Delmi, is in grade school and does not contribute much time or energy toward weaving or vending, though she does help in the marketplace and is learning how to weave. She is expected to study and help with housework. The sons, one of high school age (Santos) and the other in grade school (Israel), like their father (Juan), only sell in the marketplace during times of emergency. They do help carry heavy bags of merchandise and repair/rebuild the stall. Juan works at a factory that manufactures building construction materials.

In contrast to the typical rural pattern in Latin America of women having to pay for domestic expenses (Bourque and Warren 1981; Ehlers 1990; Nash 1970; Stephen 1991), Celia and Juan pool the money they earn and use it for both domestic expenses to maintain the household and to further their children's education. Although none of the children are discouraged from entering the *típica* market, they are encouraged to go to school. So far, Myra is the only one of their children interested in being a vendor. Aside from basic household and school expenses, which they meet equally, Celia and Juan are relatively economically independent from each other, spending and saving the surplus money they each earn as they desire. During times of illness, unemployment (Juan), and low *típica* sales (Celia), the person who brings in the money assumes responsibility for the family.

Some housework is divided according to gender. The women cook or weave, but the males generally do not do these jobs.[4] Instead, the males maintain a small milpa, which is more for symbolic reasons than for subsistence, since it does not provide them with more than a few months of maize for the family's own consumption. Males are expected to help with cleaning, such as sweeping, mopping, washing dishes, and dusting. Juan, who worked an evening shift at the factory, had the responsibility of taking care of the children during the day so Celia could run her *típica* business and develop new designs.

Both of these families described their parents' households as set up according to traditional ideals, outlined in the prior section, in which work was clearly divided according to gender. Men farmed and took care of matters outside of the house, and women wove and took care of matters within the house. According to Celia's mother, "Only when the harvest was bad did I go to work in the fields for Ladinos." The greatest change in these families and other vendor families is the increased participation of males in housework compared to their parent's generation. After dinner one Sunday at Celia and Juan's house, I joked that the men should wash the dishes, giving the women a break. As the two youngest children cleaned the table, Juan's father replied, "I didn't wash dishes back then and I'm not washing dishes now." Although members of vendor families talked about men of previous generations taking part in childcare, their participation was of their own volition. Today, men who are vendors themselves and spouses of female vendors in the Compañía de Jesús Artisan Marketplace feel that they are obligated to help take care of their children.

The increased participation of Kaqchikel males in some traditionally defined female domestic roles has meant that women have more economic and personal freedom than they had in the past, because they are relieved from daily time-consuming tasks. Furthermore, unlike cases of Maya women being restricted to their homes when their husbands are successful (see Ehlers 1990), Kaqchikel vendor women faced no such restrictions from their husbands. In fact, the economically successful women in the marketplace, who had the most personal freedom to travel independently for reasons of pleasure and business, were women whose husbands were either successful in their own respective economic pursuits or were partners in the *típica* vending business and helped with housework. Poor vendor families also followed similar patterns. However, if they had to rely on the agricultural wage labor to cover subsistence needs, then women tended to do all the housework as well as sell fewer hours per day and fewer days per week, because men worked an average of twelve hours per day in the fields. In other words, vendors who were not economically successful sometimes reverted to more traditional gendered divisions of labor.

Strategic Identities and Political Action

Marketplaces are examples of those sites described by Sallie Westwood and Sarah Radcliffe (1993: 20–21) that "serve to unify individuals who might otherwise be dispersed by the multiplicity of their interests." In such sites, both men and women can acquire the resources necessary to act politically, to communicate across gender and ethnic divisions as political subjects. Self-conscious political action entails class, ethnic, and gender dimensions, each of which informs the other and relates to specific identity configurations. In the cases of Maya vendors, it is not just the marketplace but also the interrelationship of the marketplace and the households. The tensions about resolving pragmatic problems—who does what types of work and who controls money in the marketplace and the household—contribute to one ideology and form of political action.

Moore (1994: 92) argues that "differentiated social identities are related to the exercise of power, because the very definitions of those identities are connected to normative or conventional explanations for the social order, as well as legitimations of the order." This is evident in the cases of ascriptive identities. Hence, the identity categories used in this chapter (Maya/Ladino, male/female, husband/wife, vendor/buyer, etc.) can appear to be natural, and the differential rights accorded to individuals thus categorized can also appear natural. The tourism/*típica* marketplace helps expose the power relations of these categories because it brings together diverse people, in terms of class, gender, and cultural identity, who are embedded in a socioeconomic and cultural context where local, national, international, and transnational concepts of who is Maya can conflict. In turn, this affects the ways these categories are lived by Mayas in their households.

Although the above ascriptive identities can be applied to handicraft vendors, it is productive to think about strategic identities in relation to political action. Vendors strategically use the various types of identities (including concepts of who is Maya) that are ascribed to them in the specific social and economic relationships that they are part of in the marketplace. Although Maya vendors I knew were not preoccupied with who they are, the contradictions between marketplace and household, and between local, national, and transnational contexts, contribute to the political action they take, as the earlier examples in this chapter and in the previous one illustrate, because vendors reevaluate their respective roles in the marketplace, Antigua, their hometowns, Guatemala, and the world.

Unlike the CONAVIGUA[5] widows in Guatemala, who are an organized political group with an agenda (Schirmer 1993), vendors in the Compañía de Jesús Artisan Marketplace are a group of individuals concerned with making money. Whereas CONAVIGUA came together after the harsh policies of President Ríos Montt in the early 1980s, when thousands of Guatemalan males were killed, vendors are not a cohesive political group. Additionally, the vendors do not represent a potentially revolutionary group. In fact, they labor to avoid conflict and reach compromises with Antigua's municipal government, police forces, and other businesses. Vendors are caught up in the mundane—providing for their own and their families' immediate subsistence needs, as well as individual goals of education, earning more money, and acquiring material possessions. When they have organized into political blocs (described in the previous chapters), they have been motivated by economic reasons (promotion of the marketplace for tourism) or to secure basic public services (lights, water, and trash removal). They do not envision themselves as a collective set on changing local or national politics with regard to official state policies on Mayas, marketplaces, tourism, or artisans/vendors.

Vendors conceptualize the marketplace in two significant ways that are comparable to the reorganization of gender roles in the household and the relatively equal gender participation in the political activities of vendors described in the previous chapter. First, the marketplace is not exclusively a feminine space to them. The men and women with whom I spoke did not conceptualize it in gendered terms. Both males and females could enter and conduct business. Women as well as men were admired for their economic prowess. Second, vendors identified themselves using broad categories, such as *indígenas,* Kaqchikeles, Mayas, and sometimes Guatemalans (if it would help make a sale), in addition to town and municipal affiliations. This contrasts with earlier Guatemalan marketplace descriptions by Tax (1937) and Ruth Bunzel (1959), which showed that ethnic differences prevailed at the level of town and municipality. When viewing these two changes from the perspectives of gender, class, and ethnicity, it is possible, perhaps, to conceptualize the political consciousness of the vendors.

Although individuals enter the marketplace with the pretense of buying or selling, it is also a place where ideas relating to issues of gender,

Mayas in the Marketplace

class, and ethnicity are discussed. Both male and female vendors joked about appropriate gender roles within the marketplace and in the household, but there appeared to be little consistency among them when observing their behavior. In formal interviews, men and women claimed that men made final decisions about opening their homes to tourists. However, most of the invitations to vendors' homes that were extended to me (and to tourists) came from women. Usually, the vendor would announce the decision to her spouse after the invitation had been made. Decisions about how to spend money made from vending (ranging from investment in land, increasing the handicraft inventory, contracting weavers for special orders, and specialized training in teaching, secretarial, accounting, or computer skills) could be made by either spouse, but most of the time the decision was made by women.

I do not want to give the impression that male-female roles have collapsed into each other and that the relations between genders are egalitarian. On numerous occasions, women mentioned that men were prone to wasting too much money drinking. Women also claimed that some men were irresponsible with money. Some of the poorest women in the marketplace were those whose husbands had abandoned them for work in the United States or for other women outside the marketplace. Not having a supportive husband does not determine a vendor woman's wealth. In fact, two vendors became more successful after they separated from their alcoholic and womanizing husbands. Single women and those with children have better incomes and less physically strenuous schedules than women working as agriculture wage laborers or as domestic servants. Women said, "Men just don't know how to manage money, that's why we have to hold on to ours and theirs." Vendor men who were in strong marriages even said, "My wife's money is her money, and my money is her money." Indeed, to illustrate the difference between male and female attitudes about money, men sometimes spend idle time in the marketplace gambling, but women never play these card games, even though the stakes are low. Rarely do the winnings exceed the cost of lunch, one to two dollars.

Because each has a relatively high degree of autonomy in the management of their time and in their money use, members of the opposite sex were sometimes described as promiscuous. Indeed, a common form of teasing among vendors was about how many sexual partners or spouses they had. Women would say to men, "The reason you have so many women is that you can't satisfy one enough to keep her." Among themselves, but within earshot of males (including their husbands), another would ask, "So who are you going to keep warm tonight?" with the women to whom the question was directed volunteering the name of a man other than her spouse. Other women in the group would make suggestions varying from men they thought were attractive to those who were considered hideous. Men would say to women, "I hear your husband is away. It is going to get cold tonight . . ." Suspicions of promiscuity were diffused, however, when spouses worked together or separately but with one of their children.

Although I did not witness any organized movements by vendors for women's rights or efforts to change male roles—making male roles available to women—male and female vendors did demonstrate changing perspectives on gender roles by the way they practiced their everyday lives in the marketplace and household. The marketplace should not be viewed as a feminine space invaded by men who are cutting into women's income. Prolonged success in the marketplace depends on the number of sales one makes, how well one cooperates with fellow vendors, and the support one (especially female vendors) receives from one's spouse to fulfill daily domestic tasks in the household. The fact that I met a number of men (usually spouses, but also sons and brothers) who assisted women in both the marketplace and the household demonstrates a shift away from strict sexual divisions of labor. As with political consciousness, the division of labor within households is not uniform among Maya families.

Men and women also showed interest in Maya activists such as Rigoberta Menchú and Rosalina Tuyuc (CONAVIGUA member and congresswoman). These women were seen as spokespersons for women's rights, human rights, and Maya rights. Vendors did not view them only as advocates for women's rights. I listened to women speak with pride about Menchú's work in relation to international rights for indigenous persons around the world. Male vendors spoke with concerns for the rights of women and the difficulties confronting widows and orphans from the 1980s violence. Men and women indicated a desire for the political realm to be opened to both of them. That Tuyuc and Menchú were at the forefront of international and national politics was viewed as positive for women and men, as Guatemalans and as Mayas. In fact, because of the visibility of Maya women in public cultural and political spheres (see Nelson 1999), males felt that they had more social and political maneuverability in Guatemalan society at large, even if their cultural identities were ambiguous to tourists and Ladinos.

Finally, there has been a change in the attitudes of vendors in terms of gender because families are increasingly investing in education and special training for themselves and their children. Daughters as well as sons are given opportunities to pursue nontraditional jobs in accounting, computers, engineering, and teaching. Sons are not privileged over daughters in reaping the benefits of higher education and good jobs that take them away from their town and family. In cases where unmarried daughters got pregnant, I observed several different solutions. The young women, aside from when they gave birth and a month or two of recovery/rest time, continued to work in the marketplace, pursue their studies, or perform their professional jobs. Most commonly, the young man married the woman, but the woman continued to work. Few families were opposed to the income that these women earned. For those women who did not marry, they relied on parents and siblings to help with childcare. Those who were handicraft vendors just brought their baby to the marketplace until the child was weaned, then she/he might stay at home with older members of the extended family. Young women pursuing higher education sometimes preferred to avoid getting married after becoming pregnant because new husbands tended to put pressure on their wives to dedicate themselves to childcare and domestic chores instead of their studies. In three separate cases of young women from San Antonio Aguas Calientes who were completing their high school programs or were studying in the university, all yielded to the young men's pressure to marry, dropped out of school, and went into the marketplace to sell. The parents of the women were disappointed with the respective marriages. One mother commented that her daughter was "wasting her life by throwing away a good education." Fathers and mothers of these daughters even offered to assume childcare responsibilities to help their daughters finish school. When the older sister of one of these young women became pregnant by the man she had dated for several years, she did not immediately get married. She was working in Nebaj, over 250 kilometers away, and attending graduate classes in Guatemala City. She did not give up her development position or drop out of school. Instead, with the support of her family, she put pressure on the young man to make a decision about his commitment to her, telling him that he had to "go be with her and help take care of the baby because she was not giving up her job." When the young man agreed, relocated to Nebaj, found work, and demonstrated that he would help around the house, the couple married. Unlike her sister, in addition to having her parents' support, she earned enough money that she could have hired a domestic servant to watch her baby, clean, and cook. Most young women do not have this luxury, but those impregnated by men who are considered irresponsible—prone to laziness, drinking, or fighting—also avoid getting married because, as the young woman who quit her sales job in the marketplace to do agricultural labor commented, "Being poor and having to work hard was better than living with an abusive husband who wouldn't give money or help."

The assistance that men give women in the marketplace and the redivision of housework suggest that perceptions of gender are changing among vendors, because male vendors did not feel stigmatized for having subordinate roles to women or for doing what had been defined traditionally as women's work. The international and transnational context of tourism has contributed to changes in the types of work that men and women do. Doing the work of the opposite sex has caused vendors to be more self-aware of the ways that gender relates to economic opportunities and political maneuverability.

In terms of ethnicity, vendors' concepts were not always consistent. Because of their roles as vendors to tourists, they had standardized ways of describing Mayanness. For some it was only a sales pitch, but for others it was a central way to identify themselves. In the same person and within the same family, vendors identified themselves in a variety of ways. While watching the World Cup, they might be Guatemalan, but in relation to U.S. foreign aid policies they might be Guatemalan, Maya, or Kaqchikel, framed within gendered categories. Sometimes language or particular types of dress might bring out ethnic differences.

Although vendors perform Maya identity within the context of the marketplace and with tourists in general, they face racism every day working in a city with a Ladino-run government and Ladino-owned businesses. The discrimination that Mayas experience, such as being refused service in businesses and being harassed by the police, described in various places in this book, contributes to the political action they take in Antigua—a petition drive or a protest rally in front of city hall. The differences between Ladinos and Mayas, however, do not always supplant the differences that exist between Mayas themselves.

Hale (1994) describes the conflicts and divisions between Mayas who met in Quetzaltenango on October 12, 1991, to protest the quincentenary and to plan for the future. He found that the two main groups—*indígenas,* the "Indian delegates who claimed to be unified by central elements of the worldviews, common political goals, and an expressed desire to organize first among themselves," and *populares,* those Mayas, like Menchú, who seek to build broader class-based alliances with lower- and middle-class Blacks and Ladinos (Hale 1994: 11)—were divided not only about what issues were most important but also internally. The debates revolved around issues about how to politically unify Mayas. Additional complications arose as Mayas tried to decide what type of organization best fulfills their economic needs and political objectives, because this split did not correlate with existing ethnic divisions—Mayas versus Ladinos (Warren 1998b). Like the attendees at the conference Hale and Warren write about, Maya vendors also confront issues relating to class and ethnic differences. Class consciousness, however, was least formulated by the vendors, even though they did point out differences in wealth among themselves.

Like the participants in the anti-quincentenary conference, vendors in general oppose themselves to international and Guatemalan political policies. Because they are in daily contact with foreigners and Ladinos, vendors tend to form anti-national and more international views, only participating in local community politics to gain economic advantages or protect economic interests. Voting among vendors has been inconsistent, since many do not vote if the government does not get in the way of their business. They relate to the consumers of their products as gender, ethnic, and class subjects. Which of these has meaning for the vendors shifts from moment to moment, as they tend to relate the particular tourists or Ladinos who enter the marketplace to the latest political decision made in Washington, D.C., or Guatemala City.

Conclusions

It is important to emphasize that vendors struggle with Maya identity on a daily basis. Hall (1996b: 446) writes that new concepts of Black identity that engage difference are developing in England. Vendors likewise engage difference, but it is not just between ethnic groups. Difference is also understood in gendered terms. Ethnic groups (the different Maya groups) are represented by Maya women in national and touristic discourses, which sometimes appear to make women ethnically different from men. Both men and women spoke out against this by complaining about the erasure of men from the marketplace, since the postcards and guidebooks sold in shops around Antigua and newspaper pictures of vendors favor women. They explained that although few men wore traditional clothing, they did not view themselves as Ladinos. The participation of men in the maintenance of Maya tradition was considered necessary by both men and women. The widows and women who married outside their linguistic group sometimes complained that their children were not learning a Maya language because there was no father at home who could speak it.

Vendors have engaged their differences, but they have also recognized similarities among themselves. They share the same types of market experiences. They relate to Ladino and foreign tourists, and to the ways they are reduced or demeaned by Ladinos and foreigners, in similar ways. It is in the marketplace, during lulls in business, that vendors discuss what is wrong with tourists, the Guatemalan government, and other governments. Their self-identification as Mayas or *indígenas* is informed by the changing gender concepts and roles discussed in this chapter, as they live in contemporary national and international social, economic, and political spheres, not in the imaginary feminized Maya world that is described in tourism discourses.

There is a tension, though, between the similarities they find as Mayas and the differences they encounter as Kaqchikeles or K'iche's. A tourist's action or a Ladino's comment may divide or unify vendors along ethnic lines. Some saw the appropriation of items made by one community or linguistic group as the recognition of a common Maya culture. Others felt that the appropriation of one community's crafts by another community was a form of conquest that denied them some of their agency for self-expression. Such tensions are present in the divisions between ethnic and class groups.

By taking an economic look at the market, which focuses on transactions of goods and money, the marketplace would not seem like such a contested terrain. But the *típica* marketplace is the locale where different classes, cultural groups, and genders come together. Mayas engage and confront other Mayas, Ladinos, and foreign tourists within a social terrain that is framed by gender. Few sales began and ended with just an exchange of money; just as frequently, the vendor or buyer might ask a question about the other or begin a conversion. The marketplace provides an arena that allows vendors to personally interact with the Other (the tourist) and with each other.

The *típica* marketplace is a place where men generally depend on women. By working in a marketplace where Maya women are the most culturally visible and desired by tourists, Maya men are changing their concepts about traditional gender roles outside of the marketplace and in their homes. These changes began as far back as the 1930s, when Maya women began to participate in great numbers in tourism. However, most changes related to gender and political attitudes have occurred in the 1990s, when men began to participate more in tourism and do tasks that had been considered female. Cooking, cleaning, and taking care of children has become work for males and females, just as working in a bank, managing a restaurant, and being an applied linguist are jobs that either male or female children of economically successful vendors may equally perform. These changes in the marketplace and in household organization have the potential to contribute to political change.

Chapter 6   The Places Kaqchikel Maya Vendors Call Home

Scenario I

Antonio spends an average of twenty days a month selling *típica* at the Compañía de Jesús Artisan Marketplace in Antigua. His wife, Antonieta, spends roughly ten days a month there. Although they have rented an apartment in Antigua for ten years, neither would consider Antigua their home. Comalapa is home.

Scenario II

Lisette and her daughters, Norma and Yolanda, live in Antigua and sell in the Compañía de Jesús Artisan Marketplace seven days a week. Although Lisette and her husband permanently moved to Antigua several years ago specifically to develop her *típica* business, she and her daughters do not consider Antigua their home. San Antonio is home.

Scenario III

Manuel and Francisco also sell *típica* in the Compañía de Jesús Artisan Marketplace and usually spend twenty-six days a month there. For the past four years they have rented a couple of rooms in Antigua with other male vendor friends. They do not consider Antigua home either. Solalá is home.

Introduction

Many *típica* vendors pass more hours, days, and weeks in Antigua than they do in the respective towns they call home. No matter how long they had been in Antigua, nor how familiar they were with the people and places of the city, they never considered it the place they call home. This chapter will look specifically at how Kaqchikel vendors maintain social connections to those places they call home and examine the ways that their sense of community has changed for them as a result of entering the tourism industry as vendors of *típica*. Because participation in the international tourism market has changed vendors' participation in life in their hometowns, it is productive to fuse Appadurai's (1996, 1998) concept of locality with Watanabe's concept of community. I address the theoretical concerns raised by Appadurai about how self and Other are differentiated in a particular, transnationally oriented/impacted locale, and those by Watanabe about what makes a place significant to ethnic identity, because many people throughout Guatemala, and indeed the world, have been impacted by such transnational movements. Whereas Appadurai looks at the movements of people, ideas, and things, I examine the ways that people who have not left their nation deal with, embrace, and reject these flows. It is important to recognize that place for Mayas is irreducible (Watanabe 1990). They are inscribed in that place, physically and ideologically, through their daily practices. Place (home) matters to Mayas as well as to the Guatemalan government and international tourism agencies.

In addition, this chapter looks at the ways that Mesoamerican communities have traditionally been regarded by anthropologists and seeks to explain the newer community configurations of the towns these vendors consider home. I will return to the previously mentioned people and use others to illustrate how community continues to be an important context through which Kaqchikel Maya vendors organize their lives socially and economically, despite living and working much of the time outside their hometowns.

By focusing on the similar means that *típica* vendors in Antigua use to stay connected to their home communities, this chapter lays a contextual base for the next two chapters, Chapter 7, "Home as a Place of Exhibition and Performance in San Antonio Aguas Calientes," and Chapter 8,

"Marketing Maya Culture in Santa Catarina Palopó, Guatemala." These chapters look at two different, specific cases where community and household are being redefined and contested as the result of the globalization of commodities, media, and tourism.

Background

When I began my fieldwork, I had not imagined becoming more than marginally involved with Kaqchikel vendors' hometowns. The project was to be confined to the tourism market in Antigua, with occasional visits to their respective towns to help provide contextual depth. As I spent more time studying the social relations of the vendors, it became apparent that conceptions of community, along with others like occupation, language, ethnicity, and ideology, were significant to their constructions of identity and place. Indeed, as Watanabe (1990, 1992) has shown, place and identity, localized specifically as community, continues to be one of the more prominent ways that Mayas conceive of their identities. Unlike Mesoamerican ethnographers such as John Watanabe (1992) and Alan Sandstrom (1991), who have thought critically about the concept of community, I came to study Maya communities in a similar fashion to Michael Kearney (1996), because I met Mayas who were living and working away from their hometowns, as did he with respect to the Mixtecs.

Since Robert Redfield's first ethnographies, *Tepoztlán* (1930) and *Chan Kom* with Alfonso Villa Rojas (1934), anthropological studies in Mesoamerica have tended to focus on communities (equated to small towns), which have been treated as self-contained units that could be scientifically studied in isolation from other small towns. The nature of the community as the ideal unit of investigation in Mesoamerica was further naturalized as anthropologists and other researchers drew on and reinterpreted the work of Sol Tax and Eric Wolf. Tax (1937) argued that cultural unity could be found at the level of the *municipio,* not at the level of language or ethnicity. More than by language, he found that identity was marked the most according to *municipio* when Mayas interacted within marketplaces. Wolf's (1957) concept of "closed-corporate peasant communities" contributed even more to the naturalization of small Mesoamerican towns as units of anthropological investigation. Unlike Tax's theory, which was really about difference, Wolf's theory incorporated historical and ethnohistorical research as a way to help explain the relative stability of peasant communities, their resistance to change, and their place in Latin American society. As he illustrates, different historical conditions in relationship to local cultural attitudes contribute to the degree a community is open or closed (Wolf and Hansen 1972). As Watanabe (1992: 227) notes, Wolf's concept of the closed-corporate peasant community has been misread by many Mesoamericanists because it is used as "a standard against which the 'community-ness' of actual communities is measured."[1] Although community for Wolf was an ideal type in the Weberian sense, and he never actually did community-based research, he, along with Redfield, inspired several generations of ethnographers who ignored the ways people in these places were embedded in broader socioeconomic and political contexts.

Because Kaqchikeles have been nearest to or directly but unwillingly incorporated into the mechanisms of the Guatemalan state, they have become particularly adept at resistance. As Judith Maxwell (1996: 195) puts it, "The Kaqchikeles, then, to a greater extent than many other Maya groups of highland Guatemala, have been under heavy and constant pressure to adopt non-Indian ways, particularly in language and in dress. Throughout their history, the Kaqchikeles have sidestepped direct attempts at assimilation and, whenever possible, have turned colonial policies around to serve their own ends." At first glance, community may continue to be an important geographic place and concept used to orient one's identity and serve as a base of resistance, but such a position must be looked at critically in broader social, economic, and political terms than the community itself.

Recently, anthropologists have thought about communities in terms that related them to regional, national, and global processes (Appadurai 1998; Carlsen 1997; Kearney 1996; MacCannell 1992; Nash 1993a; Sandstrom 1991; Smith 1984). When looking beyond the community that he studied, Sandstrom (1991) learned that the non-mestizo place of Amatlán, Mexico, with its local indigenous practices and knowledge, provided a base for resistance to, as well as a refuge from, dominant Mexican groups. Sandstrom, like Watanabe (1990, 1992), shows how and why the concept of community continues to be important to indigenous people in Mesoamerica and is still a pervasive way for them to conceive of identity. Instead of accepting community as a natural unit of investigation, they, like the other just-mentioned ethnographers, look at community in conceptual terms from indigenous perspectives. Community, then, is a significant unit to investigate because it reflects indigenous perspectives, and not exclusively those of the anthropologist.

Going into the field, I pointedly avoided treating the community as a natural unit of investigation—so much so, that it did not matter to me if I actually did research in a Maya town. As my life became more involved in the lives of the vendors, it became apparent that for them community meant, in Watanabe's (1990: 185) words, "relating to the world not only in particularly Mayan ways but from particular Mayan places as well." Hence, I learned from vendors that they conceived of their respective hometowns, not the marketplace in Antigua, as their communities. It is the concept of community, held in common and demonstrated through social relations and practices, that matters most to me in this chapter. For this reason, I do not focus on one particular local community.

Conceiving of and Constructing Community

Each Friday afternoon, Antonio packs his merchandise into four large *bultos* for the *cargadores* to put into storage in a warehouse across the street from the Compañía de Jesús Artisan Marketplace. Then he boards a bus for Chimaltenango, a major crossroads for travelers wanting to catch buses to numerous towns along the Pan-American Highway and beyond. There he transfers to another bus, which will take him to San Juan de Comalapa. This is his hometown, the place where he grew up, where his ancestors came from, and where his children and their spouses live. He will spend the weekend with his extended family, with the exception of his wife and one or two of his daughters, who will leave before dawn on Saturday to go to the Compañía de Jesús Artisan Marketplace. On Monday morning, Antonio will return to Antigua, where he will briefly meet his wife and daughters before they get on the bus to go back to Comalapa. Catching the buses on Friday evenings and on Monday mornings is particularly difficult because they are filled with people who commute not only from their towns to Guatemala City but also to other towns like Antigua and San Juan de Sacatepéquez, where several maquiladoras are located. On Fridays, buses bound for Comalapa are so full of riders that they often speed past Chimaltenango without stopping, which is problematic for Antonio. On some occasions when they have left Antigua after 4:30 PM on a Friday, he and his daughters have been stranded in Chimaltenango. Sometimes they return to their apartment in Antigua, but most times they catch another bus to Zaragoza, a Ladino town located on the turn-off to, and seventeen kilometers from, Comalapa, where they hope to catch a ride with someone from Comalapa who has a pickup truck. On Monday mornings from 4:00 AM to 9:00 AM, fifteen or twenty minutes apart, the buses in Comalapa fill to capacity with students heading to Chimaltenango, Antigua, Quetzaltenango, and Guatemala City; with office workers, waiters, cooks, and construction laborers commuting to work in Guatemala City, Antigua, and Chimaltenango; and with vendors going to Antigua and Guatemala City.

Similarly, other vendors leave their hometowns of San Antonio Aguas Calientes and Santa Catarina Barahona to sell handicrafts in Antigua. Like Antonio, they contend with people-packed buses and long work days in Antigua's tourism market. Because these towns are so close to Antigua, roughly seven kilometers, vendors send their spouses and children back and forth between their hometowns and Antigua on a daily basis. Family members will meet their vendor relatives in Antigua for take-out pizza from Domino's or boxed fried chicken lunches from Pollo Campero, a popular fast-food restaurant in Guatemala and El Salvador. Most days vendors from San Antonio Aguas Calientes and Santa Catarina Barahona leave their houses after an early breakfast and return to them in the evening, too tired from their day to do much other than eat dinner and watch a little television, perhaps the evening news and action-oriented programs like *Renegade* and *MacGyver.*

Manuel and his friends choose to avoid the rush-hour commutes. They travel to their homes in the Sololá–Los Encuentros area of Guatemala, between Lake Atitlán and Tecpán, during off-hours and -days. The days are spent in isolation from their families, selling in the marketplace by day and watching television or listening to the radio in the evenings. Once per month they leave Antigua on a Monday or Tuesday morning and return early Friday morning, traveling opposite the flow of commuters. As long as they are in Antigua during the busiest days for tourism, Friday through Sunday evening, they are content to travel home on the quieter weekdays.

As *típica* vendors in Antigua commute from Comalapa, San Antonio Aguas Calientes, Santa Catarina Barahona, San Juan Sacatepéquez, Santo Domingo Xenacoj, San Antonio Palopó, Santa Catarina Palopó, Sololá, and other towns, they are a small part of the commuters that travel regularly in Guatemala. Their traveling outside of their respective towns for reasons of work is considered a normal, everyday occurrence. Few people that I met on my many rides to and from these various towns had any hopes of working or studying exclusively in their hometowns. Employment and educational opportunities for most people were to be found outside their towns, in Guatemala City, Quetzaltenango, and Antigua, the places where economic and political power has been concentrated since colonial times. People confessed that, though they regretted spending time away from their families, they enjoyed the better wages and the opportunities to interact with people outside of their communities. Many Kaqchikeles under thirty years of age, males and females, have traveled between their hometowns and schools, and then to their jobs, since they were twelve years old. Commuting is a way of life for them, and it is accepted by the members of their family and town who do not leave.

As early as 1981, Nash described in a review article for the *Annual Review of Anthropology* how some ethnographers had been using the world capitalist system as one of their paradigms to better understand and contextualize the communities where they were conducting research. It was also during this same time period that Smith (1978, 1984) urged anthropologists to look at indigenous communities within regional, national, and global contexts, but to do so critically rather than blindly overlay world systems and other global theories on their ethnographic data.[2] Although Smith's (1972) early research in the 1970s on regional and national market systems in the western highlands of Guatemala certainly shed light on the economic fluidity of Maya communities, Goldín's 1985 dissertation, which analyzed the symbolic aspects of markets in the same area where Smith conducted her research, shows that marketplaces continued to be the places where Mayas recognized and maintained their differences in terms of community (or *municipio*), just as Tax (1937) had argued nearly fifty years earlier. The K'iche' Mayas that Goldín worked with conceived of themselves as morally good and of those who were outsiders (other than Ladinos, who were always evil) as ambiguous, potentially good or evil (1985: 250). Vendors from far-off towns were regarded with suspicion. Until the late 1970s or early 1980s, one usually only left one's town to work on coffee, cotton, sugarcane, or other plantations for brief periods of time.[3] Traveling vendors thus represented a minority of the population, especially those who traveled long distances from their homes. It seems that even though Maya communities were part of global systems with regard to the exchange of commodities and their dependence on (good and bad) national and global economic policies, the majority of Mayas were bound to their communities, rather than accustomed to leaving and working outside of them. However, the hottest period of Guatemala's internal war between the military and the UNRG, combined with an economic recession in the early 1980s, forced thousands of Guatemalans out of their communities (Carmack 1988; Montejo 1999).

By the late 1990s, working and living part of the time away from one's natal community, among strangers and non-kin persons, was common not only in Guatemala but also in other areas of the world. Since 1990, Appadurai (1996) has championed the theory that contemporary late-capitalist life is characterized by global flows of people, commodities, and media. In a similar vein, Gupta and Ferguson (1997) argue that direct links between people and places can no longer be automatically assumed. Appadurai (1998) theorizes that globalization has contributed to the rise in ethnic violence because the social, economic, and political dimensions of communities have changed dramatically, leading to new social meanings and roles that are misunderstood. George Marcus (1995) explains that these changes in population, commodity, and media flows have led to new methodologies as anthropologists have struggled to understand and explain the lives of contemporary people. All this suggests that the traditional anthropological concept of a bounded community is obsolete and that community-based research can only yield limited information (Kearney 1996). These scholars do not take seriously enough why specific places (home, community) can mean so much to the people they study nor why some indigenous people still try to imagine their community to be self-contained, which, by contrast, are issues Watanabe (1992) and Sandstrom (1991) address.

The changes that Appadurai, Marcus, Gupta and Ferguson, and other anthropologists describe have contributed to the new ways that community is conceived of by anthropologists and their subjects, as well as how communities are constructed by their members. No longer is the perspective of open and closed communities adequate for conceptualizing the communities constructed by Mesoamericans, be they Maya, Zapotec, Nahuatl, or any other linguistic group originally from that geographic region delineated as Mesoamerica. Open and closed communities link people to a specific town, which is now located within increasingly larger geopolitical spheres of region, nation-state, and world. A community may be open or closed in relation to the forces that act on it and the ways members of that community participate in or resist larger, more dominant nation-state and world economic and political systems.

Recent anthropological research in Mesoamerica suggests that three general types of communities can be observed. None of these community types is mutually exclusive for any one group of people, and people live in actual physical and ideological communities, which include aspects of all three types. At one pole are the types of communities that Sandstrom (1991) and Watanabe (1992) describe. These ethnographers look at how locality is reproduced and made meaningful to the members of the respective communities they studied—Amatlán, Mexico, and Santiago Chimaltenango, Guatemala. For instance, Sandstrom found that naming and ritual language were so highly localized that one was not truly a member of the community if one did not know this local knowledge. Similarly, Watanabe shows that community is constructed through the constant social interaction of persons linked linguistically and historically to a particular place. In both of these towns, residents participated in and were incorporated into larger social, political, and economic systems than the local community, but the latter could tactically be considered self-contained in terms of the knowledge and rituals specific to the place.[4]

At the other pole of community types are those studied by Michael Kearney (1996) and W. Warner Wood (2000). These anthropologists conducted the types of multisite fieldwork projects that Marcus (1995) describes. The resulting ethnographies are not "merely a different kind of controlled comparison" (Marcus 1995: 102) but ethnographies whose subjects are mobile. They live, work, and socialize in more than one place. Kearney's research with Mixtec speakers led him to a community that was located on both sides of and on the U.S.-Mexican border, in Riverside, California, in San Jerónimo, Oaxaca, Mexico, and in the border town of Tijuana, Mexico. Wood studied Zapotec speakers who constructed multisite households and communities that included their hometown of Teotitlán del Valle, Oaxaca, Mexico; other places in Mexico; and Santa Fe, New Mexico. He found that not only was community dispersed and transnational but households were dispersed and transnational. The integration of these households was maintained by the movement of people, money, and commodities among the places the households were located.

Both Kearney and Wood followed their respective subjects (à la Marcus 1995) who were constructing new communities, in part, for economic reasons. The new places where Mixtecs and Zapotecs are living relate to the types of jobs they do or can do. Hence Mixtecs go to California primarily to work in agriculture and construction, and Zapotecs go to

Santa Fe to sell specialty textiles to tourists and shopowners. In these cases, travel between the places they live and their hometowns, the original communities, tends to be limited at best to visits for special or unusual circumstances, such as town festivals, rituals, baptisms, weddings, and funerals. A person may leave home and construct satellite households and communities in contemporary Mesoamerica for numerous reasons, for example, to escape poverty or military persecution. Often this person continues to foster social and economic ties to that place designated as home, even though frequent trips back home are difficult because of the distance, the danger and expense of crossing international borders, and, depending on one's job, the reluctance to give up a job in order to go home. Despite the fact that Mixtecs and Zapotecs may have limited contact with their towns of origin, these multisite communities are integrated to some degree, and the place called home maintains special significance because remittances from the work they do in the United States helps fund rituals, festivals, house construction, and subsistence for those still in towns like San Jerónimo and Teotitlán.[5]

A third community type, which has not been given much treatment anthropologically, is one in which multisite households may be constructed, but residents of the home community have regularized social and economic relations with people who live, partly or even mostly, outside their home community. These are the types of communities constructed by the vendors that I studied, but equally by other people who commute for work, like maquiladora workers, construction workers, schoolteachers, and social workers. Often these workers establish households in the towns where they work, returning home on weekends; for vacations, family and town celebrations, and tragedies; or according to personal whim. Unlike the previous examples, these people are able to travel easily between the multiple households and places that make up their community, since they are not restricted by international boundaries or expensive travel fares. Extended family members know the vendors' households and marketplaces in Antigua as well as their households in their hometowns. The movement between places is not limited to the workers—vendors, in my case—but includes other family members who visit the places away from home out of curiosity, to carry news, or to vacation, which is the reason that Manuel's wife, children, and sister-in-law periodically visited him in Antigua.

In these three types of communities, the location of origin is a special place that residents relate to or identify with, be it of a more singular nature, as in the examples from Sandstrom and Watanabe; or of a more dispersed nature, as in the cases of Kearney and Wood; or somewhere in between, like my example. When I asked vendors why they did not just cut their ties to their hometowns, they consistently responded with horror, indignity, or bewilderment. Some commented that then they would be like me, like other Americans, who have no place and do not even know what having a place is. They would be alone (*qiyon*—literally "we are alone") in the world because family, place, and customs, to liberally paraphrase Watanabe, are what make them and their communities. What community is and how it is constructed is changing physically and ideologically, but home, the origin town, in these cases is regarded as the most significant, the most important of all the places where Mesoamericans locate themselves.

Staying Connected to Home

Kaqchikel *típica* vendors make sure that they are active members of their hometowns in relation to family, rituals, economic contributions, and general social activities with others in their community. For these activities or cultural practices to have meaning for the vendors and be recognized by their extended family and the community at large, they must be done in the place that they call home. In other words, being a member of one's community and having the right to claim a place as one's hometown has to do with public participation. If a person does not maintain his or her connection to the place and the people who live in the place on a regular basis, then that person is not a member of the community. Brothers and sisters, sons and daughters, or cousins of Kaqchikel vendors who left their town of origin are not considered part of the home community if they do not maintain regular social relations. Hence, the vision of community is maintained by the practice of excluding or writing off those who do not conform to community norms, which, as Watanabe (1990, 1992) and Warren (1989, 1998a) show, are always in process.

For example, Ramón and Everilda speak proudly of their son's success in Los Angeles, California. On several occasions they have visited him, his wife of Mexican origin, and their grandchildren, who have never been to San Antonio Aguas Calientes. Though he is their son, he is not a member of the San Antonio Aguas Calientes community. He is, they

Mayas in the Marketplace

related sadly to me on one occasion, not really even Kaqchikel, since he lives, works, and socializes in the United States with English and Spanish speakers.

Throughout the rest of this section, I map out and describe how vendors use selected economic, ritual, and social activities to retain their membership in their respective communities. Although I look at these activities as separate categories for analysis, they clearly overlap each other. This vantage point from which to view Maya communities does not yield any monolithic descriptions of what these communities are like, but demonstrates, instead, the efforts vendors make to belong to their respective communities.

MILPAS

The most important of all social, family, and economic activities that help connect vendors, especially men, to their hometown is cultivating one's *awän* (milpa, or cornfield). In my early visits to San Antonio Aguas Calientes, Santa Catarina Barahona, San Juan Sacatepéquez, San Juan de Comalapa, and other towns, one of the first things that my hosts did was show me their milpa, if they grew one, or that of a close relative who did. The significance of working a milpa in terms of subsistence, collective identity, and ritual is well documented in Mesoamerican ethnography.

Alicia Re Cruz (1996) illustrates that Mayas in Chan Kom, Mexico, refer to their jobs in the tourism industry as "their other milpa." Watanabe (1990: 187) describes subsistence maize agriculture as one of the "three constants [that] continue to shape Chimalteco life and livelihood." Growing maize is one of the foundations for building one's soul. According to Watanabe (1992: 92), "those who cease to work regularly in their *milpas* . . . fall somewhat in the estimation of their neighbors." To emphasize the importance of the milpa, Annis (1987: 60) comments, "Within the Indian sphere, the *milpa,* not commodity production, was the basis of local economies and social organization." Richard Wilson (1995: 121) explains that "the planting [of maize] serves as a forum for expressing and creating collective identities."

Although women tend not to participate directly in the agricultural cycles associated with maize, except in some areas where they help with weeding and harvesting (Wilson 1995: 42), they do perform roles that connect them to maize and are equally socially significant. Watanabe (1992: 35) reports that women take lunch, which includes corn tortillas, to men working in the milpa. Making tortillas is one of the practices by which women in Santiago Chimaltenango acquire their soul (Watanabe 1992: 92). Among Q'eqchi' Mayas, tortilla making by women is important female knowledge, without which men claim "that they would starve" (Wilson 1995: 41). What is commonly overlooked in these and other ethnographies about Mesoamerica (Annis 1987; Cohen 1999; Ehlers 1990; Sandstrom 1991; Stephen 1991; Warren 1989) is the sociality of maize preparation for women. Maya girls and women, who rise early in the morning to take their corn to be ground, meet other girls and women with whom they socialize around the noisy mill. Maya women also work together at weddings, baptisms, religious confirmations, and funerals to prepare maize-based ceremonial dishes like tamales. Female vendors stayed connected to their hometowns by participating in these activities.

In the above examples, maize farming constitutes a major part of the social and economic lives of these ethnographers' subjects. By contrast, for handicraft vendors, the milpa was often of minimal economic importance. Some, such as Antonio, put great emphasis on growing maize. He and his wife purchased additional land to meet the subsistence needs of their family. Teaching his sons to "make milpa" and seeing them continue to plant is important to him because it demonstrates to the community at large that they keep up traditions, have a good work ethic, and provide for their families. When one of his sons does not help, which happens more frequently because they have teaching and publishing jobs that take them away from their hometown of Comalapa, he describes them as "*q'oran*" (lazy). In fact, to be called *q'oran* is one of the more powerful insults one can give.

For Kaqchikel vendors, planting maize and being a maize farmer have more symbolic than economic value. The symbolic value of maize for them, however, is more mundane than the examples provided by Sandstrom (1991), Watanabe (1992), and Wilson (1995). Many of the male vendors and the husbands of female vendors from the towns of San Antonio Aguas Calientes and Santa Catarina Barahona that do not plant a milpa do plant a few plants of maize within their household compounds. Early in my fieldwork, when I surveyed vendors selling in the Compañía de Jesús about the types of work identities they assumed, they corrected the category *campesino,* which not one person ascribed to. Instead, they informed me, they were *tikonela',* "farmers," or literally "those who plant."

They were emphatic that they were not campesinos. These men also impressed upon me their knowledge of maize farming, explaining planting schedules, maintenance of the plants, and harvests. On the household altars of both Protestant and Catholic families, they placed four colors of maize: *räx ixim* (black), *säq ixim* (white), *q'än ixim* (yellow), and *käq ixim* (red), symbolizing the four cardinal directions, the four basic elements of the world, and the "four races of humanity." Saying that they are *tikonela'*, planting maize plants, and placing maize in their household altars are ways that men, in particular, connect with the past, the community, and the spiritual realm.

For vendors like Antonio and Manuel, who plant maize for household consumption, cultivating their *awän* signifies hard work and demonstrates that one is a *samajel*, a "worker," to others in their community. It also demonstrates to them that the vendors are still members of the community because they must go from their house located in the *tinamït* (town or city) where they live to their fields in the *juyu'* ("countryside," or literally "hill"). Along the way they pass neighbors and walk with other men who have fields nearby or adjoining theirs. Kaqchikeles explained that *tinamït* is where people live. The *juyu'* is where wild plants and animals live. The *awän* is one of the things that symbolically links these two realms together, being literally in between them, a point that Warren (1989) explained in her ethnography of San Andrés Semetabaj. Vendors who keep a milpa have to return home to their fields periodically in order to plant, tend, and harvest the maize. The trips home and the fieldwork are publicly noted. Neighbors comment favorably on well-tended milpas, and owners modestly reply that their *awän* are "sickly, barely alive."

PATRONIZING LOCAL STORES AND PERIODIC MARKETPLACES

Additional economically related practices that link *típica* vendors to their home communities include regularly patronizing a neighborhood *tienda* (store) and attending the local periodic marketplace. Although some male vendors participate in these arenas, women tend to be the primary participants, as has been well documented in the ethnography of Mayas in Guatemala (Bossen 1984; Bunzel 1959; Ehlers 1991; Glittenberg 1994; Swetnam 1988; Tax 1953; and others). Generally in Guatemala, as in other

vendor is a male or when a female vender is marrying a man from the same town. Although the party is initially closed to uninvited guests, once the meal has been served, just about anyone can join the celebration, regardless of religious faith. The Protestant weddings I attended were relatively more restricted, but even in those, when the meal was over, uninvited guests came,[10] and they were never asked to leave.

One Protestant couple from San Antonio Aguas Calientes explained why having a big church wedding was important to them. They had had a civil marriage seven years prior to their church wedding and had demonstrated to their respective families and members of the community their commitment to each other and later to their children. For persons eighteen or older, few in the community think anything unusual about two people uniting and living as a married couple. A civil ceremony is regarded as a Ladino requirement, which does not fulfill spiritual and community expectations. However, for the community to sanction the union, a church wedding is proper. The couple explained that the wedding would honor both their parents and the people in the town. They could have easily married quietly in their church and saved a great deal of money. Instead, they staged an elaborate wedding, paying for it themselves. They are relatively successful vendors and sold one of their two pickup trucks to pay for the party. A small wedding procession led from the groom's father's house in San Andrés Ceballos (an *aldea* [neighborhood, hamlet] of San Antonio, though residents consider it a separate town) to the bride's parents' house, centrally located in San Antonio, eventually arriving at their church in Santa Catarina Barahona. By the time it had reached the church, several hundred people were present, and no one could doubt that the couple were committed to both of their families and the town.

Cofradía PARTICIPATION

The previous examples also illustrate that spiritual or religious practices help vendors stay connected to their hometowns. One practice they participate in—though of lessening importance to vendors these days—is the *cofradía*. The *cofradía,* or *cargo* system, has been described by various anthropologists working in Mesoamerica.[11] *Cofradías* in contemporary Guatemala have little to do with the civil government, and some priests, especially charismatic ones, want to end the *cofradías.* In some towns, such as Santiago Atitlán and Panajachel, *cofradías* exist outside of the church. Whether they operate with or without the support of the Catholic Church, *cofradías* are time-consuming and expensive organizations to participate in. In addition to contributing money and labor to the titular festival and numerous smaller ceremonial dances and rituals during their year of service, participants must keep the church (or the *cofradía* house) clean and the saints fed and happy with candles, flowers, and hard liquor. Participation for *típica* vendors is even more difficult than for other members of the community because they work in other towns. To compound matters, *cofradía* participation among Kaqchikeles requires the participation of both spouses. Those who are not married, or whose spouse refuses to participate, cannot serve in the *cofradía*. Because female vendors work and sell in the marketplace with their husbands, it is difficult to fulfill *cofradía* duties and run the *típica* business. For couples who rely on *típica* sales for their subsistence needs, *cofradía* service is impossible, especially for younger couples. Older couples with nearly grown children can participate in the *cofradía* more easily than younger couples because their children can watch their booth in the marketplace and help out with some of the menial work that must be done for the *cofradía*.

Despite the difficulties, vendors do participate in the *cofradía,* although more do so indirectly by contributing money to their relatives who wish to participate. *Cofradía* service is recognized by vendors as a sacrifice and burden on the officeholders. Among the couples who work in the Compañía de Jesús Artisan Marketplace and had recently served in a *cofradía,* every one of them said that they would never take a *cofradía* office again. One man and his wife, from Santa Catarina Palopó, complained that their responsibilities were so rigorous that they almost lost their *típica* business. On another occasion, I made an offhand remark to an older (in her sixties) vendor woman from San Antonio Aguas Calientes that the Kaqchikel verb *-samäj* (to work), and the word for "worker," *samajel,* were about the same as *ajsamaj,* the generic name for a masculine *cofradía* position. Her reply was that of course they were from the word *work* because serving in the *cofradía* is work. She went on to explain that participation in the *cofradía* is good for a number of reasons. It shows that spouses can work together, that they have the moral and economic support of their extended families, and that they are members of the community. She and her husband, who helps her in the marketplace but is a *tikonel* and spends most of his time in the milpa, have participated in the *cofradía* a few times.

The most important purely social activity for vendors is the titular festival of their hometown. All Kaqchikel vendors try to go home for their *nimaq'ij*. During festival days, which are scheduled for the week around the day commemorating the patron saint, vendors from that town leave Antigua. For example, around June 13, vendors from San Antonio Aguas Calientes and San Antonio Palopó spend most of the week in their towns celebrating Saint Anthony of Padua. During the week of June 24, vendors from Comalapa return home to honor their patron, Saint John the Baptist. Residents from Santa Catarina Barahona and Santa Catarina Palopó celebrate Saint Catherine of Alexandria on November 25, and so it goes with the patron saints of all the other towns vendors come from. During the dates of titular festivals, vendors went out of their way to extend invitations to me to visit them and attend the festivities by offering room and board. "You don't have to pay. We are inviting you," I was assured as the *nimaq'ij* approached. According to them, their town was at its finest and the people were happy during the festival.

A *nimaq'ij*, or titular festival, in a Maya town includes several days of *cofradía* activities (the most important occurring on the feast day of the saint). There are fireworks, folk dances, processions, live music, discos, special foods, Ferris wheels and other amusement park rides, games of chance, and plenty of alcoholic beverages to drink. The fiestas, while honoring Catholic saints, are not exclusive to Catholics and are also attended by Protestants, especially children, who enjoy the food and the rides. The festivals are open and widely attended by Mayas and Ladinos alike. Female residents of the town hosting the festival spend months weaving new *p'ot* (*huipiles*, or "blouses"). Men and boys purchase new pants and shirts. In addition to fair food like candy, corn on the cob, and sweet bread, special foods like *xaq q'utu'n* in San Antonio Aguas Calientes and Santa Catarina Barahona, *ruyal q'utu'n* in Comalapa, and *pulik*[12] in San Antonio Palopó and Santa Catarina Palopó are served at almost every meal. For vendors, it is an important time to be seen and to get confirmation from others that they are still members of the community. At the same time, they prove they are members of their community by participating in fun activities, eating traditional foods, and, especially for females, dressing in new, community-specific clothing.

Each of the examples of means of maintaining ties to their hometown illustrates the social relations that vendors foster in their communities. These include participation in activities, which shows their neighbors that they are materially and spiritually connected to the place. They particularly try to engage in public social events where others can see them. In other instances, like milpa farming and even *cofradía* participation, where they may not be seen, the results of their labor are seen by their fellow townspeople. Because *envidia,* or "jealousy," long a topic in Mesoamerican ethnography,[13] is commonly expressed in vendors' hometowns, vendors are also expected to demonstrate that they are only as successful as their neighbors, hiding other evidence of greater material success within parts of their homes to which visitors do not have access. For example, vendors often have a small television in a common area, such as a kitchen or parlor, but the big color television, sometimes with the cable connection, was located in a room that was restricted to immediate family members and close friends. Basically, vendors were expected to and did conform to community norms with regard to displays of consumption. Those who flagrantly ignore these norms are ostracized by their fellow townspeople.

Why Belonging Means So Much

Providing examples of how Kaqchikel Maya vendors stay connected to and part of their respective hometowns does not, however, explain what compels them to want to belong, to be part of a community, especially for those who live most of the time in Antigua. If community is related to local knowledge (Sandstrom 1991) and maintaining specific social relationships within a specific place (Watanabe 1990, 1992), why would vendors, like Lisette and her family as well as others who spend the majority of their time in Antigua, work hard to be members of communities they do not live in or are away from most of the time? To phrase it in another, more general way, why would individuals in the people-commodity-media-idea-flowing postmodern world (Appadurai 1996; MacCannell 1992) work hard to be part of a community that may be, according to Watanabe (1990: 302), "divided by tensions between old and young over household resources and political power . . . , by economic inequities of the extended family household cycle . . . , by the atomism of kinship, residence, and economic necessity . . ."?

Although anthropologists no longer take community for granted, noting instead how people and commodities enter and leave their respective communities, how the national dominant society acts on indigenous communities, and, in some cases, how these communities have become tourism objects (see Carlsen 1997; Castañeda 1996; García Canclini 1993; Kearney 1996; Nash 1993; Sandstrom 1991; Smith 1984; Stephen 1991; Watanabe 1992), they have less to say about why people put energy into belonging to a community. Even though this may be so, these researchers do not see community membership as automatically given, as does Robert Redfield (1960) in *The Little Community*.

A possible explanation for the desire to belong to one's hometown may have to do with land ownership or access, but for vendors this is inadequate because they are content to plant their symbolic maize plants in the courtyard of their houses and not buy and farm milpa land. Xavier Albó (1997: 142) explains that Aymaras migrate to La Paz, Bolivia, because they can't earn sufficient wages in their hometowns. What keeps them tied to their home communities is land or, they hope, future access to land. Certainly, access to a small piece of milpa land is a reason that vendors such as Antonio and Manuel return home. For vendors and others in these towns who still have some land, planting milpa helps them stay connected. Others who purchased land did not plant it themselves, but rented it out to nonvendors in their respective community. Though this does not have the symbolic import that planting a milpa does, it does keep them connected to their hometown. Purchasing land, especially if it is land that one rented from or on which one worked as a laborer for Ladinos, may have important symbolic meaning because it inverts earlier patterns of ownership and economic exploitation (Warren 1989). Antonio's land purchases may also be interpreted in this way. Mayas from his town of Comalapa and others were forced to work for Ladino landowners in earlier periods (Carey 2001; McCreery 1994; Petrich 1996a, 1996d; Smith 1990b; Williams 1994). However, when his grade-school-age daughter was asked to write an essay in school about her family being forced to work for Ladino-owned coastal or nearby plantations, her family members exclaimed that they had never worked for Ladinos. Although it is highly unlikely that no one in his family worked for Ladino landowners, purchasing arable land reduced the amount of labor Mayas were required to do during early periods of Guatemala's history (Handy 1984; McCreery 1994), and purchasing land today is considered a form of insurance by vendors and other Mayas.

Land alone does not explain why Lisette and numerous other vendors do not break ties with the towns where they were born. For vendors, who do not own farmland or even want to own it, landownership or the prospect of it does not influence their decisions to integrate themselves into their communities.

A potentially more productive theory—which can be articulated using Appadurai's (1996: 178–200) concepts of locality and Watanabe's (1990: 184–185) ideas of community, both of which explain processes of belonging—is found in Teófilo Altamirano and Lane Hirabayashi's (1997) "Construction of Regional Identities in Urban Latin America." They outline four "needs" that migrants to cities respond to: community, services, employment, and political empowerment. Here I pursue only the need for community. According to Altamirano and Hirabayashi, migration to cities by peasants or indigenous persons entails facing "barriers due to their class and social status" (14). The immigrants contend with social isolation, language differences, and low wages. Although the authors do not mention it, I would assume that being part of a community alleviates some of these problems.

Like Maya handicraft vendors, migrants in Mexico City and Lima, Peru, are concerned with keeping active ties with their hometowns, despite the fact that some live permanently in the large city. Indeed, in studies of dispersed or rural-to-urban communities in Mexico and Peru,[14] rural migrants frequently formed social clubs, sports clubs, and neighborhood associations with others from their hometown or region, which served, among other things, to help them reinforce kinship ties, maintain hometown reciprocal work obligations, lobby the government for basic public services, provide support networks for peers to find jobs, and share cultural values and interests among themselves. Typically, the residents in the urban neighborhood maintain connections to their original hometowns. Although people in both places eventually influence each other in terms of consumptive patterns, political organization, and mutual assistance, the construction of urban communities around associations and clubs also served to buffer migrants from their new and sometimes harsh city environs and help them retain cultural practices they valued.

Although the natal language of the *típica* vendors in question is different from the natal language of Ladinos and tourists, language differences were minimal, since all were fluent in Spanish and many knew basic English. Second, most vendors are urbanites who live in one urban setting and commute to another for work. Third, they are generally not socially isolated and tend to make better wages than most other indig-

and commuting to work from one's hometown to another town within the same country, community linked to a particular place continues to be important to indigenous Mesoamericans.

Homi Bhabha (1994: 230) claims that the "agency of the community-concept 'seeps through the interstices of the objectively constructed, contractually regulated structure of civil society,' class-relations, and national identities. Community disturbs the grand globalizing narrative of capital, displaces the emphasis on production in 'class' collectivity, and disrupts the homogeneity of the imagined community of the nation." Certainly, in relation to such grand social structures as states and world capital economic systems, community appears to be and can be their opposite. However, it is more than this and more than a social space that falls through the cracks of the dominant political and economic institutions. Communities are not merely opposed to, but are also part of, the state and global economic systems.

Kaqchikel vendors' communities, like other communities, may be dispersed in terms of where people live and work. However, the location referred to as home, especially in the cases of Kaqchikel vendors, is still linked to a particular place. This place, its physicality and history, can serve multiple functions, such as a place of refuge from the dominant society, a base for some types of collective identity, a vantage point from which one can understand the world, and a place to leave from and return to. This special position and function of community, linked to a particular place even though its membership may be widely dispersed, helps root Kaqchikel Maya vendors as they engage other places and people.

Chapter 7

Home as a Place of Exhibition and Performance in San Antonio Aguas Calientes

Introduction

In Antigua, there are five-hundred-odd *típica* vendors competing for clients. All sell similar products. All are aware that most tourists will go to other towns like Chichicastenango and Panajachel with similar *típica* marketplaces and products. Vendors are also under pressure from self, family, and fellow townspersons to fulfill obligations in their homes and in their hometowns. In order to outcompete rival vendors and to comply with hometown obligations, some vendors from San Antonio Aguas Calientes have strengthened the links between their town and Antigua and the connection between household and tourism through performances of domestic life for tourists.

In a 1912 article in the *Diario de Centro América*, promoting tourism to Guatemalans and foreigners, San Antonio Aguas Calientes is described as one of the towns "most frequently visited by tourists for its beautiful panoramas." With descriptions of clothing, occupations, and community traditions, it distinguishes women as an attraction by noting that when they are "on the street they use colorful and clean outfits." The article also calls attention to the economic links *antonecos* have with Antigua and Guatemala City, where they go to buy thread for weaving and to sell produce and other items such as mats. The article encapsulates aspects of life in San Antonio Aguas Calientes that are still present today: cultural and economic exchanges with tourists, economic ties outside the community, and the differences between indigenous people and Ladinos.

The links to the nation-state and to global economic and cultural phenomena are further strengthened when it is recognized that San Antonio was one of the first indigenous towns in Guatemala to be missionized by Protestants. Reportedly, a school was founded by U.S. missionaries in 1874 (Brown 1998: 3). By 1909, the Central American Mission had established a permanent clinic and nurses training program (Garrard-Burnett 1996: 34). And in 1917, Cameron Townsend, the founder of the Summer Institute of Linguistics/Wycliffe Bible Translators, arrived in San Antonio, where, over the next twelve years, he would translate the Old Testament into Kaqchikel Maya (Garrard-Burnett 1998: 53; Stoll 1982: 33). Since the beginning of the twentieth century, tourism and missionary activity have intensified.

Instead of looking at the relationship between tourism, craft production, and religion, a topic addressed by scholars doing research in San Antonio (Annis 1987) and other areas of Latin America (Ariel de Vidas 1995; Deitch 1989; Ehlers 1990; García Canclini 1993; Nash 1993a; Stephen 1991; Tice 1995), I explore the use of households as sites for touristic performances. By focusing on these public performances, I explain how gender relations are changing in some households in San Antonio Aguas Calientes.

A well-known tourism destination, San Antonio Aguas Calientes is a relatively prosperous town located near Antigua Guatemala with an indigenous population of 6,262 out of 6,740 people (Rodríguez 1996: 172). Additionally, San Antonio was one of the favored sites for international development when Annis arrived in the late 1970s to conduct fieldwork there, because for over fifty years farmers there had earned "a reputation for being technically progressive, literate, and willing to innovate" (Annis 1987: 44). Although economic development projects are not as common in San Antonio as they were in the past, in part because it is now considered to be relatively developed, educated *antonecos,* as managers and caseworkers, are a common presence in various development agencies operating throughout Guatemala. And farmers have not ceased being innovative, as in the case of one who turned a chance meeting in Antigua with an English traveler into an opportunity to surf the Internet and gather information on making organic fertilizer with earthworms. He now produces more fertilizer than he can use on his own fields and is beginning to sell it.

San Antonio was a well-known tourist destination when I first arrived there in 1987; since then it has become even better known. Kaqchikel women there are world-renowned weavers whose products are collected by American, European, and Japanese aficionados of indigenous clothing. Tourism has grown to be a part of the lives of nearly every person there.

Mayas in the Marketplace

Antonecos keep themselves informed of world events by listening to the radio, reading the newspaper, and, especially, watching television, which they tell me allows them to gain insight into the practices of other peoples and cultures. They use this information to help them figure out tourists. Increasingly, more of them have cable television, which they use to watch programs in English, French, and German to learn new words and strengthen their school lessons in those languages. They also use it to follow teams in the National Basketball Association and the latest goings-on in Hollywood. Some have traveled (and frequently travel) to the United States and to Europe to visit family, conduct business, and vacation.

These flows of people, media, ideas, and commodities in late-twentieth-century San Antonio Aguas Calientes are common aspects of life for people in many places around the globe. In recent years, scholars have studied and commented on the effects of globalization. Specifically, Kearney (1996) focuses on people and economics; Morley and Robins (1995), on global media; Castañeda (1996), on anthropological inquiry and tourism; MacCannell (1992), on tourist consumption; and García Canclini (1993, 1995), Nash (1993a), and Tice (1995), on crafts, to mention but a few. Like the works by Nash (1993b) and Tice (1995), this chapter contributes to the understanding of how indigenous people respond to global cultural, economic, and media flows.

Touristic Performances: Some Background and Contexts

Almost since the first tourists arrived in San Antonio, performance has been a part of textile marketing. Guidebooks and Internet sites frequently portray *antoneca* women seated at their backstrap looms. As Annis (1987: 13) observes, "The image of the San Antonio woman at the loom—clad in her *huipil* of blue and red and orange and a dozen other colors—has become a national icon for use on tourism and export promotion brochures." Indeed, depictions used in tourism literature showing a woman weaving in the courtyard of her home with a child nearby clearly link women to household and domestic chores. Such images purport to be inside, intimate looks at women's work and homes.

Most touristic images of Kaqchikel women, like early visits by tourists to San Antonio, assume a passive subject to be gazed on by the tourist. As far back in time as they can remember, residents of San Antonio tell of tourists wandering through their town looking into their houses and taking pictures, in blatant attempts to get a glimpse of their lives. Women in San Antonio, however, were not and are not oblivious to the tourists' gaze (e.g., Urry 1990). By accommodating tourists, by letting them watch and then offering them woven items for sale, women essentially became part of a global economy of handicraft sales.

The first truly organized performances of indigenous household activities came during the dictatorship of Jorge Ubico (1931–1944) in the Feria de Agosto.[1] Also described as the "national fair 'La Aurora' " and the "Summer Fair," it was regularly held in Guatemala City during Ubico's tenure as dictator. A "Pueblo Indígena" (Indigenous Town) was built as one of several exhibits showcasing Guatemalan industries, development, and people, which were offered along with amusement park rides. Over the years that the fair was held, the Pueblo Indígena was consistently described in the Guatemalan press as the exhibit drawing the largest attendance.

Tourists from Guatemala, Europe, and the United States visited the Pueblo Indígena to see how Mayas lived. Wattle-and-daub houses, called *ranchos,* were constructed, and the village was populated by Maya representatives from various highland communities, who enacted their lives before the gaze of those visiting the fair. Mayas (men, women, and children) were told to weave; fabricate bricks, tiles, and soap; and make fishnets, pottery, and candles. They played music and danced, demonstrated "ancient rituals" (*Diario de Centro América,* August 23, 1932), and otherwise lived in their *ranchos* for the duration of the fair. Women are featured in pictorials caring for children, weaving, and carrying baskets and pots (*Diario de Centro América,* September 8, 1932). *Antonecos* were described as "skillful at certain weavings, such as *güipiles* [blouses], *fajas* [belts], and *ceñidores* [sashes]" (*Diario de Centro América,* August 13, 1932).

Without going into a more thorough description of Ubico's Summer Fair, it is significant to note that households and women were prominently featured in the Pueblo Indígena. Thinking back to her childhood participation in the fair, one now elderly woman explained that it provided an opportunity for women and children "to travel to Guatemala City and meet *indígenas* from all over Guatemala." It was also, she explained, when they began to realize the economic potential of weaving for the tourist market. Even so, Mayas were ordered by Ubico to participate in the fair (*Diario de Centro América,* November 16, 1932; October 29, 1936) as part of a plan to stimulate international tourism and help forge a sense of Guatemalan national identity (*Diario de Centro América,* November 5, 1936; November 19, 1936). The objective was not to provide them with expanded economic and social opportunities. In conjunction with the fair, trilingual (English, Spanish, and German) picture books were published with photographs of San Antonio women weaving at backstrap looms while seated on reed mats in front of *ranchos* (Rubio 1938). Although the fair is now long defunct, tourism packages from companies such as Clark Tours and Kim' Arrim still attract foreign tourists by promising stops in indigenous villages and marketplaces.

Today in San Antonio the performance of household activities takes a variety of guises. The most common is the *típica tienda,* where residents who live along the road entering the town on the way to the Catholic church set up little stores in the street-side room of their houses. These stores, as noted by Annis (1987: 19–21), tend to consist of one room where woven items are offered for sale and a loom is set up for weaving. Weaving allows women to produce more inventory, alleviate the boredom of waiting for tourists, and provide tourists with a show. During the course of my fieldwork, tourists frequently explained that they were enticed into marketplace locales or San Antonio *tiendas* by the sight of indigenous women weaving.

The Pérez family, one of the families Annis (1987: 148 n. 20) describes as having a "monopolistic grip on the local tourist industry," have made use of two other versions of touristic performance. For the past thirty years, they have been the only family officially endorsed by INGUAT, the Guatemalan government's tourism office, and supported by all of the major tour companies operating in Guatemala partly because they pay commissions to guides. One type of performance is presented in a private textile museum in Antigua Guatemala, where weaving demonstrations are offered and mannequins dressed in *traje* are located in displays of household rooms. It is an "in situ" style of exhibit in which household life and the importance of textiles in Maya life are interpreted through a combination of artifacts, constructed settings, and actors. According to Barbara Kirshenblatt-Gimblett (1998: 19), in an "in situ" exhibit, "the object is a part that stands in a contiguous relation to an absent whole that may or may not be re-created." Thus, carefully selected items— a mannequin dressed in a *huipil* and *corte,* a *mano y metate* next to a *comal,* and a few ears of maize, as in one of the exhibits—serve to represent and mimic San Antonio life. Similar displays show female mannequins taking care of children. In the courtyard of the colonial-style house, a group of women weave together, joke with tourists, and answer questions in a form of improvisational theater. The combination museum, retail store, and theater is presented as a type of neutral arena in which tourists can learn the most about Maya life in the shortest amount of time, without having to actually go to a Maya town or household.

The other type of performance, presented at the entrance to San Antonio, is in a store-restaurant where weaving demonstrations are given and local dishes are served. Here tourists watch brief weaving demonstrations and listen to explanations of weaving techniques and the uses of pieces of clothing. They are then invited to purchase and try traditional San Antonio cuisine, such as *pepián,* a dish of stewed chicken smothered in a sauce made from peppers, tomatoes, and onions. The restaurant overlooks the town, offering one of those splendid panoramic views frequently mentioned by tour guides. As part of the performance in this locale, tourists are told of the dangers of San Antonio. It is full of thieves, rabid dogs, and diseases because of its unsanitary conditions. Indeed, upon rereading my journal from my pre-anthropology tourist days in July 1987, my first visit to San Antonio ended at the Pérez *tienda,* when I followed Alida Pérez's advice and did not venture into the town.

These performative arenas are presented as neutral to tourists, but *antonecos* reported feeling combinations of jealousy, anger, and shame that the Pérez family has dominated the tourism market in the Antigua–San Antonio area.[2] Many *antonecos* are so infuriated by the Pérez family that just mentioning their name yielded scathing commentaries on how they "have stolen all the tourists for themselves," "make pacts and payoffs with INGUAT and tour guides," have preyed on the misfortunes of *antonecos* by purchasing prized pieces of handwoven clothing at low prices when families are strapped for cash, and are misinterpreting various traditions— Catholic and Maya. The Pérez family is Protestant, going back several generations. During the celebrations for the *cofradía* Dulce Nombre on January 20, 1998, some *antonecos* constructed a float for the procession that satirized the Pérez family's tourism/textile business. A living diorama, depicting a touristic scene with a marimba, some men dressed in *traje,* and obese women holding up pieces of shabby textiles, was constructed in the back of a pickup truck, which was labeled "Hotel/Posada Alida." Following the float were other *antonecos* dressed as tourists—wearing short pants and sunglasses and taking pictures of each other, the crowd, and the float. As the float passed through the streets, the crowd roared with laughter. For days following the procession, *antonecos* talked about the float—both how hilarious it was and how the Pérez family should feel ashamed for blocking the tourism business from others.

Since the late 1980s, some women in San Antonio, working against the hegemony of the Pérez family, have taken their performances out of their *tiendas* and into Antigua's marketplaces and Spanish language schools, where they weave, tell stories, and answer questions about daily life. As crime increased in Guatemala in the last ten years of the twentieth century, Spanish language schools encouraged these performances, which allow students to see weaving demonstrations within the safe confines of the school. A typical performance with a question-and-answer period lasts less than an hour. Gladys, one of the women performing in Spanish schools, explained that she was not making much money selling to tourists at the Tanque de la Unión marketplace, so she offered to give free weaving demonstrations at Spanish schools. One school near her vending location agreed, and she began giving periodic performances. According to one tourist, it was "the best thing I saw in Antigua. It gave me a chance to learn something about how Indian women live." The tourist ended up purchasing close to $100 worth of merchandise. Some women have forged international connections this way and have given weaving demonstrations and descriptions of household life in the United States and Europe.

It must be realized that these self-conscious performances by *antoneca* women take a very different tone than those described by MacCannell in "Cannibalism Today" (1992), which examines the often hostile interactions between "ex-primitive[s]" and "postmoderns," or in "Reconstructed Ethnicity: Tourism and Cultural Identity in Third World Communities." In these articles, MacCannell describes the tensions between tourists looking for "primitive" people and those people who are deemed appropriately primitive. The "primitives" can fail to live up to the tourists' expectations, in part because they are savvy capitalists who may angrily reject the touristic stereotypes ascribed to them. The women are neither hostile toward tourists nor intent on reconstructing collective identity for either themselves or tourists. They attempt to stage a slice of San Antonio life that will, in turn, capitalize on tourists' curiosity and money. However, because most tourists are not fools and are mildly skeptical, the transparent presentations of San Antonio life and identity are sometimes regarded as inauthentic. Kirshenblatt-Gimblett (1998: 72–74) discusses the intricacies of "staging culture," noting that when the performance becomes spectacle, authenticity is called into question. The issue facing producers is "to present rather than represent that life" (74). The distinction that Kirshenblatt–Gimblett (1998: 75) is making here relates to how culture is performed and who performs it, namely, that real cultural practices are presented by the people who use and perform them in everyday life, not represented by a group of actors. The women in the Cooperativa Ixchel and other women are aware of these distinctions as they live/perform their daily lives for others.

Presenting is a complex and difficult task for Kaqchikel women because the presentation of their culture through performance runs the risk of becoming a show.[3] The staged productions by the Pérez family and those women giving weaving demonstrations in Spanish language schools, while usually interesting to tourists, were often considered to be solely for their benefit. In the words of one tourist, the performance was "not really the real thing, but it was good."

Women such as Gladys, the Pérez sisters, and those of the López family, whom I will address in the following section, all commented that it is not enough to act out their domestic chores and weave in front of a group of tourists. "Nik'o nuk'u'x. Nik'o kik'u'x," commented one woman: "It bores me. It bores them." The better performers are constantly modifying their presentations to keep tourists interested and to help ensure that tourists believe the presentation is real. The López family, in particular, attempts to make their presentations interesting and authentic.

Cooperativa Ixchel: Transformation of Household Space to Performance Space

Twice a day Ana López prepares her family's house for tourists and students of Spanish. Tourists, independent travelers, and those on guided tours who visit the López home come primarily from the United States, Europe, Korea, and Japan. Although the students may come from all these areas of the world, they tend to be mainly from the United States. They participate in language programs that stress an immersion method of learning. Ana's parents, Alejandra and Tomás, both in their seventies, cannot remember a time when there were no tourists. In addition to the street-side rooms in private homes that have been transformed into *típica tiendas*, a daily *típica* marketplace is located in the *plazuela*. Whereas these stores sell material goods, the Lópezes sell stories and daily life. Both tourists and students visit their home to get a glimpse of "Indian" life—in the hope of seeing what indigenous people do when tourists are not looking.

Despite the Pérez family's monopoly with INGUAT and the major tour companies, enough other tourists and Spanish students studying in Antigua make trips to San Antonio to make *típica* sales worthwhile for other families there. Competition is fierce among vendors, who are always trying to figure out new ways to attract customers. Some vendors go so far as to guide tourists from Antigua to San Antonio. It is not enough to just set up a *tienda* on the main road and wait for tourists to show up, so vendors visit Spanish language schools, travel agencies, restaurants, and hotels to invite tourists to visit San Antonio and to distribute flyers. But as these businesses became inundated with solicitations and the owners and managers began turning vendors away, vendors conceived of new strategies to improve their sales.

Some vendors from San Antonio who sell in Antigua have agreements with businesses that cater to tourists. Sometimes the relationship is symbiotic, as when vendors are permitted to sell in a business locale with the expectation that their presence will attract tourists, who will stay in the hotel or buy a meal. In other instances, the relationship is economic. The vendors pay the proprietor rent for the right to sell *típica* in the establishment. Vendors who make these arrangements are very territorial and expect other vendors not to infringe on their space.

CONCEPTION OF THE MAYA PERFORMANCE

Since the mid-1980s, various women in the López family have been selling *típica* in front of the ruins of the Capuchinas Convent and as street peddlers in Antigua. As they watched their sales decline over the years from 1994 through 1996, they conceived of one of the more innovative strategies to attract customers. They announced that they were a weaving/vending cooperative and named themselves Cooperativa Ixchel (after the goddess of weaving). They printed business cards, the back of which lists their services: showing exhibitions; selling traditional clothing for ceremonies, *cofradías,* marriages, and daily use; and selling typical food such as tortillas and *pepián.* Next, they planned a program for tourists, consisting of five parts: (1) welcome and traditional stories that include courting practices and gendered work activities common in "traditional"

Maya households, (2) dressing the students in *traje* for various ceremonial occasions, such as *cofradía* rituals and marriage ceremonies, after which they do mock enactments, (3) a weaving demonstration in which visitors are invited to try their hand at weaving, (4) tortilla making and eating *pepián,* and (5) informal conversation and sales. They went to Spanish language schools to sell their idea, making sure to point out that no one was obligated to purchase anything, but Q10 (about US$1.50) would be required to cover the cost of the meal. Spanish schools tended to mark up this price to Q30–Q60 ($5–$10), claiming that it was to cover transportation and fees for the teachers who accompanied the students.

The Lópezes established regular business relations with the Christian Spanish Academy, Amerispan, Spanish School San José, and Centralamerica Spanish Academy. Other schools and organizations visited periodically, including the Instituto Guatemalteco Americano from Guatemala City, a group from the U.S. embassy, the Oxlajuj Aj Kaqchikel class, and a women's association from the Japanese embassy, among others. To get this business, the Lópezes used a number of strategies to convince potential clients it was worth the trip to San Antonio. First and foremost, they de-emphasized the economic relationship. They stressed that they were not a *tienda* but a real household. According to Ana, they opened their home to let "guests see what a Maya family lives like and hear traditional stories."

Second, in an example of Mayan capitalism, they promoted themselves as a cooperative. This decision came after years of experience selling *típica* on the streets of Antigua. Tourists frequently asked them if their products were made by a weaving cooperative. Although they are not officially recognized as a cooperative, Ana and her older sister, Zoila, explained that tourists are more sympathetic to cooperatives.[4] To make themselves more like a cooperative, they spoke to other weavers in San Antonio, offering to sell their products on consignment and pass special orders back to them. Some profits are then donated to sponsor activities associated with the Catholic Church, such as purchasing clothing and school supplies for needy children and providing food for elderly or incapacitated persons.

Third, they explained that the performance/exhibition is participatory and social. Few foreigners and non–Maya Guatemalans have opportunities to socialize and visit in a Maya household. This is partly because tourists and Spanish students generally do not have the time to meet and develop a rapport with Mayas. Also, families recounted stories of failed encounters with tourists who did not like the food, the living conditions, or the sanitary practices in these settings. They felt insulted by their tourist guests' behavior and were hesitant to invite other foreigners into their homes. The Lópezes, on the other hand, expect these behaviors. Although they prefer that the tourist guests eat the food that is prepared, they are not offended if they do not.

Fourth, they offered to take the performance/exhibition to the school if students could not visit San Antonio. The Instituto Guatemalteco Americano agreed to host a performance at its Guatemala City school. School personnel were so impressed with the performance that they now make periodic trips with their students to the López household. This pattern of presenting at a school, followed by students from the school visiting the López home, was repeated, in part, because the Lópezes explained to students, teachers, and administrators that Maya life is more than stories and weaving demonstrations. Students have to be in the house, smell tortillas cooking on the *comal* (griddle), and hear the town around them to get a more realistic feel for life as a Guatemalan Maya.

Despite some altruistic motivations, it is important to remember that the Cooperativa Ixchel, like other businesses, was founded to help the López family outcompete other *antoneco* vendors and make money. By opening their home to tourists, categories such as global and local conflate. But this conflation is not simply a blending of cultures or a new hybrid form of household. As tourists visit the López household, and the Lópezes themselves modify and adjust their performance, their household organization and attitudes in relation to gender roles change. At the same time, they maintained distinctions between themselves and tourists in and out of different performative contexts (Butler 1993).

PERFORMING MAYA LIFE

On days when a group of tourists or Spanish students are expected to visit, the López family transforms the physical space of their home into a theater-in-the-round. This involves partitioning off private areas of the home and removing electrical appliances and other signs of non-Maya material culture, a process that is similar to the construction of *National Geographic* photographs (see Lutz and Collins 1993). Ordinarily, their household plot has three clear divisions, since Tomás and Alejandra, who purchased the land over thirty years ago, have since given one-third portions of the property to two of their sons. Their houses are located to either side of Tomás and Alejandra's, built of reinforced concrete with tile floors, and equipped with refrigerators and gas stoves—both contemporary houses for San Antonio. Tomás and Alejandra's house, on the other hand, is of an older style of construction, with cane walls and packed-dirt floors. Although it has electricity, that is made inconspicuous to tourist visitors.

One of the first orders of business is putting up partitions between the three households. This is done by stringing laundry cord across the courtyard and hanging bolts of *corte* material (used for wraparound skirts) and handwoven tablecloths on it. On some performance days, Tomás helps rig the laundry cord for partitions and moistens the dirt yard with water and sweeps it to keep the dust down. Then he goes to work in his fields. Alejandra, her daughters, Ana and Zoila, their sister-in-law Agripina, and Tomás's younger sister, Bernarda, hang two backstrap looms and prepare a meal of *pepián* and tortillas, saving back some of the *masa* (corn dough) so that their guests can learn to make tortillas. Tomás's grandchildren, male and female, help out with the preparations as they can, but most of the time they are attending school.

When the guests arrive, they pass through a fence made of cane, walk

Figure 7.1. Preparing *pepián* at Cooperativa Ixchel. Photograph by author.

Mayas in the Marketplace

along a wall decorated with various pieces of *típica,* and pass into a small courtyard that is bounded on two opposing sides by walls of *corte* and *típica* and on the other two opposing sides by a kitchen and multipurpose room that serves as a warehouse, religious altar, and formal meeting room. Both are made of cane. Off to the side of the courtyard is a large *jocote* tree, which *antonecos* say produces San Antonio's typical, or traditional, fruit. The guests are surrounded by Maya material culture: textiles are everywhere, bags of maize and beans from Tomás's fields rest to the side of the general purpose room, and the smell of tortillas, *pepián,* and pine fills the air. Alejandra, Ana, Zoila, and Bernarda greet their guests dressed in their finest San Antonio–style brocaded *huipiles.*

The self-conscious performance of Maya culture is not limited to tourists; Mayas also present their culture to themselves. An interesting example of this is when Catholic Action leaders in San Andrés Semetabaj dramatized rituals in the late 1980s as a way to help revitalize Mayan culture. These enactments of rituals played on the distinctions between *cofradía* rituals and scenes of daily life. In this case, the performances were not for international tourists, but for diasporic and local youth who had not learned or lived these practices.

Figure 7.2. Tourists watch a weaving demonstration at Cooperativa Ixchel. Photograph by author.

The artist Coco Fusco writes in "The Other History of Intercultural Performance" that "the construction of ethnic Otherness [is] essentially *performative* and located in the body" (1995: 40; emphasis in original). Her essay, which both satirizes white European and American colonial practices of displaying Others and describes her and Gómez-Peña's artistic experiment "Two Undiscovered Amerindians Visit . . ." (see Chapter 1), explains how "human exhibitions dramatize the colonial unconscious of American society" (1995: 47). Although two purposes of their original performance piece and the essay were to expose the ways in which persons mainly of white European descent view the Other and to show the imposed, but seemingly natural, boundaries between themselves and their Others, it is relevant to the analysis of the Lópezes' tourist performance. According to Fusco, "actual encounters [with the Other] could threaten the position and the supremacy of the appropriator unless boundaries and concomitant power relations remain in place" (1995: 46).

Like Fusco and Gómez-Peña, the López family is self-conscious about its performance. Whereas Fusco and Gómez-Peña construct a performance to expose "white people's" practices of making an Other, the Lópezes construct an equally sophisticated performance playing on tourists' practices, desires, and beliefs. Fusco and Gómez-Peña were interested in constructing and playing with boundaries that mark and separate "whites" from their "Others" in ways that may produce reflection, anger, doubt, complicity, or some other response that causes them to react to or to think about their relation to the people in the cage. The Lópezes, too, are concerned with constructing boundaries, but they do not challenge tourists to doubt their beliefs or their exposed unconscious desires projected onto the body and artifacts of the Other. They try to use the interests, desires, and curiosities of tourists to draw them into the performance, to confirm their beliefs about the exotic, different Other. The tourists and Spanish students who visit want to see and experience someone and something contrary to themselves. If the Lópezes are too much like the tourists, the performance fails. Hence, attending to boundaries is fundamental to the success of the performance and subsequent sales of *típica*. In other words, the Lópezes must consciously make themselves different from tourists.

To ensure their difference is maintained, they speak to each other—usually giving stage instructions—in Kaqchikel Maya. Ana and Zoila have the most verbal interaction with guests, with Ana serving as the narrator who tells stories and describes San Antonio life. She tells her guests, "Please

Mayas in the Marketplace

excuse my poor Spanish. If I speak slowly, it is because Spanish is my second language, and it is difficult for me to find the correct words." She and her sister interpret for their mother, "who knows only a few words in Spanish." Their brothers, who live in the houses to either side of the performance area, are kept out of the performance. One is employed at the Nestlé fruit-processing plant between San Antonio and Antigua and, in another way, is also participating in the global economy. The other brother, a skilled carpenter and talented sculptor, is involved in Maya political activism and likes to discuss why neither Marxism nor capitalism is for *antonecos*. Furthermore, they explain that the success of their cooperative helps them carry on traditions such as weaving and maintaining the *cofradías* and shows their children that Maya culture is aesthetically and economically valuable.

They used me to help make them different to tourists, too. Most *antonecos* know something about anthropology through direct contact with persons who conducted or are conducting research in San Antonio, such as Sheldon Annis (1987), R. McKenna Brown (1991), Margaret Wilhite (1977), myself, and others. They know that anthropologists study traditions, material artifacts, and other aspects of culture. In fact, vendors advised me to read *National Geographic* magazine, especially the October 1989 issue, "La Ruta Maya," which was reprinted and easily found in Guatemala. The Lópezes called my presence to the attention of the tourists, telling them that I was there to study the people of San Antonio because their traditions are unique and special. They engaged me in conversations in Kaqchikel and occasionally had me interpret for them because some things could "only be explained in Kaqchikel." In reference to the Lópezes' remarks about their inadequate Spanish skills, it is important to note that all of them read and write Spanish and conduct most public activities and even some private home activities in Spanish.

Their practices of making themselves different, though usually successful, always ran the risk of derailing because of skeptical tourists. This was the case during one performance when a well-traveled woman in her fifties from San Francisco announced to her classmates in English, "I think the Lacandón Indians are the most authentic Mayas. They haven't changed as much as those here. They are not as commercial." Another student asked me if this was true. My vague reply that both groups were equally authentic led to three of the students debating this for a few minutes. Eventually they decided, despite this woman's opinions, that the Lópezes were authentic Mayas, just different from the Lacandones.

Mirroring anthropology, the core of the López performance of Kaqchikel Maya life and household practices is the construction and maintenance of tradition. Traditions are what link them to place and past.[5] In the world that the López women describe, male and female gender roles are clearly defined. Women weave, cook, and care for children. Men farm, manage the finances, take care of the saints, and deal with outsiders. Their guests, tourists or students, never questioned the contradiction before them, that they, as outsiders, were interacting with women who were, according to Ana, "timid with strangers."[6] In the two dozen or so performances I watched, the Lópezes' guests always expressed their gratitude for being allowed into their home and permitted some time to see how "real Mayas" live. Even the skeptical tourist mentioned earlier told me how "surprised and fortunate" she was for having had the opportunity to go into a "real home."

HOUSEHOLD AS HOME

The Lópezes' house is a real home. When it is not transformed into a stage, it is where they live, especially Tomás and Alejandra and their daughter Ana, since their other children's homes are never used as places of performance. Home and stage are one. The Lópezes are characters portraying Mayas, but they are also Mayas. Actually, they call themselves Mayas while performing for tourists but Kaqchikeles and *indígenas* in all other contexts of their life. This helps them maintain boundaries and distinguish between the life they show and tell to their Others and the life that they do not perform. The maintenance of boundaries is common in all social situations, not just in tourism settings. Following Butler (1993), it is more appropriate to conceive that we are performing all the time and presenting self-images to others in different contexts, but Bourdieu (1977) would argue that habitus crosses out any self-consciousness. De Certeau (1984) would contend, as I do, that their acting out in front of tourists is not merely a semantic degree of difference, because it is a staged life, stylized and simplified. One of the problems that the Lópezes confront, because their house is both home and stage, is that they do not always live, or even want to live, in the ways that they portray themselves.

Bruner and Kirshenblatt-Gimblett (n.d.: 68–71) explain that the Maasai and the Mayers face a similar problem, because the Mayers Ranch is both home and stage for them. And like the Maasai, "it becomes essential to keep the boundaries straight, to distinguish between who is and who is not in the picture, and to know precisely when the picture begins and when it ends" (n.d.: 70). Just as it is necessary to construct and maintain boundaries for tourists, boundaries are important to the Lópezes, too, because they help them separate the house as home from the house as stage. They allow the family to pursue their normal lives when they are not actors following a script anchored in, and constrained by, tradition. That life is often in contradiction to the life that is performed. Although they live without televisions and blenders during performances, they make use of them when the house is not a stage. In truth, they are more preoccupied with their children and grandchild who are attending college than with whether they strictly follow the traditions they describe.

At the same time, some traditional activities are not included in the household performances. Not once did the Lópezes discuss doing performances of curing rituals, taking care of the saints, honoring the dead, planting rituals, or preparing commonly eaten food like *ichaj*.[7] These distinctions allow *antoneco* families such as the Lópezes to distinguish between the household as stage and the household as home. But they also allow them to mask from tourists the ways that they practice their lives, pursue interests that may not be considered traditionally Maya, and modify traditions to better fit contemporary life.

HOUSEHOLD GENDER DYNAMICS

In the cases of the López family, the Pérez family, and others mentioned briefly, the persons maintaining boundaries and defining who are Mayas, Kaqchikeles, and *indígenas* are women. The performance of "Maya life" in contemporary San Antonio is a "gender-specific activity" (Nash 1993b). Nash's discussion of the ways Maya households have changed in light of the penetration of the world market in Amatenango, Mexico, has some parallels with San Antonio. In Amatenango, pottery production tended to be a gender-specific activity for women, which complemented men's semisubsistence agricultural activities. It was and is a component of a woman's "identity as a wife and manager of a household" (Nash 1993b: 133). Pottery sales were not viewed as the way for families to achieve subsistence. However, as men migrated out of the community in search of work, and as tourism touched Amatenango, women increasingly began supporting themselves and their families from pottery sales—especially to tourists. This resulted in a number of changes in the gendered relations of Amatenango life. In one case, a man helps his wife in producing pottery. Only one man made pottery, but he began making sculptural objects for tourist sales. As pottery prices and demand for pottery have risen, pottery production "can be used to subsidize agriculture" (1993b: 135). It also made it possible for women to support children without the aid of men, making them more economically independent and powerful within the community. According to Nash (1993b: 139), "the changing value of women's contribution through the greater intensity of artisan production is affecting betrothal customs, marital relations, and the redistribution of wealth within the family." The major threat to men was the control over pottery sales by women.

As a result of tourism and strong *típica* sales, gender relations in San Antonio have changed, too. The Pérez sisters, Alida and Carolina, are two of the most wealthy and powerful people in San Antonio because of their successes in the *típica* market. After Alcides López, one of Annis's key informants (not related to Tomás and Alejandra), was killed by a death squad in 1979,[8] his wife and daughters went from being a relatively poor farming family to relatively successful *típica* weavers and vendors. Their houses are filled with luxuries like cable television and stereos. In San Antonio households, selling *típica* has provided women with an economically viable activity. In some cases, like those mentioned above, and in the case of the Lópezes' tourist performances combined with sales, women become the primary breadwinners, deciding how to use family finances, choosing when and whom to marry.

Take, for example, the *k'utunïk,* one of the traditional practices involved when a young man and his parents ask a young woman's parents for their daughter's hand in marriage. In the past, a man and his parents were responsible for providing a gift of a basket filled with bread, fine textiles woven by female family members or purchased from a vendor, bottles of hard liquor, honey, bread, and chocolate to the mother of his betrothed. According to the vendor women I worked with and the López family, the *k'utunïk* is not as widely practiced anymore. It is harder for men to come up with the money, and women say that it is not reasonable to require a man to provide such a gift when the women make more money and want to decide for themselves whom to marry. In some cases, smaller, less expensive baskets are given to future mothers-in-law because of the symbolic value of them. It puts the man in good graces with his in-laws. The *k'utunïk* is also used in some of the Lópezes' performances.

By inviting tourists into the home, the Lópezes' household has changed in other ways not influenced by economics and local politics. This contact has led to changes related to gender roles and taste and aesthetic sensibilities. Tomás farms but has changed his routine to support the activities of the female members in his household. He now helps with kitchen chores and watches children, freeing the women to visit potential clients. In some other households, when guests were present, women served men and ate apart from them on reed mats. At the López house, men and women ate together. Males are expected to help serve food and take away dishes at the end of the meal.

During the informal conversation and socializing portion of the performance, the Lópezes and their guests swap stories about cultural differences and pose for pictures. This has resulted in them exploring new types of food, experimenting with the ways they take pictures of themselves, and thinking about the ways men treat women. One of the more common comments by their visitors is how women's and men's work can be so separate and women so subordinate to men. Ethnographic literature abounds for Mesoamerican cases where women are subordinated to men (see Bossen 1984; Ehlers 1990; Nash 1993a; Stephen 1991). However, like successful women in San Antonio, the López women run their households, controlling finances and making decisions about how leisure time is spent and what leisure items are purchased. Interaction with tourists who make comments about gender inequalities has stimulated conversations about women's roles in Guatemalan society and resulted in their reflection about appropriate sexual behavior and alcohol consumption. But for tourists, they explain that though their work is different and separate from men's, it is not subordinate. In fact, as Ana tells them, "It helps us maintain order and avoid confusion. Men do what men do, and women do what women do."

Not all households are as peaceful as the López household. In a couple of others, also run by successful businesswomen, men have become abusive and turned to excessive drinking. Such behavior is not condoned by the community, and San Antonio women have not been run out of town or killed for their successes, as was the president of the pottery cooperative in Amatenango (Nash 1993b). Women in San Antonio are recognized by community members as important contributors to the maintenance of the town, economically and culturally. In late December 1997, the plazuela vendors began developing a performance piece for tourists that showcased traditional women's work. My wife, my daughter, and I became guinea pigs as the women tested the performance on us. The mayor and other city government officials attended the trial run (as of 2003, they still have not performed for tourists) to show their solidarity with the women, and they pledged to help them attract tour companies and gain INGUAT approval. Until 2000, the Pérez family was the only family/group with INGUAT approval, but in 2000, the women plazuela vendors were also given this approval.

The men I work with in San Antonio frequently mention that women uphold traditions and cultural markers such as language, clothing, and food, and that Kaqchikel, *indígena,* and Maya culture originates and is reproduced by women. Although I met men who were jealous of women's economic successes and the prominent representation of women in INGUAT and international tourism promotional materials, they were proud, too, of the recognition that San Antonio women have received nationally and internationally. What men are somewhat reluctant to admit is that women also bring new ideas about how to run households and how to guide economic, political, and religious committees that are integrated in local, state, and global contexts.

INGUAT and the Pérez Family

As a consequence of making their household public, the López family is having some problems within their community and is facing some obstacles with the Guatemalan government. One of the local problems relates to the plazuela vendors' jealousy of the Lópezes' success. Jealousy, as discussed in the previous chapter, is not unique to this situation but can be found in other tourism settings and throughout Mesoamerica. Prior to the Lópezes' success, their family, the plazuela vendors, and other vendors and weavers felt a sense of camaraderie because they were getting roughly the same number of customers. Additionally, they were united against the Pérez family's hegemonic position in the textile/*típica* and tourism business. Although the Lópezes only attract a fraction of the tourism business that the Pérez family does, plazuela vendors commented that they must have cut underhanded deals and offered textiles at artificially low prices. One accused me of using my connections (of which I have none) to help the Lópezes' business. After a couple of tense weeks and some discussion, the plazuela vendors reconsidered my role and decided that even if tourists were going to the López household first, they

Mayas in the Marketplace

were at least in the town and looking around at other *tiendas*. Besides, most plazuela vendors, like the Lópezes, are Catholics and continually found themselves involved with the Lópezes in church activities. This was a marked difference from their dealings with the Pérez family, who are Protestants. Because the Pérez family's *tiendas* are on the road just outside of San Antonio and they discourage tourists from venturing into San Antonio because it is "dangerous," the more affluent tourists who visit their stores never go into San Antonio. Even those who still desire to visit the town center are talked out of it by their guides and bus drivers.

The other local problem faced by the López family relates directly to the Pérez family. As Carolina and Alida Pérez watched small buses shuttle groups of ten to twenty tourists past their *tiendas* to the López household, sometimes as often as twice a day, five days per week, they decided to take measures to increase their hold on tourism in San Antonio. One strategy was to approach Spanish schools that took students to the López house. When that failed, they spoke with INGUAT, since they are the only family endorsed by the government tourism agency. Before waiting to see if INGUAT would shut down the López operation, they visited them and threatened them with violence. The Lópezes made the threat public knowledge, and this helped them improve the strained relations they were having with other vendors, because threats from the Pérez family were commonly known. Far from stopping their performances, they proceeded to make them even more official. Ana's father and brothers made repairs on the buildings used in the performances and constructed a modern bathroom with a toilet and washbasin. When Ana was satisfied with the oral part of her performance and the other women felt at ease with the tourists and Spanish students who visited, they decided to court INGUAT and the biggest tour companies operating in Guatemala, such as Kim' Arrin Travel and Clark Tours. These companies and others, including STP Guatemala and Neys Viajes y Turismo, S.A., tend to patronize businesses that are endorsed by INGUAT.

For a few months, they tried to make contact with INGUAT officials who were instrumental in giving INGUAT approval to tourism businesses. After visiting INGUAT's offices in Guatemala City several times and calling by telephone on numerous occasions, they learned that a contingent from INGUAT would come to watch their performance and inspect their house. They came in late May 1998. The performance went without complications. The inspectors approved of the house, calling attention to how "traditional" it was, with its cane walls and packed-dirt floors. They liked the large religious altar adorned with candles, statues of saints, flowers, pre-Columbian pottery shards, and incense. The textiles exhibited received high marks, and the performance was considered authentic and entertaining. The bathroom exceeded all their expectations. Ana and Alejandra explained to me that they felt INGUAT approval was assured and that their household would be listed on INGUAT promotional materials and they would be recommended to the large tour companies. This would make their home more public and thrust their household activities even more into the global realm. However, when the decision was made, they learned that they would not get INGUAT endorsement. The reason, they were informed, had nothing to do with their house or performance. It was, according to one of the officials, the "best portrayal of *indígena* life" he had seen. The reason had to do with the town. The streets had to be cleaned, and it needed to be made more traditional. Only Spanish colonial-style buildings or cane-style buildings would be acceptable. More people in San Antonio had to wear *traje* and speak Kaqchikel. They suggested that the Lópezes talk to their neighbors and the mayor about making these changes. Tomás commented to me that the requested changes are unreasonable and unpractical. The López women pledged to continue working with Spanish schools, and despite lack of endorsement from INGUAT, they went directly to Clark Tours to try to convince the company to take tourists to their home. As time has passed, however, they are not hopeful about reaching an agreement with Clark Tours.

Conclusions

In this chapter, I have described measures the residents of San Antonio Aguas Calientes have taken to make the performance of household activities an economic activity within global tourism flows. In the transformation of private space to public space, some San Antonio women have opened their homes to tourists, Spanish students, tour guides, anthropologists, and Guatemalan government officials. In particular, the López women have drawn on traditions commonly known by *antonecos* to exhibit their house, present domestic activities, and tell stories about Maya life. This has placed their household into public spheres of debate, from local to international contexts, as townspeople, government officials, and tourists enter their household, consume their production, and comment on it.

As numerous chapters in Nash's (1993a) edited volume illustrate, Mesoamerican artisans, households, and towns have changed as a result of entering or being absorbed into late-capitalist systems of global economic flows. *Antonecos* are no exception. However, in the case of Nash's study (1993b) and in Ehlers's (1993) analysis, the households and towns of the producers have relatively little direct contact with tourists. In San Antonio, on the other hand, the town and its residents have been objects of tourism for nearly a century. The López family's use of their household as a performance space intensified interactions with tourists and led to changes in the management of the household, finances, and gender relations that did not occur when the women were just street peddlers of *típica*.

The Lópezes' performance calls attention to the differences between how they perform their lives and how they live their lives outside of the performance.[9] What they claim are transparent presentations of their lives increasingly become constructed traditions as they modify them in order to satisfy their tourist and Spanish student guests. At one time or another, members of the López family have commented on the strain of being "traditional." For the López women, my apartment in Antigua became a place of refuge where they could watch television, joke around, and try my "gringo food" away from other *antonecos* and tourists (who sometimes spotted them in Antigua out of San Antonio *traje*).

The complications of performing and exhibiting to tourists have been discussed by Bruner and Kirshenblatt-Gimblett (1994), Castañeda (1996), Fusco (1995), Karp and Lavine (1991), Kirshenblatt-Gimblett (1998), MacCannell (1992), Mitchell (1988), and Picard (1995). Most have reviewed tourism performances and exhibitions of ethnic Others within the contexts of U.S. and European colonial practices. Indeed, the concept of who Mayas, in particular, and *indígenas,* in general, are is inextricably linked first to colonial and then later to anthropological and touristic discourses in which the developed "West" sees and makes its Others.

Unlike most Latin American cases studied by academics,[10] some *antonecos,* such as the Pérez and the López families, are taking the exhibition and performance of Mayas (or Guatemalan *indígenas*) into their own hands. Many, even those not connected with performance or *típica* sales to tourists, recognize, at the very least, that tourists want to see the types of Mayas that guidebooks and brochures promise. What they find frustrating is being represented in touristic contexts where they have no control or access to potential economic benefits from said representations. They feel that it is their right to present and represent themselves in ways that are economically advantageous to them. The difference between this and the Western practice of exhibiting Others is that *antonecos* decide who is exhibited, what is performed, and how performances are made. They, then, control the money made from the exhibitions/performances. Here is another instance in which the general concerns of Maya handicraft vendors and Pan-Mayanists converge (see Warren 1998a), since both groups are concerned with who manages and gains politically and economically from representations of Mayas.

Bruner and Kirshenblatt-Gimblett (n.d.: 71) comment that a "Maasai performance constructed for tourists becomes reproduced as *the* Maasai, and comes to stand not only for all Maasai but for African tribesmen, for the primitive." Certainly, there is a potential for *antonecos* to be viewed as *the* Maya, especially since some are presenting the "Maya household," whether in an actual house setting or at a school or other location. When I asked *antonecos* if they were Mayas, they always corrected me, saying that they are the "descendants of Mayas." However, when it was time to sell *típica* and exhibit themselves and their household activities, they became Mayas.

Antonecos cannot expect to use their house as a refuge from tourism and tourists if that house becomes public space where the women have to be self-conscious about how they portray themselves to outsiders. The irony of this is that the performance of "Maya life" gets farther away from the ways *antonecos* actually live in private. Sandstrom (1991) discusses ethnicity as being defined by contextual, situational, and strategic considerations, and certainly it is for the women in San Antonio who portray "Maya life." However, unlike for the people of Amatlán, Mexico, in Sandstrom's ethnography, the household and the community are not always places where people can be themselves.

Chapter 8

Marketing Maya Culture in Santa Catarina Palopó

Introduction

Matilde Tax is described by her family and other members of Santa Catarina Palopó as an ideal contemporary young woman. "Purely one of us, a good person" (*Puro qawinaq, jeb'ël runa'oj*), people commented to me. They and Matilde recognize the importance of self-representation and the representation of Santa Catarina to outsiders for economic gain. Matilde is considered one of the best at it, because pictures of her are on postcards, in books, and on magazine covers (Figure 8.1). She speaks Kaqchikel Maya unashamedly inside and outside of the community. She only dresses in the latest Santa Catarina–style *po't,* and she embodies characteristics that other *catarinecos* consider important, such as being virtuous, well traveled, a practicing Catholic, and a good salesperson.

I first met Matilde and a number of other women and children from Santa Catarina Palopó in Antigua in 1994, when Matilde was a teenager. These women, who patiently listened and made fun of my initial struggles to learn Kaqchikel Maya, were easy for me to identify as Kaqchikel speakers and appropriate persons with whom to use my budding language skills. Smith (1995: 723) remarks, "More often than not, women bear the burden of displaying the identifying symbols of their ethnic identity to the outside world, whether these be items of dress, aspects of language, or distinctive behavior." Anthropological research about Mayas in Guatemala, such as Irma Otzoy's (1996, 1998) and Carol Hendrickson's (1995) on identity and dress, and about Quechuas in Peru, such as Marisol de la Cadena's (1991) on women in Cusco, certainly bear this out. According to Smith (1995: 724), the reasons that Maya women bear "the emblems of the stigmatized position of a lower-order ethnic group" have to do with the particular historical conditions of gender relations and ideology in which Maya women live in Guatemala in relation to Ladinos and Maya men. The predominant ethnic symbol in Guatemala is *traje.* As Hendrickson

(1995: 62–63) notes, paralleling Otzoy, Maya women continue to wear *traje,* and men do not wear it because of the ways each has intersected with the Guatemalan labor economy. Both Hendrickson and Otzoy also explain how women, as weavers, have maintained a cultural practice and product that is considered an important symbol for Maya identity. Diane Nelson's (2001) thesis, that Maya women are a crutch that supports Maya,

Figure 8.1. Matilde on travel agency trade magazine. Cover, *Recommend* magazine, photography by Terence Murphy. Courtesy of Rick Shively, executive editor, and Terence Murphy, associate publisher.

Mayas in the Marketplace

Ladino, and Guatemalan national identities, goes beyond Smith's, Hendrickson's, and Otzoy's theories but focuses primarily on the politics of the representation of Maya women. All this is not to imply that men are not concerned with maintaining community traditions. They are. In contrast to the men in San Antonio Aguas Calientes, some men in Santa Catarina still wear *traje,* but their work lives intersect with tourism— mainly as laborers, gardeners, and construction workers—in different ways than women's lives do.

Like the above anthropologists, in this chapter I place the ways women from Santa Catarina represent and maintain their culture in contemporary economic contexts as the result of specific historical conditions. I show that a number of changes in Guatemala, particularly in relation to tourism, have significantly broadened the acceptable economic and social roles open to *catarinecas*. At the same time, I demonstrate that these women increasingly and willingly take on additional responsibilities to maintain the traditions and customs of their town. While this is common among successful Maya women who sell handicrafts to foreign tourists, it is not necessarily the case for women who do other work. For example, in nearby San Andrés Semetabaj, Maya women, but especially youths, are ambivalent about maintaining traditions (Warren 1998a).

Three contradictions are examined in this chapter. One concerns the differences between my research findings and those of earlier anthropologists. Although some of the differences are explainable through historical contextualization, one is not resolved by that means, namely, that of women traveling independently of men during the 1930s and 1940s. A second contradiction involves the usage of several terms—*culture, tradition,* "Maya," and "Kaqchikel." The multiple ways these terms are used in this chapter reflect, in part, differences in how anthropologists, *catarinecos,* tourists, and the Guatemalan government apply their own particular meanings to them. In other words, the specific meanings of these terms relate to the different discourses in which they are used.

The third contradiction relates to *catarinecos'* view of their community as both open and closed, socially and economically (Wolf 1955, 1957). Residents speak of Santa Catarina as an open community when they look outward for economic opportunities, social alliances, and spiritual concerns. Specifically, *catarinecas* who maintain and promote community traditions are not homebound women but are often well-traveled vendors, frequently in contact with non-Mayas. However, extensive travel is not required to have intense contact with Others, since one merely has

to go four kilometers by paved road to Panajachel, a well-known destination for international and national tourists. The residents of Santa
Catarina are in regular contact with tourists, because the latter visit the
town in increasing numbers to see a "pristine, picturesque indigenous
village." Despite the openness of these economic relationships, *catarineco*
discourses evoke the concept of a closed-corporate community when
they pertain to the social, spiritual, and economic self-sufficiency of the
town. James Scott (1990: 1415) theorizes that when a subordinate group
has intense contact with others who are economically and politically
dominant, the subordinate group uses "hidden transcripts" to critique
the dominant group's discourses and practices, but they express criticisms
of the dominant group indirectly or within contexts that cannot be traced

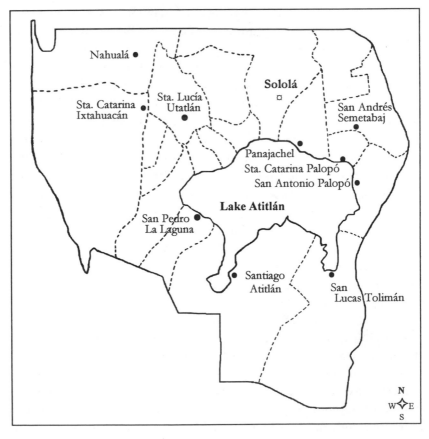

Figure 8.2. Department of Sololá. Map by author.

Mayas in the Marketplace

back to them. In effect, the discourse of closed community in Santa Catarina is similar to that of hidden transcripts, which help create safe spaces for political dissidence and hide some cultural practices.

Residents of Santa Catarina envision their town in this closed way because it helps them conceive of it as orderly and unified. Communities such as Santa Catarina Palopó and other smaller towns throughout Mesoamerica have been viewed by both the residents themselves and some anthropologists as closed-corporate communities. By looking at these communities historically, including the actual socioeconomic exchanges of the residents, a quite different view of them emerges, one in which characteristics of both closed-corporate communities and open communities are present (Kearney 1996: 16).

Ethnographic Background and Contexts

Santa Catarina Palopó is located on the banks of Lake Atitlán, four kilometers east of Panajachel (Figure 8.2). Most of the houses are located on the steep side of the mountain that leads down to the lake from a plateau, which peaks a little over 1,758 feet above the town. Of the 1,581 residents counted in the 1994 census, 1,469 are described as *indígenas,* or Indians (INE 1996). When one enters Santa Catarina, one may never encounter any resident who is not, or does not consider herself or himself to be, *indígena,* in this case, Kaqchikel Maya. The town is so overwhelmingly *indígena* that nearly all women wear some form of traditional handwoven outfit, and many men do so as well. The predominant language in the household, the street, and places of business is Kaqchikel. It is spoken by the majority of the populace, from the very youngest to the very oldest.

LAND USE AND SALES

By Guatemalan standards, the *municipio* of Santa Catarina is small, a mere eight square kilometers, making it relatively land-poor compared to other neighboring *municipios.*[1] Farming, both for economic and subsistence purposes, is a diminishing source of livelihood for *catarinecos,* like other traditional Santa Catarina occupations such as fishing and mat making.

According to Felix McBryde (1947: 123), around 1911, K'iche' Mayas from Santa Lucía Utatlán bought from *catarinecos* roughly one thousand acres of fairly level land 1,968 feet above Santa Catarina. In 1936, *catarinecos* also rented out eight terraced fields (*tablones*) to *panajacheleños* who planted onions. This was more than twice as many fields as the *catarinecos* had planted for themselves (McBryde 1947: 123). Tax (1946: 19) reports that Ladinos from San Andrés Semetabaj "bought up considerable parts" of the arable land above Santa Catarina. According to one *catarineco* (Petrich 1996a: 26), "Before in Santa Catarina there had been many landowners and they [*catarinecos*] sold all of it, but nobody [*catarinecos*] did anything good with the money."

The shortage of land was further exacerbated as most of the real estate along the banks of the lake was purchased, beginning in the 1950s, by wealthy Guatemalans and foreigners (Petrich 1996b: 13) for the construction of vacation homes, though most real estate development on Lake Atitlán did not take place until the late 1980s, when political violence had slowed and roads were improved, making it easier for *capitalinos* (residents of the capital, Guatemala City) to travel to the lake for weekend getaways. One column in a Guatemalan tourism magazine, *Revue* (July 1998, page 64), even went so far as to describe the "tumultuous growth" of lakeside real estate development in the 1990s. Today, aside from the municipal soccer field and the public beach and docks, the flat shore land is owned by the Villa Santa Catarina, a first-class hotel, and by other wealthy non-*catarinecos*, who have built chalets for weekend retreats.

Despite the shortage of land and the steep, rocky features of the terrain, Santa Catarina has been a densely populated town for a long time. Rather than following settlement patterns common in some other Maya areas, such as Chichicastenango, Guatemala (Bunzel 1959), and Zinacantán, Mexico (Cancian 1965), where the town center is relatively depopulated and the residents live in outlying hamlets, most *catarinecos* live within the town limits. In the 1994 census (INE 1996), only 243 out of 1,581 people lived outside the town proper. McBryde (1947: 123) reported that the population density of Santa Catarina in 1936 was much greater than that of Panajachel. Tax (1946: 22) reported "that there are but 350 people in town, and that the town is more closely packed than any in the United States." He counted 90 households in 1936 (Tax 1946: 68), but by the 1994 census (INE 1996: 85), the town had grown to 309 households, occupying the same area that it had in 1936.

In the 1930s the town was nearly four times smaller in population size than it is today, and nearly all its families owned "a few cords of milpa"[2] (Tax 1946: 19). Now, by comparison, many families do not own milpa land, and those who do own some do not harvest enough maize or beans to sustain their households, much less to sell in the marketplace. What is striking about this comparison, aside from the fact that today Santa Catarina is even more densely populated, is that most *catarinecos*, especially males and some females too, still identify themselves as "*tikonela'*"—farmers who plant and sell agricultural products from land that they own and manage.[3] This perspective reflects the view of *catarinecos* that Santa Catarina is relatively self-sufficient and that *tikonela'* are independent and self-sufficient farmers who do not work the land of others—when, in fact, most of them do not own land today.

SHIFTING PATTERNS OF LABOR

In the 1930s and 1940s, it was common for *catarinecos* to work on plantations, because they lacked land and other economic resources (Tax 1953: 185). In 1936, *catarinecos* survived by working on Ladino-owned milpas (Tax 1946: 19), picking coffee near the lake, and harvesting cotton on plantations on the Pacific coast, not by planting their own milpas. Furthermore, Tax (1953: 99) wrote, in regard to agricultural laborers, that "others are transients, chiefly from Santa Catarina, who seek work (and advances on their wages) almost house to house, although of course they know who is likely to hire them at a particular season, such as the coffee harvest." Even at the time Tax conducted his fieldwork, the majority of *catarinecos*, according to their definition of *tikonela'*, were not actually *tikonela'* but dependent wage laborers.

The lack of land or other viable work options drove *catarinecos*—along with other poor people throughout Guatemala—to work on the plantations in order to comply with the antivagrancy laws imposed by Jorge Ubico (1931–1944) and avoid incarceration (Petrich 1996b: 11). It was common for women with children to accompany their husbands and work alongside them (Petrich 1996c: 44–58; 1996d: 14–19). Most older (over thirty years of age) women I interviewed or had conversations with went to the plantations to work in their youth. On separate occasions, Maltide's mother, María; her aunt Petrona; and other elderly women explained that if the husband was too drunk, injured, or sick, women and children went to work on the plantations without their husbands. They also explained that, on occasion, women traveled to buy and sell salt and vegetables in surrounding markets without their fathers, husbands, or adult sons.[4]

Later, in 1965, Robert Hinshaw (1975: 153) collected data that indicated that more than 50 percent of the households in Santa Catarina migrated annually for work. In comparison, only 2 percent of the households in Panajachel and less than 1 percent of those in San Pedro La Laguna migrated annually for jobs. In 1965 Santa Catarina was one of the poorest towns on the lake, but this was also true during Tax's fieldwork in the 1930s and mine in 1990s. It had and has difficulty generating income within its municipal boundaries, so its residents did and do look outside the town for work.

The other traditional economic activities that *catarinecos* participated in were selling handwoven reed mats, fish, and crabs in numerous highland marketplaces, such as Panajachel, Sololá, Patzún, Tecpán, San Andrés Itzapa, San Andrés Semetabaj, and others (see Figures 0.4 and 8.2). According to Tax (1946, 1953) and McBryde (1947), fishing was one of the primary ways that *catarinecos* distinguished themselves and were distinguished by others around the lake. Some *catarineco* merchants also bought vegetables in Sololá and then sold them on the Pacific coast (Tax 1953: 127). Additionally, fishermen made house-to-house fish sales in Panajachel and Sololá (Tax 1953: 133). This practice continues to this day but with a new focus: rather than selling to private individuals in Panajachel, fishermen now tend to sell fish to the restaurants in Panajachel serving national and international tourists.

In Santa Catarina today, most residents make a living taking care of the vacation homes along the lake shore or working in nearby Panajachel in jobs related to some aspect of the tourism industry, such as vendors and weavers of *típica,* hotel managers, housekeepers, cooks, waiters, and construction workers. Manual laborers earn as little as Q200 per month, but the most successful vendors can earn as much as Q2,000 or more per month. Some still plant a milpa, but it is only for self-consumption. A few work in the Ladino-owned fields located on land above the town. Although some still sell fish and crabs in highland marketplaces, mat production and vending has died out because the reeds (*tul*) used to weave the mats no longer grow along Santa Catarina's shoreline or are now on chalet property owned by Ladinos and foreigners.

Tourism Background and Contexts

The shift from earning a living primarily from agricultural labor to earning one from tourism marks a profound change in the ways that *catarinecos* interrelate with national and global economies, especially with regard to women's participation. Fifty years ago, women's work was mainly in the home taking care of children, weaving, and preparing meals. Tax (1946: 19, 21) observed that, other than going to the market with their husbands or helping their husbands in the fields, women tended to stay at home, not even socializing with neighbors. Because women in Santa Catarina were less needed for agricultural work than those in Panajachel, a few *catarinecas* wove *huipiles* for Panajachel women (Tax 1953: 152); like sales of fruit and salt in Panajachel, Sololá, and San Andrés Semetabaj, such weaving provided meager amounts of cash.

For the most part, the labor and social practices recorded by Tax (1946) indicate that, unlike most women, men from Santa Catarina were well integrated into the regional economy through market selling and buying. They were also part of the national and international economies as temporary migrant laborers.[5] *Catarinecos* gradually became less dependent on migratory work as tourism developed beginning in the 1930s. By the late 1970s, men and women had ceased working on cotton, sugarcane, and coffee plantations.

THE GROWTH OF TOURISM

When Tax did his initial fieldwork, tourists only trickled into Panajachel, sometimes visiting Santiago Atitlán and taking a boat tour of the lake. The boats stopped for a few minutes in San Antonio Palopó, which was then and is now much larger that Santa Catarina. Although one of the guidebooks from this period—*Guía manual de turismo—1933*—lists Santa Catarina, it is not described in detail, but Santiago Atitlán is (Valladares 1934: 97–98, 169). That guidebook and another one, *Album de Guatemala* (Rubio 1938), which makes no reference to Santa Catarina, refer to and show pictures of San Antonio Palopó, which is Santa Catarina's neighbor to the east. One of the earliest touristic descriptions of Santa Catarina can be found in the guidebook *Guatemala, from Where the Rainbow Takes Its Colors* (Muñoz 1940: 198). It describes the town as an "attractive small village. . . . Quaint little church and thatch-roofed huts. Easily accessible on [sic] foot, horse, or boat."

Despite the lack of tourism in Santa Catarina Palopó and the relatively small numbers of tourists visiting the Lake Atitlán area compared to Guatemala City and Antigua, which had hundreds of visitors, some *catarinecos* were aware of the economic potential that tourism represented.

In 1935, Gertrude Tax (in Sol Tax 1946: 108) encouraged *catarinecas* to sell textiles:

> Now, also: the women here do very nice weaving. See how nice the material of your trousers is. Yet, isn't it true that they weave only for their own and your use? Why? If they would weave more, they could sell it to tourists for a lot of money. Do you know that more and more tourists—Americans are coming here—and that everybody likes to buy Indian textiles? They buy a lot at S. Pedro [La Laguna], and your things are as nice as theirs.

Two years later, Sol Tax (1953: 18) described what may have been the beginning of *catarinecas'* selling of *típica* to tourists and indicated the particular economic relationship that he and his wife had established with some of the *catarinecas*:

> The Indian women of neighboring Santa Catarina weave red *huipiles* that make attractive tablecloths in the eyes of Americans. In 1937 the Catarinecas were not engaged in any considerable tourist trade, but we were buying such *huipiles*. At first we paid $2.50 or $3, bargaining as is customary in such cases, and purchased quite a few. The women came with greater and greater frequency; and since they were making the cloths primarily for us, we felt an obligation to continue buying. In order to put a stop to it, we lowered our price, and began paying no more than $2. They kept coming. We lowered our price to $1.50 and eventually to $1, and still they kept coming. (How foolish we had been to pay $2.50!) Eventually, a particular friend who had not come to sell us textiles came to offer a *huipil* she had made; she wanted $3 and would not come down in price. When we told her what we had been paying, she asked to see the textiles; a comparison showed that hers weighed at least twice as much as those we were currently buying. The Catarineca women had simply kept pace with our price, and nobody could of course complain.

Mayas in the Marketplace

Some aspects of the foregoing quotation deserve comment. First, some textiles from Santa Catarina were being sold to tourists even though they were not visiting the town. The closest that most tourists came to Santa Catarina was when their boat passed by it en route to San Antonio (Jackson 1937; Mitchell-Hedges 1931). This suggests that *catarinecas* probably left their town in order to sell textiles to tourists, since even the Taxes were not staying in Santa Catarina but were offered *huipiles* for sale.

Second, the *catarinecas* made the Taxes their *patrones*, establishing a combined economic and social relationship with them. This relationship is quite complex and can seem confusing in the context of marketplace economic transactions, because more is involved than merely exchanging money for a product or one product for another. In cases of patronage, the economic relationship becomes "strongly personalized" (Wolf and Hansen 1972: 156), and the *patrón* is obligated to help the dependent person. Typical patron-dependent relationships (such as shopkeeper-customer or hacienda owner-peon) can be similar to that of consumer-vendor, especially if the relationship is regularized.[6] As *patrones*, the Taxes were, to some degree, obligated to help the women.

Third, *catarinecas* adjusted the quality of their product to match the price they got from the Taxes. Aside from indicating that *catarinecas* were aware of the relationship between the price of the finished product and the cost of thread and time spent weaving, this adjustment also shows a lack of haggling by the women—in contrast to the typical consumer-vendor relationship between *indígenas* and Ladinos of that time. Indeed, there tended to be more bargaining between *indígenas* and non-*indígenas* than among *indígenas* (Tax 1952: 72). Based on my broad reading of Tax's fieldnotes (1946), what may be gathered from his anecdote is that the *catarinecas* regarded the Taxes as *patrones* because they were affluent and influential in comparison to themselves, and as non-Ladinos because they were not bargaining but buying at the offered price.

TOURISM FINDS TRADITION AND MAYAS IN SANTA CATARINA

Clearly, in the 1930s the town of Santa Catarina was on the periphery of tourism, and *catarinecas* were only marginally involved in tourism. This certainly is not the case today. Since the late 1980s, most *catarinecas* have become involved in tourism, primarily by weaving *típica* and selling it to tourists. By the early 1990s, Santa Catarina was one of the most men-

arrived tourists may think that she really was from Santa Catarina, they were not bothered by this. One of the women explained that it might convince the tourists to visit Santa Catarina Palopó or to at least buy something from one of them in Antigua.

I mention these various representations because, in most cases, *catarineca* vendors are aware of them. They have looked through the Lonely Planet and other guidebooks that tourists carry. They have seen their images on posters, postcards, and book covers in the shops around Antigua and Panajachel. They talk about these representations among themselves and speculate about how much money is being made from them. Women find the images disturbing because others are making money from their images,[11] and because the representations are usually not as they would have portrayed themselves. This, some women explained, was because the photographer did not ask to photograph them, or if they were asked, they were posed by the photographer. When some of my friends in Santa Catarina asked me to take their pictures, they gave me detailed instructions on how I was to take the pictures. They chose the locations, holding the camera and looking at the background to ensure that it was what they desired. Then they explained how much or how little of their bodies I was to include in the camera's frame; no head shots were permitted. I was also not allowed to take candid shots, but only those in which they posed, deciding to smile or not to smile to convey a particular mood. Even in that situation, where *catarinecos* had a great deal of control over where they posed, how their picture was taken, and how much of them was in the picture, they were not always satisfied with the results. In general, urban Guatemalan Mayas have a great deal of experience taking photographs and shooting videotape at weddings, baptisms, festivals, school gatherings, conferences, and other functions.

In contrast to their reactions to tourism representations of themselves, my *catarineca* friends did not have problems with the Ladina INGUAT employee. She and the tourists who purchase and wear clothing from Santa Catarina are walking advertisements for the town's textiles. Unlike postcards or other media representations, which may distort who they are and exclude them economically, textiles from Santa Catarina are produced by them. When someone wears an item of clothing from Santa Catarina, then somebody from Santa Catarina has made some money and has had control over the production of the item. Usually, this is not the case with photographic and other representations.

Catarineca *Vendors*

Catarineca típica vendors can be found at most of Guatemala's principal tourism sites: Panajachel, Chichicastenango, Antigua, and, occasionally, Tikal and the coastal ports (Puerto Quetzal on the Pacific Ocean and Puerto Barrios on the Atlantic Ocean, where cruise ships dock). It is possible to make some generalizations about *catarineco* vendors' selling strategies, travel schedules, and social and economic partnerships. The majority of the vendors are women accompanied by their children. Some men also sell in these various towns and locations, but usually when they accompany their wives and children. Most of the forty-three vendors (including a few male and female youths who sold *típica*) with whom I had regular contact worked in Antigua and Panajachel, but occasionally they also sold in Chichicastenango, Guatemala City, and other locations.

The majority of *catarineca* vendors in Antigua (as well as in Panajachel) are ambulatory, selling in the main plaza and in various strategic locations where tourists are found, such as first-class hotels, restaurants, Spanish language schools, and Spanish colonial ruins. Unlike most of the *típica* vendors from towns close to Antigua, who pick one of these strategic locations, display their products, and stay there, *catarinecas* are highly mobile. The women and their children spend the day wandering from one tourism locale to another, trying to predict where to find customers. By traveling among numerous places, they encounter a large number of people from various towns and countries, as well as from various ethnic and linguistic groups.

Although vendors had regular schedules, selling in Antigua on weekends and in Panajachel and other towns on the remaining days of the week, few admitted to it. On numerous occasions I asked *catarinecas,* as they prepared to leave Antigua, when they would return. I knew in advance that if they followed the patterns that I had observed, they would arrive in Antigua Thursday evening or Friday morning and then return home to Santa Catarina the following Monday morning. Also, most vendors spend three or four days in Antigua—at least Friday, Saturday, and Sunday—and then three or four days in Panajachel, where they can spend mornings and evenings at home in Santa Catarina. My *catarineca* friends rarely replied that they would be back in Antigua the following Thursday. Instead, they joked that they would return in a month, two months, or never. Warren (personal communication 7/17/02) explains that in San

Andrés, people respond to strangers in a similar fashion. Indeed, given the history of Guatemalan politics, in which people never know who may be a spy who could put their life or a family member's life in jeopardy (see Carlsen 1997; Stoll 1993), it is understandable that Mayas are suspicious of surveillance in any form. However, in the case of Santa Catarina, vendors did not tell other residents and often did not even tell immediate family members their schedules. Because Santa Catarina has been less connected to Guatemala's legacy of violence in comparison to other towns, I suspect that their ambiguity relates more to protecting business interests and avoiding the jealousy of other *catarinecos*.

NEGOTIATING SOCIOECONOMIC RELATIONS AND PERSONAL SECURITY

Catarineca vendors are quite adept socially, navigating easily between tourists and local police. In order to make sales to tourists and skillfully avoid problems with local authorities, they must politely interact with both. Although ambulatory vendors in Antigua generally employ similar strategies in dealing with tourists and the police, *catarineca* vendors rarely confronted Antigua authorities, whereas those from San Antonio Aguas Calientes did. While the latter felt it was their right to sell *típica* in Antigua, *catarinecas* acted more like visitors. Even those *catarinecas* who had spent several years selling *típica* in Antigua, including three families who had enrolled their children in Antigua schools and lived there most of the year, felt that they were temporary visitors.

While I was in the field, *antoneco* vendors promoted various political actions (organizing petition drives to sell legally in Antigua, going to the human rights office to report abuses by the police, visiting the mayor's office to complain about lack of city services in marketplaces), but *catarinecos* (women and men) did not participate in any of them. They, unlike male *antoneco* vendors, were never thrown in jail, either. Most tried to avoid conflict with adversaries (rival vendors, police officers, and Ladinos) and to foster economic relationships with tourists and Ladinos.

Like the women who sold textiles to the Taxes in the 1930s, some *catarinecas* establish patron-client relationships with Ladinos. This contact helps provide them with places to sleep and emergency cash while they are in Antigua. One of the problems facing ambulatory vendors, especially those from Santa Catarina because it is far from Antigua, is finding safe, affordable housing. Many Ladino property owners will not rent to Mayas (or "*indios*," to use their word), as I learned when I looked for a larger apartment to better accommodate the indigenous vendor friends who visited me and my growing fieldwork materials. They are especially opposed to *catarineca* vendors. In my apartment search, several Ladino landlords recognized me and said that they would not rent to "a friend of those *catarineco* animals," and similar comments. For this reason, first-time *catarineca* vendors find themselves sleeping on the street and worrying about thieves. Vendors commonly fear being robbed, but this fear was greatest among *catarinecas.*

A few Ladinos and expatriates from various countries, primarily owners of small hotels and textile retailers, act as a form of traveler's aid service. Some hotel owners charge *catarinecas* a small amount of money for a place on the floor in a corridor. For instance, from 1996 through 1998, a local posada charged only Q1 (US$0.17) for such an accommodation. Even though the accommodations are very modest, the arrangement allows vendors to keep their expenses down and protects them from thieves.

When vendors lacked cash needed for daily expenses and emergencies, some boutique owners, even when they did not need the merchandise, bought textiles from vendors at slightly over cost. Although vendors did not make much profit from these sales, such sales did provide them with some much needed cash. Vendors made larger profits when they left textiles on consignment with boutique owners. Some of the vendors used the money they made on consignment sales as a form of insurance—they watched their accounts but avoided using the money unless it was absolutely necessary.

BARGAINING WITH TOURISTS

Like the Maya vendors that the Taxes knew, contemporary *catarineca* vendors also avoid bargaining. This is not to say that I did not see them haggle, as they will bargain when it is necessary. If a tourist wants to bargain, then the vendor will haggle over the price of the item. However, when a vendor offered a price and the tourist countered with another, lower price, the vendor would immediately state her bottom selling price. If the tourist insisted on yet a lower price, the vendor would hold other items up for sale. According to most *catarinecas,* haggling over prices made them uncomfortable, especially when buyers tried to get merchandise below cost. Usually, the prices Santa Catarina ambulatory vendors charged were less than the prices that boutiques in Antigua charged, sometimes less than half.

Catarineca vendors felt offended by tourists and Ladinos who badgered them to sell at very low prices. For example, in one case, a tourist countered an initial selling price of Q1,000 (about US$167) for a well-made *po't* (*huipil* or blouse) with the ridiculously low offer of Q25 (about US$4.15). The vendor said that she would sell at Q600 (US$100), her bottom price. The tourist countered with a Q75 (US$12.50) offer. The vendor stood fast at Q600, but the tourist insisted on buying at Q75, not willing to raise her offer if the vendor did not lower her price some more. The vendor took out another blouse, which was worn and in need of repair but matched the amount of money the tourist indicated that she was willing to pay. "This," she said "I will sell to you for Q75." When it was clear that the vendor was serious, the tourist left without purchasing anything. The vendor turned and said to me, referring to the first blouse, "It is a sin (*xajan*) that she wants to buy at such a low price."

According to *catarineca* vendors, such behavior by tourists is rude, insulting, and ignorant, because both purchasers and sellers should know roughly what a reasonable price is. In fact, it is common practice for *catarinecas* to ask each other the prices of items they have purchased. They even grill tourists about how much they spent on backpacks, clothing, and portable electronic equipment. Thus, not knowing a price range reflects one's ignorance, but pretending to ignore a price range is rude and insulting. These patterns of vending, bargaining, and substituting inferior items to match an offered price followed a similar pattern to that described by Tax (1946, 1952, 1953) over sixty years ago.

SOCIOECONOMIC RELATIONS OF VENDOR FAMILIES

The greatest change in relation to *catarinecos'* participation in tourism has to do with a shift in magnitude. During Tax's fieldwork, only a few *catarinecas* participated in tourism. Today, most *catarinecos* participate in some aspect of tourism, by weaving, vending, or working in construction and hospitality services. By changing from dependency on plantation

Mayas in the Marketplace

wage labor and fishing to work related to tourism, *catarinecas* have become more mobile and have increased their access to money.

Numerous references in Tax (1946, 1952, 1953) indicate that women rarely traveled or conducted business without their husbands and fathers nearby. In Perla Petrich's (1996a, 1996b, 1996c, 1996d) oral history volumes about people from Lake Atitlán, women and children commonly traveled with their husbands and fathers to work on plantations in other regions and at marketplaces in other towns. Today, women travel extensively throughout Guatemala without their husbands but often with their children. Many have established regular business relationships and their own personal contacts in Antigua. Even in the three cases in which husbands regularly accompanied their wives and children to Antigua, the women made the decisions about where they sold, how business was conducted, where they spent the night, and how their finances were managed. Husbands and children turn over the money they make in sales to their wives or mothers, who then decide what to do with it.

Women explained that if they did not keep watch over their spouses and children, the latter would squander their meager profits. The men would drink it away, and the children would buy sweets and toys. This is a common household economic pattern in rural Latin America (Bossen 1984; Bourque and Warren 1981; Nash and Safa 1976). The three husbands who periodically worked with their wives complained about their wives' miserly ways, but they recognized that tourists purchased more items from women than from men. Most men, however, did not participate in their wives' vending lives.

Unmarried vendor women who were of marriageable age managed their own finances. They claimed that they did not have to give money to their parents, that they could spend their earnings as they saw fit. Although they used their money to buy clothing and some luxury items, such as radios and televisions, most continued to make contributions to the maintenance of their parents' household in Santa Catarina. For instance, Matilde, the young vendor woman I mentioned at the beginning of this chapter, maintains strong ties to her parents' household and town while being socially and economically independent in her vending activities. She is one of the more successful ambulatory vendors selling in Antigua. She used the money she earned from sales to tourists to buy well-made clothes, to occasionally eat in restaurants, and to purchase jewelry and a radio, but she also gave some of her earnings to assist her parents and her siblings, chipped in for various construction projects at her parents' home, and contributed to numerous Catholic Church–related functions.

TAKING TOURISTS HOME

At home, women scheme about how to attract tourists to their town. A number of *catarinecos* rent rustic rooms to tourists and students desiring to spend a couple of days in Santa Catarina. Most often, tourists are made aware of these simple accommodations by *catarineca* vendors in Antigua and Panajachel, who will literally take tourists and students home with them. For example, in July 1998, on invitation from *catarineca* vendors, the Oxlajuj Aj Kaqchikel Maya Language and Culture class took advantage of *catarineco* hospitality and stayed with six different families. They, like the tourists before and after them, ate meals with their *catarineco* hosts; participated in such celebrations as birthdays, baptisms, and memorial services that coincided with their stay; and learned how to weave and make bracelets. In addition to paying rent, all of the Kaqchikel students purchased textiles from their hosts, just as tourists and students before them had.

To coordinate activities such as weaving, vending, and attracting tourists, household members must cooperate. Most often, female vendors take interested tourists home, leaving them with male and older female family members. These extended family members entertain their guests, who may not see again the vendor woman who originally brought them. This strategy places the tourist in a setting that eliminates practically all of the household's competition. Tourists in this situation are dependent on their host families for meals, entertainment, and companionship. Because houses are located on paths that wind and twist up and down the mountainside, tourists frequently get lost. They depend on members of the host family, usually children, to guide them around the village. Tourists tend to gain a sense of belonging during their stay and often feel obligated to purchase items exclusively from their hosts. For the most part, *catarinecos* respected each other's boundaries when it came to the exclusive rights to particular tourists' business. Tourists were expected to purchase something from their hosts before they purchased something from anyone else.

Overwhelmingly, *catarineca* vendors selling in Antigua and other locations view tourism in a positive light. They play a crucial role in the

Mayas in the Marketplace

production of wealth in Santa Catarina Palopó. By vending in Antigua, Panajachel, and other tourism locales, they find outlets for *catarineca* weavers. By bringing tourists to their homes to rent rooms, they involve their extended families in processes that bring cash into their households. The more successful female vendors make decisions about general household expenses that male family members respect, since these same women have become more economically successful than others in their town. They are also relatively more independent and mobile than most men, because they have established economic and social contacts on their own, apart from other family members. Despite the increased economic and social freedom open to these women, most elect to maintain strong ties to their families and town.

Traditions and Community Boundaries

Based on data collected in the year 1965, Hinshaw (1975: 152) noted the relative strengths and weaknesses of several traditional and newer institutions present in eight of the towns located on Lake Atitlán. The traditional ones included service in the *cofradía*[12] and reliance on shamans, both strong practices in Santa Catarina. Newer institutions included schools, Catholic Action, and Protestantism, all weak there. Santa Catarina was one of the more conservative towns on the lake, as well as one of the towns most dependent on work outside of the community.

Hinshaw's observations led him to conclude that Santa Catarina had changed little in the thirty intervening years since Tax did his fieldwork. Residents were resistant to economic development and assistance from outsiders, did not embrace Protestantism, avoided service in the Guatemalan military, and clung to traditional economic practices such as fishing, crabbing, and mat making (Hinshaw 1975: 166–167). Since Hinshaw's fieldwork in the 1960s, most of these traditional economic activities have experienced rapid declines. Although weaving textiles remains vigorous to this day, the design and color schemes of Santa Catarina clothing have changed from primarily red and white stripes to deep blue, purple, and green geometric shapes. This change in clothing design relates to the availability of blue, purple, and green thread produced in the Cantel, Guatemala, factory and of imported thread, and to *catarinecas'* personal tastes, including their realization that no other Maya community weaves clothing using these colors. Most likely the color scheme changed because of individual family experimentation. Hendrickson (1995) describes how *huipil* fashions come and go as weavers experiment with new patterns and color combinations in the Kaqchikel town of Tecpán. These practices are common throughout highland Guatemala, despite the rhetoric of tourism guidebooks, which tend to locate *huipiles* as timeless, unchanging cultural artifacts.

CONTINUING TRADITIONS

Much of daily life in Santa Catarina appears to follow patterns similar to those observed by both Tax and Hinshaw. Men leave home to work (on the lake, in fields, or at construction sites) outside of Santa Catarina, and women stay home, weaving, watching children, washing clothes, and preparing meals. Had my introduction to Santa Catarina been from going to the town and not from meeting *catarineca* vendors in Antigua, my impressions of the town and the people would have been very different. The peaceful, traditional-looking town belies the economic and social relations in which it participates. As Kearney (1996) explains, residents of small, traditional towns are also increasingly members and direct participants in transnational work forces and commodity flows. Unlike Appadurai (1996), who concentrates on flows of media, people, and commodities, Kearney is concerned with the local ways that transnational subjects maintain their community and traditions, despite the fact that they may live and work months or years away from the place that they call home. Like the residents of San Jerónimo, Mexico, where Kearney did fieldwork, Santa Catarina's residents are participants in global economic practices who maintain a very traditional-looking town.

To the outsider, the Santa Catarina traditions most easily observed include weaving, *cofradía* activities, village-specific clothing, the Kaqchikel language, adobe house construction, and food such as *pulik richin ëk'* (chicken stew thickened with cornmeal) and *sub'an* (corn tamales with no filling). A casual conversation with a man would reveal that the important male-related traditions include *cofradía* service, wearing Santa Catarina–specific clothing, fishing, and milpa farming. Men clearly recognize that fishing, especially with a net for sardine-sized fish, and milpa farming are dying traditions, but the memory of these economic activities is still fresh. A similar conversation with a woman would reveal that important female-related traditions are weaving, wearing Santa Catarina–specific clothing, *cofradía* participation, and preparing certain foods. These types of traditions are still an active part of their daily life.

THE ROLE OF TOURISM IN THE MAINTENANCE OF TRADITIONS

The survival of some of these traditions, such as weaving, wearing traditional clothing, and participating in the *cofradía,* is partially related to tourism and encouraged by the national government.[13] *Catarinecos* are well aware that foreign tourists are particularly interested in seeing "Indians" who wear their traditional clothing and practice weaving. In Santa Catarina, women often weave publicly, setting up their looms where a passing tourist can easily observe them. The slightest pause by the tourist results in them being invited in, given a brief weaving demonstration, and offered items for sale.

In rural towns and hamlets that are not designated tourism sites, weaving and other household activities are done in private. When hiking around the hamlets of Tecpán, Totonicapán, Santa Lucía Utatlán, and Comalapa, I watched most women drop what they were doing and hide from me, something that may not have happened had I been a Kaqchikel-speaking Maya woman. However, foreign women are likewise regarded with suspicion by rural women (Adams 1998; Nelson 1999). The women sometimes acknowledged my presence only after I greeted them and quickly stated my business in the appropriate language (Kaqchikel or K'iche'). On the other hand, women in Santa Catarina interact very differently with outsiders such as tourists. They are open and talkative, and they showcase their clothing and weaving techniques. Some even offer their guests a taste of traditional foods, such as stew (*pulik richin ëk'*) and tamales (*sub'an*). They showcase these traditions because they attract tourists who spend money on textiles and rent rooms in the town.

The combination of colorful, blue-purple clothing, the sound of Kaqchikel, the view of Lake Atitlán with the surrounding volcanoes, and the friendliness of the residents distinguishes Santa Catarina from most other towns in Guatemala. As men and woman alike realize, should these traditions cease to be practiced, tourists would probably not visit Santa Catarina. For this reason, men cooperate by wearing traditional clothing while in Santa Catarina (although they dress in "American-style" clothing when they go to work in other areas of Guatemala), by supporting

government soldiers and became suspicious of any kind of surveillance (Stoll 1993).

Although *catarinecos* did not even serve in the Guatemalan army, they feel that Maya rituals would have been squelched if they had been practiced in public where soldiers and Protestants could learn of them. After an elaborate memorial service for his father, performed by an *ajq'ij,* Diego explained to me how, in the past, he went to the cemetery and to a small nearby cave to do the rituals. "Today, you do not know if a Protestant or someone in the army may be watching," he said. Maya curing ceremonies, birthday blessings, and memorial services are all performed behind guarded, closed doors.

Why, then, has the *cofradía* not died or at least gone underground, as have Maya ritual practices? I can only partially answer this. Like some other traditions that are actively maintained, particularly weaving and wearing traditional clothing, the *cofradía,* especially during the titular festival, has sparked the interest of tourists. During the week of the November festival in 1997, the Villa Santa Catarina, the first-class hotel located between the town center and the lake shore, filled to capacity. On each of the four principal days, tour companies took boatloads of tourists to watch *cofradía* ceremonies in the church and town center. The activities in the *cofradía* houses, however, were not open to tourists.

On one of the festival days, a group of French tourists arrived in time to listen to the marimba bands in the plaza, before watching Santa Catarina Alejandría's procession leave the Catholic church. While the tour group was a source of amusement for the *catarinecos* when the tourists danced to the marimba music,[15] *catarinecas* seized the opportunity to sell some locally made textiles to them. No tourist who enters Santa Catarina in order to see *cofradía* or other church activities escapes the watchful eyes of the women and children,[16] just as no traditional activity that interests tourists is discouraged. It is rare to see a tourist leave the town without purchasing something.

THE ROLE OF WOMEN
IN THE MAINTENANCE OF COMMUNITY TRADITIONS

Some traditions (and the gendered division of them) are easily observed, but often one cannot casually observe the actors who maintain those traditions. Although men make economic contributions to the maintenance of their households, the town festival, and other *cofradía* activities where Santa Catarina's traditions are reproduced, women are the main reproducers of tradition, including *ajq'ija'*. The anthropological literature is filled with examples of the important roles that women play in reproducing people, material items, food, and knowledge (also see Bossen 1984; Hendrickson 1995; Moore 1988; Nash and Safa 1976; Stephen 1991). The central place of tourism in the economic lives of *catarinecos* helps explain why they maintain these various cultural practices. The use of *traje* and weaving in public view mark them as indigenous to tourists. However, individual and community rituals, in addition to the consumption of foods like *ichaj* and *pulik,* can be used to delineate boundaries between them and tourists. Throughout Latin America the reliance on indigenous women to reproduce local cultural items, knowledge, and practices has been challenged by changing economic and social contexts. As indigenous communities become economically stratified, socially and economically marginalized women have stopped maintaining ethnic and local community traditions (Bourque and Warren 1981; de la Cadena 2000; Ehlers 1990; Nash 2001).

Women in Santa Catarina do play important roles in the production of wealth, partly because their weaving and vending activities bring in cash. The money earned from sales to tourists has been used to cover the costs of weaving clothing for self and family consumption, to pay *ajq'ija'* to perform ritual ceremonies, to financially support the *cofradía* system, and to contribute to the titular festival, an annual celebration in which the town's patron saint is honored.

Women and girls continue to weave their own clothing, but there is a general decline in the number of men who wear *traje* on a daily basis. Men who did not own traditional clothing were often in the poorest families, who could afford to weave only female clothing. This contrasts with trends in other Kaqchikel towns like San Andrés Semetabaj (Warren 1989), San Juan de Comalapa, and Tecpán (Hendrickson 1995), where the poorer men wear *traje.*

Among the *catarinecas* I met, there was not one vendor woman who did not make major financial contributions to community ritual practices. The *ajq'ija'*'s ritual performances, which are done by both men and women individually as well as by male and female pairs, and the accompanying accouterments of candles, incense, hard liquor, tobacco, sugar, chocolate, and bread, can add up to Q300–Q400 (US$50–$67) for a single ceremony. A great deal of *cofradía* service involves labor and time, but, as in years past, it also includes great outlays of cash that reach well over Q2,000 (US$333) for the main participants, who must keep fresh flowers in the church, provide the saints with clothing, purchase hard liquor and beer for ceremonial activities in the *cofradía* houses, rent costumes for dances on scheduled ceremonial days throughout the year, hire a marimba band (in addition to the three bands hired to play in the plaza during the titular festival) for the *cofradía* house, and weave and purchase special items of clothing for them to wear during ceremonies and celebrations. The contributions of roughly Q20–Q200 (US$3.33–$33.33) that *catarinecos* make for the titular festival are minor compared to the costs of clothing, *ajq'ija'* ceremonies, and *cofradía* service. Successful vendors spent more money on clothing than did unsuccessful vendors and weavers, and they also made some of the largest contributions to the titular festival.

Though it is necessary to recognize that the combined incomes of many female vendors and their husbands are modest, only between Q400 and Q700 (US$66.67 and $116.67) per month, which covers their basic subsistence expenses, some women make much more money. The amount of money that successful vendor women make also greatly exceeds what men typically make in the tourism services or as construction laborers and farmworkers, their most common jobs. The best-paying jobs for males in Santa Catarina are at the Villa Santa Catarina, which pays *catarineco* bartenders, cooks, housekeepers, and gardeners Q20 (US$3.33) per ten-hour day. Although the Guatemalan government's official minimum wage for agricultural work is around Q25 (US$4.27) per day, most *catarinecos* reported making only around Q15 (US$2.50) per day. Unskilled construction laborers reported that they earned wages similar to farmworkers and employees in tourism services. This means that men's monthly salaries ranged from Q375 to Q675 (US$62.50–$112.50), if they even had a job. Many younger men were underemployed or unemployed.

Successful female vendors, on the other hand, sometimes made Q100–Q200 (US$16.67–$33.33) per day. On occasion, *catarineca* vendors asked me to keep money for them in my Antigua apartment after they had made large sales of over Q200. Most of the time, I learned the amounts of money they earned by listening to them sell to tourists. Then I compared the amount they received from tourists to the amount that they paid weavers and other wholesale providers. Vendors also gave me the U.S. dollars they earned to exchange them for quetzales.[17]

Among *catarineca* vendors, Matilde was the most open with me about the money she made on any particular day. Consistently, Matilde had days when she cleared Q100 in sales. I do not quite understand why she started showing me her daily expenses, since I never once asked her or any other *catarineca* vendor how much they made. After people in Santa Catarina established friendships with me, they freely discussed how much they paid for all the items they purchased, but they did not talk about how much they made, only commenting that they were poor. Numerous people mentioned to me that the amount of wealth an individual or family had would always be downplayed to everyone outside the immediate family.

After providing for household subsistence and improving their homes by adding such items as sinks/wash basins (*pilas*), griddle stoves (*pollos*), and improved saunas (*tuj*), *catarinecas* put part of their money into Santa Catarina–style clothing, the *cofradía,* and the titular festival. On three different occasions, men over age sixty proudly modeled the clothing their wives had made for them. In each case, their pants were of the highest quality, a heavy red-and-white-striped cotton that was entirely covered with animal, plant, and human motifs in shades of blue, green, and purple. The designs were made of silk and *cedelina* (two of the more expensive types of thread available in Guatemala), and the pants cost between Q1,000 and Q1,500 (US$167.67 and $250) to make. These prices were confirmed by describing the pants to two different weavers and then asking them how much they would charge. Each of these men proclaimed proudly that not only had their wives woven the pants, but their success as *típica* vendors allowed them to afford such expensive threads. Although the women I worked with did not weave or purchase such elaborate pants as did the wives of these three elderly men, they did provide their husbands and male children with more modest traditional clothes or new "American-style" clothing for special occasions, such as birthdays and weddings.

Female *típica* vendors do more than dress themselves and their families; they make monetary contributions that allow family members to participate in the *cofradía.* Even though Matilde is not yet married and thus is ineligible to take a *cofradía* post, she contributed money to various family members to cover parts of their *cofradía* obligations. Martín, who works with his wife in the Compañía de Jesús Artisan Marketplace in Antigua (and who is among three nonambulant vendors from Santa Catarina), explained that he could not have fulfilled his obligations to the *cofradía* had it not been for his wife and her *típica* business. Couples younger than age thirty who participate in the *cofradía* tend to get the money they need from the wife's *típica* sales.

In addition to physically reproducing and financially supporting Santa Catarina traditions, *catarinecas* have been particularly resistant to Protestantism and national public education. Unlike vendors from San Antonio Aguas Calientes, who have a long, strong tradition of Protestantism, *catarineca* vendors are overwhelmingly Catholic. They still practice *costumbre*, which Warren (1989: 27) describes as traditions inherited from ancestors. In Santa Catarina, as in San Andrés Semetabaj, *costumbre* is tied to the *cofradía* system and a belief system that, when practiced, helps bring order to the community. As Warren (1989: 49) explains, "The first Indian ancestors who 'invented' *costumbre* became models for correct behavior, which was 'rewarded by a long life, many children, and successful plantings and harvests.'"

In many communities, such as San Andrés Semetabaj (Warren 1989), San Antonio Aguas Calientes (Annis 1987), San Antonio Ilotenango (Falla 1978), and Santiago Atitlán (Carlsen 1997), practitioners of *costumbre* have conflicted with Catholic Action catechists and Protestants over the proper ways to practice Christianity. The emphasis on local community-focused practices of *costumbre* rather than a recognition of universalist ideology tied to a hierarchically ordered church is often at the center of these groups' differences. Although conflict between Catholics and Protestants in San Antonio Aguas Calientes was minimal at the time of this writing (2003), *catarineca* vendors still spoke strongly against the Evangelical Protestants, saying that they were "crazy" (*chuj*), "lost" (*xsach*), or "evil" (*itzel*). When Anastasia, a teenager in one of the families that regularly participates in the *cofradía,* openly practices *costumbre,* and weaves and sells *típica* to tourists, took me to see if the pastor of one of the Protestant churches would let the Oxlajuj Aj Kaqchikel Maya class use one of its rooms, she warned me not to speak to him in Kaqchikel. Although the pastor was a native speaker and a lifelong resident of Santa Catarina, Anastasia said that he was trying to encourage *catarinecos* to give up Kaqchikel and *costumbre.* As it turned out, we were not allowed to use one of the church rooms because the course supported the traditions and taught the language that he was discouraging. Vendor women and their husbands frequently called the Protestant sermons "noise" (*bulla*) and said of the flock, "they scream, they don't sing" (*yesik'in, man yeb'ixan ta*). When the younger children of some vendors made pig sounds and said that they were "acting like Evangelicals," their parents encouraged the children by laughing and asking them to repeat the behavior.

Regarding the public school and education in general, *catarinecas* and their husbands did not think going to school was bad for their children. Most, however, did very little to encourage them to go or to stay in school. Petrich (1996a: 19, 31) correctly assesses the relationship between the poverty of Santa Catarina and the pressure that girls feel to give up their studies so they can sell bracelets, shirts, and small handwoven textiles to tourists to assist with basic household expenses. It is difficult for girls and young women to see the benefits of going to school. Inscription fees and the costs of materials appear to be a waste of money, because no women and few men have reaped any benefits from a school education. Besides, going to the school places them in classrooms with Ladino teachers, with whom they do not feel comfortable because of cultural differences. Ladino teachers are also associated with mistreatment of Mayas and ethnic discrimination.

Those who periodically go to school, like Matilde and her youngest sisters or the daughters of another family, do not receive very much monetary or emotional support from their parents, most of whom are illiterate. Unpublished statistics for 1994 from the Instituto Nacional de Estadísticas (National Institute of Statistics) office in Guatemala City indicate that illiteracy in Santa Catarina Palopó at that time was a little over 55 percent. In 1955, according to Petrich (1996a: 13), 93.3 percent of all older children and adults in Santa Catarina were illiterate. It would appear that Santa Catarina has made great improvements in literacy over the intervening thirty-nine years, but it is still lower than that of many other indigenous communities. For instance, San Antonio Aguas Calientes had a literacy rate of 84 percent in 1994. It is doubtful that the current statistics are very accurate, since the "literate" people did not go beyond first or second grade and have not practiced their rudimentary reading and writing skills since leaving school.

On the other hand, traditional forms of education, especially for girls, were encouraged and supported. Mothers and grandmothers taught their daughters how to cook traditional foods and to weave. They took their daughters with them to sell *típica* in Panajachel, Antigua, and other tourism sites, where they learned how to sell and interrelate with tourists, Ladinos, and other Mayas. Younger girls literally grow up selling *típica* and can see the benefits of being a good salesperson. They personally know successful role models. Besides, a successful vendor makes more money than a teacher, who earns between Q700 and Q1,200 (US$116.67– $200) per month.

Conclusions

Like the residents of San Jerónimo, Mexico, studied by Kearney (1996), *catarinecos* live in a sociocultural space that defies traditional anthropological categorization. When residents of Santa Catarina say that they are farmers (*tikonel*), Maya, Kaqchikel, *indígena,* or *catarineco,* the terms reflect the social and conceptual fields in which they live, such as the Guatemalan state and international tourism. They participate in a wage economy and aspire to own, if they do not already, material items such as televisions, refrigerators, and cars. By describing themselves as *tikonel,* Maya, *indígena,* Kaqchikel, and *catarineco* they are not trying to recapture their traditions and heritage or release some latent primitivism that is trapped inside themselves, practices common among Northern Europeans and U.S. Americans (see MacCannell 1992). Because *catarinecos* historically conceive of themselves as persons who practice *costumbre,* and because they maintain traditions such as backstrap weaving and the *cofradía,* *catarinecos* have a strong sense of traditional collective identity and community.

In contemporary Santa Catarina Palopó, *catarinecos* feel direct physical and genealogical connections to place and to certain traditional practices. They do not just remember their traditions (including net fishing and reed mat weaving); they still know how to perform them. Women in Santa Catarina have particularly important roles in the practice and maintenance of tradition. They also provide a significant amount of the economic base that makes possible the reproduction of these traditions. Without the cash that *catarinecas* earn from sales to tourists, the strength of community traditions would probably erode because women would not be able to provide the money for clothing, festivals, and the *cofradía.*

Men in Santa Catarina, of course, have not given up traditions wholesale. They also help contribute to household subsistence and to the maintenance of the *cofradía* and the annual town festival. They just do not make as much money as some of the women. Also, men's jobs in construction, tourism, and agriculture do not directly relate to community beliefs about what is traditional. Traditional occupations such as reed mat weaving, milpa agriculture, and fishing are weak or nonexistent for most men, although most of them still considered themselves *tikonela'* (farmers) or fishermen. Even the few men who are *típica* vendors tend not to make and sell textiles indigenous to Santa Catarina. Instead, they sell key chains, decorated T-shirts, and inexpensive jewelry—generic products that can be found in tourist marketplaces throughout the Americas. Thus, women continue to practice their economic lives in ways that relate to numerous community traditions, but men usually do not.

Like the residents of other communities in Guatemala and Mexico, *catarinecos* perform economic activities to sustain themselves that increasingly take them outside their home community (e.g., Annis 1987; Ehlers 1990; Kearney 1995, 1996; Nash 1993a; Re Cruz 1996). Whereas the jobs men perform frequently take them away from Santa Catarina and the traditional practices described in this chapter, women contribute economically by both staying and leaving. They have made Santa Catarina traditions and identity a commodity for sale to tourists. This economic strategy entails women leaving Santa Catarina to sell *típica* and then bringing tourists home, where traditions are presented to them. Although *catarinecas* sell textiles throughout Guatemala, they also sell an image of their town to tourists, which is that of a traditional closed-corporate community, unchanging in time and in beliefs. Tourism has helped *catarinecos* think of their town as a closed community because of the traditions that interest tourists the most: traditional clothing, the *cofradía,* the titular festival, and Maya rituals and language. Most of these traditions are generally not open or easily accessible to outsiders such as tourists.

Despite the conservativeness of Santa Catarina (in terms of *cofradía,* Catholic and Maya spiritualism, community clothing, and Kaqchikel language), *catarinecos* have transformed both their town and themselves. Revisiting Tax's 1935 (1946: 19) fieldnotes reveals how great the physical transformation has been over time:

> Santa Catarina is known to the Government health officials, as well as to the Indians of other towns, as an exceptionally dirty place. . . . But the personal habits of the people have not been changed and their reputation hasn't suffered. Partly because of their use of lake water for all purposes (and this is the only lake town where drinking

water is taken from the same spot where clothes are washed), partly because of the general filth, Santa Catarina is notorious for disease.

As Santa Catarina became a recognized tourism site and, at the same time, less notorious for poor sanitary conditions, *catarinecas* did not give up the roles they performed when Tax conducted his fieldwork. Instead, they have expanded traditional women's economic, social, and ritual practices to embrace a larger social and economic universe. Although they direct their economic gains inward, toward home and community, they are participants in a world economic system. Men spoke proudly of their wives', sisters', mothers', and daughters' economic successes and contributions to conserving Santa Catarina traditions. Female and male children spoke admirably of successful vendor women and considered them role models.

In the sixty-plus years since Tax's fieldwork in Santa Catarina Palopó, women have had increasingly important roles in earning money and maintaining community traditions. These practices have led to the dual and contradictory *catarineco* view of Santa Catarina as both a closed community, in regard to some religious traditions, and an open community, in regard to tourism. It is in this sociocultural context that women have balanced community traditions with economic enterprises.

Mayas in the Marketplace

Conclusion: Traditions and Commodities

One afternoon I listened to a group of friends from Santa Catarina Palopó talk about recent encounters they had had with "tourists," which in this case included a film crew, a photographer, and an anthropologist. The tourists were interested in witnessing and recording aspects of traditional culture in this small Kaqchikel Maya town. For instance, a film crew from Germany came to document traditional life in Santa Catarina, but they became frustrated when they discovered too many corruptions of modernity, such as gas cooking stoves, radios, an occasional television, and mass-produced prepackaged foods. In an effort to capture traditional Maya life on film, they encouraged *catarinecos* to hide modern artifacts and stage traditional life (c.f. Lutz and Collins 1993). One woman explained, "They wanted us to weave without our radios and cook without our stoves. They wanted me to cook a meal on top of rocks."

Jokingly, another woman commented, "They wanted me to be in the movie, but my *pollo*[1] was too big. There was no room for me to cook on the ground."

Another said, straight-faced, "I was going to be in the movie, but my television was too big. I told them it had to be [in it] so I could see myself in their movie." At this they all laughed.

Like the film crew, the photographer and the anthropologist had wandered through their town looking for tradition—the former with a camera, the latter with a tape recorder. As with the film crew, Maya tradition either had been "corrupted" or had eluded them. My friends explained how they intentionally placed items near them that they knew the photographer would not think were traditional, like radios, Coca-Cola containers, and Disney toys. When the anthropologist passed by with his tape recorder, they spoke in Spanish, mixing in some English words. "I don't know why he wanted to record our language. He couldn't even speak it," said one of the women.

Since they thought all of this was pretty funny, I asked them why they treated these "tourists" like this when they did not treat most other tourists in such a fashion (although vendors from other towns say similar things about tourists, anthropologists, and photographers). One of them explained, "They want to know everything about us, but who are they? They want to ask questions and get answers and take pictures, but they don't give us anything. Other tourists pay to take pictures. They buy *típica* from us, and they don't bother us with questions and try to tell us what to do."

This book has looked at the socioeconomic relationships of Kaqchikel Maya vendors, attending to how they use various conceptualizations of identity and tradition to sell to foreign and national tourists. Vendors play upon and react to these stereotypes in the selling strategies they use. Often their commodification of the mundane is a response to these stereotypes that gives them the opportunity to carve out new economic niches and alter tourists' perceptions.

Tradition

Típica vendors are more than willing to sell tradition to tourists and anthropologists. However, as one friend said bluntly with regard to tourists and anthropologists who are consumed with discovering Maya traditions and do not learn what really matters to them, "We'll tell you something you want to hear, but it probably won't be true—not all of it. We Mayas are good at lying." These types of commentaries by Mayas demand that anthropologists reexamine how they think about their subjects and how their subjects think about them, as has been done in recent ethnographies by Fischer (2001) and Warren 1998a).

Watanabe (1995: 33) asks anthropologists to "unimagine the Maya" and shows how anthropologists have imagined Mayas in two modalities: "the romantic and the tragic." The first focuses on exotica, the traditions that link them to pre-Columbian Maya civilization. The second focuses on the ways that Mayas have been the victims of Spanish colonialism, national liberal economic projects, religious missionizing, and other ideological and economic policies by those who have politically, economically, or militarily dominated them. According to Watanabe (1995: 34), "Clearly, neither romance nor tragedy sufficiently explains what being Maya is all about or even why Maya should remain Maya."

I have tried to push Watanabe's call to unimagine the Maya even further by asking scholars to examine whether the analytical categories they bring with them when they come to learn about Mayas are appropriate. Appadurai (1996), García Canclini (1995), Gupta and Ferguson (1997), and Hall (1997a, 1997b) have endeavored to redefine the categories anthropologists use to understand anthropological subjects, but they have limited themselves in a number of ways. Appadurai suggests looking at the world in terms of global flows of people, commodities, and media that are reconfiguring localities and transforming place-bounded communities into cybernetic, multisite communities. Similarly, Gupta and Ferguson say that the concept of culture as the connections between people and a specific bounded place is antiquated, since too many people have left their homelands. As Gupta (1998) demonstrates in his research on Indian peasants, some anthropological subjects actually live and think about their lives in ways that do not make distinctions between traditional and modern or global and local, although they are clearly part of both of these conceptual fields.

Appadurai (1996: 44) writes:

> What is new is that this is a world in which both points of departure and points of arrival are in cultural flux, and thus the search for steady points of reference, as critical life choices are made, can be difficult. It is in this atmosphere that the invention of tradition (and of ethnicity, kinship, and other identity markers) can become slippery, as the search for certainties is regularly frustrated by the fluidities of transnational communication. As group pasts become increasingly parts of museums, exhibits, and collections, both in national and transnational spectacles, culture becomes less . . . a habitus . . . and more an arena for conscious choice, justification, and representation, the latter often to multiple and spatially dislocated audiences.

As I have illustrated throughout this book, Kaqchikel Maya *típica* vendors do not have difficulties constructing steady points of reference. They, in particular, have adjusted quite well to transnational flows of commodities, ideas, and people as they sell to international tourists, surf the Internet, watch international cable television channels, and sometimes travel themselves. They know where home is, who populates that place, and what they need to do to exist and participate in it.[2] If anything, the invention of tradition only becomes "slippery" for these Mayas when they debate what they should present and sell to anthropologists and tourists. They are also quite aware of how Mayas are represented in touristic discourses and Guatemalan, Mexican, and Honduran museums. This knowledge helps them market Mayanness in ways that are often framed in terms of past traditions. However, among Mayas themselves, tradition really refers to ongoing localized sets of life practices and social relations, not to some unchanging or past cultural practice. This practice of "tradition," or *costumbre,* is also demonstrated by Mayas in the research of other scholars (e.g., Warren 1989; Watanabe 1992). This is not to imply that Mayas' direct, often personal participation—not indirect, as Smith's (1978, 1984, 1990a) research illustrates—in the global economy has not resulted in them changing some of the ways they live and conceive of themselves. The point is that vendors are not in a state of crisis with regard to their cultural identity.

Appadurai, García Canclini, and Hall (1996a, 1996b, 1997a, 1997b) all offer potential outcomes, in terms of identity, for people who are caught up in the global system. García Canclini and Appadurai argue that the movements of people into and out of modernity (to use García Canclini's (1995) cultural-studies-inflected phrasing) or between traditional and modern have resulted in people becoming cultural hybrids. Certainly, in terms of material items, this also seems to be the case with Kaqchikel vendors. Those Kaqchikel Mayas (including nonvendors) that I know do not think using such things as cellular telephones, computers, gas stoves, refrigerators, televisions, and cars makes them less Maya. In fact, these things allow them to be even more Maya because they make it easier to maintain basic and special cultural practices. Furthermore, as Kaqchikel Mayas see it, they do not move between the traditional and the modern, the local and the global. According to them, it is all the same thing, all mixed up, just the way life is.

Within the political context of Guatemala, hybridity, or rather *mestizaje,* is being used to defuse Maya political and cultural movements. Warren (1998a) discusses this issue at some length from the Maya perspective, as does Hale (1996) from the Ladino perspective. Some Ladinos, such as Mario Roberto Morales, a self-styled culture critic and Guatemalan newspaper columnist, use concepts of *mestizaje* (hybridity) to delegitimize the Maya movement. By trying to prove Mayas are really the same as (or close enough to) Ladinos, they seek to deny them voice and agency within Guatemalan political arenas. Vendors have avoided these debates by avoiding "Maya" as a term of collective identity within national political contexts. However, within the context of the tourism marketplace, they will use indigenous languages and other markers. Like Maya politicians and political/cultural activists, Maya vendors need to distinguish themselves from Ladinos. In part, vendors do it because they know that tourists do not come to Guatemala to see Ladinos and learn about Ladino life. Even though Mayas stage certain aspects of their lives, even invent some of it for tourists, they practice their lives differently from Ladinos. And despite Ladino political rhetoric about Mayas really being mestizos, I met few Ladinos who really thought Mayas were like them. In fact, Ladinos complained to me that they were fearful that Mayas would resort to ethnic cleansing, as in Bosnia, since the Maya movement promotes culture and most Guatemalans are ethnically Maya. Warren (2002) explains that this issue was used to catalyze the anti-Maya vote in the 1999 referendum. Most Mayas thought this position was laughable, precisely because Mayas consider themselves different from Ladinos, who effectively resorted to ethnic cleansing in the early 1980s.

Hall's (1997a: 33–34) argument is that some people choose between local and global, usually opting for the local over the global because the global is too complicated and too inclusive. Others have become de-centered and marginalized to such an extent that "new subjects, new genders, new ethnicities, new regions, new communities" are emerging. Mayas, however, especially those vendors who are in the midst of transnational tourism, commodity, and idea flows, do not choose between local and global. Nor are they forming new identities and communities because they are de-centered and marginalized. If anything, they have a more centered, less marginalized, and more expansive conception of who they are now than they did in the past. The very global forces that Hall (and other theoreticians) says are fragmenting and tearing apart the old identities and communities of many people around the world have in fact served to reinvigorate Maya cultural, political, and economic practices. To some extent, this has to do with the fact that Mayas, specifically Kaqchikel Maya vendors, do not choose between the global and the local. These are not categorical distinctions for them. However, both Maya and Guatemalan nationalisms are, and they choose not to participate in them.

The Commodification of Social Life

One of my underlying themes has been the extent to which some Kaqchikel Maya vendors have commodified their social life and put it up for sale on the global market. Unlike the artisans and vendors discussed by García Canclini (1993) and in Nash's (1993a) edited volume, they have gone beyond the manufacture of handicrafts for the global market. Some market mundane life practices, such as cooking, weaving, and taking care of children. Not only are the handicrafts for sale, so is Maya life, especially what has been described in anthropological literature as the domestic sphere. Indeed, Castañeda (1996) makes a forceful argument about the role anthropology has had in shaping cultural identity in tourism sites.

Hall (1997a: 30) contends that "capital is constantly exploiting different forms of labor force, constantly moving between the sexual division of labor in order to accomplish its commodification of social life." With regard to Kaqchikel Mayas, how should the forces of capital be regarded? What motivates or compels them to enter the handicraft trade and, then, to eventually sell the life that happens behind and around the fabrication of handicrafts? I have discussed several different mechanisms that explain why this has happened: increased demand for handicrafts, ease of travel, high levels of unemployment and underemployment combined with poor or low wages, land shortages, and low capital investment. Aside from Ubico's requirement that Mayas present the domestic side of life to Ladinos and international tourists during the fairs he staged in the 1930s, there has been no law or mandate for Mayas to commodify the domestic sphere. Mayas today do not have to sell this to tourists, but they do so primarily to outcompete their vendor neighbors, who are selling the same basic handicrafts.

Hall's statement, however, makes capital appear to be an agent and process similar to the Borg, a cyborg collective from the *Star Trek* family of television series that absorbs other societies and technologies into their own communal mind and body at the expense of the individual. From the perspective of Kaqchikel vendors who perform domestic life for tourists, capital does not work that way. They choose to commodify or not to commodify social life, no matter how much tourists desire to see it. Even those who do perform for tourists decide what and how much they will share. Most decide that, aside from giving weaving demonstrations, it is not worth the trouble to perform mundane domestic life for tourists, who more often than not complain that Maya homes are too dirty or too modern.

The commodification of the domestic sphere is connected to the commodification of place. In fact, the household is one of the places, like the artisan marketplace, where local, national, and transnational political, social, and economic spheres are integrated in Mayas' daily life practices. Mayas demonstrate this pragmatically in the approaches they take to working and socializing in the marketplace, in their towns, and in their households. Identity and place are interrelated, and vendors use them strategically, invoking specific ones to get what they need out of tourists and government officials. In contrast to activists in the Pan-Maya movement, they perform to their audiences but refuse to be pegged with one particular identity—ethnic, national, or class—just to get international tourism money or maneuver through Guatemala's sociopolitical terrain. Basically, Mayas who perform life for tourists' consumption are selling a package that includes the handicraft, the life behind the handicraft, a place, and their cultural identity.

The touristic construction of and use of places (household, marketplace, Antigua, Guatemala) by Mayas to enact culture are tied to the ways identity is presented and used in relation to particular types of Others. In this context, global processes are part of localities that provide a space for new economic and political uses of identity to operate. This touristic borderzone (appropriating from Bruner [1996b, 1999]) is constantly changing because tourism spaces in Guatemala are not controlled by the Guatemalan nation-state, but are contested and negotiated by a number of different social, economic, and political actors: Maya vendors, international tourists, Guatemalan and foreign government officials, Guatemalan and international businesspersons, non-Maya Ladinos, and others. Within the tourism borderzone, two contradictory processes occur: (1) global and transnational economic and political forces become part of the local context, and (2) new localisms, differences, and nationalisms emerge. These two contradictory processes give Kaqchikel Mayas more space to avoid essentialized identities (political or otherwise) and to invoke identities recognizable to others. This helps them place their products—handicrafts, their towns, and themselves—in ways that tourists can recognize them. As they are keenly aware, if their buyers do not recognize them, then they cannot sell themselves, their locality, or their handicrafts.

Final Thoughts

I have focused herein on tourism/*típica* marketplaces, marketing *típica* to foreign tourists, and the interplay of transnational processes and community and household life. Kaqchikel Maya vendors critically and creatively engage the tourism borderzone, and this engagement relates to the state and touristic terrains of power and representation that make Mayas both their subjects and their objects. These vendors tend to ignore the Maya movement, just as they tended to ignore the guerrillas and Guatemalan government unless forced to pay attention. Like the nationalism promoted by the Guatemalan state, the concepts of plurality and Pan-Mayanism promoted by leaders of the Maya movement are not monolithic or hegemonic. Although the Maya movement's cultural revitalization agenda has certainly influenced vendors, vendors have different frames of reference and different pragmatic concerns, based on the manner in which they live in the world.

Critical to vendors' sense of identity and their ultimate success in the marketplace, their hometowns, and their households are the strategies they use to maintain ongoing social relations among themselves and with others. In addition to the interconnections between marketplace and hometown, as demonstrated through social relations, local indigenous perspectives on identity, place, and what can be sold are embedded in broader national and transnational processes. My concern was to describe the specific ways that vendors lived, used, and thought about their lives in the tourism borderzone, as well as how they critiqued Guatemalan Ladino nationalism, Maya movement nationalism, and international tourism, as each related to identity concepts of who Mayas are.

The themes pursued throughout this book include understanding transnational processes of tourism in Guatemala, conceptualizing touristic Guatemala as a borderzone, and trying to describe Kaqchikel Maya identities within the transnational dimensions of tourism. I have tried to understand in socioeconomic terms "ethnic groups as reflections of an evolving transnational system" (Stack 1981: 40–41) and how this "transnational system" can conflict with the nation-state (Appadurai 1996).

Although ethnicity is one of the ways that vendors express their identity, it is not the only form of identity that emerges from the social relations in which they are embedded. Ethnic identity is related to the nation-state (see Stephen 1991; Toland 1993; and Weber 1946: 159–179), but the Guatemalan nation-state, as a political/economic force, is, for the most part, questioned by Kaqchikel Maya vendors and probably most other Mayas (see Smith 1984: 150). However, Mayas do recognize its existence and the power it has had, especially when violently repressing them (see Green 1999; Montejo 1999; Nelson 1999; Warren 1998a, 1998b, 2002).

Asking what the "real" identities of Kaqchikel Maya vendors are or, for that matter, those of all Mayas parallels an anecdote that Clifford Geertz (1973: 29) relates in *The Interpretation of Cultures*. Upon discovering that Indians believe that the world rests on the back of a turtle, an Englishman asks, "What did the turtle rest on?" "Another turtle" was the response. "And that turtle?" Answering him, the Indian man replies, "After that, it is turtles all the way down." Such is the state of things with Maya identity, too: Maya all the way down.

Wilson (1995: 305) makes an insightful observation about Maya identity: "Mayas have sought to elude the uniform and controlled identities conferred by a system of dominance and find new, untrammeled cultural domains which then serve as foundations for alternative visions of identity." Certainly, within Ladino systems of dominance, Mayas continually try to find new and different expressions of identity. However, it is something that has been forced upon them, as Smith's (1990a, 1990b) and Nelson's (1999) research so powerfully indicates. At different points in Guatemalan history (the development of export agriculture, for example), white elites and, later, Ladinos needed Maya identity to be different from theirs.

Within the socioeconomic dimensions of tourism, both Ladinos and Mayas need to be different from each other, too. However, Maya vendors use a subtle combination of difference and identification in their socioeconomic relations with tourists because they are aware that being completely different means that there is no communication across cultural borders. In Antigua, Kaqchikel Maya *típica* vendors from San Antonio Aguas Calientes and Santa Catarina Palopó buy cups of coffee from two different cafés owned by American expatriates, Tostaduría Antigua and Café Condesa. They claimed to tourists and to me that they only want to drink the best coffee in Antigua. Never, in the numerous times that I drank coffee in their homes, did I drink anything that resembled the taste of the coffee they bought in the cafés. Coffee serves as a way for vendors to identify with their Others—tourists—in a way that acknowledges, albeit in a small way, a commonality with them: their joint membership in global, transnational culture.

In their own small ways, tourists also want to identify with their Others. For example, during one afternoon, I was sitting on a bench in Antigua's Central Plaza, organizing fieldnotes that I had written earlier that day, when a female tourist came up to me. For an hour, one after another, peddlers selling *típica* had walked up to her and asked her to buy something. When they got to me, however, they put away their merchandise and conversed with me. During a break in the parade of vendors, the woman approached me and asked, "Why don't the Indians try to sell you something? They act like they're your friends."

I replied, "They are my friends."

Before walking back to her bench, she commented, "It would be nice to talk to them like that."

"Real" Maya identities are composed within a complex matrix of social, economic, and political arenas, where difference from and identification with other individuals are manifested in continually shifting ways. Hall (1997b: 47) explains that getting at identity is really about subjectivity. "It makes us aware that identities are never completed, never finished; that they are always as subjectivity itself is, a process."

The best that anthropologists can do is to examine those forces that make Mayas subjects and contribute to Maya self-concepts of identity. Warren (1989) does this when looking at *costumbre* and the introduction of Catholic Action to San Andrés and, later, when looking at the Maya movement (Warren 1998a). The partial matrices that she describes include community, nation, and transnational forces that are involved in Maya subjectivity. In explaining Maya subjectivity, Wilson's (1995) partial matrix concentrates on the interplay between the dominance of the state and local community history and tradition. Watanabe's (1992) partial matrix focuses on the internal dynamics of community itself.

With respect to anthropology, it is probably impossible to map, describe, and understand the totality of Maya subjectivity/identity (even though this is what we should strive to do both descriptively and theoretically), in part, because of the discipline's emphasis on the particularities of locality and certain types of individuals. My own partial matrix has focused on the interrelations among transnational forces, nation, community, and household within the contexts of international tourism. In this matrix, complexes of social relations between Kaqchikel Maya vendors and others, including other Mayas, significantly contribute to their subjectivities and expressed identities, including strategic and tactical forms that can rearticulate with other aspects of identity. While scholars continue to confront such dilemmas, Maya handicraft vendors will continue to conceive of creative ways to market their products, make their livelihoods, and construct their identities within the transnational tourism borderzone.

Epilogue

In the months between my annual trip to Guatemala to teach and conduct research, profound changes occurred in the Antigua handicraft market. It would be remiss of me to not outline these changes and summarize vendors' opinions about their future in handicraft sales.

When I left Guatemala in August 2002, an annex to the new Handicrafts Marketplace (that which was constructed in 1998 and is behind the Pollo Campero restaurant) was near completion, and the Spanish government's renovations of the Compañía de Jesús were also beginning in and around the areas of the artisan marketplace there. The Compañía de Jesús Artisan Marketplace vendors knew their time in that location was limited and had been lobbying the city government for several years to allow them to set up smaller-scale, self-regulated vending locations in or near tourism attractions throughout Antigua. City officials did not consider this option, so vendors awaited the impending move with some trepidation, but not without letting the government know of their dissatisfaction.

In September, all vendors—handicraft and utilitarian—throughout Antigua rallied to protest the city's failure to provide adequate trash removal. As described in the *Prensa Libre* (September 21, 2002), vendors argued that because "Antigua is a tourism place," the city needs to improve the municipal market and provide basic sanitation services. Handicraft vendors explained to me in July 2003 that the protest was also meant to signal to the mayor that vendors of all classes were united.

In November 2002, some Compañía de Jesús vendors who work with Maya Works, a not-for-profit organization that imports Guatemalan textiles, visited me in Chicago. They explained that they had been notified that the Compañía de Jesús Artisan Marketplace would be closed and vendors would be relocated to the newly completed annex in February. By March 2003, I received e-mails from vendors and anthropologist colleagues that the marketplace was closed.

What I did not expect when I returned to Guatemala in June 2003 was that all handicraft vendors selling on public land in Antigua had been ordered to relocate to the new annex. The marketplaces described in this book, and familiar to students, scholars, and tourists who know Antigua, were closed. According to vendors, this would not have happened had sales been strong and tourist numbers high. Many of them explained that declining sales and tourist visitors were related to the September 11, 2001, terrorism attacks on the United States, the wars in Afghanistan and Iraq, and the general downturn of the world economy since the fall of 2000. To make the situation worse, consumers are buying fewer Latin American handicrafts (Chibnik 2003). Small-scale exporters reported to me that they have nearly dropped all textiles from their catalogues.

The closure of the Antigua handicraft marketplaces resulted in three general trends on the part of vendors. Economically successful vendors moved into the annex marketplace and took it upon their own initiative to promote the new location. Because the majority of the now more than four hundred vendors in the new marketplace were from the Compañía de Jesús Artisan Marketplace, the annex was given that name. However, the start-up costs of over US$400 to enter the annex were prohibitive to many vendors. Those who could not afford them either returned to their hometowns or now work as street vendors, constantly under police pressure to desist selling handicrafts.

It is still too early to predict the long-term economic impact of the marketplace closings, but the *cargadores,* the owners of the *bodegas,* and the women who catered food to handicraft vendors throughout the city lost their financial base and are out of work. Some of the *cargadores* and food vendors have themselves become street vendors of handicrafts. The empty *bodegas* languish in the slow tourism economy, as the owners are unable to attract new clients.

This new annex, the new location of the Compañía de Jesús Artisan Marketplace, symbolizes a bittersweet victory for handicraft vendors. After years of being under threat by officials to leave Antigua, these vendors, aided by their successful organizing and demonstrations of unity, were rewarded by an official handicraft marketplace, but not the one they wanted. Located far from the tourism sites of Antigua and surrounded by the dust and exhaust of the municipal bus terminal, vendors have mixed expectations about tourists visiting and buying.

What the forced unification of handicraft vendors has done is to politicize them further. Even at this early stage in the development of the new marketplace, vendors repeatedly explained that they are more unified and are a more powerful political force than before the consolidation. Instead of being divided into fragmented competitive groups, they are working together to plan strategies to promote the marketplace. They intend to confront the city government for charging high rents, using the electricity for which they pay, and interfering with weavers and middlepersons selling handicrafts to the marketplace. As one vendor friend commented to me, "The economy will get better, we'll develop new products to sell, and there will be a new mayor of Antigua." It is such optimism and a long history of experience that will allow them to adjust to the dramatic changes of the past couple of years.

Appendix

A. *Datos generales*

Nombre:

Locación:

1. ¿En qué lugar nació usted?
2. ¿Dónde vive actualmente?
3. ¿Cuál es su religión?
4. ¿Cuáles idiomas habla usted?
5. ¿Cuál es el grado más alto que cursó en la escuela?
6. ¿Cuántos años tiene usted?
7. ¿Está casado, soltero, divorciado, viudo?
   Si está casado, ¿en qué lugar nació él?/ella?
8. ¿Cuánto tiempo tiene de tener este lugar?
9. ¿Desde hace cuántos años se dedica al negocio de artesanía?
10. ¿Tiene usted otras fuentes de ingreso de dinero? ¿Cuáles?
11. ¿Tiene hijos en edad de ayudarlo?
    ¿Colaboran ellos con usted en este negocio?
    ¿Qué hacen ellos?
12. ¿Cuáles idiomas hablaron sus padres?
13. ¿Cuáles idiomas hablaron sus hijos?
14. ¿Tiene familia que trabajan en el mercado?
    ¿Cómo se llaman?
15. ¿Tiene compadres, comadres, padrinos, madrinos, ahijados en el mercado?
16. a. ¿Lee el diario?
    b. ¿Mira la televisión?
    c. ¿Escucha la radio?
17. ¿Cómo se auto identifica?

    a. ladino   c. indígena   e. Kaqchikel/K'iche'/Ixil

    b. maya   d. guatemalteco f. otro

Observaciones:

B. *Manejo del negocio*
18. ¿Qué cosas vende? Lista:
19. ¿Produce usted mismo algunos de los productos que vende?
    Sí. No. ¿Cuáles?
20. ¿Tiene empleados o emplea personas para producirlos?
21. ¿Cuáles días de la semana vende?
22. ¿Trabaja para otra persona? Sí. No. ¿Qué hace?
23. ¿Le ayuda a su esposo/a? Sí. No. ¿Qué hace él/ella?
24. ¿Tiene que pagar impuestos para su local? Sí. No. ¿Cuánto?
25. ¿De qué municipios provienen sus productos? Lista:
26. ¿Aproximadamente cuántos proveedores tiene usted y de qué pueblos son?
27. ¿Cuál de los siguientes arreglos utiliza usted con sus proveedores?
    a. paga al contado
    b. recibe mercadería en consignación
    c. paga un porcentaje al recibir la mercadería y otro más tarde
    d. suministra los materiales al proveedor
    e. otra forma
28. ¿Compra de vendedores ambulantes? Sí. No.
29. ¿Negocia con turistas y proveedores sobre los precios? Sí. No.
30. ¿Cuáles se aplica a usted?

a. comerciante	c. propietario	e. ambulante	g. tejedor
b. revendedor	d. mayorista	f. campesino	h. artesano

Observaciones:

C. *Exportación*
31. ¿Exporta usted mercadería directamente al extranjero?

TÄQ TZIJ RUMA RI SAMAJ PA RI K'AYIB'ÄL
(POCAS PALABRAS SOBRE EL PROYECTO EN EL MERCADO)

Tab'ana utzil, rik'in ri grabadora, tab'ij kik'in jun, ka'i', oxi' awach'alal
jub'a tzij k'atzinel:
(Por favor, con su grabadora, dígales a su familia unos cuentos
importantes:)
Tab'ij pe chwe jub'a tzij ruma ri ak'aslem ojer kan.
¿Achike nana' ruma ak'aslem ojer kan?

¿Achike xab'än pa ak'aslem?
(Por favor, relata la historia de su vida.
¿Qué memorias tiene sobre su juventud y su crecimiento?
¿Qué ha hecho en su vida?)

Tab'ij pe chwe jub'a tzij ruma asamaj pa k'ayib'äl.
¿Achike ruma yasamaj pa ri k'ayib'äl?
¿Achike nab'än pa k'ayib'äl?
¿Awetaman jun ti q'oloj ruma ri k'ayib'äl o ri turista?
(Dígales unos cuentos sobre su trabajo en el mercado.
¿Qué trabajo hace en el mercado?
¿Por qué trabaja usted en el mercado?
¿Sabe usted un chiste sobre el mercado o los turistas?)

Tab'ij pe chwe jub'a tzij k'atzinel ruma atinamit.
¿Awetaman jun tzijon kan ruma atinamit?
¿Achike ruma ri tzijon kan k'o k'atzinel wakamin?
(Dígales unos cuentos importantes sobre su pueblo.
¿Sabe usted un cuento de folklore o cuento antiguo sobre su pueblo?
¿Por qué ese cuento es importante hoy en día?)

¿Achike k'o ri winaqi' Maya'? K'o winaqi' Maya' wakamin o xaxe ojer
Kan?
(¿Quiénes son los mayas? Hay mayas hoy en día?)

¿Achike ruma ri *indígena* man junam ta ri *ladino*? o ¿Achike ruma junma
ri *indígena* chuqa' ri *ladino*?
¿Achike nanojij toq jun *ladino* (o ri winaq man *indígena* ta nuk'ayij ri
tzyaq *indígena*?
¿Achike nanojij toq jun "gringo" nukusaj ri tyaq *indígena*?
(¿Por qué los indígenas y los ladinos no son iguales? o ¿Por qué los
indígenas y los ladinos son iguales?
¿Qué piensa usted cuando un ladino o persona no indígena se pone la
ropa indígena?
¿Qué piensa cuando una gringa se pone la ropa indígena?)

QUESTIONNAIRE FOR TOURISTS

Date: Location:

General Data
Age:
Sex:
Occupation:
Level of Education:
Country of Origin:

Survey Questions:

1. Is this your first trip to Guatemala?
    If not, when was the previous trip?
    How long was that trip?
2. How many days, weeks, months long is your current trip?
3. Are you:
    a. on a guided tour?   c. a Spanish student?
    b. an independent traveler?   d. a business traveler?
4. What places have you visited on this trip (and previous trips)?
5. What motivated you to travel to Guatemala instead of some other destination?
6. Have you purchased any *artesanía*?
    What items?
    How much did you pay?
7. In general, are you satisfied with the prices you paid?
8. Why did you make these purchases?
    personal use   gifts   *recuerdos*/mementos
9. How much money do you plan to spend on *artesanía*?
10. Do you know who are:
    a. Mayas   b. Ladinos   c. Indians (*indígenas*)
11. What artisan markets have you visited?
    Which ones do you anticipate visiting?
12. Why did/do you want to visit markets?
13. Do you feel safe in marketplaces?
14. Is there some significance about your trip? What?
15. Additional comments:

Notes

INTRODUCTION

1. In Guatemala, the term "Ladino" refers to a complex social construction. It is not synonymous with a particular phenotype, nor does it gloss easily into *mestizo* (indigenous and Spanish hybrid), non-Maya, or *non-indígena*. Greg Grandin (2000: 239) explains that in Guatemala "the use of Ladino has historically suggested a His-panicized or European cultural identity."

2. Also see Richard Wilson (1995), who discusses local markers of identity, espe-cially related to geography, such as mountains and mountain spirits.

3. Watanabe (1992) makes a similar point about Maya identity, but I show how this works for translocal Mayas as well.

4. Also see Fischer (1996a), who contextualizes the controversy over population figures, explaining how Mayas have been undercounted by Ladino census takers.

5. See Fischer (1996a). The hearth group literally consists of all the people who regularly eat and socialize within a household.

6. Some anthropological projects have been situated in multiple sites, as Marcus recognizes in his review with the inclusion of Smith's (1976) volume on regional analy-sis. Although Nash (1981) does not specifically call the world-systems-oriented ethnog-raphy that emerged in the late 1960s and 1970s multisited ethnography, the term cer-tainly applies to some of it. Research on networks in Africa, done by the "Manchester School," represents another form of multisited ethnography (see Werbner 1984).

I. GUATEMALA AS A LIVING HISTORY MUSEUM

1. See also Anzaldúa (1987), Bhabha (1994), Fusco (1995), García Canclini (1995), Gómez-Peña (1993), and Rosaldo (1989).

2. According to Michel de Certeau (1984: 117; italics in original), "A place (*lieu*) is the order (of whatever kind) in accord with which elements are distributed in rela-tionships of coexistence. . . . A place is thus an instantaneous configuration of positions. It implies an indication of stability." He posits that "a *space* exists when one takes into consideration vectors of direction, velocities, and time variables. Thus space is com-posed of intersections of mobile elements. It is in a sense actuated by the ensemble of movements deployed within it . . . *space is a practiced place.*"

3. This was a travel-tourism company based in Florida that began taking tour groups to the Amazon in the 1980s and then expanded its destinations to include Guatemala in the early 1990s.

4. Mitchell (1988: 7–13) describes three features of exhibitions: apparent realism, organization around a common center, and position of the visitor as occupant of the center.

5. Exhibits that challenge and contradict the dominant classes tend to get short shrift (see Wallace 1981), but exhibitions by Fusco (1994) and Gómez-Peña (1993), performed in the Field Museum of Natural History in Chicago, successfully challenged dominant class ideologies.

6. Boon (1991: 266) describes how museum patrons viewed samples in "a world of as-if merchandise. . . ." Such commodification of the "Other" possibly grew out of the Industrial Revolution (Hinsley 1991) and is rooted in European traditions of describing and collecting "exotic" people and things (Hodgen 1964; Said 1979).

7. In order to make museums more profitable, museum personnel utilize Disney's strategies of corporate sponsorship (Wallace 1987, 1989). Linkages between museums (including living history museums) and multinational corporations have benefited sponsors, leading to views of other cultures and countries as "benign, if exotic, fairy tale[s]" (Wallis 1994: 279).

8. It is estimated that over 200,000 people, most of them Mayas, were killed in the thirty-five-year conflict and tens of thousands were displaced within the country or forced into exile. See the Catholic Church's report (REMHI 1998), *Guatemala: Nunca más,* on the Project for the Recovery of Historical Memory. Also see *Violencia institucional en Guatemala, 1960 a 1996: Una reflexión cuantitativa* (Ball, Kobrak, and Spirer 1999); *Guatemala, memoria del silencio* (CEH 1999); and a report on the displaced population by FNUAP (1997), *La población desarraigada en Guatemala.* For economic and development indicators, see the United Nations report (SNUG 1998), *Guatemala: Los contrastes del desarrollo humano.*

9. With regard to authenticity, anthropologists focus on the processes in which people, concepts, and things become authentic, rather than on objective, pure, and unchanging categories (see Bruner 1989; Castañeda 1996; Clifford 1997; Kirshenblatt-Gimblett 1998). Although this dynamic, processual approach to authenticity, which corresponds to anthropological concepts of culture, may be problematic to curators and tourists, it has inspired critics of indigenous activism to defame the efforts of indigenous leaders as inauthentic, since the latter take advantage of advanced degrees and utilize computers and other technology to get their work done (Nash 2001; Warren and Jackson 2002a).

10. By the mid-1990s, fast-food chains from Mexico and the United States and cable television offering programs from all over the world were present in Guatemala's major cities and tourism centers. See Watson (1998), who illustrates the multiple ways that fast-food chains are indigenized and used by diverse local populations.

11. Airplanes and airports fit into the category of "non-places," which, according to Marc Augé (1995: 94), are "spaces formed in relation to certain ends (transport, transit, commerce, leisure), and the relations that individuals have with these spaces." Marin's "limit" is such a place. With regard to airports, Augé's perspective is limited. Handicrafts, locally grown coffee, national liquors, and traditional food are sold in Guatemala's Aurora International Airport, all of which give multiple meanings to the space of the airport: waiting room for transit, a showcase for Guatemalan national products, and a place to consume local and international food and other products.

12. Not all tourists had this perspective. Some read extensively, especially tourists who studied Spanish. Books such as Francisco Goldman's *The Long Night of the White Chickens,* Rigoberta Menchú's *I, Rigoberta Menchú,* and Linda Schele and David Freidel's *A Forest of Kings: The Untold Story of the Ancient Maya* were commonly read by some tourists prior to their visit.

13. Foucault takes Bentham's concept of panopticon, a vantage point from which a prison warden or factory manager, for example, can watch inmates or workers to monitor their behavior but cannot be seen by them, in order to argue that those individuals under surveillance eventually internalize and self-monitor their behavior. This is a form of objectification that makes humans into subjects.

14. An early guidebook that emphasizes Guatemala's crafts is David and Marian Greenberg's (1955) *Shopping Guide to Mexico, Guatemala, and the Caribbean.*

15. Dean MacCannell (1992: 28) writes of another ethnic tourism locale: "The commercialization of the touristic encounter extends to the point of commodification not merely of the handicrafts and the photographic image, but to the person of the ex-primitive. Southwest American Indians complain that tourists have attempted to pat up their hair and arrange their clothing before photographing them, and that they receive unwanted offers from tourists to buy the jewelry or the clothing they are actually wearing."

16. See the annual magazine *Destination Guatemala;* the monthly magazine *La Visión del Mundo Maya* (Vol. 1, No. 1, 1994); *Guatemala: Jaguar of the Americas* (December 1992), by the Guatemalan Development Foundation; *Vida y Color de Guatemala,* by the Chamber of Guatemalan Tourism; and *Viva Guatemala* (Vol. 1, No. 4, 1990), by the Guatemalan Development Foundation.

17. Statistics from *Crónica* 538, Supplement (August, 7–13), *1998, Guatemala en números: Las cifras más importantes de la sociedad, economía y las finanzas.*

18. Explanations and analyses for attacks on women for suspected child stealing can be found in a report by the Centro de Estudios de Guatemala (1995), as well as in Adams (1998), Nelson (1999), and White (1994).

19. This police force was formed in August 1996. Recruits take a two-month course from SNUG (Sistema de Naciones Unidas en Guatemala; United Nations System in Guatemala) on law and human rights. The primary function of this force is to prevent crime by maintaining a visible presence in Antigua. One of its duties is to

escort foreign tourists and local Guatemalans who wish to visit the Cerro de la Cruz. Between August 1996 and March 1998, 19,776 individuals took advantage of this service.

20. Castañeda (1996: 220) notes that Yucatec Maya vendors at Chichén Itzá learn English phrases to catch the attention of tourists and provide a counterdiscourse to that of the guides. He does not note if or how tourists regard this language use.

21. Banco de Guatemala (1994) and *Crónica* (1998).

22. Numerous scholarly perspectives on the consumption of souvenirs may be applied to Guatemala as well. According to Anath Ariel de Vidas (1995: 67), "A *souvenir*, in the context of tourism . . . , is something kept as a reminder of a place or event." Susan Stewart (1984: 150; quoted in Dorst 1989: 208) contends that purchasing souvenirs contributes to the restoration of "a conservative idealization of the past." According to Penelope Harvey (1996: 158–169), visitors at the 1992 Universal Exhibition in Seville, Spain, purchased and collected souvenirs less for their material value or their association with a particular country than because the "Expo had become a brand which could market objects . . . through an evocation of a future need for a memory of the Expo visit itself." For Nelson Graburn (1989: 33), souvenirs are evidence of travel completed, places visited. He contends that the souvenirs purchased correspond to the type of tourism of which one partakes. Tourists in Guatemala may be motivated to purchase specific types of items by these concerns and others related to their perceptions of authenticity, but their motivation may be as simple as the desire to own something that is handmade, not mass-produced in China (Kay Warren, personal communication 7/17/02).

2. PLACE AND PEOPLE IN A TRANSNATIONAL BORDERZONE CITY

1. See Díaz (1927), Idell (1949), Popenoe (1973), Valladares (1934), and Zamora (1943).

2. See Rosaldo (1989: 198–204) on culture and Wolf (1982) about how history has been denied to non-Europeans.

3. ANTIGUA *típica* MARKETS AND IDENTITY INTERACTION

1. *Ma* is a term of respect for men in Kaqchikel Maya.

2. The daily wage for unskilled manual laborers during most of the 1990s was roughly twenty quetzales (US$3.34).

3. This comment is based on dozens of informal conversations with tourists, documented sources such as tourism guides and brochures (Little 1995), and a survey (Little and Walton n.d.) indicating that 32 percent of tourists in Antigua believe indigenous

people in Guatemala are Mayas. Forty-nine percent of the tourists surveyed responded that the vendors were "Indian." The remaining 19 percent chose Ladino.

4. The study of Latin American indigenous producers of handicrafts for foreign markets is well documented: García Canclini (1993) and Stephen (1991) for Mexico, Nash (1993c) for Mexico and Central America, and Tice (1995) for Panama.

5. As Fischer (2001: 150–162) notes, *k'u'x* is a key word in Kaqchikel Maya that does not translate easily into English. He explains that *k'u'x* is used in relation to the cosmos, to ritual, to curing, to the body, to the soul, to states of mood, and to qualities or traits that all things have. He argues that "cognitive models of *k'u'x* are an important mechanism of cultural commonality." For Maya vendors, *k'u'x* serves as a metaphor for certain places and particular states of being, which, in the case of the plaza, can come together in the same place.

6. For example, during my research, Maya and Ladino vendors frequently described Antigua as a Ladino *municipio* and San Antonio Aguas Calientes as an *indígena municipio*.

7. When I asked tourists in Antigua to describe the marketplaces they visited, most did not mention the Compañía de Jesús marketplace unless I specifically asked if they had been there.

4. MERCADO DE ARTESANÍA COMPAÑÍA DE JESÚS AND THE POLITICS OF VENDING

1. Shana Walton, Sergio García, and I (Little and Walton n.d.) found that 32 percent of the tourists surveyed identified vendors as Mayas, and 49 percent of them identified them as Indians.

2. Fischer and Brown (1996b), Nelson (1999), Warren (1998a), and Watanabe (1995) analyze the Maya movement. Little (1998 and n.d.) critiques the movement from the perspectives of *típica* vendors.

3. See *Tourist Guide—Guía de Turismo* (no date, but published in the 1960s by the Junta Departamental de Turismo de Sacatepéquez) and Jickling (1964).

4. A thorough discussion of development projects and the impact they had and continue to have is beyond the scope of this section and this book.

5. Ehlers (1993) analyzes the development of weaving cooperatives and the problems and benefits experienced by the residents of San Antonio Palopó as they entered the world market. Also see "The Peace Corps in Guatemala" (US Government 1981), doc. no. AA 1.17: 4200.48.

6. See Hendrickson (1995) for a discussion of Maya textile meanings and uses.

7. Artisan production increases preoccupied Guatemalan scholars, who were concerned about the deterioration of artisan products because of tourism (Gil 1983; Molina 1978; Rodríguez 1985; Rosales 1978).

8. In the central Peruvian Andes, rural vendors and merchants followed similar patterns. Furthermore, the development of the local tourism economy in Chiuchín provided entrepreneurial opportunities for women, such as tending stores, renting sleeping rooms, and serving meals, the proceeds from which were invested in their children (Bourque and Warren 1981).

9. In Guatemala in the 1930s, Mayas and their products were similarly commercialized for Guatemala's National Fair (described in Chapter 7). Marketplaces oriented toward tourists are common in other parts of Latin America, such as Chichén Itzá, Yucatán (Castañeda 1996); Mexico City (García Canclini 1993); Oaxaca, Mexico (Stephen 1991; Wood 2000); San Cristóbal, Mexico (van den Berghe 1994); Panama City (Swain 1989; Tice 1995), and Otavalo, Ecuador, and Puno, Peru (Ariel de Vidas 1995).

10. In summer 2001, the Compañía de Jesús Artisan Marketplace still existed, and vendors reported that they were less worried about being expelled. Even a few who got spaces in the new Handicrafts Marketplace returned to Compañía de Jesús because the business and the camaraderie were better there. Vendors reported that the municipality had plans to eventually relocate all of them to an annex of the new Handicrafts Marketplace, but construction had not yet begun.

11. See Montejo (1999) for a scholarly treatment by a Maya on the impact and the chilling effect of violence on Mayas.

5. GENDERED MARKETPLACE AND HOUSEHOLD REORGANIZATION

1. Henrietta Moore (1988: 89–93) suggests that the women may predominate in marketplaces because they can begin with small amounts of capital. Few women, however, are successful at making large quantities of money.

2. Note that in San Andrés Semetabaj, Kaqchikel widowers can hire young girls to do domestic work if they do not live close to their parents (Kay Warren, personal communication 7/17/02).

3. Some cases in Africa, where women have a great deal of economic autonomy and play central roles in household decision making, are comparable. Şaul (1989: 189) points out that Bobo women in Burkina Faso rely on close kin (male and female) for support of their entrepreneurial activities and negotiations with their husbands over conjugal and domestic responsibilities. Clark (1994) details how Ashante women resolve conflicts between entrepreneurial activities and domestic work through the support of matrilineal kin, especially mothers and older daughters. Because Ashante households are organized differently from Maya models, which generally follow a Chayanovian model of members pooling resources, Ashante concepts of property, decision making, and economic rights are different. "[W]omen traders actually said they would avoid accepting capital from their husbands because this would end their claims to child

support and allow him or his heirs to claim ownership of the business later" (Clark 1994: 334).

4. Men in the neighboring towns of San Antonio Aguas Calientes and Santa Catarina Barahona learn to weave on a backstrap loom (Pancake 1993). Two male vendors (one from each town) in the Compañía de Jesús Artisan Marketplace divide their labor between weaving, farming, and vending. Males are prompted to weave for economic reasons. As one Kaqchikel explained, "Men know they can make a lot of money from a well-made *po't*." This practice also relates to changing attitudes about the division of labor according to gender. Mothers in the 1960s encouraged their sons to learn to weave, and their fathers did not discourage them. Nevertheless, most men do not weave in adulthood, nor do they weave for self-consumption, as do women; they weave only for the market.

5. CONAVIGUA (Coordinador Nacional de Viudas de Guatemala; National Coordinator of Widows of Guatemala).

6. THE PLACES KAQCHIKEL MAYA VENDORS CALL HOME

1. The uses and abuses of Wolf's concept of "closed-corporate peasant communities" are also addressed in several chapters of *Articulating Hidden Histories: Exploring the Influence of Eric R. Wolf,* edited by Schneider and Rapp (1995).

2. Tsing (2000) makes a more forceful argument about the temptations and pitfalls of not treating critically those theoretical concepts and other economic and social conditions that utilize the modifier "global."

3. See Fischer (1996b) for a brief overview of economic development and its relationship to Maya identity in Guatemala.

4. Looking at the diasporatic nature of Mayas before Hispanic contact also makes it obvious that the closed-corporate community is a construction. See Sharer (1995) for an example.

5. Jennifer Burrell (personal communication May 1998) relates that residents of Todos Santos Cuchumatanes, Guatemala, have left home to go to Michigan for both economic and political reasons. As the war subsided, they, like Mixtecs and Zapotecs, began sending money home to Todos Santos. In the case of Maya refugees, however, Montejo (1999) shows that there is a generational rupture with regard to the significance of home that resulted from the political violence, a lack of communication with home communities, and the inability to cross international borders safely.

6. Ana now sells most days of the week in the new Handicrafts Marketplace behind Pollo Campero, but during the period that I conducted fieldwork, her schedule was Saturday through Monday morning in Antigua.

7. *Ichaj* is a strong marker of difference between Ladinos and Mayas. In marketplaces in Chichicastenango, Tecpán, San Francisco el Alto, and Sololá, one can pur-

chase meals with *ichaj* from Maya-owned restaurants. In Ladino-owned restaurants, it is not served. Additionally, my Ladino friends, in-laws, and acquaintances never served *ichaj*. As explained by one Ladina who rented a room to me, "*Ichaj* is Indian food. Here, we don't eat their food."

8. A ritual gift given by the groom and his family to the bride's parents when the groom formally asks the young woman and her parents for the young woman's hand in marriage. They reciprocate by having a brief ceremony and serving a meal to both extended families.

9. Over the period that I conducted extensive fieldwork, June 1996 through August 1998, no vendors or their family members died. No examples are included because I did not witness vendors returning for funerals. However, since that fieldwork period, the brother of the women running Cooperativa Ixchel, discussed in Chapter 7, and a male vendor from Santa Catarina Palopó, the town discussed in Chapter 8, died. In both cases, my friends reported that the funerals were well attended, drawing to the respective towns friends and family who worked in distant locations.

10. My use of "invited" and "uninvited" is probably inaccurate, since no one is technically not invited to the wedding or the party. However, only select, formally invited guests are allowed to participate in all wedding activities.

11. The literature on this topic is extensive. Brandes (1988), Brintnall (1979), Bunzel (1959), Cancian (1965), Carlsen (1997), Falla (1978), Oakes (1951), Reina (1966), Smith (1977), Warren (1989), Wasserstrom (1976), and Watanabe (1992) represent only a few of the researchers who have described and analyzed the *cofradía*.

12. *Xaq q'utu'n,* or *pepián,* is a sauce made primarily of roasted peppers and tomatoes; *pulik* is a thick maize-based stew; and *ruyal q'utu'n* is a stew made with vegetables. Each dish is also prepared with some kind of meat, usually beef or chicken. All three are served with *sub'an,* an unfilled maize tamal that has been wrapped in a green maize leave and steamed until the maize dough (*masa*) is stiff and holds its shape.

13. See Foster (1965, 1988) for an early theoretical treatment about how envy is a form of social control that can help maintain community equilibrium.

14. This literature is extensive. Some important studies that address rural-to-urban migration and urban associations include Altamirano and Hirabayashi (1997), Bourque and Warren (1981), Hirabayashi (1986), Kemper (1977), Smith (1989), and Turino (1993).

7. HOME AS A PLACE OF EXHIBITION AND PERFORMANCE IN SAN ANTONIO AGUAS CALIENTES

1. The fair was described in all the Guatemalan newspapers of the day, such as *Diario de Centro América, El Imparcial,* and *El Liberal Progresista,* during the months of August and September for about ten years, but was also noted in the *New York Times,* August 8, 1937.

2. While studies of peasants have discussed envy (Foster 1988), it is important to note that in front of tourists, *antonecos* are careful to mask any jealousy they may feel among themselves .

3. My intent is not to measure *antoneco* performances against an ethnographic original to gage their authenticity. MacCannell (1976, 1992) has discussed authenticity and tourism in depth. Indeed, while authenticity is an issue for some tourists, it was not for the women presenting or for me. See Bruner and Kirshenblatt-Gimblett (n.d.: 27), who contend that it "serves no useful purpose to denigrate tourist performances as inferior reproductions, but seems more reasonable to take such performances as topics worthy of serious scholarly inquiry."

4. According to Annis (1987: 173), the "artisan coop is moribund." Cooperatives may not have taken hold in San Antonio because *antonecos* had easy access to services typically offered through cooperatives, such as marketing, credit, supplies, and technical assistance (Annis 1987: 45). They frequently explained that cooperatives failed for several primary reasons: families put themselves before the cooperative, individuals feuded with each other over the proper management of the cooperative, the cooperative stifled the creativity of individual weavers and consequently led to inferior products, and, the most cited reason, the cooperative fell under the control of the Pérez family.

5. See Watanabe (1990) and Wilson (1995) for discussions about the ways that Mayas link identity and tradition to geographical space.

6. The traditions that they present are commonly known to *antonecos* and to persons from Santa Catarina Barahona, a neighboring town. I took a transcript of one of the Lópezes' performances to two of my Kaqchikel teachers, who confirmed that the stories were true. Also, I tested my newfound knowledge on my vendor friends, who commented that they were impressed that I was actually learning something relevant, not just watching them deal with Ladinos and tourists.

7. See Warren (1998a) for an explanation of this type of selectivity in the context of San Andrés Semetabaj. Basically, the manifestations of culture that are selected relate to reasoning based on context-specific situations and politics. She shows how different segments of the Maya population (university students, agriculturalists, activists, linguists, and others) select and emphasize specific cultural practices in order to further relevant economic, political, and social concerns.

8. The tragic story of Alcides's murder is told by Annis in Carmack's edited volume *Harvest of Violence* (1988).

9. See Warren and Jackson (2002b), who argue that there has been a tendency for us anthropologists to demand consistency in the lives and practices of the people we study, but the objects of our study, individually and collectively, are generally not concerned with this issue.

10. Scholars working in other areas of the world have also analyzed the ways that

indigenous people represent themselves when dealing with tourists (e.g., Adams 1995, 1997; Errington and Gewertz 1989; MacCannell 1992).

8. MARKETING MAYA CULTURE IN SANTA CATARINA PALOPÓ

1. Sololá is ninety-four square kilometers, Panajachel is twenty-two square kilometers, San Antonio Palopó is thirty-four square kilometers, and San Andrés Semetabaj is forty-eight square kilometers.

2. A cord (*cuerda* in Spanish) is a basic measure of land area that varies in Guatemala from community to community; in the region of Santa Catarina Palopó and Panajachel, it is equivalent to 0.178 acre, or 0.0712 hectare. A milpa is a field planted with corn, usually in combination with beans and squash.

3. Not just Kaqchikel Mayas from Santa Catarina Palopó, but all Kaqchikeles and many K'iche' Mayas that I worked with distinguished *tikonel* (plural *tikonela'*) from *campesino*. The latter term they related to landless persons who did agricultural work for wages.

4. Although the reference of my female informants to independent travel by women contradicts the data collected by Tax in the 1930s and 1940s and the oral histories edited by Petrich in the 1990s, I suspect that this was merely an oversight on the part of the investigators.

5. Unlike residents of other indigenous communities (Adams 1995; Schirmer 1998) and even other Kaqchikel communities (Carey 2001), *catarinecos* explained that they did not participate in the army as a means of livelihood, either voluntarily or through forced conscription. Older (fifty years of age or more) male vendors and agriculturalists from Comalapa and San Antonio Aguas Calientes explained that although they had received harsh treatment at the hands of their Ladino superiors during their military service, they had seen other parts of Guatemala and, most usefully, had gained basic literacy skills.

6. During my fieldwork, I learned firsthand of *patrón*-dependent relationships. First, some older vendors from San Antonio Aguas Calientes, Santo Domingo Xenacoj, and San Juan Sacatepéquez described the persons who regularly bought *típica* from them in the 1950s, 1960s, and 1970s as their *patrones,* not their clients. Second, in June 1999 I learned that I, as a co-director of a Kaqchikel Maya course, was regarded as a *patrón* by the owner of the bus company the course had contracted in past years. On presenting me with an unusually large bill for estimated services, he explained how slow business had been and that he was "looking forward to my help."

James Scott (1990: 62–63) argues, however, that patron-client relations go beyond "a network of dyadic (two-person) reciprocities always articulated vertically," as typically described by anthropologists, to include "horizontal linkages between subordinates."

7. Some of the guidebooks include Brosnahan (1994), Gorrey (2001), Greenberg

and Wells (1976), Janson (1996), Knopf Guide (1995), Norton and Whatmore (1993), Ramírez and Zúñiga (1996), Schaeffer (1974), Whatmore and Eltringham (1993).

8. A *petate,* glossed incorrectly in the guidebook, is a mat woven from reeds.

9. Mayas are bothered by Ladinas who are paid to portray Maya women in international tourism exhibits. Women in San Antonio Aguas Calientes are opposed to any representation of Mayas by Ladinos, and Kay Warren (personal communication 7/17/02) reports that people from San Andrés are infuriated by such paid performances, in part "because of racist concepts of beauty." That Maya and Ladino aesthetics and general concepts of beauty differ and have been used by Ladinos but contested by Mayas in creative ways has been discussed by Hendrickson (1995) and McAllister (1996).

10. One of the ways that male and, especially, female *catarinecos* (but also Mayas from San Antonio Aguas Calientes and Santa Catarina Barahona) distinguished Maya women from Ladinas was according to who wears makeup. While I watched Mexican soap operas and movies on several occasions with different groups of female friends from Santa Catarina and their children, they explained that prostitutes and Ladinas wore makeup, but they did not.

Warren (personal communication 7/17/02) reports that young Maya women from San Andrés Semetabaj who worked outside the community may use cosmetics. However, among vendors, only one from San Antonio Aguas Calientes applies makeup on a regular basis, for which she is teased by other vendor women. One twenty-one-year-old vendor from Santa Catarina returned from a business trip to the United States in 2001 with cosmetics that she and her friends apply in the privacy of her room, but not in public.

11. My predissertation (Little 1995) describes the response of two *catarineca* girls to a couple of tourists who wanted to take a picture without their permission. When the tourists ignored their request to stop and then their demand for monetary compensation, the girls commenced to throw rocks and make faces.

12. In Guatemala, the *cofradía* is a Catholic brotherhood, the members of which are responsible for taking care of saints (the physical statues and their "spirit"), cleaning the church, and other tasks.

13. I owe the latter observation to Kay Warren (personal communication 7/17/02), who notes that "the 'survival' of weaving raises the issue of the counterinsurgency danger of marking oneself ethnically."

14. Nash (1960) reports that several sects of Protestants were operating in Panajachel prior to the 1960s.

15. *Catarinecos* do not dance outside of the *cofradía,* and within the *cofradía* they dance in same-sex pairs.

16. Warren (personal communication 7/17/02) recalls that in the 1970s, while she was conducting research in San Andrés Semetabaj, the Catholic church in Santa Catarina was robbed of images of saints.

17. When vendors knew that I was going home, they sought me out to exchange

dollars for quetzales, thinking that the exchange would benefit us both economically, since it costs more quetzales to buy dollars than one gets when one sells dollars for quetzales. I matched the best bank rates for dollars, and then they did not have to put up with the ethnocentric and demeaning comments of bank employees, who sometimes denied them service. The economic exchanges, however, were not in my favor, because I drew from an account in dollars in the United States. In order to buy their dollars, I had to sell my own dollars to a bank for quetzales. I did reap untold fieldwork benefits from these exchanges: vendors' confidence in me increased, I got a glimpse of the amounts of money they made, and I learned more about the ethnic-racial tensions between Mayas and Ladinos.

CONCLUSION

1. A *pollo* is a large, usually wood-fueled griddle on a masonry hearth that is used for making tortillas and as a stove top.

2. It is important to note that the Maya vendors described in this book were not displaced by the political violence of the late 1970s through the 1980s. Such extreme situations, where refugees are separated from their traditional economic, material, and cultural bases, can rupture Mayas' connections to a particular place (Montejo 1999).

Bibliography

Adams, Abigail

1998   *Gringas,* Ghouls, and Guatemala: The 1994 Attacks on North American Women Accused of Body Organ Trafficking. *Journal of Latin American Anthropology* 4 (1): 112–133.

Adams, Kathleen

1995   Making up the Toraja. *Ethnology* 34: 143–153.

1997   Ethnic Tourism and the Renegotiation of Tradition in Tana Toraja. *Ethnology* 36: 309–320.

Adams, Richard N.

1995   *Etnicidad en el ejército de la Guatemala liberal (1870–1919).* Debate 30. Guatemala City: FLACSO (Facultad Latinoamericana de Ciencias Sociales).

Albó, Xavier

1997   La Paz/Chukiyawu: Two Faces of a City. In *Migrants, Regional Identities, and Latin American Cities,* edited by Teófilo Altamirano and Lane Hirabayashi, pp. 113–150. Society for Latin American Anthropology Publication Series, Vol. 13. Washington, D.C.: American Anthropological Association.

Altamirano, Teófilo, and Lane Ryo Hirabayashi

1997   The Construction of Regional Identities in Urban Latin America. In *Migrants, Regional Identities, and Latin American Cities,* edited by Teófilo Altamirano and Lane Hirabayashi, pp. 7–24. Society for Latin American Anthropology Publication Series, Vol. 13. Washington, D.C.: American Anthropological Association.

Anderson, Jay

1984   *Time Machines: The World of Living History.* Nashville, Tenn.: The American Association for State and Local History.

Annis, Sheldon

1987   *God and Production in a Guatemalan Town.* Austin: University of Texas Press.

1988   Story from a Peaceful Town: San Antonio Aguas Calientes. In *Harvest of Violence,* edited by Robert M. Carmack, pp. 155–173. Norman: University of Oklahoma Press.

Anzaldúa, Gloria

1987   *Borderlands: The New Mestiza = La Frontera.* San Francisco: Aunt Lute Press.

Appadurai, Arjun

1986   (ed.) *The Social Life of Things: Commodities in Cultural Perspective.* Cambridge:

Cambridge University Press.

1990   Disjuncture and Difference in the Global Cultural Economy. *Public Culture* 2 (2): 1–24.

1991   Global Ethnoscapes: Notes and Queries for a Transnational Anthropology. In *Recapturing Anthropology: Working in the Present,* edited by Richard G. Fox, pp. 191–210. Santa Fe, N.Mex.: School of American Research Press.

1996   *Modernity at Large: Cultural Dimensions of Globalization.* Minneapolis: University of Minnesota Press.

1998   Dead Certainty: Ethnic Violence in the Era of Globalization. *Public Culture* 10 (2): 225–248.

2000   Grassroots Globalization and the Research Imagination. *Public Culture* 12 (1): 1–19.

Ariel de Vidas, Anath

1995   Textiles, Memory, and the Souvenir Industry in the Andes. In *International Tourism: Identity and Change,* edited by Marie-Françoise Lanfant, John B. Allcock, and Edward Bruner, pp. 67–84. London: Sage.

Asturias, Miguel Angel

1923   *Sociología guatemalteca: El problema social del indio.* Guatemala City: Tipografía Sánchez y de Guise.

Asturias de Barrios, Linda

1994   Mano de mujer, mano de hombre: Producción artesanal textil en Comalapa, Guatemala. Ph.D. diss., SUNY-Albany.

Augé, Marc

1995   *Non-Places: Introduction to an Anthropology of Supermodernity.* London: Verso.

Babb, Florence E.

1987   Marketers as Producers: The Labor Process and Proletarianization of Peruvian Marketwomen. In *Perspectives in U.S. Marxist Anthropology,* edited by David Hakken and Hanna Lessinger, pp. 166–185. Boulder: Westview Press.

1998   *Between Field and Cooking Pot: The Political Economy of Marketwomen in Peru,* rev. ed. Austin: University of Texas Press.

Babcock, Barbara A.

1993   Bearers of Value, Vessels of Desire: The Reproduction of Pueblo Culture. *Museum Anthropology* 17 (3): 43–57.

Ball, Patrick, Paul Kobrak, and Herbert F. Spirer

1999   *Violencia institucional en Guatemala, 1960 a 1996: Una reflexión cuantitativa.* New York: American Association for the Advancement of Science.

Banco de Guatemala

1994   El turismo en Guatemala: 1993. *Boletín Informativo* 5 (105): 1–7.

Barth, Fredrik

1969   (ed.) *Ethnic Groups and Boundaries.* Boston: Little, Brown.

Baudrillard, Jean

1983   *Simulations.* Translated by Paul Foss, Paul Patton, and Phillip Beitchman. New

York: Semiotext.

1988   *America*. London:Verso.

Bell, Elizabeth, and Trevor Long

1993   *Antigua Guatemala:An Illustrated History of the City and Its Monuments*. Guatemala City: Impresos Industriales.

Bennett, Tony

1995   *The Birth of the Museum: History, Theory, Politics*. London: Routledge.

Bereskey, Andrew E.

1991   (ed.) *Fodor's Central America*. New York: Fodor's Travel Publications.

Bhabha, Homi

1994   *The Location of Culture*. London: Routledge Press.

Bohannan, Paul, and George Dalton

1962   (eds.) *Markets in Africa*. Chicago: Northwestern University Press.

Boon, James

1991   Why Museums Make Me Sad. In *Exhibiting Culture:The Poetics and Politics of Museum Display*, edited by Ivan Karp and Steven D. Lavine, pp. 255–277. Washington, D.C.: Smithsonian Institution Press.

Bossen, Laurel

1984   *The Redivision of Labor:Women and Economic Choice in Four Guatemalan Communities*. Albany: State University of New York Press.

1989   Women and Economic Institutions. In *Economic Anthropology*, edited by Stuart Plattner, pp. 318–350. Stanford: Stanford University Press.

Bourdieu, Pierre

1977   *Outline of a Theory of Practice*. Translated by Richard Nice. Cambridge: University of Cambridge Press.

Bourque, Susan C., and Kay B. Warren

1981   *Women of the Andes: Patriarchy and Social Change in Two Peruvian Towns*. Ann Arbor: University of Michigan Press.

Brandes, Stanley

1988   *Power and Persuasion: Fiestas and Social Control in Rural Mexico*. Philadelphia: University of Pennsylvania Press.

Brintnall, Douglas E.

1979   *Revolt against the Dead:The Modernization of a Mayan Community in the Highlands of Guatemala*. New York: Gordon and Breach.

Brosnahan, Tom

1994   *Guatemala, Belize, and Yucatán: La Ruta Maya*. 2d ed. Hawthorn, Australia: Lonely Planet Publications.

Brown, R. McKenna

1991   Language Maintenance and Shift in Four Kaqchikel Towns. Ph.D. diss., Tulane University.

1998   Case Study Two: San Antonio Aguas Calientes and the Quinizilapa Valley. In *The Life of Our Language: Kaqchikel Maya Maintenance, Shift, and Revitalization,* edited by Susan Garzon, R. McKenna Brown, Julia Becker Richards, and Wuqu' Ajpub' (Arnulfo Simón), pp. 101–128. Austin: University of Texas Press.

Bruner, Edward M.

1989   Tourism, Creativity, and Authenticity. *Studies in Symbolic Interaction* 10: 109–114.

1994   Abraham Lincoln as Authentic Reproduction: A Critique of Postmodernism. *American Anthropologist* 96: 397–415.

1996a   Tourism in Ghana: The Representation of Slavery and the Return of the Black Diaspora. *American Anthropologist* 98: 290–304.

1996b   Tourism in the Balinese Borderzone. In *Displacement, Diaspora, and Geographies of Identity,* edited by Smadar Lavie and Ted Swedenburg, pp. 157–179. Durham: Duke University Press.

1999   Return to Sumatra: 1957, 1997. *American Ethnologist* 26 (2): 461–477.

Bruner, Edward M., and Barbara Kirshenblatt-Gimblett

1994   Maasai on the Lawn: Tourist Realism in East Africa. *Cultural Anthropology* 9: 435–470.

n.d.   Mayers' Ranch and the Kedong Maasai Manyatta. Draft ms. 1986.

Bunzel, Ruth

1959   *Chichicastenango: A Guatemalan Village.* Seattle: University of Washington Press.

Butler, Judith P.

1990   *Gender Trouble: Feminism and the Subversion of Identity.* New York: Routledge Press.

1993   *Bodies That Matter: On the Discursive Limits of "Sex."* New York: Routledge Press.

Cancian, Frank

1965   *Economics and Prestige in a Maya Community: The Religious Cargo System in Zinacantan.* Stanford: Stanford University Press.

1972   *Change and Uncertainty in a Peasant Economy: The Maya Corn Farmers of Zinacantan.* Stanford University Press.

1992   *The Decline of Community in Zinacantan: Economy, Public Life, and Social Stratification, 1960–1987.* Stanford: Stanford University Press.

Carey, David, Jr.

2001   *Our Elders Teach Us: Maya-Kaqchikel Historical Perspectives Xkib'ij Kan Qate' Qatata'.* Tuscaloosa: University of Alabama Press.

Carlsen, Robert

1997   *The War for the Heart and Soul of a Highland Maya Town.* Austin: University of Texas Press.

Carmack, Robert M.

1988   (ed.) *Harvest of Violence: The Maya Indians and the Guatemalan Crisis.* Norman: University of Oklahoma Press.

Castañeda, Quetzil

1996   *In the Museum of Maya Culture: Touring Chichén Itzá.* Minneapolis: University of Minnesota Press.

1997   On the Correct Training of Indios in the Handicraft Market at Chichén Itzá: Tactics and Tactility of Gender, Class, Race, and State. *Journal of Latin American Anthropology* 2 (2): 106–143.

CEH (Comisión para el Esclarecimiento Histórico)

1999   *Guatemala, memoria del silencio.* Informe presentado por la Comisión para el Esclarecimiento Histórico, Guatemala City.

Centro de Estudios de Guatemala

1995   *El negocio más infame: Robo y tráfico de niños en Guatemala.* Guatemala City: Editorial Nuestra América.

Chibnik, Michael

2003   *Crafting Tradition: The Making and Marketing of Oaxacan Wood Carvings.* Austin: University of Texas Press.

Clark, Gracia

1994   *Onions Are My Husband: Survival and Accumulation by West African Market Women.* Chicago: University of Chicago Press.

Clifford, James

1988   On Collecting Art and Culture. In *The Predicament of Culture,* pp. 215–251. Cambridge: Harvard University Press.

1991   Four Northwest Coast Museums: Travel Reflections. In *Exhibiting Culture: The Poetics and Politics of Museum Display,* edited by Ivan Karp and Steven D. Lavine, pp. 212–254. Washington, D.C.: Smithsonian Institution Press.

1997   *Routes: Travel and Translation in the Late Twentieth Century.* Cambridge: Harvard University Press.

Coe, Michael D.

1987   *The Maya.* London: Thames and Hudson.

Cohen, Jeffrey H.

1999   *Cooperation and Community: Economy and Society in Oaxaca.* Austin: University of Texas Press.

Colby, Benjamin, and Pierre L. van den Berghe

1969   *Ixil Country: A Plural Society in Highland Guatemala.* Berkeley: University of California Press.

Comaroff, John, and Jean Comaroff

1992   Of Totemism and Ethnicity. In *Ethnography and the Historical Imagination,* pp. 49–68. Boulder: Westview Press.

Cone, Cynthia A.

1995   Crafting Selves: The Lives of Two Mayan Women. *Annals of Tourism Research* 22 (2): 313–327.

Cook, Scott, and Leigh Binford

1990   *Obliging Need: Rural Petty Industry in Mexican Capitalism.* Austin: University of Texas Press.

Coordinator of Inter-American Affairs

1944   *Guatemala: Volcanic but Peaceful.* Washington, D.C.: Coordinator of Inter-American Affairs.

Crónica

1998   *1998, Guatemala en números: Las cifras más importantes de la sociedad, economía y las finanzas.* Supplement to *Crónica* 538 (August 7–13).

Crowther, Geoff

1986   *South America on a Shoestring.* Berkeley: Lonely Planet.

Cojtí Cuxil, Demetrio (Waqi' Q'anil)

1991   *La configuración del pensamiento político del pueblo maya.* Quetzaltenango, Guatemala: Asociación de Escritores Mayances de Guatemala.

1995   *Ub'aniik ri una'ooj Uchomab'aal ri Maya' Tinamit* (La configuración del pensamiento político del pueblo maya). Guatemala City: Editorial Cholsamaj.

1997   *Ri Maya' Moloj pa Iximulew: El movimiento maya (en Guatemala).* Guatemala City: Editorial Cholsamaj.

de Certeau, Michel

1984   *The Practice of Everyday Life.* Translated by Steven Rendall. Berkeley: University of California Press.

Deere, Carmen Diana, and Magdalena León de Leal

1981   Peasant Production, Proletarianization, and the Sexual Division of Labor in the Andes. *Signs* 7 (2): 338–360.

Deitch, Lewis

1989   The Impact of Tourism on the Arts and Crafts of the Indians of the Southwestern United States. In *Hosts and Guests: The Anthropology of Tourism,* edited by Valene L. Smith, pp. 223–236. Philadelphia: University of Pennsylvania Press.

de la Cadena, Marisol

1991   "Las mujeres son más indias": Etnicidad y género en una comunidad del Cusco. *Revista Andina* 9: 7–47.

2000   *Indigenous Mestizos: The Politics of Race and Culture in Cuzco, Peru, 1919–1991.* Durham: Duke University Press.

Díaz, Víctor

1927   *La romántica ciudad colonial: Guía para conocer los monumentos históricos de la Antigua, Guatemala.* Guatemala City: Tipográfico Sánchez y De Guise.

Dorst, John D.

1989   *The Written Suburb: An American Site, an Ethnographic Dilemma.* Philadelphia: University of Pennsylvania Press.

Eco, Umberto

1986   *Travels in Hyperreality: Essays.* San Diego: Harcourt Brace Jovanovich.

Edelman, Marc

1999   *Peasants against Globalization: Rural Social Movements in Costa Rica.* Stanford: Stanford University Press.

Ehlers, Tracy

1990   *Silent Looms: Women and Production in a Guatemalan Town.* Boulder: Westview Press.

1991   Debunking Marianismo: Economic Vulnerability and Survival Strategies among Guatemalan Wives. *Ethnology* 30 (1): 1–16.

1993   Belts, Business, and Bloomingdale's: An Alternative Model for Guatemalan Artisan Development. In *Crafts in the World Market: The Impact of Global Exchange on Middle American Artisans,* edited by June Nash, pp. 181–199. Albany: SUNY Press.

Engels, Friedrich

1972   *The Origin of the Family, Private Property, and the State, in the Light of the Researches of Lewis H. Morgan.* With an introduction and notes by Eleanor Burke Leacock. New York: International Publishers. [Orig. pub. 1884]

Enloe, Cynthia

1989   *Bananas, Beaches, and Bases: Making Feminist Sense of International Politics.* Berkeley: University of California Press.

Errington, Frederick, and Deborah Gewertz

1989   Tourism and Anthropology in a Post-Modern World. *Oceania* 60: 37–54.

Esquit Choy, Alberto, and Víctor Gálvez Borrell

1997   *The Mayan Movement Today: Issues of Indigenous Culture and Development in Guatemala.* Guatemala City: FLACSO.

Fabian, Johannes

1983   *Time and the Other.* New York: Columbia University Press.

Falla, Ricardo

1978   *Quiché rebelde: Estudio de un movimiento de conversión religiosa rebelde a las creencias tradicionales, en San Antonio Ilotenango, Quiché, 1948–70.* Guatemala City: Editorial Universitaria de Guatemala.

Field, Les W.

1999   *The Grimace of Macho Ratón: Artisans, Identity, and Nation in the Late-Twentieth-Century Western Nicaragua.* Durham: Duke University Press.

Fischer, Edward F.

1996a   The Pan-Maya Movement in Global and Local Context. Ph.D. diss., Tulane University.

1996b   Induced Culture Change as a Strategy for Socioeconomic Development: The Pan-Maya Movement in Guatemala. In *Maya Cultural Activism in Guatemala,* edited by Edward F. Fischer and R. McKenna Brown, pp. 51–73. Austin: University of Texas Press.

1999   Cultural Logic and Maya Identity: Rethinking Constructivism and Essentialism. *Current Anthropology* 43 (4): 473–499.

2001   *Cultural Logics and Global Economies: Maya Identity in Thought and Practice.* Austin: University of Texas Press.

Fischer, Edward F., and R. McKenna Brown

1996a   Introduction: Maya Cultural Activism in Guatemala. In *Maya Cultural Activism in Guatemala,* edited by Edward F. Fischer and R. McKenna Brown, pp. 1–19. Austin: University of Texas Press.

1996b   (eds.) *Maya Cultural Activism in Guatemala.* Austin: University of Texas Press.

Fjellman, Stephen

1992   *Vinyl Leaves: Walt Disney World and America.* Boulder: Westview Press.

Flores Martini, Carlos

1974   Preservation. Pp. s-13 to s-15 in supplement to *Américas.*

FNUAP (Fondo de Población Naciones Unidas)

1997   *La población desarraigada en Guatemala: Cifras actualizadas y situación socioeconómica.* Guatemala City: FNUAP.

Foster, George

1965   Peasant Society and the Image of Limited Good. *American Anthropologist* 67 (2): 293–315.

1988   *Tzintzuntzan: Mexican Peasants in a Changing World.* Prospect Heights, Ill.: Waveland Press. [Orig. pub. 1967]

Foucault, Michel

1979   *Discipline and Punish: The Birth of the Prison.* New York: Vintage Books.

1986   Of Other Spaces. *Diacritics* 16 (1): 22–27.

2000   The Subject and Power. In *Power,* edited by James D. Faubion, pp. 326–348. Vol. 3 of *The Essential Works of Foucault, 1954–1984.* New York: The New Press.

Friedlander, Judith

1975   *Being Indian in Hueyapan: A Study of Forced Identity in Contemporary Mexico.* New York: St. Martin's Press.

Fusco, Coco

1995   *English Is Broken Here: Notes on Cultural Fusion in the Americas.* New York: The New Press.

Fussell, Paul

1980   *Abroad.* Oxford: Oxford University Press.

Gable, Eric, Richard Handler, and Anna Lawson

1992   On the Uses of Relativism: Fact, Conjecture, and Black and White Histories of Colonial Williamsburg. *American Ethnologist* 19: 791–805.

García Canclini, Néstor

1993   *Transforming Modernity: Popular Culture in Mexico.* Translated by Lidia Lozano. Austin: University of Texas Press.

1995   *Hybrid Cultures: Strategies for Entering and Leaving Modernity.* Translated by Christopher L. Chiappari and Silvia L. López. Minneapolis: University of Minnesota Press.

Garrard-Burnett, Virginia

1998   *Protestantism in Guatemala: Living in the New Jerusalem.* Austin: University of

Texas Press.

Geertz, Clifford

1973   *The Interpretation of Cultures.* New York: Basic Books.

Gil Aguilar, Julio Roberto

1983   *Políticas de protección y desarrollo artesanal.* Tesis de Licenciado, Universidad de San Carlos de Guatemala, Guatemala City.

Glassman, Paul

1988   *Guatemala Guide.* New York: Passport Press.

Glittenberg, Jody

1994   *To the Mountain and Back: The Mysteries of Guatemalan Highland Family Life.* Prospect Heights, Ill.: Waveland Press.

Goffman, Erving

1959   *The Presentation of Self in Everyday Life.* New York. Anchor Books.

Goldín, Liliana R.

1985   Organizing the World through the Market: A Symbolic Analysis of Markets and Exchange in the Western Highlands of Guatemala. Ph.D. diss., SUNY-Albany.

1987a   De plaza a mercado: La expresión de dos sistemas conceptuales en la organización de los mercados del occidente de Guatemala. *Anales de Antropología* 24: 243–261.

1987b   The "Peace of the Market" in the Midst of Violence: A Symbolic Analysis of Markets and Exchange in Western Guatemala. *Ethnos* 53 (3–4): 368–383.

Goldín, Liliana R.

1999   (ed.) *Identities on the Move: Transnational Processes in North America and the Caribbean Basin.* Albany: Institute for Mesoamerican Studies.

Goldman, Francisco

1992   *The Long Night of the White Chickens.* London: Faber and Faber.

Gómez-Peña, Guillermo

1993   *Warrior for Gringostroika.* Saint Paul, Minn.: Graywolf Press.

Gorrey, Conner

2001   *Guatemala.* Victoria, Australia: Lonely Planet Publications.

Graburn, Nelson

1976   Introduction: Arts of the Fourth World. In *Ethnic and Tourist Arts: Cultural Expressions from the Fourth World,* pp. 1–31. Berkeley: University of California.

1984   The Evolution of the Tourist. *Annals of Tourism Research* 11: 393–419.

1989   Tourism: The Sacred Journey. *Hosts and Guests: The Anthropology of Tourism,* edited by Valene Smith, pp. 21–36. Philadelphia: University of Pennsylvania Press.

1993   Ethnic Arts in the Fourth World. In *Imagery and Creativity: Ethnoaesthetics and Art Worlds in the Americas,* edited by Dorothea S. Whitten and Norman E. Whitten, Jr., pp. 173–204. Tucson: University of Arizona Press.

Grandin, Greg

2000   *The Blood of Guatemala: A History of Race and Nation.* Durham: Duke University Press.

Green, Linda

1999   *Fear as a Way of Life: Mayan Widows in Rural Guatemala.* New York: Columbia University Press.

Greenberg, David, and Marian Greenberg

1955   *The Shopping Guide to Mexico, Guatemala, and the Caribbean.* New York: Trade Winds.

Greenberg, Arnold, and Diana Wells

1990   *Guatemala Alive.* New York: Alive Publications.

Grimes, Kimberly M., and B. Lynne Milgram

2000   (eds.) *Artisans and Cooperatives: Developing Alternative Trade for the Global Economy.* Tucson: University of Arizona Press.

Gupta, Akhil

1998   *Postcolonial Developments: Agriculture in the Making of Modern India.* Durham: Duke University Press.

Gupta, Akhil, and James Ferguson

1992   Beyond "Culture": Space, Identity, and the Politics of Difference. *Cultural Anthropology* 7: 6–23.

1997   (eds.) *Culture, Power, Place: Explorations in Critical Anthropology.* Durham: Duke University Press.

Hale, Charles

1994   Between Che Guevara and the Pachamama: Mestizos, Indians, and Identity Politics in the Anti-quincentenary Campaign. *Critique of Anthropology* 14 (1): 9–39.

1996   *Mestizaje,* Hybridity, and the Cultural Politics of Difference in Post-revolutionary Central America. *Journal of Latin American Anthropology* 2 (1): 34–61.

1997   Cultural Politics of Identity in Latin America. *Annual Review of Anthropology* 26: 567–590.

Hall, Stuart

1996a   The Meaning of New Times. In *Stuart Hall: Critical Dialogues in Cultural Studies,* edited by David Morley and Kuan-Hsing Chen, pp. 223–237. London: Routledge.

1996b   New Ethnicities. In *Stuart Hall: Critical Dialogues in Cultural Studies,* edited by David Morley and Kuan-Hsing Chen, pp. 441–450. London: Routledge.

1997a   The Local and the Global: Globalization and Ethnicity. In *Culture, Globalization, and the World-System: Contemporary Conditions for the Representation of Identity,* edited by Anthony King, pp. 19–40. Minneapolis: University of Minnesota Press.

1997b   Old and New Identities, Old and New Ethnicities. In *Culture, Globalization, and the World-System: Contemporary Conditions for the Representation of Identity,* edited by Anthony King, pp. 41–68. Minneapolis: University of Minnesota Press.

Handler, Richard, and William Saxton

1988   Dyssimulation: Reflexivity, Narrative, and the Quest for Authenticity in "Living History." *Cultural Anthropology* 3: 242–260.

Handy, Jim

1984   *Gift of the Devil: A History of Guatemala.* Toronto: Between the Lines Press.

Harvey, Penelope

1996   *Hybrids of Modernity: Anthropology, the Nation State, and the Universal Exhibition.* London: Routledge Press.

Hawkins, John

1984   *Inverse Images: The Meaning of Culture, Ethnicity, and Family in Postcolonial Guatemala.* Albuquerque. University of New Mexico Press.

Hendrickson, Carol

1995   *Weaving Identities: Construction of Dress and Self in a Highland Guatemala Town.* Austin: University of Texas Press.

Hervik, Peter

1998   The Mysterious Maya of National Geographic. *Journal of Latin American Anthropology* 4 (1): 166–197.

Hinshaw, Robert

1975   *Panajachel: A Guatemalan Town in Thirty-Year Perspective.* Pittsburgh: University of Pittsburgh Press.

1988   Tourist Town amid the Violence: Panajachel. In *Harvest of Violence,* edited by Robert M. Carmack, pp. 195–205. Norman: University of Oklahoma Press.

Hinsley, Curtis M.

1991   The World as Marketplace: Commodification of the Exotic at the World's Columbian Exposition, Chicago, 1893. In *Exhibiting Culture: The Poetics and Politics of Museum Display,* edited by Ivan Karp and Steven D. Lavine, pp. 344–365. Washington, D.C.: Smithsonian Institution Press.

Hirabayashi, Lane Ryo

1986   The Migrant Village Association in Latin America: A Comparative Analysis. *Latin American Research Review* 21: 7–29.

Hodgen, Margaret T.

1964   *Early Anthropology in the Sixteenth and Seventeenth Centuries.* Philadelphia: University of Pennsylvania Press.

Holston, James, and Arjun Appadurai

1996   Cities and Citizenship. *Public Culture* 8 (2): 187–204.

Hooper-Greenhill, Eileen

1989   The Museum in the Disciplinary Society. In *Museum Studies in Material Culture,* edited by Susan M. Pearce, pp. 62–72. Leicester, England: Leicester University Press.

Huxley, Aldous

1960   *Beyond the Mexique Bay.* New York: Vintage Books. [Orig. pub. 1934]

Idell, Albert

1949   *Doorway in Antigua: A Sojourn in Guatemala.* New York: William Sloane Associates.

Instituto Indigenista Nacional

1948   *San Antonio Aguas Calientes: Síntesis socio-económica de una comunidad indígena guatemalteca.* Publicaciones Especiales del Instituto Indigenista Nacional, No. 6. Guatemala City: Ministerio de Educación Pública.

Instituto Nacional de Estadística [cited as INE]

1996   *X Censo Nacional de Población y V de Habitación, 1994.* Guatemala City: INE.

Jackson, Joseph H.

1937   *Notes on a Drum: Travel Sketches in Guatemala.* New York: MacMillan.

Janson, Thor

1996   *Thor Janson's Guatemala.* Guatemala City: Editorial Artemis Edinter.

Jickling, David

1964   *Two Walking Tours of Antigua.* Antigua Guatemala: Tourist Office.

Karp, Ivan, and Steven D. Lavine

1991   (eds.) *Exhibiting Cultures: The Poetics and Politics of Museum Display.* Washington, D.C.: Smithsonian Institution Press.

Kay, Cristóbal

1989   *Latin American Theories of Development and Underdevelopment.* London: Routledge Press.

Kearney, Michael

1995   The Local and the Global: The Anthropology of Globalization and Transnationalism. *Annual Review of Anthropology* 24: 547–565.

1996   *Reconceptualizing the Peasantry: Anthropology in Global Perspective.* Boulder: Westview Press.

Kemper, Robert Van

1977   *Migration and Adaptation: Tzintzuntzan Peasants in Mexico City.* Beverly Hills: Sage.

King, Anthony

1997   The Global, the Urban, and the World. In *Culture, Globalization, and the World-System: Contemporary Conditions for the Representation of Identity,* edited by Anthony King, pp. 149–154. Minneapolis: University of Minnesota Press.

Kinnaird, Vivian, and Derek Hall

1994   *Tourism: A Gender Analysis.* Chichester, England: Wiley.

Kirshenblatt-Gimblett, Barbara

1998   *Destination Culture: Tourism, Museums, and Heritage.* Berkeley: University of California Press.

Knopf Guide

1995   *Route of the Mayas.* New York: Alfred Knopf.

Kratz, Corinne A., and Ivan Karp

1993   Wonder and Worth: Disney Museums in World Showcase. *Museum Anthropology* 17: 3: 32–42.

Lanfant, Marie-Françoise, John B. Allcock, and Edward Bruner

1995   (eds.) *International Tourism: Identity and Change.* London: Sage.

Little, Walter E.

1995   Not Who We Expected to Meet: A Discussion of Ethnic Tourism in Guatemala and Critique of Textual Discourses Describing the Maya. Predissertation, Department of Anthropology, University of Illinois at Urbana-Champaign. Unpublished ms.

1998   Ignoring the Pan-Maya movement or What Really Matters to Maya Vendors. Paper presented at the American Anthropological Association 97th annual meeting, "Population: Two Hundred Years after Malthus," Philadelphia, Pennsylvania (December 2–6).

n.d.   In Between Social Movements: Dilemmas of Indigenous Handicraft Vendors in Guatemala. Forthcoming in *American Ethnologist.*

Little, Walter E., and Shana Walton

n.d.   Survey of Tourists in Antigua. Unpublished ms.

Lugo, Alejandro

1997   Reflections on Border Theory, Culture, and the Nation. In *Border Theory: The Limits of Cultural Politics,* edited by Scott Michaelson and David E. Johnson, pp. 43–67. Minneapolis: University of Minnesota Press.

Luján Muñoz, Jorge

1966   *Permanencia de Antigua.* Guatemala City: Universidad de San Carlos de Guatemala.

Lutz, Catherine, and Jane Collins

1993   *Reading National Geographic.* Chicago: University of Chicago Press.

Lutz, Christopher H.

1994   *Santiago de Guatemala, 1541–1773: City, Caste, and the Colonial Experience.* Norman: University of Oklahoma Press.

MacCannell, Dean

1974   Staged Authenticity: Arrangements of Social Space in Tourist Settings. *American Journal of Sociology* 79 (3): 589–603.

1976   *The Tourist: A New Theory of the Leisure Class.* New York: Shocken.

1992   *Empty Meeting Grounds: The Tourist Papers.* London: Routledge.

Marcus, George

1995   Ethnography in/of the World System: The Emergence of Multi-Sited Ethnography. *Annual Review of Anthropology* 24: 95–117.

Marin, Louis

1984   *Utopics: The Semiological Play of Textual Spaces.* Atlantic Highlands, N.J.: Humanities Press International.

Maxwell, Judith M.

1996   Prescriptive Grammar and Kaqchikel Revitalization. In *Maya Cultural Activ-*

ism in Guatemala, edited by Edward F. Fischer and R. McKenna Brown, pp. 195–207. Austin: University of Texas.

McAllister, Carlota

1996   Authenticity and Guatemala's Maya Queen. In *Beauty Queens on the Global Stage: Gender, Contests, and Power,* edited by Colleen Cohen, Richard Wilk, and Beverly Stoeltje, pp. 105–124. New York: Routledge.

McBryde, Felix

1933   Sololá: A Guatemalan Town and Cakchikel Market-Center. *Middle American Research Series,* Publication No. 5, Pamphlet 3: 4–152.

1947   *Cultural and Historical Geography of Southwest Guatemala.* Smithsonian Institution of Social Anthropology No. 4. Washington, D.C.: U.S. Government.

McCreery, David

1994   *Rural Guatemala: 1760–1940.* Stanford: Stanford University Press.

McLaren, Deborah

1999   The History of Indigenous Peoples and Tourism. *Cultural Survival Quarterly* 23 (2): 27–28.

Meillassoux, Claude

1971   (ed.) *The Development of Indigenous Trade and Markets in West Africa.* London: Oxford University Press.

Meisch, Lynn A.

1995   Gringas and Otavaleños: Changing Tourist Relations. *Annals of Tourism Research* 22 (2): 441–462.

Menchú Tum, Rigoberta

1984   *I, Rigoberta Menchú: An Indian Woman in Guatemala.* Edited by Elisabeth Burgos-Debray. Translated by Ann Wright. London: Verso.

Mintz, Sidney

1961   Pratik: Haitian Personal Economic Relationships. In *Proceedings of the Annual Spring Meeting of the American Ethnological Society,* edited by Viola Garfield, pp. 54–63. Seattle: University of Washington Press.

1964   Peasant Market Places and Economic Development in Latin America. Occasional Paper No. 4, pp. 1–9. Nashville, Tenn.: The Graduate Center for Latin American Studies, Vanderbilt University.

1971   Men, Women, and Trade. *Comparative Studies in Society and History* 13: 247–269.

Mitchell, Timothy

1988   *Colonizing Egypt.* Berkeley: University of California Press.

1991   (ed.) *Questions of Modernity.* Minneapolis: University of Minnesota Press.

Mitchell-Hedges, Frederick Albert

1931   *Land of Wonder and Fear.* New York and London: The Century Co.

Molina Rodríguez, María Antonio

1978   *Incidencias de turismo en las tradiciones populares de Guatemala.* Tesis de Licenciada, Universidad de San Carlos de Guatemala, Guatemala City.

Montejo, Victor

1999   *Voices from Exile: Violence and Survival in Modern Maya History.* Norman: University of Oklahoma Press.

Moore, Henrietta

1988   *Feminism and Anthropology.* Minneapolis: University of Minnesota Press.

1994   *A Passion for Difference: Essays in Anthropology and Gender.* Cambridge: Polity Press.

Morales, Mario Roberto

1998   La identidad y la patria del ladino (o el síndrome de Maximón). In *La construcción de la nación y la representación ciudana en México, Guatemala, Perú, Ecuador y Bolivia,* edited by Claudia Dary, pp. 411–446. Guatemala City: FLACSO.

Morley, David, and Kevin Robins

1995   *Spaces of Identity: Global Media, Electronic Landscapes, and Cultural Boundaries.* London: Routledge Press.

Muñoz, Joaquín

1940   *Guatemala, from Where the Rainbow Takes Its Colors.* Guatemala City: Tipografía Nacional.

Nash, June

1960   Protestantism in an Indian Village in the Western Highlands of Guatemala. *Alpha Kappa Delta Quarterly* 30: 490–503.

1970   *In the Eyes of Ancestors; Belief and Behavior in a Maya Community.* New Haven: Yale University Press.

1981   Ethnographic Aspects of the World Capitalist System. *Annual Review of Anthropology* 10: 393–423.

1993a   (ed.) *Crafts in the World Market: The Impact of Global Exchange on Middle American Artisans.* Albany: SUNY Press.

1993b   Introduction: Traditional Arts and Changing Markets in Middle America. In *Crafts in the World Market,* edited by June Nash, pp. 1–24. Albany: SUNY Press.

1993c   Maya Household Production in the World Market: The Potters of Amatenango del Valle, Chiapas, Mexico. In *Crafts in the World Market,* edited by June Nash, pp. 127–154. Albany: SUNY Press.

2001   *Mayan Visions: The Quest for Autonomy in an Age of Globalization.* New York and London: Routledge Press.

Nash, June, and Christine Kovic

1997   The Reconstitution of Hegemony: The Free Trade Act and the Transformation of Rural Mexico. In *Globalization: Critical Reflections,* edited by James H. Mittelman, pp. 165–185. Boulder: Lynne Rienner Publishers.

Nash, June, and Helen Safa

1976   (eds.) *Sex and Class in Latin America.* New York: Praeger.

Nelson, Diane

1994	Gendering the Ethnic-National Question. *Anthropology Today* 10 (6): 3–7.

1999	*A Finger in the Wound: Body Politics in Quincentennial Guatemala.* Berkeley: University of California Press.

2001	Stumped Identities: Body Image, Bodies Politic, and the *Mujer Maya* as Prosthetic. *Cultural Anthropology* 16 (3): 314–355.

Norton, Natascha, and Mark Whatmore

1993	*Central America.* London: Cadogan Books.

Núñez de Rodas, Edna

1981	*Cultural Policy in Guatemala.* Paris: UNESCO.

Oakes, Maud

1951	*The Two Crosses of Todos Santos: Survivals of Mayan Religious Ritual.* Bollingen Series, no. 27. Princeton, N.J.: Princeton University Press.

OKMA (Oxlajuuj Keej Maya' Ajtz'iib')

1993	*Maya' Chii': Los idiomas mayas de Guatemala.* Guatemala City: Cholsamaj.

Ortner, Sherry B.

1995	Resistance and the Problem of Ethnographic Refusal. *Comparative Studies in Society and History* 137 (1): 173–193.

1997	Fieldwork in the Postcommunity. *Anthropology and Humanism* 22 (1): 61–80.

Otzoy, Irma

1996	*Maya' Banikil Maya' Tzyaqb'äl: Identidad y vestuario maya.* Guatemala City: Cholsamaj.

Pancake, Cherri M.

1993	Las fronteras de género reflejadas en los estudios de tejedores indígenas: El caso de Guatemala. *Mesoamérica* 26: 267–280.

Pardo, Joaquín

1944	*Efemérides para escribir la historia de la muy noble y muy leal ciudad de Santiago de los Caballeros de Guatemala.* Guatemala City: Tipografía Nacional.

Petrich, Perla

1996a	(ed.) *La educación en los pueblos del Lago Atitlán.* Guatemala City: Cholsamaj.

1996b	(ed.) *Vida de los ancianos del Lago Atitlán.* Guatemala City: Cholsamaj.

1996c	(ed.) *Vida de las mujeres del Lago Atitlán.* Guatemala City: Cholsamaj.

1996d	(ed.) *Vida de los hombres del Lago Atitlán.* Guatemala City: Cholsamaj.

Picard, Michel

1995	Cultural Heritage and Tourist Capital: Cultural Tourism in Bali. In *International Tourism: Identity and Change,* edited by Marie-Françoise Lanfant, John B. Allcock, and Edward Bruner, pp. 44–66. London: Sage.

Plattner, Stuart

1975	The Economics of Peddling. In *Formal Methods in Economic Anthropology,* edited by Stuart Plattner, pp. 55–76. Special Publication of the American Anthropological Association, no. 4.

1989a	Economic Behavior in Marketplaces. In *Economic Anthropology,* edited by Stuart Plattner, pp. 209–221. Stanford: Stanford University Press.

1989b   Markets and Marketplaces. In *Economic Anthropology,* edited by Stuart Plattner, pp. 171–208. Stanford: Stanford University Press.

Popenoe, Dorothy

1973   *The Story of Antigua Guatemala.* Dalton, Mass.: Studley Press. [Orig. pub. 1933]

Price, Sally

1989   *Primitive Art in Civilized Places.* Chicago: University of Chicago Press.

Ramírez, Isaac, and Mynor Zúñiga

1996   *Guatemala.* Barcelona: Grupo Editorial Norma.

Re Cruz, Alicia

1996   *The Two Milpas of Chan Kom: Scenarios of a Maya Village Life.* Albany: SUNY Press.

Redfield, Robert

1930   *Tepoztlán: A Mexican Village.* Chicago: University of Chicago Press.

1956   The Relations between Indians and Ladinos in Agua Escondida, Guatemala. *América Indígena* 16: 253–275.

1960   *The Little Community and Peasant Society and Culture.* Chicago: University of Chicago Press.

Redfield, Robert, and Alfonso Villa Rojas

1962   *Chan Kom: A Maya Village.* Chicago: University of Chicago Press. [Orig. pub. 1934]

Reina, Rubén E.

1966   *The Law of the Saints: A Pokomam Pueblo and Its Community Culture.* Indianapolis: Bobbs-Merrill.

REMHI ([Proyecto Interdiocesano de] Recuperación de la Memoria Histórica)

1998   *Guatemala: Nunca más.* Guatemala City: Oficina de Derechos Humanos del Arzobispado.

Richardson, Miles

1982   Being-in-the-Market versus Being-in-the-Plaza: Material Culture and the Construction of Social Reality in Spanish America. *American Ethnologist* 9 (2): 421–436.

Robbins, J. Stanton

1947   *Preliminary Report on Tourist Development in Guatemala.* Washington, D.C.: Inter-American Development Commission.

Rodríguez Rouanet, Francisco

1985   *Breve introducción al estudio de las artesanías populares de Guatemala.* Guatemala City: Subcentro Regional de Artesanías y Artes Populares.

1996   *Diccionario municipal de Guatemala.* Guatemala City: Instituto de Estudios y Capacitación Cívica.

Rosaldo, Renato

1989   *Culture and Truth: The Remaking of Social Analysis.* Boston: Beacon Press.

Rosales Arenales de Klose, Margarita

1978   *Mercadeo de textiles artesanales.* Tesis de Licenciada, Universidad Rafael Landívar,

Bibliography

Guatemala City.

Rubio, Julio Alberto

1938   *Album de Guatemala.* Guatemala City: Imprenta[?] Electra.

Said, Edward

1979   *Orientalism.* New York: Vintage.

Sandstrom, Alan R.

1991   *Corn Is Our Blood: Culture and Ethnic Identity in a Contemporary Aztec Indian Village.* Norman: University of Oklahoma Press.

Sassen, Saskia

1996   Whose City Is It? Globalization and the Formation of New Claims. *Public Culture* 8 (2): 205–225.

Şaul, Mahir

1989   Separate and Relation: Autonomous Income and Negotiation among Rural Bobo Women. In *The Household Economy: Reconsidering the Domestic Mode of Production,* edited by Richard Wilk, pp. 171–193. Boulder: Westview Press.

Schaeffer, Phillip

1974   *Lake Atitlán.* Guatemala City: Phillip Schaeffer Productions.

Schele, Linda, and David Freidel

1990   *A Forest of Kings: The Untold Story of the Ancient Maya.* New York: Quill Books.

Schirmer, Jennifer

1993   The Seeking of Truth and the Gendering of Consciousness: The CoMadres of El Salvador and the CONAVIGUA Widows of Guatemala. In *"Viva": Women and Popular Protest in Latin America,* edited by Sallie Westwood and Sarah A. Radcliffe, pp. 30–64. London: Routledge Press.

1998   *The Guatemalan Military Project: A Violence Called Democracy.* Philadelphia: University of Pennsylvania Press.

Schneider, Jane, and Rayna Rapp

1995   (eds.) *Articulating Hidden Histories: Exploring the Influence of Eric R. Wolf.* Berkeley: University of California Press.

Scott, James

1990   *Domination and the Arts of Resistance: Hidden Transcripts.* New Haven: Yale University Press.

Sharer, Robert

1995   *The Ancient Maya.* 5th ed. Stanford: Stanford University Press.

Shaw, Carolyn Martin

1995   *Colonial Inscriptions: Race, Sex, and Class in Kenya.* Minneapolis: University of Minnesota Press.

Sinclair, M. Thea

1997a   (ed.) *Gender, Work, and Tourism.* London: Routledge Press.

1997b   Issues and Theories of Gender and Work in Tourism. In *Gender, Work, and Tourism,* edited by M. Thea Sinclair, pp. 1–15. London: Routledge Press.

Skinner, G. William

1967   Marketing and Social Structure in Rural China. In *Peasant Society: A Reader,* edited by Jack Potter, May Diaz, and George Foster, pp. 63–97. Boston: Little, Brown, and Company.

Smith, Carol

1972   The Domestic Marketing System of Western Guatemala. Ph.D. diss., University of Wisconsin.

1974   Economics of Marketing Systems: Models from Economic Geography. *Annual Review of Anthropology* 3: 167–201.

1975   Examining Stratification Systems through Peasant Marketing Arrangements: An Application of Some Models from Economic Geography. *Man* 10 (1): 95–122.

1976   (ed.) *Regional Analysis,* Volumes 1 and 2. New York: Academic Press.

1978   Beyond Dependency Theory: National and Regional Patterns of Underdevelopment in Guatemala. *American Ethnologist* 5 (2): 574–617.

1984   Local History in Global Context: Social and Economic Transitions in Western Guatemala. *Comparative Studies in Society and History* 26 (2): 193–228.

1990a   Failed Nationalist Movements in Nineteenth-Century Guatemala: A Parable for the Third World. In *Nationalist Ideologies and the Production of National Cultures,* edited by Richard G. Fox, pp. 148–177. American Ethnological Society Monograph Series, No. 2. Washington, D.C.: American Anthropological Association.

1990b   (ed.) *Guatemalans and the State, 1540 to 1988.* Austin: University of Texas Press.

1995   Race-Class-Gender Ideology in Guatemala: Modern and Anti-Modern Forms. *Comparative Studies in Society and History* 37: 723–749.

Smith, Gavin

1989   *Livelihood and Resistance: Peasants and the Politics of Land in Peru.* Berkeley: University of California Press.

Smith, Valene L.

1989   (ed.) *Hosts and Guests: The Anthropology of Tourism.* Philadelphia: University of Pennsylvania Press.

Smith, Waldemar R.

1977   *The Fiesta System and Economic Change.* New York: Columbia University Press.

SNUG (Sistema de Naciones Unidas en Guatemala)

1998   *Guatemala: Los contrastes del desarrollo humano.* Guatemala City: SNUG.

Solares, Carlos

1964   *Guía turística, kilométrica, demográfica de la República de Guatemala Centro América.* Guatemala City: Editorial Martí.

Stack, John, Jr.

1981   Ethnic Groups as Emerging Transnational Actors. In *Ethnic Identities in a Transnational World,* edited by John Stack, Jr., pp. 17–43. West Point, Conn.: Greenwood Press.

Stephen, Lynn

1991   *Zapotec Women*. Austin: University of Texas Press.

1993   Weaving in the Fast Lane: Class, Ethnicity, and Gender in Zapotec Craft Commercialization. In *Crafts in the World Market: The Impact of Global Exchange on Middle American Artisans,* edited by June Nash, pp. 25–58. Albany: SUNY Press.

Stewart, Susan

1984   *On Longing: Narratives of the Miniature, the Gigantic, the Souvenir, the Collection.* Baltimore: Johns Hopkins University Press.

Stoler, Ann L.

1991   Carnal Knowledge and Imperial Power: Gender, Race, and Morality in Colonial Asia. In *Gender at the Crossroads of Knowledge,* edited by Micaela di Leonardo, pp. 51–101. Berkeley: University of California Press.

Stoll, David

1982   *Fishers of Men or Founders of Empire? The Wycliffe Bible Translators in Latin America.* London: Zed Press.

1993   *Between Two Armies in the Ixil Towns of Guatemala.* New York: Columbia University Press.

Stoller, Paul

1997   Globalizing Method: The Problems of Doing Ethnography in Transnational Spaces. *Anthropology and Humanism* 22 (1): 81–94.

2002   *Money Has No Smell: The Africanization of New York City.* Chicago: University of Chicago Press.

Swain, Margaret B.

1989   Gender Roles in Indigenous Tourism: Kuna Mola, Kuna Yala, and Cultural Survival. In *Hosts and Guests: The Anthropology of Tourism,* edited by Valene L. Smith, pp. 83–104. Philadelphia: University of Pennsylvania Press.

1993   Women Producers of Ethnic Arts. *Annals of Tourism Research* 20 (1): 32–52.

1995   (ed.) *Gender in Tourism.* Special Issue of *Annals of Tourism Research* 22 (2).

Swetnam, John J.

1975   The Open Gateway: Social and Economic Interaction in a Guatemalan Marketplace. Ph.D. diss., University of Pennsylvania.

1978   Interaction between Urban and Rural Residents in a Guatemalan Marketplace. *Urban Anthropology* 7 (2): 137–154.

1988   Women and Market: A Problem in the Assessment of Sexual Inequality. *Ethnology* 27 (4): 327–338.

Subcentro Regional de Artesanía y Artes Populares (SRAAP)

1990   *Distribución geográfica de las artesanías de Guatemala.* Guatemala City: SRAAP.

Tax, Sol

1937   The *Municipios* of the Midwestern Highlands of Guatemala. *American Anthropologist* 39: 27–42.

1941   World View and Social Relations in Guatemala. *American Anthropologist* 43: 27–42.

1946   The Towns of Lake Atitlán. Microfilm Collection of Manuscripts on Middle American Cultural Anthropology, No. 13. Chicago: University of Chicago Library.

1952   (ed.) *Heritage of Conquest: The Ethnology of Middle America*. New York: Coopers Square Publishers. [Reprinted 1968]

1953   *Penny Capitalism: A Guatemalan Indian Economy*. Smithsonian Institute of Social Anthropology, No. 16. Washington, D.C.: Smithsonian Institution Press.

Tice, Karin

1995   *Kuna Crafts, Gender, and the Global Economy*. Austin: University of Texas Press.

Toland, Judith D.

1993   (ed.) *Ethnicity and the State*. Political and Legal Anthropology Series, vol. 9. New Brunswick, N.J.: Transaction Publishers.

Tsing, Anna

2000   The Global Situation. *Cultural Anthropology* 15 (3): 325–456.

Turino, Thomas

1993   *Moving Away from Silence: Music of the Peruvian Altiplano and the Experience of Urban Migration*. Chicago: University of Chicago Press.

Tzian, Leopoldo

1994   *Kajab'aliil Maya'iib' Xuq Mu'siib': Ri Ub'antajiik Iximuleew/Mayas y ladinos en cifras: El caso de Guatemala*. Guatemala City: Cholsamaj.

Urry, James

1990   *The Tourist Gaze: Leisure and Travel in Contemporary Societies*. London: Sage.

1992   The Tourist Gaze "Revisited." *American Behavioral Scientist* 36 (2): 187–199.

U.S. Government

1981   The Peace Corps in Guatemala. Doc. no. AA 1.17: 4200.84. Washington, D.C.: U.S. Government.

Valladares, Julio

1934   (ed.) *Guía manual de turismo—1933*. Guatemala City: Tipografía Nacional.

van den Berghe, Pierre

1994   *The Quest for the Other: Ethnic Tourism in San Cristóbal, Mexico*. Seattle: University of Washington Press.

1995   Marketing Mayas: Ethnic Tourism Promotion in Mexico. *Annals of Tourism Research* 22: 568–588.

Villatoro, Ana María

1988   La importancia de la industria indígena en el municipio de Panajachel y su aceptación en el turismo interno y receptivo. *Cultura de Guatemala* 9 (3): 71–132.

Wallace, Michael

1981   Visiting the Past: History Museums in the United States. *Radical History Review* 25: 63–96.

1987   The Politics of Public History. In *Past Meets Present*, edited by Jo Blatti, pp. 37–53. Washington, D.C.: Smithsonian Institution Press.

1989   Mickey Mouse History: Portraying the Past at Disney World. In *History Museums in the United States: A Critical Assessment,* edited by Warren Leon and Roy Rosenzwerg, pp. 158–180. Urbana: University of Illinois Press.

Wallis, Brian

1994   Selling Nations: International Exhibitions and Cultural Diplomacy. In *Museum Culture: Histories, Discourses, Spectacles,* edited by Daniel J. Sherman and Irit Rogoff, pp. 265–282. Minneapolis: University of Minnesota Press.

Warren, Kay

1989   *The Symbolism of Subordination: Indian Identity in a Guatemalan Town.* Rev. ed. Austin: University of Texas Press. [1st ed. 1978]

1992   Transforming Memories and Histories: The Meanings of Ethnic Resurgence for Mayan Indians. In *Americas: New Interpretive Essays,* edited by Alfred Stephan, pp. 189–219. Oxford: Oxford University Press.

1998a   *Indigenous Movements and Their Critics: Pan-Maya Activism in Guatemala.* Princeton: Princeton University Press.

1998b   Indigenous Movements as a Challenge to the Unified Social Movement Paradigm for Guatemala. In *Cultures of Politics / Politics of Culture: Re-visioning Latin American Social Movements,* edited by Sonia E. Alvarez, Evelina Dagnino, and Arturo Escobar, pp. 165–195. Boulder: Westview Press.

2002   Voting against Indigenous Rights in Guatemala: Lessons from the 1999 Referendum. In *Indigenous Movements, Self-Representation, and the State in Latin America,* edited by Kay B. Warren and Jean E. Jackson, pp. 149–180. Austin: University of Texas Press.

Warren, Kay B., and Jean E. Jackson

2002a   (eds.) *Indigenous Movements, Self-Representation, and the State in Latin America.* Austin: University of Texas Press.

2002b   Introduction: Studying Indigenous Activism in Latin America. In *Indigenous Movements, Self-Representation, and the State in Latin America,* edited by Kay B. Warren and Jean E. Jackson, pp. 1–46. Austin: University of Texas Press.

Wasserstrom, Robert

1976   The Exchange of Saints in Zinacantan: The Socioeconomic Bases of Religious Change in Southeastern Mexico. *Ethnology* 17: 197–210.

Watanabe, John M.

1990   Enduring Yet Ineffable Community in the Western Periphery of Guatemala. In *Guatemalan Indians and the State: 1540 to 1988,* edited by Carol A. Smith, pp. 183–204. Austin: University of Texas Press.

1992   *Maya Saints and Souls in a Changing World.* Austin: University of Texas Press.

1995   Unimagining the Maya: Anthropologists, Others, and the Inescapable Hubris of Authorship. *Bulletin of Latin American Research* 14 (1): 25–45.

Watson, James

1998   (ed.) *Golden Arches East: McDonald's in East Asia.* Stanford: Stanford University Press.

Weber, Max

1946   *From Max Weber: Essays in Sociology.* Translated, edited, and introduction by Hans Gerth and C. Wright Mills. New York: Oxford University Press.

Werbner, Richard P.

1984   The Manchester School in South-Central Africa. *Annual Review of Anthropology* 13 (157–185).

Westwood, Sallie, and Sarah A. Radcliffe

1993   Gender, Racism, and the Politics of Identities in Latin America. In *"Viva": Women and Popular Protest in Latin America,* edited by Sallie Westwood and Sarah A. Radcliffe, pp. 1–29. London: Routledge Press.

Whatmore, Mark, and Peter Eltringham

1993   *Guatemala and Belize: The Rough Guide.* London: Rough Guides.

White, Isobel

1994   Who Is Stealing Guatemala's Children? Behind the Attacks on U.S. Tourists. *Report on Guatemala* 15 (2): 2–5.

Wilhite, Margaret

1977   First Language Acquisition: Textile Design Terminology in Cakchikel (Mayan). Ph.D. diss., Washington University.

Williams, Robert G.

1994   *States and Social Evolution: Coffee and the Rise of National Governments in Central America.* Chapel Hill: University of North Carolina Press.

Wilson, Richard

1995   *Maya Resurgence in Guatemala: Q'eqchi' Experiences.* Norman: University of Oklahoma Press.

Wolf, Eric

1955   Types of Latin American Peasantry. *American Anthropologist* 57: 452–471.

1957   Closed Corporate Peasant Communities in Mesoamerica and Central Java. *Southwestern Journal of Anthropology* 13 (1): 1–18.

1982   *Europe and the People without History.* Berkeley: University of California Press.

Wolf, Eric, and Edward Hansen

1972   *The Human Condition in Latin America.* New York: Oxford University Press.

Wood, W. Warner.

2000   Flexible Production, Flexible Households, and Flexible Fieldwork: Participant Observation among Petty Commodity Producers in the Era of Late Capitalism. *Ethnology* 39 (2): 133–148.

Zamora, Pedro

1943   *Guía turística de las ruinas de la Antigua Guatemala.* Guatemala City: Tipografía Nacional.

Index

Radcliffe, Sarah, 169
Re Cruz, Alicia, 189
Redfield, Robert, 180, 181, 198
Richardson, Miles, 99–100
Ríos Montt, Efraín, 170
Rosaldo, Renato, 84, 282n.2(Ch.2)
Ruta Maya (Mundo Maya), 13, 44, 67, 217, 238

samajel, 191, 195
San Andrés Semetabaj, 160, 191, 215, 229, 232, 234, 241–242, 256, 270
San Antonio Aguas Calientes, 3, 13, 25–26, 29, 30–31, 60, 61, 74, 104, 105, 107, 119, 121, 126, 134, 164, 166–168, 183, 188–189, 200, 203–226, 229, 269
Sandstrom, Alan, 180, 181, 185–186, 226
San Francisco el Grande Church, 104–105, 112
San Juan de Comalapa, 29, 96, 104, 119, 126–127, 143, 165–166, 182–183, 190, 192, 200
Santa Catarina Barahona, 30–31, 105, 107, 120, 164, 183, 189, 200
Santa Catarina Palopó, 13, 25–26, 29, 164, 200, 227–260, 261–262, 269
Santa Cruz del Quiché, 5
Santa María de Jesús, 91, 107
Santiago Chimaltenango, 190
Sassen, Saskia, 76, 78
Scott, James, 230–231, 288n.6
simulacra, 77
Sinclair, Thea, 11
Smith, Carol, 96–97, 102, 114, 145, 153, 156, 184, 227, 264, 269
Smith, Gavin, 18
social construction of people, 42–43, 45–50, 74–76

social construction of place, 37–43, 47–50, 58, 69–74, 98–100, 267
socioeconomic conditions, 7, 22, 51–52, 254–255
souvenirs, 40, 62, 103, 280n.6, 282n.22
Stephen, Lynn, 128
Stoller, Paul, 12–13
street vendors. *See ambulantes*
subjectivity, 16–17; anthropological, 19–21, 30
Swain, Margaret, 11, 12
Swetnam, John, 28, 74, 97, 106, 123, 124, 128–129, 149

tamal, 29
Tax, Gertrude, 236
Tax, Sol, 14, 15, 16, 25, 32, 95, 100–101, 141, 170, 180, 184, 232–334, 236, 260
tianguis, 105–106
tikonel(a'): defined, 190–191, 233, 288n.3
típica, 60, 126; defined, 51. *See also traje*
típica tienda, 207; defined, 4
típica vendors: defined, 7. *See also* vendors
tourism companies, 50–51. *See also* Clark Tours
tourism routes in Guatemala, 13, 19, 36–37, 44–45, 47–48, 94
tourism theory, 11–12, 13, 41, 142, 151, 209, 225–226. *See also* borderzone; Bruner, Edward; Castañeda, Quetzil; Urry, James
tourist gaze, 46, 67–68
touristic performance, 41–42, 204, 207, 209–210, 211–218, 225–226, 261–262
touristic surveillance, 49, 60, 61, 65–68, 242

Mayas in the Marketplace